Marx, Engels, and Marxisms

Series Editors
Marcello Musto, York University, Toronto, ON, Canada
Terrell Carver, University of Bristol, Bristol, UK

The Marx renaissance is underway on a global scale. Wherever the critique of capitalism re-emerges, there is an intellectual and political demand for new, critical engagements with Marxism. The peer-reviewed series Marx, Engels and Marxisms (edited by Marcello Musto & Terrell Carver, with Babak Amini, Francesca Antonini, Paula Rauhala & Kohei Saito as Assistant Editors) publishes monographs, edited volumes, critical editions, reprints of old texts, as well as translations of books already published in other languages. Our volumes come from a wide range of political perspectives, subject matters, academic disciplines and geographical areas, producing an eclectic and informative collection that appeals to a diverse and international audience. Our main areas of focus include: the oeuvre of Marx and Engels, Marxist authors and traditions of the 19th and 20th centuries, labour and social movements, Marxist analyses of contemporary issues, and reception of Marxism in the world.

Rémy Herrera

Confronting Mainstream Economics for Overcoming Capitalism

palgrave
macmillan

Rémy Herrera
National Center of Scientific Research
Paris, France

ISSN 2524-7123 ISSN 2524-7131 (electronic)
Marx, Engels, and Marxisms
ISBN 978-3-031-05853-0 ISBN 978-3-031-05851-6 (eBook)
https://doi.org/10.1007/978-3-031-05851-6

This Palgrave Macmillan imprint is published by the registered company Springer Nature Switzerland AG
The registered company address is: Gewerbestrasse 11, 6330 Cham, Switzerland

Series Foreword

Titles Published

1. Terrell Carver & Daniel Blank, *A Political History of the Editions of Marx and Engels's "German Ideology" Manuscripts*, 2014.
2. Terrell Carver & Daniel Blank, *Marx and Engels's "German Ideology" Manuscripts: Presentation and Analysis of the "Feuerbach Chapter,"* 2014.
3. Alfonso Maurizio Iacono, *The History and Theory of Fetishism*, 2015.
4. Paresh Chattopadhyay, *Marx's Associated Mode of Production: A Critique of Marxism*, 2016.
5. Domenico Losurdo, *Class Struggle: A Political and Philosophical History*, 2016.
6. Frederick Harry Pitts, *Critiquing Capitalism Today: New Ways to Read Marx*, 2017.
7. Ranabir Samaddar, *Karl Marx and the Postcolonial Age*, 2017.
8. George Comninel, *Alienation and Emancipation in the Work of Karl Marx*, 2018.
9. Jean-Numa Ducange & Razmig Keucheyan (Eds.), *The End of the Democratic State: Nicos Poulantzas, a Marxism for the 21st Century*, 2018.
10. Robert X. Ware, *Marx on Emancipation and Socialist Goals: Retrieving Marx for the Future*, 2018.
11. Xavier LaFrance & Charles Post (Eds.), *Case Studies in the Origins of Capitalism*, 2018.

12. John Gregson, *Marxism, Ethics, and Politics: The Work of Alasdair MacIntyre*, 2018.
13. Vladimir Puzone & Luis Felipe Miguel (Eds.), *The Brazilian Left in the 21st Century: Conflict and Conciliation in Peripheral Capitalism*, 2019.
14. James Muldoon & Gaard Kets (Eds.), *The German Revolution and Political Theory*, 2019.
15. Michael Brie, *Rediscovering Lenin: Dialectics of Revolution and Metaphysics of Domination*, 2019.
16. August H. Nimtz, *Marxism versus Liberalism: Comparative Real-Time Political Analysis*, 2019.
17. Gustavo Moura de Cavalcanti Mello and Mauricio de Souza Sabadini (Eds.), *Financial Speculation and Fictitious Profits: A Marxist Analysis*, 2019.
18. Shaibal Gupta, Marcello Musto & Babak Amini (Eds.), *Karl Marx's Life, Ideas, and Influences: A Critical Examination on the Bicentenary*, 2019.
19. Igor Shoikhedbrod, *Revisiting Marx's Critique of Liberalism: Rethinking Justice, Legality, and Rights*, 2019.
20. Juan Pablo Rodríguez, *Resisting Neoliberal Capitalism in Chile: The Possibility of Social Critique*, 2019.
21. Kaan Kangal, *Friedrich Engels and the Dialectics of Nature*, 2020.
22. Victor Wallis, *Socialist Practice: Histories and Theories*, 2020.
23. Alfonso Maurizio Iacono, *The Bourgeois and the Savage: A Marxian Critique of the Image of the Isolated Individual in Defoe, Turgot and Smith*, 2020.
24. Terrell Carver, *Engels Before Marx*, 2020.
25. Jean-Numa Ducange, *Jules Guesde: The Birth of Socialism and Marxism in France*, 2020.
26. Antonio Oliva, Ivan Novara & Angel Oliva (Eds.), *Marx and Contemporary Critical Theory: The Philosophy of Real Abstraction*, 2020.
27. Francesco Biagi, *Henri Lefebvre's Critical Theory of Space*, 2020.
28. Stefano Petrucciani, *The Ideas of Karl Marx: A Critical Introduction*, 2020.
29. Terrell Carver, *The Life and Thought of Friedrich Engels, 30th Anniversary Edition*, 2020.
30. Giuseppe Vacca, *Alternative Modernities: Antonio Gramsci's Twentieth Century*, 2020.

31. Kevin B. Anderson, Kieran Durkin & Heather Brown (Eds.), *Raya Dunayevskaya's Intersectional Marxism: Race, Gender, and the Dialectics of Liberation*, 2020.
32. Marco Di Maggio, *The Rise and Fall of Communist Parties in France and Italy*, 2020.
33. Farhang Rajaee, *Presence and the Political*, 2021.
34. Ryuji Sasaki, *A New Introduction to Karl Marx: New Materialism, Critique of Political Economy, and the Concept of Metabolism*, 2021.
35. Kohei Saito (Ed.), *Reexamining Engels's Legacy in the 21st Century*, 2021.
36. Paresh Chattopadhyay, *Socialism in Marx's Capital: Towards a Dealienated World*, 2021.
37. Marcello Musto, *Karl Marx's Writings on Alienation*, 2021.
38. Michael Brie & Jörn Schütrumpf, *Rosa Luxemburg: A Revolutionary Marxist at the Limits of Marxism*, 2021.
39. Stefano Petrucciani, *Theodor W. Adorno's Philosophy, Society, and Aesthetics*, 2021.
40. Miguel Vedda, *Siegfried Kracauer, or, The Allegories of Improvisation: Critical Studies*, 2021.
41. Ronaldo Munck, *Rethinking Development: Marxist Perspectives*, 2021.
42. Jean-Numa Ducange & Elisa Marcobelli (Eds.), *Selected Writings of Jean Jaurès: On Socialism, Pacifism and Marxism*, 2021.
43. Elisa Marcobelli, *Internationalism Toward Diplomatic Crisis: The Second International and French, German and Italian Socialists*, 2021.
44. James Steinhoff, *Automation and Autonomy: Labour, Capital and Machines in the Artificial Intelligence Industry*, 2021.
45. Juan Dal Maso, *Hegemony and Class Struggle: Trotsky, Gramsci and Marxism*, 2021.
46. Gianfranco Ragona & Monica Quirico, *Frontier Socialism: Self-organisation and Anti-capitalism*, 2021.
47. Tsuyoshi Yuki, *Socialism, Markets and the Critique of Money: The Theory of "Labour Notes,"* 2021.
48. Gustavo Moura de Cavalcanti Mello & Henrique Pereira Braga (Eds.), *Wealth and Poverty in Contemporary Brazilian Capitalism*, 2021.
49. Paolo Favilli, *Historiography and Marxism: Innovations in Mid-century Italy*, 2021.

50. Levy del Aguila Marchena, *Communism, Political Power and Personal Freedom in Marx*, 2021.
51. V. Geetha, *Bhimrao Ramji Ambedkar and the Question of Socialism in India*, 2021.
52. Satoshi Matsui, *Normative Theories of Liberalism and Socialism: Marxist Analysis of Values*, 2022.
53. Kei Ehara (Ed.), *Japanese Discourse on the Marxian Theory of Finance*, 2022.
54. Achim Szepanski, *Financial Capital in the 21st Century*, 2022.
55. Stephen Maher, *Corporate Capitalism and the Integral State: General Electric and a Century of American Power*, 2022.

Titles Forthcoming

Vesa Oittinen, *Marx's Russian Moment*

Kolja Lindner, *Marx, Marxism and the Question of Eurocentrism*

Adriana Petra, *Intellectuals and Communist Culture: Itineraries, Problems and Debates in Post-war Argentina*

George C. Comninel, *The Feudal Foundations of Modern Europe*

Spencer A. Leonard, *Marx, the India Question, and the Crisis of Cosmopolitanism*

Joe Collins, *Applying Marx's Capital to the 21st Century*

Jeong Seongjin, *Korean Capitalism in the 21st Century: Marxist Analysis and Alternatives*

Marcello Mustè, *Marxism and Philosophy of Praxis: An Italian Perspective from Labriola to Gramsci*

Shannon Brincat, *Dialectical Dialogues in Contemporary World Politics: A Meeting of Traditions in Global Comparative Philosophy*

Francesca Antonini, *Reassessing Marx's Eighteenth Brumaire: Dictatorship, State, and Revolution*

Thomas Kemple, *Capital After Classical Sociology: The Faustian Lives of Social Theory*

Xavier Vigna, *A Political History of Factories in France: The Workers' Insubordination of 1968*

Attila Melegh, *Anti-migrant Populism in Eastern Europe and Hungary: A Marxist Analysis*

Marie-Cecile Bouju, *A Political History of the Publishing Houses of the French Communist Party*

Peter McMylor, Graeme Kirkpatrick & Simin Fadaee (Eds.), *Marxism, Religion, and Emancipatory Politics*
Mauro Buccheri, *Radical Humanism for the Left: The Quest for Meaning in Late Capitalism*
Tamás Krausz, Eszter Bartha (Eds.), *Socialist Experiences in Eastern Europe: A Hungarian Perspective*
Martin Cortés, *Marxism, Time and Politics: On the Autonomy of the Political*
João Antonio de Paula, Huga da Gama Cerqueira, Eduardo da Motta e Albuquer & Leonardo de Deus, *Marxian Economics for the 21st Century: Revaluating Marx's Critique of Political Economy*
Zhi Li, *The Concept of the Individual in the Thought of Karl Marx*
Lelio Demichelis, *Marx, Alienation and Techno-capitalism*
Dong-Min Rieu, *A Mathematical Approach to Marxian Value Theory: Time, Money, and Labor Productivity*
Salvatore Prinzi, *Representation, Expression, and Institution: The Philosophy of Merleau-Ponty and Castoriadis*
Agon Hamza, *Slavoj Žižek and the Reconstruction of Marxism*
Éric Aunoble, *French Views on the Russian Revolution*
Terrell Carver, Smail Rapic (Eds.), *Friedrich Engels for the 21st Century: Perspectives and Problems*
Patrizia Dogliani, *A Political History of the International Union of Socialist Youth*
Alexandros Chrysis, *The Marx of Communism: Setting Limits in the Realm of Communism*
Paul Raekstad, *Karl Marx's Realist Critique of Capitalism: Freedom, Alienation, and Socialism*
Alexis Cukier, *Democratic Work: Radical Democracy and the Future of Labour*
Christoph Henning, *Theories of Alienation: From Rousseau to the Present*
Daniel Egan, *Capitalism, War, and Revolution: A Marxist Analysis*
Genevieve Ritchie, Sara Carpenter & Shahrzad Mojab (Eds.), *Marxism and Migration*
Emanuela Conversano, *Capital from Afar: Anthropology and Critique of Political Economy in the Late Marx*
Marcello Musto, *Rethinking Alternatives with Marx*
Vincenzo Mele, *City and Modernity in George Simmel and Walter Benjamin: Fragments of Metropolis*

David Norman Smith, *Self-emancipation: Marx's Unfinished Theory of the Working Class*
José Ricardo Villanueva Lira, *Marxism and the Origins of International Relations*
Bertel Nygaard, *Marxism, Labor Movements, and Historiography*
Fabio Perocco (Ed.), *Racism in and for the Welfare State*
Marcos Del Roio, *Gramsci and the Emancipation of the Subaltern Classes*
Marcelo Badaró, *The Working Class from Marx to Our Times*
Tomonaga Tairako, *A New Perspective on Marx's Philosophy and Political Economy*
Matthias Bohlender, Anna-Sophie Schönfelder, & Matthias Spekker, *Truth and Revolution in Marx's Critique of Society*
Mauricio Vieira Martins, *Marx, Spinoza and Darwin on Philosophy: Against Religious Perspectives of Transcendence*
Jean Vigreux, Roger Martelli, & Serge Wolikow, *One Hundred Years of History of the French Communist Party*
Aditya Nigam, *Border-Marxisms and Historical Materialism*
Fred Moseley, *Marx's Theory of Value in Chapter 1 of* Capital*: A Critique of Heinrich's Value-Form Interpretation*
Armando Boito, *The State, Politics, and Social Classes: Theory and History*
Anjan Chakrabarti & Anup Dhar, *World of the Third and Hegemonic Capital: Between Marx and Freud*
Hira Singh, *Annihilation of Caste in India: Ambedkar, Ghandi, and Marx*
Salvatore Engel-Di Mauro, *An Introduction to Ecosocialism*

Presentation

The objective of this book is twofold. On the one hand, it offers, from a Marxist point of view, a radical criticism of the mainstream currently dominating in economics—that is, the neoclassical mainstream, or "neoclassicism" (Part I)—as well as of some "soft heterodoxies" (Part II) that are today fashionable and particularly influencing (neoinstitutionalist schools, neo-Keynesian schools, Amartya Sen's methods, or Thomas Piketty's positions, among others). And, on the other hand, the book shows the need to enter into intellectual dissidence and scientific resistance by demonstrating the relevance of the conceptual, methodological, and theoretical instruments of Marxism (Part III). In this direction, it not only analyzes in depth the destructive character of capitalism—illustrated by the actual systemic crisis of capital, the imperialist wars that are linked to it, and the catastrophic effects on the environment, natural resources, and climate change—but also seeks the necessary alternatives to capitalism through the engagement of socialist transition processes in our societies.

In the First Part, the main aspects of the neoclassical paradigm are analyzed and criticized. Three related but distinct fundamental themes are examined: ideology (Chapter 1), growth (Chapter 2), and development (Chapter 3). A precise and thorough knowledge of the mainstream is absolutely essential for any heterodox in economics who wishes to stand out from it.

The book begins with a preliminary—essentially epistemological and historical—reflection on the scientific status of economics as a discipline.

Chapter 1 explains that we are presently facing the domination of a certain current of thought in economic theory, which can provisionally be characterized as the "neoclassical-neoliberal-orthodox" mainstream. However, in a field where the comparison and contrast of theoretical references are inherent to the work of the researcher, it is disturbing that such a consensual paradigm, or "single thought," is even thinkable. In what strange way do mainstream economists make themselves at home formulating presumably scientific truths about the (extraordinarily unfair) ways the world works, thus constantly calling into question their neutrality as researchers? This chapter discusses the one-track thinking of mainstream economists and its history. It asks whether this one-dimensional thinking is inventing its own history, and if economics now constitutes an "anti-historical science." It shows that the tendency of the mainstream to want to impose this "single thought," elaborated around the neoclassical fiction of *homo oeconomicus*, denies the necessity of confrontation in economic theory, and consequently reduces the neoclassical mainstream to a "scientific ideology." And the following two chapters of this First Part of the book aim to provide evidence for this.

Indeed, Chapter 2 is a radical critique of the neoclassical growth theory, showing its limits and justifying ways out of mainstream economics. To begin with, we shall analyze growth theories from the classical representations to the most contemporary neoclassical models (endogenous growth). Then, we demonstrate (without giving the math) that the "new growth theory" is not a break with older neoclassical formalizations. We show that both exogenous and endogenous neoclassical models prove to be incapable of explaining growth over the long term. We concentrate on the ambiguities surrounding the hypothesis of a single agent, as well as on the role of the State, in particular when it is considered as a "planner" by the neoclassicals. Endogenous growth models do not correspond to macrodynamization of the Walrasian general equilibrium, nor do they have solid microeconomic bases. Let us insist on the fact that, each time, the theoretical aspects are discussed—making the models as accessible as possible, even to non-economists—as well as the properly ideological functions of the neoclassical assumptions and formalizations. However, no recourse to mathematics will be made at this time, so as not to exclude any readers.

In Chapter 3, we shall see that development economics, the branch of economics that attempts to show how the world's poor economies can develop, had its origins in the 1940s and 1950s. One of its earliest ideas was that the economies of the less developed countries were mired in a cycle of poverty and needed a "Big Push" to develop. This push was seen as a large boost in investment, helped by the State's infrastructural and social spending, as well as by private foreign capital spending and aid from the governments of the developed nations. Much of development economics was expressed in a narrative form; it was one of the least formal and mathematically modeled branches of economics. For this reason, and others as we shall see, it fell out of favor less than a generation after it began. Mainstream economics thought of itself as a rigorous "science," and in the eyes of its economists, what was not rigorously mathematical was simply not economics. Nevertheless, in the late 1980s, development economics began to take off again, thanks to its reformulation in more "scientific" terms. We study this revival and also identify its limits. The thesis of a disappearance-reappearance of development theory is now shared by a majority of specialists. This chapter takes strong issue with the mainstream interpretation of development economics. It intends to show how neoclassical economics, which has now absorbed development as one of its components, is the prisoner of a deep crisis, and how mainstream domination in this theoretical field is inseparable from that of neoliberal development policies.

In the Second Part, the critical work will be extended to related currents of the neoclassical mainstream, which were originally satellites of it, but have now been fully absorbed into it. Such are the cases of the various neoinstitutionalist and neo-Keynesian schools, including certain currently well-known authors like Thomas Piketty. Theorists like Oliver Williamson, Douglass North, Joseph Stiglitz, and Paul Krugman will also be targeted.

In Chapter 4, we examine how dominant economics has long wondered about the mechanisms by which institutions intervene in economic activities, in particular in the interactions between markets and their modes of structuring and functioning, as well as in the dynamic processes of transformation of economies. This field was first explored by theorists who came from a fairly mistrustful trend toward *homo oeconomicus* and who wanted to distance themselves from utilitarianism, such as Thorstein Veblen or the "American Institutionalist School." However, their non-formalized methodologies exposed them to the criticism of those who would go on to form the new orthodoxy in economics. But, for the neoclassical corpus, the institutions are generally endowed with an exogenous status. The "endogenization" of institutions within the various analytical frameworks claiming to be "Walrasians," by O. Williamson or D. North, for example, has been one of the major developments in the neoclassical research program in recent decades, that we shall present and criticize, especially for their systematic attachment to the theory of general equilibrium and their absolute defense of property rights. Although the neoinstitutionalist authors are very diverse and sometimes contradictory in their definitions and their arguments, the immense majority of them agree on the essential questions; more precisely, they agree in their allegiance to the fundamentals of the neoclassical paradigm, namely the theory of the general equilibrium of markets.

To continue, Keynesianism will be analyzed by going back to the root (or rather one of the roots) of the problem: John Maynard Keynes' view of money, which is very reductive compared to Karl Marx's conception of money. So, Chapter 5 will propose a theoretical analysis, from a Marxist point of view, of the relationships between the most famous British economist of the Twentieth Century and the economic mainstream of his time, as well as those between him and K. Marx, especially concerning the theories of money and, more generally, those of the crisis and the State. It presents the theoretical elements of capitalist crisis developed by J. M. Keynes. One of the main limitations here is that he does not consider money as capital, contrary to what Marx quite rightly did. Another one is Keynes' conception of entrepreneurs' behavior and that of the capitalist State. We shall finally criticize, in the context of our current crisis, today, the possibility for a return to so-called "Keynesian" policies—i.e., pro-cyclical State interventions aimed at saving capitalism—including when undertaken by governments said to be "right-wing" or "conservative," as is the case with the Republicans in the United States.

Thomas Piketty, a much weaker theorist than Keynes, also recommends regulating capitalism through taxation. Showing the limits and inconsistencies of the reasoning of T. Piketty—who, however, has the merit of shining a spotlight on inequalities—will be the subject of Chapter 6. The latter will be a critique, from a Marxist perspective, of *Le Capital au XXIe siècle* by Piketty. Firstly, we shall present the book's conception of the fundamental contradictions of capitalism and of inequalities, and the history of this system will be emphasized. Then, we shall underline some of his misinterpretations, highlighting the many elements that separate Piketty's book from Marx's *Capital*, before proposing some Marxist explanatory elements of the current return to power of capital during the "neoliberal" era. Finally, the difficulties and the inconsistencies of a so-called "fiscal revolution" as supported by Piketty will be discussed, as well as the deep ambiguities and the real limits of the form of democracy he claims for our modern societies.

The Third Part of the book will allow us, finally, to enter Marxist analysis directly, both in theory and in practice. This will be done by broadening the discussion beyond mere theoretical questions and combining economic theory with an in-depth examination of fundamental current problems of the present time. Three will be discussed: firstly, the interpretation of the current capitalist crisis (Chapter 7); secondly, its relations with imperialist wars, principally led by the United States and NATO (Chapter 8); and thirdly, the effects of the capitalist system on climate change, the environment and natural resources (Chapter 9).

In Chapter 7's analysis of the current crisis, we shall insist not only on its systemic character, but also on the Marxian concept of "fictitious capital," to understand the process of capital over-accumulation that we have been witnessing for several decades. Here, we underline the fact that a frequent error in interpreting this crisis is that it is seen as a financial crisis which is contaminating the sphere of the "real economy." Rather, it is, in fact, a crisis of capital, of which one of the most visible and publicized aspects has emerged within the financial sphere because of the extreme degree of financialization of contemporary capitalism. We are indeed dealing with a systemic crisis that is affecting the very heart of the present capitalist world system, i.e., the power center of high finance which has been controlling capital accumulation over the past four decades. It is not due to conjunctural factors; it is a structural phenomenon. We shall present an original Marxist interpretation of the current crisis of capital, utilizing and explaining in particular Marx's concept of fictitious capital. It will analyze the origins, manifestations, and effects of this crisis, and present a critique of the orthodox anti-crisis policies, as well as of the so-called "Keynesian" ones. We argue that there is a very high probability that the present crisis will become more acute as a systemic crisis of capital, since all the conditions are present for that to happen.

After that, we shall turn to the question of military expenditure and defense, analyzed from the perspective of Marxist theory, to show how crises and wars are closely linked. Thus, Chapter 8 shows that defense, generally regarded as the sovereign function *par excellence*, is a peculiar category of public spending. Within the framework of "defense economics," this topic has been the subject of numerous, more and more technical contributions by leading theoreticians, from Wassily Leontief to Kenneth Arrow. Nevertheless, the paradox is that, until now, these studies have failed to reach clear, convincing conclusions. Strengthened by the opacity and scarcity of information on defense, the complexity of this field is partly due to the fact that its analyses involve a political-strategic dimension. As a consequence, the researcher who investigates this area faces very specific difficulties. In addition, even if defense represents an example of a "public good," whose characteristics would theoretically justify the intervention of the State, ultraliberal economists have challenged the public good character of defense. On the basis of anti-State positions clearly in favor of private property and free trade, "libertarian" theoreticians even recommend a privatization of the national defense. We shall examine such ideas and, of course, criticize them. We also suggest that economic links exist between the capitalist crisis and imperialist wars. First, we shall insist on the necessity to give up the framework of the neoclassical mainstream to understand this issue in its full complexity; then, analyze the timing of this crisis and wars in which the hegemonic power of the world system is involved; and examine the control exercised by high finance over the military sector, including the military-industrial complex and private military companies. Finally, this chapter studies the effects of the links between crisis and wars on the exacerbation of the current capitalist contradictions.

And finally, in Chapter 9, we shall show how Marxist theory can provide a radical analysis of political ecology. The management of natural resources and the protection of the environment constitute the typical example for which the arguments formulated by neoclassicism and by the timorous and inconsistent "reformists" prove to be dangerously limited and ineffective, in the face of the dominant forces of capitalism and their destructive tendencies as this system has come to threaten even life on earth. This chapter argues that capitalism has become essentially destructive of nature as well as social formations and is today the most dangerous threat to Humanity and life. The chapter presents and then criticizes the techniques of mainstream modeling of the relations between the environment (or natural resources) and growth within the neoclassical current. It shows that the "soft" proposals (such as the market of polluting rights) and that of "degrowth" constitute false alternatives. It sketches the outline of a democratic management of the natural resources of the planet and protection of the environment. This shows that Marxists consider such issues extremely seriously and that they consider them to belong to the heart of the matter in the perspective of rebuilding radical social projects.

This invites us to reconsider post-capitalist social transformations and the alternatives to a capitalist economy, which more and more of the peoples, in spite of their differences, hopes to be socialist. The outline of a project of social emancipation and transition to socialism must be drawn. We advocate in favor of rehabilitating State intervention in social areas and of reactivating Marxist theoretical reflections regarding social planning and class analysis in our current time of structural crisis of the capitalist world system. In this concluding chapter, the book demonstrates the necessity to categorically reject the neoclassical mainstream as well as the theoretical "false alternatives" represented by neoinstitutionalist, neo-Keynesian, and reformist economists, nowadays, and to adopt Marxist theory. It is indeed Marxist theory that most effectively allows us to account for the crisis of current capitalism, and also to grasp, theoretically and practically, the transformations of our societies toward social emancipation and the transition to socialism.

In the four Appendices proposed to the readers, the works of several emblematic authors of the successive mainstreams in economics, of classical, Keynesian, and neoclassical inspirations or emanations, respectively, will be presented and dissected: Jean-Baptiste Say, Walt W. Rostow, Robert Barro. And, to finish, the "institutionalist" Amartya Sen, one of the gurus of the international organizations, will also be examined.

Contents

About the Author

Rémy Herrera (France) is an economist, researcher at the National Center of Scientific Research (CNRS). Graduated from Business School (École supérieure de Commerce, 1988), the Institute of Political Studies (Institut d'Études politiques, 1990) and the University of Paris 1 Panthéon-Sorbonne (Master of Philosophy, 1994; Ph.D. in Economics, 1996), he supervises students in Ph.D. at the Centre d'Économie de la Sorbonne. He started working in financial audit (1988), the Secrétariat général de la Défense nationale (1991), the OECD (1992–1997), and also for the World Bank (1999–2000). He was member of the CNRS National Committee (2000–2005) and of the Scientific Council of Paris 1 (2001–2006). He taught at various universities in France (especially at Paris 1 [1993–2013]) and abroad, including at the Universities of Aleppo (1998), Cairo (1999–2000), Vitoria in Brasil (2006), Complutense in Madrid (2009–2013), and Lingnan in Hong Kong (2018). He was adviser to research programs at the Chubu University (Nagoya). He is or was associated with the: Third World Forum (Dakar), Union of Radical Political Economics (New York), International Initiative for Promoting Political Economics (London), Sociedad de Economía Política Latinoamericana (São Paulo), and Asociación Nacional de Economistas de Cuba (Havana). He was the World Forum of Alternatives (WFA)'s executive secretary. He is member of the Global University for Sustainability and of the International Crisis Observatory. He currently organizes the

"Marx in the Twenty-First Century" seminar at La Sorbonne. He also works with the Centre Europe-Tiers Monde (Geneva), supporting it in its advisory role to the Human Rights Council of the United Nations.

PART I

Toward a Radical Criticism of Mainstream Economics

CHAPTER 1

On Ideology: Is There a Single Thought in Economics?

Let us endeavor, before undertaking a critical journey through "neoclassicism,"[1] to attach the thread of our discourse to the reality of the present world, whose evidence is brutal. At the risk, deliberately accepted, of appearing to privilege the percept over the concept and of falling from *logos* to *pathos*, let us contemplate for a brief moment what this world, such as it functions, gives to see of its differences. They are first of all, elsewhere, far away, in the South, the masses of innumerable human beings without voice, deprived of everything, an anonymous people of the shantytowns as far as the eye can see, miserable peasantry struggling to feed itself, the lacks, the brutality of the conditions of existence and work, the humiliation, the inhumanity. And what we have in front of our eyes, in this rich North this time, are wandering specters that we still look at but do not see anymore, without roof, dispossessed of their rights, impersonal "new poor," "untouchables" of our countries, offended, dehumanized, often lonely old men, with deformed faces, sometimes even children, to whom we have given up helping.

This sentimental, subjective, and highly partisan vision is, however, quite consistent with the apparent neutral and rigorous objectivity of

[1] This chapter has been written, primarily, from the author's three articles: Herrera (2000, 2001, 2012).

R. Herrera, *Confronting Mainstream Economics for Overcoming Capitalism*, Marx, Engels, and Marxisms,
https://doi.org/10.1007/978-3-031-05851-6_1

the statistics. The richest 20% of the world's population (classified by country) would have nearly 85% of the total income, while the share of the poorest 20% would not exceed 1% of this income.[2] Today, the gross national product *per capita* would be 38,500 U.S. dollars in the high-income economies, with a population of about 950 million inhabitants, compared to approximately 3,800 U.S. dollars for the so-called "rest of the world"—including Russia and Eastern Europe—where more than three billion people are estimated to be living (or surviving) in extreme poverty.[3] The income gap between transnational corporate executives and informal sector workers is abysmal and growing in the United States,[4] where the income structure may be as unequal as, or even more unequal than, that of a (caste-bound) country like India.[5] Impressive: the 85 richest people in the world would own more than the 3.5 billion poorest.[6]

These figures are certainly exaggerated. As a matter of fact, in reality, they *under*estimate the inequalities (those according to gender or skin color in particular) and ignore the essential, that is to say, the private property of assets, and especially the property of the means of production. Nonetheless, despite their very approximate nature, these figures bear witness to inequalities whose consequences in terms of the hardship of life for the peoples of the periphery and, more generally, for the working classes throughout the world, including the most precarious workers in the center, can be seen even in the indicators of life expectancy. In the years 2010, life expectancy at birth was estimated at 77 years in the "most developed" countries, against 67 years in the "least developed" ones, and only 56 years in Africa.[7] In France, for example, life expectancy at age 35 and without disability was 47 years for senior executives, but only 41 years for blue-collar workers.[8]

[2] See: Ortiz and Cummings (2011). And, for a comparison over time: United Nations Development Programme (1992, p. 39–40).

[3] The World Bank (2014).

[4] Frydman and Saks (2008).

[5] See the rankings established according to the Gini indicator: The World Bank (2013).

[6] Oxfam (2014). And: Crédit Suisse (2013).

[7] Based on data from the United Nations Population Division. Read here: Observatoire des inégalités (2011).

[8] Cambois, Laborde and Robine (2008).

These data show a polarization[9]: that of a system that is now called "globalized" so as not to have to say "capitalist," and even less "imperialist"—two expressions that make smile because they are supposed to be archaic, retrograde, or even nostalgic for a totalitarianism. Nevertheless, although they reveal a state of affairs, these data do not provide any analytical tools for understanding the chain of mechanisms articulating markets and organizations that produce this systemic polarization, consubstantial with the very dynamics of capital, and that reproduce it on an ever-expanding scale. These analytical tools can only be discovered in and through theoretical investigation.

But what do we observe in economic theory at the present time? The domination of a current of thought, "neoclassicism"—we will qualify it very provisionally as "neoclassical-neoliberal-orthodox"—which, faced with the reality of these extraordinarily violent inequalities, chooses to exclude the latter from its field of vision by negating, from the very outset and its presuppositions, of any relevance of the concepts and methods likely to account for this polarization, and by the compensatory edification of a fictitious paradigm made of optimal equilibria and imaginary harmonies, claiming to be scientific and universal, but always apologetic of a capitalism seized as the only thinkable one in the theory and as an unsurpassable horizon of history.

This leads us straight to the following question: by what strange effect do the cohorts of "neoclassical-neoliberal-orthodox" economists adapt so well to having to formulate scientific and universal truths about the functioning of this world that is so inequitable and unreasonable in which they are immersed and which cuts right through their neutrality as researchers?

1.1 Is a "Single Thought" Thinkable?

The existence of a "single thought" in political economy cannot be considered *a priori* as merely conceivable. Insofar as it is a constituent part—along with sociology, political science, and, to a certain extent, history, anthropology, and law—of the core of the social sciences, which has been institutionalized in its courses and researches since the Nineteenth Century, economics is one of those domains in which the confrontation of theoretical referents is inherent to the work of

[9] On the concept of "polarization": Herrera (2001).

the researcher.[10] Basically, there always remains an irreducible conflict between irreconcilable opposing positions, a conflict to be understood as the very propulsive engine that allows this discipline to unfold, to deploy itself, and to find meaning only in contradiction.

No more than the sociologist or the political scientist, the economist can free himself or herself from the hold and influence that ideology has on his or her practice, nor can he or she divest himself or herself of a subjectivity that refers his or her judgment to the philosophical landmark and reference point that is more or less consciously his or her own. A *Weltanschauung* (or conception of the world) which is some rare times *gegen der Storm*, that is to say, against the tide or the stream, but generally *geschlossene*, i.e., in unison, "homogeneous" as some used to say at the time when the philosopher Martin Heidegger was still rector at the university of *Freiburg im Breisgau*... As a particular person, attached to a group of particular persons, this economist is led to be able to claim only a relative universality and truth, always opposed to other competing particularist conceptions.

Therefore, his or her universalism conceals a particularism—sociocentric or ethnocentric, for example[11]—which can be oppressive in the sense that the representative of the current holding power generally finds the state of things that is favorable to him or her "natural"; in the same way that his or her science masks an ideology, potentially mystifying in that it tends to deny to scientific truth its fundamentally historical nature.

Moreover, this co-presence of science and ideology leaves its mark even in the indeterminacy of economics to encircle what is its own object of analysis, so pervasive is the influence of the political stakes it underlies. The elegant formula chosen by Jean-Baptiste Say to define economics as the science that studies the way in which "wealth is formed, distributed and consumed,"[12] induces the curious impression that wealth does so "if not on its own, at least in a manner that is somehow independent of man's will," added Léon Walras, who very pertinently emphasized: "[w]hat seduced the economists in this definition [the one provided by J.-B. Say (Appendix A)] is precisely this exclusive coloring of natural science that it gives to all political economy. As a matter of fact, this point

[10] Commission Gulbenkian (1996).

[11] Here: Preiswerk and Perrot (1975). And: Said (2000).

[12] Say (1803). Also: Say (1852).

of view singularly helped them in their struggle against the socialists. Any plan for organizing property was rejected by them a priori and, so to speak, without discussion."[13]

And further on, L. Walras, who was a prudent supporter of a reformist gradualism that was both social and liberal, continued as follows: "Unfortunately, it must be said that the economists have so far less demonstrated their *laissez-faire laissez-passer* than they have affirmed it against the socialists, old and new, who, for their part, assert, without demonstrating it further, the intervention of the State. I feel that in expressing myself in this way I am going to offend some sensibilities."[14]

From all this stems the impossibility of identifying in this discipline an "axiomatic core"—at the conceptual, methodological and theoretical levels—that would form a common *corpus* for the different schools of economic thought and that would be likely to drive research in a spontaneous and generalized way. The accretion of economic knowledge can only take place around distinct paradigms, exclusive of each other—although it may give rise to certain attempts at "synthesis," as was the case between neoclassical orthodoxy and the "Keynesian revolution," through the efforts of authors such as John Richard Hicks in the UK or Paul Anthony Samuelson in the United States.[15]

In our view, the deepest divide that is localizable within the (so fictitious) "scientific community" of the economists separates, in the final analysis, supporters and opponents of the capitalist system; the former who, for one reason or another, stop short of challenging its social order, which they believe could be amended, and the latter who engage in its radical critique and do not believe in the possibility of a capitalism "with a human face." In other words, the line of demarcation is between those who claim to reform, regulate, in fact try to repair the dominant economic system, and those who aspire to deform it, to transform it, in short to recast it in order to re-found it.

We can perceive here what irremediably distinguishes political economy, and with it the other social disciplines, from the so-called "hard" sciences, more especially mathematics and physics. In mathematics, a certain unity is emerging between branches in increasingly direct

[13] Walras (1988 [1874–1877], p. 30).

[14] Ibidem, p. 233.

[15] On this point, for example: Blanchard (2008).

communication, beyond traditional antagonisms and fields of specialization. Physics, as for it, offers to all researchers, in spite of the absence—or the expectation—of a unified theory of forces, a matrix of fundamental equations. The sciences of matter and life (chemistry, biology…) can also progress from a secure theoretical core in a cumulative and, in a very particular sense, transcendent way, by successive widening and deepening of their knowledge.

Some analysts argue that the natural sciences advance through paradigm shifts that lead to the rejection of old theories and pre-established truths.[16] However, even in these disciplines, where a statement can be massively recognized as correct and be the object of a broad agreement between specialists, the existence of a "single thought" is quite uncertain, if not inconceivable. For example, in the physical sciences, there remain polemics whose outcome is open and not definitively decided, because they refer to epistemological points of view, and *in fine* to deeper intellectual debates, situated upstream, or below physics, that is to say, in the element of ***meta***physics.

Let us think of the clearly different treatments of the concept of infinity that has made of it philosophy, on the one hand, since the frontal clash between the Parmenidian paradoxes of Zeno of Elea and the paralogisms of Aristotelian *Physics*,[17] and mathematics, on the other hand, from the concomitant discovery of the differential calculus by Gottfried Wilhelm Leibniz and Isaac Newton (only a few decades after the pioneering works of Pierre de Fermat) to the invention of the transfinite by Georg Cantor.[18]

Thus, no more in political economy than in any other science the idea of a "single thought" is strictly speaking thinkable. In the economic discipline, it can only be a question of dominant thoughts, even if they are hegemonic, but always contingent, because they are constantly competing.

1.2 What is the "Single Thought"?

The fact remains that the figure of a "single thought" with economistic contours has been denounced, in the media, by some authors. Extending the Anglo-Saxon debate on "economic correctness" and engaging in

[16] Kuhn (1996).

[17] Aristotle (1931, p. 61).

[18] Dauben (1979).

polemics with the well-meaning advocates of political alternation without economic alternatives, progressive journalists in France from the mid-1990s onwards have castigated this "translation into ideological terms with a universal pretension of the interests of a set of economic forces, those of international capital in particular," stifling "rebellious reasoning," and establishing a "globalitarian regime."[19] Certainly justified, this denunciation was supported by some intellectual authorities and a certain number of economists grouped around a "call to get out of the single thought" and enter into the "ideological resistance."[20]

The paradox and, for us, the interest of this mobilization come from the fact that not only did the aforementioned expression of "single thought" flourish, but also from the fact that its success exceeded the ambitions of the circle of its initiators, to the point of becoming one of the major and recurrent themes of the discourse of those whom it precisely aimed at and intended to condemn. Indeed, in France, for example, and among many Northern countries, "market journalists" and other *ejusdem farinae* who were brought into line during the first Gulf War and who had just returned from their condemnation of the great strikes and social movements of 1995, sank comfortably into this "rebellion, as well as almost the entire national political class, whether it is the traditional right, of course, or a large majority of the "socialist left"—which is neither "left" nor "socialist" anymore, and which we will soon have to resolve to call by its name: a "new right."

These newly enlisted troops joined some of the most famous representatives of the dominant forces of the world system: Alan Greenspan, former chairman of the U.S. Federal Reserve, who warned the markets against their "exuberant irrationality"[21] ; Joseph Stiglitz, former chief economist of the World Bank, who intended to "regulate financial flows"[22]; or the speculator and financial group leader George Soros (worth 24 billion U.S. dollars alone—that is to say, one Côte d'Ivoire,

[19] Ramonet (1995).

[20] See, for example, the issue n° 137 of May 1996 of the review *Alternatives économiques*.

[21] Greenspan (1996).

[22] Stiglitz (2003).

or two Mali—), who nurtures the hope of the possibility of "saving capitalism from neoliberalism."[23]

The thought of the owners thus easily melted into the "critical" arguments of their opponents. Indeed, this was not due to the effect, however dreadfully effective, of its centripetal force, but rather because most of these anti- "single thought" attacks left the essential intact; the essential, that is to say, the perpetuation of the capitalist world system, beyond the layout and the adjustment of its forms, and the permanence within it of the U.S. hegemony, beyond the rearrangement and the redevelopment of its forces. For, these condemnations have been those of an anti-neoliberalism, but (almost) never those of an anti-capitalism. Nevertheless, now, of the two, only the latter fully belong to the *socialist* project.

Such a critique of "the unique thought," by censoring from its analyses any theoretical and historical reference to the perspectives of an end of exploitation, an abolition of class differences, a social appropriation of the means of production, the construction of a society which would be (not nominally or fictitiously, but) authentically democratic, but also the perspectives of the anti-imperialist struggle by the peoples, a sovereign and self-centered development—is all this really so outdated today?—does not it at the same time obliterate in the debates the possibility of glimpsing a *non*-capitalist horizon?[24]

Yet this path, which is that of *post*-capitalism, is also being sought at present in the radicalization of demands and claims aimed, among other things, at establishing the conditions for democratic control over the huge banking and financial oligopolies, in order to put an end to the predominance of speculative operations, to redirect investments toward productive activities and to promote regional stabilization of exchange rates; to reform the international monetary and financial systems by questioning the functions (and perhaps even the existence) of the International Monetary Fund (IMF) and the World Bank; to boost a global tax system based on principles of justice that go beyond a "Tobin tax"; to redefine the norms of access to markets, in particular by dismantling the rules of the World Trade Organization (WTO) and dislocating the privileges of

[23] Soros (1998).

[24] Rightly, Alain Badiou rather spoke of a "semaphore of communism." See: Badiou (1998).

transnational corporations; to engage in the democratic re-foundation of the United Nations Organization (UNO) reconciling the requirements of universalism and the socio-political rights of individuals and peoples...[25]

It is by refusing such discussions, which are those of a beyond of globalized capitalism and the engagement of concrete processes of deep social transformations, that one forbids oneself to define the criteria allowing to draw the border between the inside and the outside of the said "single thought." It is by closing these perspectives that one condemns onself to make yesterday's realities, which have disappeared today—whether it is the Welfare State in the West (let us call it "national social capitalism"), authoritarian statism in the East (most often assimilated to a particular type of "capitalism without capitalists"), or national-bourgeois developmentism in the Third Worlds (which was indeed a "peripheral capitalism")—the *capitalist* utopias of tomorrow.

1.3 Does the "Single Thought" Have a History?

Under these conditions, the "single thought" that we are so often told about cannot be basically understood otherwise than as single thought of capitalism; that is to say, what Karl Marx and Friedrich Engels had already qualified a long time ago as "the dominant ideology of the dominant class."[26] If we can hold, according to them, that this thought has no history "of its own,"[27] it is nevertheless possible for us to decipher a history of the single thoughts of capitalism that have succeeded one another, since economic science became autonomized and institutionalized in a precise space–time: in the Nineteenth Century and at the center of the capitalist world system (Western Europe/North America).[28] It will also be a question for us of spotting and tracing the evolution of the class content of these successive thoughts, up to the current domination of high finance over world capitalism—some of whose features we will return to in the last chapters of this book.

This history began with the bourgeois single thought deployed during the Nineteenth Century, i.e., the "classical" ideology of liberalism, that

[25] See: Amin and Herrera (2000).

[26] Re-read: Marx and Engels (1968, p. 44–45).

[27] About that: Althusser (1995, p. 209).

[28] Amin (1997, p. 27–46).

of small proprietors attached to the principles of the preponderance of (self-regulated) markets and (anti-monopoly) free competition, engaged in an industrial revolution in which State intervention already played a fundamental role in the formation of the market society, *laissez-faire* and the original (called "primitive") accumulation of capital. This thought of bourgeois civilization knew how to become that of "human rights" in discourse, while accepting European colonization and the rise of white racism in action.[29]

The history of the single thoughts continued, between the end of the Nineteenth Century and the Second World War, with a "monopolistic liberalism" resulting from the transformations of capitalism by a bank-industry merger powerfully supported by a State which, at the center of the world system, had completed its national integration and considerably increased its expenditures. In Europe, this single thought was able to perfect bourgeois "democracy" on the basis of political blocs of classes, through the alliance of capital with the middle and/or aristocratic classes, turning when the time came into fascism, or one of its by-products, where the working class, won over to communism after 1917, threatened its hegemony too directly: Spartakist Revolution in Germany, Council movement in Italy, Republic in Spain, Popular Front in France...

Then, from 1945 until the beginning of the 1970s, the single thought of capitalism transformed, under the combined pressure of Soviet military victories, the trade union and party struggles of the Western proletariat, and the successes of anti-colonialist peripheral popular movements, turning into a "national-social" liberalism. This thought, cemented in the North around the "Keynesian compromise," was able to reconcile wage increases and social progress within the country with genocidal colonial wars, criminal support for neo-fascist dictatorships, and systematic State support for the crudely imperialist strategies of the big Western transnational corporations.

These actions have of course also been supra-State and have mobilized, among other actors, the World Bank. Besides, the latter did not take off until after 1968 and the assumption of office by President Robert Strange McNamara, who had already been involved, from 1961 onwards (with his collaborator and friend Walt Whitman Rostow [Appendix B], as we will

[29] Herrera (2018, 2022).

see) in the "development" of Vietnam as Secretary of Defense—before apologizing, to the (only) U.S. people, for "the mistakes made."[30]

The end of the 1960s marked, as we know, the entry into crisis of the capitalist system in the countries of the center, which was particularly noticeable in the decline of profit rates recorded in most of the major Western countries from that time on. This crisis became generalized during the following decade, with the tipping of the center of the world system into monetary and financial chaos, mass unemployment, and the explosion of inequalities in the 1970s. The foundations of the Western Welfare State—thanks to which wages and productivity gains were growing in tandem—which had proved their effectiveness for three decades in ensuring the post-war boom, became inoperative.

The conjunction of the profound questioning of Keynesian regulatory model of capitalism in the North—brought on in the 1970s by stagflation, the simultaneous increase in unemployment and prices—the failures of the national-bourgeois developmentist projects in the South—highlighted by the debt crisis of the 1980s—and the collapse of the Soviet bloc in the East—completed by the early 1990s—was to provoke, on a worldwide scale and in the short space of about fifteen years, a nothing less than gigantic change in the capital-labor relations.

It is, therefore, only in this new global context of the retreat of the positions conquered by the workers of the center and by the peoples of the peripheries, following their common victories over fascism and colonialism, as well as of the consequent reorientation of economic policies intended to consolidate the return to power of high finance in the United States during the 1970s, that it is possible to truly understand the globalized deployment of the offensive of "neoliberalism."[31]

1.4 "Neoliberalism"

The neoliberal doxa is well known. At the national level, it is, cursorily, on the one hand, to conduct an aggressive anti-State strategy, resulting in the privatization of public enterprises, that is to say, the mut(il)ation of the ownership structure of capital to the benefit of the private sector, and in

[30] McNamara (1995). For the Vietnamese position, see: Tran (2021, p. 141–156).

[31] Supposedly to be "competitive" in its French version. For more details: Herrera (2010, Chapter 5).

the reduction of budgetary expenditures, associated with the dismantling of social protection, and, on the other hand, to impose wage austerity, made possible by the elimination of "union rigidities," as the pivot of a disinflation[32] that takes priority over any other consideration, i.e., a sharing of added value favorable to capital and the maintenance of high interest rates in real terms.

Applied at the global level, neoliberal dogmas aim mainly at perpetuating the supremacy of the U.S. dollar over the international monetary system, through the adoption of flexible exchange rates—hence its European counterpart of a single currency that subjects to its ruthless law the entire economic policy of the member countries of the euro zone, as well as multiple problems posed to all the other countries of the world—and at promoting free trade, through the lowering of protectionist barriers and the liberalization of capital transfers.

The planetary standardization of this strategy of market "deregulation"—that is, "*re*-regulation" of the markets by the globally dominant capital exclusively—is part of the functions of the complex made up of the international organizations (first and foremost the IMF, the World Bank, the WTO, etc.) and local monetary and financial authorities, starting with the self-proclaimed "independent" Central Banks (but who do they obey if the political power no longer controls them?), the ministries of Finance and the Treasury departments... The whole device is placed, to this day, under the hegemony of the United States, whose military component guarantees, as a last resort, through war if necessary, the global reproduction of the polarizing operating conditions of the world capitalist system.

Nearly thirty-five years before the bursting of the "financial bubble" in the so-called subprime segment in the United States, neoliberal policies, conducted under the aegis of a high finance that had taken over the reins, were already seeking to "manage" the crisis of the expansion of capital. So, this "management" consisted, in the face of insufficient opportunities of profitable investment for the enormous masses of profits derived from capitalist exploitation, in trying to constantly enlarge the outlets for the surplus of floating capital in order to avoid its devalorization.

Although they did not succeed, for more than four decades, in bringing the system out of its structural crisis, these policies could seem, in a certain

[32] Ibidem, Chapter 6.

sense, "rational," from the point of view of *capital*: in fact, they offered it the possibility, on liberalized capital markets, of a headlong rush into speculative financial investments, extremely lucrative for it, and ensured the continuity of transfers of surplus from the South to the North, thanks to the various strategies of "management" (i.e., of repayment of the service) of the debt and to structural adjustment programs, imposed unilaterally on poor countries by the force of international institutions under U.S. control.

Nonetheless, this choice of "management" of the long crisis of capitalism—should it be remembered?—has made and continues to make victims, very numerous, that we should maybe one day learn to count in physical units—that is, in the deaths of human beings—and to locate spatially—for the most part of them, in the peripheries of a capitalist world system within which the circulation of all commodities is "free," with the exception of one, a very particular "commodity": labor.

The offensive of neoliberal thought launched since the 1970s is, therefore, nothing other than the ideological product derived from major transformations registered in the conflictual order of social relations on a global scale. It owes nothing to the illusory triumph of the "reasoned" doctrine of neoliberal intellectuals over the "unreasoned" arguments of their adversaries in the ethereal sphere of ideas: it is the result of the profound evolution of a balance of power observed on the fields of production and circulation which has suddenly and massively shifted to the advantage of capital, and above all of its new hegemonic fraction: high finance.

The conversion, also brutal and massive, of "social democracy" to neoliberalism has maintained a lie[33]: that according to which this neoliberal thought would identify with modernity. The fact remains that, at present, the supremacy of the philosophical values and political preferences of neoliberalism is manifested in close solidarity with the predominance in economic theory, almost unchallenged since the beginning of the 1980s, of "neoclassicism," or neoclassical mainstream, whose pretension claiming to scientificity has reinforced the discourse of neoliberal thinking of capitalism.

[33] In France, this evolution had the consequence of turning the "cohabitation" from exception into rule under the Fifth Republic, before the ideological lines of the traditional right and of what is still curiously called the "socialist" party ended up converging. See: Herrera (2020).

1.5 A Thought that Invents Its Own Economic History…

In order to impose itself as a system of referential and rational representations, this new neoliberal single thought of capitalism still needs to try to rewrite its own history, which it will present as the only possible reading of the succession of ideas and doctrines; in short, as the *single* history of thought.

To do this, the mainstream genealogists and epistemologists have taken it upon themselves to invent prestigious—all too prestigious—theoretical filiations for neoclassicism and for what we will generously call neoliberal "philosophy." The first, neoclassicism, is accommodatingly and artificially inscribed in the lineage of the works of the greatest classics,[34] which it would logically prolong and surpass; the second, the supposed neoliberal "philosophy," is pegged to the doctrines elaborated by the liberal theoreticians[35] of the Eighteenth and Nineteenth Centuries.

This reconstruction of the histories of economic and philosophical thoughts is carried out through a movement of inversions: crucial ruptures in theory are presented as continuities, while strong theoretical continuities, as far as they are concerned, are considered to be ruptures. Thus, where an in-depth critical analysis reveals scientific regressions and step backward in the history of the bourgeois single thoughts of capitalism, an ideologically built historical-mythical narrative will reveal *progress*.

All that will remain for the mainstream to do is to underline, in support of its vital (for it) claims to scientificity and universality, the richness of its "new theories," when the economic research whose production it institutionally controls no longer provides, in the opinion of some of its most eminent representatives—in France, for example, Edmond Malinvaud in the lead, to quote here only a former director general of the National Institute of Statistics and Economic Studies (called INSEE in French),

[34] With K. Marx, we will call "classics" the scientific economists, like and since Pierre Le Pesant de Boisguilbert, and the polymath William Petty. *Cf.* Marx (1978, p. 83).

[35] By "liberals," we will mean the thinkers of the liberal society in formation: David Hume, Adam Smith, Anne Robert Jacques Turgot… For an enlightening introduction: Vergara (2002).

professor at the *Collège de France* and first president of the Pontifical Academy of Social Sciences—the least significant innovative result.[36]

The neoclassical current has thus become accustomed to presenting itself as the sole descendant and beneficiary, in direct line, of the great classical thinkers. Nevertheless, the ruptures it was forced to make with the latter—breaks necessitated by the Marxian developments, destructive and creative, at the same time, and so close to classical thinking, but leading through unsuspected paths to the theory of the extortion of surplus value—were decisive for the trajectory that modern economic science was to take thereafter. These "epistemological hyphenations," which the orthodox of neoclassicism often try to conceal or resolve to the point of retroactively making them into simple growth crises of "the" science of economics, can be seen at the methodological, theoretical, and conceptual levels.

First of all, in method: with methodological individualism, any socio-historical vision of capitalism disappears within bourgeois thought, thus blocking the recourse to analyze conceived in terms of social classes and long trends. Secondly, at the theoretical level: because of a focus on utility, which reduces all social reality to a collection of *homines œconomici*, the bridge between the theory of value and that of exploitation is broken, and with it a certain relationship between economics and politics. Finally, with respect to concepts: due to the substitution of a long-term equilibrium (through quantity adjustment) by a short-term equilibrium (through price adjustment), the understanding of cycles and, even more profoundly that of prolonged crises, is condemned, which is rather worrying these days—we shall return to this at the end of this book (Part III).

Consequently, a double reversal of ruptures into continuities (from classical to neoclassical economists) and of continuities into ruptures (between the classics and Marx) allow the mainstream to transform the ideological correspondence between the "universal harmony" of the historical and social theories of the classics and the "optimum equilibrium" of the anhistorical and asocial pseudo-theorems of the neoclassicals into a purely theoretical *continuum*. Or how to make all of them commune—except Karl Marx!—in a *unified* apologetic vision of capitalism…

[36] Malinvaud (1993, 1996).

The *camera obscura* effect is sometimes visible to the naked eye, so crude is the misappropriation of classical writings, as well as is summary their manipulation. A typical example is provided by William Stanley Jevons, who attributes the paternity of utility-value to David Ricardo by exploring a blind spot in economic analysis (the value of a work of art).[37] Another is the recovery, at all costs, in the theory of international trade, of the law of comparative advantage of the same D. Ricardo by neoclassical antiquarian merchants turned into zealous servants of free trade.[38] However, certain orthodox authors have sometimes found the means to mobilize more subtlety as was the case (we shall show it in Chapter 2), with the neoclassical "new theory" of growth, known as "growth with endogenous technical progress."

1.6 ... Its Philosophical History...

For the effectiveness of the "single thought" to be fully operating, these inversions-inventions must also function in the element of philosophy. That underlying the publications of the contemporary neoliberal authors (such as the theoreticians of ultraliberalism, for the majority of them) is thus most often presented as being situated in the direct extension of the ideas of the liberals of the Eighteenth and Nineteenth Centuries.

Therefore, an economist, like Milton Friedman, for example, whose individualist, anti-statist, and monetarist positions have been placed at the basis of economic policies implemented in the main Western countries for nearly four decades, in the context of the social transformations that we have recalled, is frequently considered to be an heir by blood of Adam Smith, A.R.J. Turgot, Jeremy Bentham, or David Ricardo, with whom he would quite naturally share, through the same community of mind, the choice of "freedom" as the ultimate ethical criterion.

Would a simple prefix (neo-) be enough to divide their visions of what "liberalism" would be? Moreover, does not Milton Friedman state that "as liberals, we [that means, as "we" continue the work of liberals...] take the freedom of the individual as the permanent ultimate goal for judging

[37] Jevons (1957 [1871], p. 239–241).

[38] For example, Dornbusch, Fischer and Samuelson (1977); or: Krugman and Obstfeld (2003).

social institutions"[39]? However, this is to omit the fact that the natural law of some (A.R.J. Turgot, Nicolas de Condorcet, Thomas Jefferson...) and the utilitarianism of others (David Hume, A. Smith, J. Bentham...) never elevated "the freedom of the individual" to the status of a primary criterion; and it is also to conceal the profound alteration that the "new" liberals have introduced into the theory of the old ones.

Indeed, the young *neo*liberal generations, as well as the *ultra*liberal ones, are characterized by a very loose eclecticism in the determination of their philosophical criteria of judgment. Friedrich Hayek, among others, is exemplary of this vacillation, which makes him constantly hesitate between several criteria and abandon, at the discretion of his rhetoric, the argument based on "the maximum of freedom," in order to fall back randomly, sometimes on the (unique) criterion chosen by the supporters of natural law—the "conformity to justice," according to A.R.J. Turgot, for instance—[40]sometimes on the (unique) criterion adopted by utilitarians—"the greatest happiness of the greatest number," for A. Smith in particular.[41]

These ethical ambivalences, present in F. Hayek's work, as much as they could be revealed in the study of M. Friedman's writings, logically contaminate the fields of economic policy. There, the recommendations for State intervention remain most often imprecise, even ambiguous, if not contradictory. The State of Hayekian libertarianism intends to respect the principle of "increasing the chances for all participants to satisfy their needs," but it will have to "ensure protection for all against extreme destitution in the form of a guaranteed minimum income, at the level of resources below which no one can fall"; while at the same time affirming, in order not to risk appearing to want to reinforce a social State of law, that "such a minimum of resources must be provided outside the market to all those who, for whatever reason, are unable to earn enough in the market to live on"[42]! And so, "progress" for the poor derives from a delegitimization of the ideal of social justice and, to put it with André Tosel,

[39] Friedman (1986, p. 12).

[40] Turgot (1788 [1766]).

[41] Hayek (1976, p. 125, 309).

[42] Hayek (1981, vol. 3, p. 169–170).

from a return to "Nietzsche's worst"—that is, the condemnation of the "resentment of the weak."[43]

Besides, we also find in Milton Friedman the idea that it is private charity that should regulate redistribution, together with the idea of "negative taxation," leading peacefully to the suggestion of a "minimum income." The environment will be privatized to the end, but the Friedmanian currency will be public; whereas it must be totally private for Hayek, but the government is welcome to promote major infrastructure works. The important thing here is not the coherence of the argument, but the mobilization, in the service of the powers of the market, of all the wills of domination—from the Nietzschean conception to the Heideggerian one, in Hayek's case—and of "policing" the *polis* of this ideal liberal society.

In certain respects, such confusion, both ethical and practical, is found even in the apparent rigor of the "Pareto optimum"[44] of general equilibrium demonstrations. An "indeterminacy theorem" is even called upon to maintain the order of social inequalities. Once the impossibility of comparing all the agents' preferences on a common scale has been mathematically proven, (the reason for) the economic optimum can no longer have any connection with (the passion for) the distribution of income. Would we try to upset the social order by forcibly redistributing what the wealthiest "1 percent" is unwilling to give up to the 99% least fortunate? Science would be unable to support this change with its "welfare economics." On what pretext? This one: the gain of the poorest 99% is not formally comparable to the loss of the richest 1%, which makes it impossible to consider our better world preferable to the old one in terms of social utility. It is, furthermore, into this breach, as we shall see, that the astute Amartya Sen will rush (Appendix D).

This laborious effort to reconstruct the history of thought, intended to ensure, over and above the oppositions between these different bourgeois schools and sometimes even the internal contradictions of their own demonstrations, the properly ideological unity of *all* the supporters of the capitalist order, is still at work when these authors have to take a position on the subject of State interference in the allocation of resources. It is then to the "non-interventionist" Turgot and Smith that one will appeal, in the

[43] Tosel (1992, p. 119).

[44] Pareto (1964 [1897]).

scrum of the polemics of the present time, to support some categorical anti-State argument—and this, even in the field of education.

Therefore, according to Milton Friedman's views, for example, State intervention beyond the educational services spontaneously offered by the market "is not necessary" and would even lead to a situation "much worse than that which would have developed if cooperation [i.e., the market] had continued to play an increasing role."[45] This thesis cannot, however, be deduced in any way from the writings of classical liberals: neither from Adam Smith, aware of the requirement to make the exercise of citizenship compatible with the functioning of capitalism,[46] nor from John Stuart Mill, who was confronted even more directly with the rise of working-class protests in the Nineteenth Century.[47]

On the contrary, it presents similarities with what Frédéric Bastiat declared, all muscles stretched in defense of private property against "the disastrous deviations of our revolutions": "Since the Republic, there has been much talk of free instruction. (…) It is Communism applied to a branch of human activity. (…) Instruction is free! And it is not only free instruction that one should ask the State, but free food, etc. But what! Is not food even more necessary? Let us be careful. The people are almost there. Fooled by a word, we have taken a step toward Communism; what reason do we have not to take a second step, then a third one, until all freedom, all property, all justice have disappeared? (…) *Primo vivere, deinde philosophari* [i.e., first live, then philosophize], the people will say, and I really do not know what to say to them in reply."[48]

1.7 …And Its Universal History

Here we should recognize the similarities between this meticulous work of inversion carried out in the history of ideas and a much larger basic enterprise, which always goes hand in hand with it, of inventing the history of facts—of the *universal* history—long started by mainstream thinkers. So

[45] Friedman (1986, p. 197). The World Bank for its part says: "the development of education should be encouraged (…), the best way to proceed is to support the action of the private sector in this area [because] private schools often provide better education at a lower cost" (The World Bank [2000], p. 44–61).

[46] Smith (1937 [1776]).

[47] Mill (1865).

[48] Bastiat (1864 [1855], vol. 4, p. 477, 295, respectively).

true is it, as Immanuel Wallerstein notes, that "the history of the distant past always depends on the events of the near past," because, contrary to the dominant logico-deductive schemas, it is "the present [which] determines the past and not the other way around."[49]

Martin Bernal has thus shown how, of the two great versions of Greek history which clashed, one—which he describes as the "Aryan model"—presenting ancient Greece as being of essentially European origin, and the another—the so-called "old" model—like a civilization located at the crossroads of African (Egyptian) and Asian (Semitic) areas and resulting from a fruitful mixture of the different cultures of the Eastern Mediterranean, it is the first one that Western teachings have imposed and in which common sense has *de facto* most naturally placed its belief.

Moreover, the author has also shown how this "Aryan model" was created from scratch during the first half of the colonial Nineteenth Century, then further radicalized during the imperialist era, especially during the rising wave of anti-Semitism, from the years 1890 to 1920, in its negation of the fact—yet attested by many Greek thinkers of the period of antiquity—of extra-European colonizations, and in its recognition of the only civilizational contribution of the Hellenes of Nordic origin and of the Indo-European language to the peoples of the so-called "pre-Hellenic" Aegean. M. Bernal said: "If it turns out that I am right to want us to debunk the Aryan model, it will not only be necessary to rethink the bases of 'Western civilization,' but also to recognize the influence of racism, of 'continental chauvinism,' in our historiography. The old model [was] absolutely intolerable in the eyes of the racist ideologues of the Eighteenth and Nineteenth Centuries [as was also the idea] that Greece, in whom they saw the quintessence of Europe, and which embodied the purity of the European childhood, could have been the result of a mixture of native Europeans and African and Semitic colonizers. It was therefore necessary (…) to replace it with something that was more bearable."[50]

From an equally anti-Europeocentric perspective, Cheikh Anta Diop maintained that the black identity of ancient Egypt was "for all the authors prior to the grotesque and surly falsifications of modern Egyptology, and contemporary of the ancient Egyptians (…) an obvious fact

[49] Wallerstein (1997, p. 151–152).

[50] Bernal (1996 [1987], p. 24).

which made sense, that is to say which fell under the eyes, and thus that it would have been superfluous to demonstrate"—whereas today it demands of us an effort to tear ourselves away from the ideological gravity which makes us, so to speak by reflex, "cut off" ancient Egypt from the rest of the African continent.[51] It was on the basis of this thesis of a "Negro origin of Egyptian-Nubian civilization" that this author had succeeded, in order to awake "the memory of humanity that the slavery of the Negro had rendered amnesic with regard to the past of this people," in going back to an "African and Negroid origin of humanity and civilization" and in retracing "the contribution of Negro thought to Western civilization in the sciences, letters and arts," and "the formation of African States [after the decline of Egypt] throughout the continent and the continuity of the historical-cultural bond until the dawn of modern times."[52]

What is true for the historical facts of the most remote times continues to be valid, all the more so, for the events of the contemporary period, on which the hold of the dominant ideology, generator of mythologies and mystifications, is almost total. W. Stetson Kennedy, before Howard Zinn, Noam Chomsky or William Blum, knew how to reveal some unspoken sections of the interior and exterior history of the United States.[53] As far as France is concerned, the colonialist, collaborationist, and neo-imperialist detours of its history still remain largely to be written.[54] Our aim is not so much to unmask, through these lines, a plot orchestrated by the cynicism of professional ideologists, whose constructions in economics are only one of the cogs, but rather to state the biases systematically introduced and complacently repeated in the history of ideas and facts, through the inversions, inventions, unspoken that we have underlined, and to denounce their permanent reorientation to the advantage of the dominant powers of the capitalist world system.

[51] Diop (1981, p. 9).

[52] Diop (1979, p. 5–6).

[53] See: Kennedy (2008 [1955]); Zinn (1980); Chomsky (2005); and Blum (2002).

[54] Fortunately, there are exceptions, a few of which are heroic, such as: Alleg (2006).

1.8 The Impossibility for Economics of Constituting Itself in a Science Against History

As regards economics more specifically, the consolidation of the bourgeois "single thoughts" of capitalism has gained in efficiency, obviously, with the changes in a disciplinary field whose expansion has continuously sought to make people forget that it is itself a by-product of the evolution of the capitalist system. The discipline has indeed slowly transformed from "political economy" to "pure economics." "Political economy" is the form in which it appeared in the Seventeenth Century, thanks to mercantilists like Antoine de Montchrestien and Sir William Petty,[55] reflecting the new prevalence of the economic over the political following the affirmation of capitalism; then under which it was improved from the Eighteenth Century on, by Adam Smith and the classical contributions. "Pure economics" is what it claims to have become since the end of the Twentieth Century, and even more so at the start of the Twenty-First Century. The central part of the chronological triptych is certainly represented by the formulation of a (Walrasian) "pure political economy" in the last decades of the Nineteenth Century.

As it became more detached from philosophy and law, and as political science (dealing with the State) and sociology (focusing on civil society) separated from it, the changing economic discipline claimed, in its movement of institutionalization and its unrestrained search for an appearance of scientificity, an increasingly openly normative, nomothetic and anti-idiographic vocation.

By taking up the task of overthrowing historical and holistic methods in favor of atomism and the subjectivism of methodological individualism, the neoclassics were not only able to advance the idea that the behavior of *homo œconomicus* was only the reflection of an individualistic psychology that can be perfectly universalized, rather than of socially built institutions, but also to affirm the "natural" character of the *laissez-faire laissez-passer* principles and, more generally, of the very foundations of the capitalist market system.

[55] The term "political economy" came to us with the *Traicté de l'œconomie politique* (1615) by A. de Montchestien. As to him, W. Petty spoke of *Political Arithmetick* (1690).

This is obviously and decisively the case with the recognition of private ownership of the means of production. And this, even if it means appealing to the Robinsonades that Frédéric Bastiat was so fond of, for their ability to make the social relationship disappear, as if by magic, in the definition of *capital*. Let us read him on this subject: "Economic laws act on the same principle, whether it is a question of a numerous agglomeration of men, of two individuals, or even of a single one, condemned by the circumstances to live in isolation. (…) Tools, materials, provisions, this is what Robinson will call his *capital* (…). Let us now place ourselves within the social order. Capital will also consist of the instruments of labor, materials and provisions without which, neither in isolation nor in society, nothing can be undertaken in the long term. Those who find themselves provided with this capital will have it only because they will have created it by their efforts or by their privations."[56]

We will subsequently find "our Robinson" on a mission almost everywhere in the theoretical literature, since the demonstrations of the existence of subjective value in the absence of exchange made by W.S. Jevons ("an isolated individual…"), through the descriptions of the economizing man given by Carl Menger ("…suffering from myopia on a desert island…"), or by the illustrated explanations of the decrease in marginal utility according to Alfred Marshall, to the heart of the theory of capital and interest proposed by Eugen von Böhm-Bawerk ("… in his remote cabin in the middle of a virgin forest…") and even, this time lost in the mathematical analysis of rational choices, in the midst of a diagram of indifference curves, with Francis Y. Edgeworth[57]—before one of the "masters" of contemporary microeconomics (and chief economist at Google), Hal Ronald Varian, put it in his "generalized Edgeworth box."[58]

This is because mathematics constitutes a field where, as J.C.F. Gauss and, later, the Bourbaki group had foreseen, the unification of the march of the discipline is relatively strong, and maximal the autonomy of its upliftment to reality—and *a fortiori* in relation to historical time. Does it not seem in fact, especially since the appearance of non-Euclidean

[56] Bastiat (1864 [1855], Chapter 7, "Capital," vol. 6, p. 204 *et s*).

[57] See, respectively, Jevons (1957 [1874], p. 80); Menger (1950 [1871], p. 133); Marshall (1920 [1890], p. 129); Böhm-Bawerk (von) (1959 [1890], p. 2; Edgeworth (1967 [1881], p. 28).

[58] Varian (1984, p. 224).

geometries to which the names of Nikolai Lobachevsky, János Bolyai, or Bernhard Riemann are attached, that "mathematics and reality are almost completely independent, and their contacts more mysterious than never"?[59]

In mathematics, the history of thought seems to be that of progression through abstraction and the only reciprocal determination of its concepts, "oriented by an internal dialectic of notions," to speak like Jean Cavaillès.[60] A "dialectic" which, besides, would perhaps not be entirely reducible to an interpretation giving rise to thought only from historical conditions. J. Cavaillès,[61] so Spinozist here, continues: "I believe that we grasp the necessary everywhere. Necessary, the sequences of mathematicians; necessary (...) the stages of mathematical science, also necessary this struggle that we are waging" (as far as he was concerned, as a communist against fascism during World War II). Science would even then seem to attain something of a purity.

How could our neoclassical theorists have escaped the temptation—they who have this "superiority" over physicists to have achieved the feat of identifying not only *the* elementary particle (unique: *homo œconomicus*), but also *the* fundamental force (also unique: the maximization of profit or utility under constraint)—in order to appropriate a little of the prestige of mathematical science to establish their laws, "true" in any place and all time for all and everyone?

As a consequence, the result could only be catastrophic. Also the followers of neoclassicism, of whom it must be said in passing that a majority did not receive an authentic mathematical training, and who nevertheless strive to develop an objective knowledge of "social reality," have plunged back, by an unfortunate *salto mortale*, in precisely what they intended to flee: intellectual speculation.

There arises, thus, a fictitiously "apolitical" economic discipline, but very concretely dominated, or even crushed within the academy, by an extremely dogmatic hegemonic current which makes it tend toward a "scientific ideology"—in the sense given to the expression by Georges Canguilhem, who re-found "the Marxist concept of ideology, as being

[59] Quote from Jean Dieudonné, taken from: Dahan-Dalmedico and Peiffer (1986, p. 159).

[60] Canguilhem (1996, p. 29).

[61] Engels (1978, p. 69).

the representation of natural or social reality whose truth does not reside in what it says but in what it silences."[62] Or toward what we have called, elsewhere, an "economic science (-fiction)"[63]—as Louis Althusser had been able to speak of "political science-fiction (…) whose anti-social role is obvious."[64]

To conclude, the term "single thought" has, therefore, been chosen by the currently dominant forces of the capitalist system to name its own ideology. The bourgeois thought of capitalism that succeeds in imposing itself is the one that responds in the most appropriate way to the immediate historical needs of the dynamics of capitalism.

In short, this "single thought":

1. articulates an economic theory (neoclassical) with scientific pretensions—i.e., neoclassicism—and a political philosophy (neoliberal) with a universal vocation, in order to build a *total* "cultural" and "societal" project;
2. incorporates, by subsuming it and overcoming its contradictions, any external and/or critical thesis as one of the components of its own unity;
3. functions with "persecutive unanimity"[65] through the interplay of a necessary pluralistic and "democratic" (in the bourgeois sense of the word) freedom of thought and authoritatively normalized academic and media apparatuses;
4. excludes popular masses from all the most fundamental processes of economic and political decisions, by the polarization of the knowledge and the technicization of the tasks;
5. derives from a real-life balance of power between capital and labor on a global scale, reflecting the rise of high finance to hegemony;
6. relies on the threatened but still effective unipolar hegemony of the United States, based on oligopolies, including that of armed force, as a last resort;

[62] Canguilhem (1977, p. 43).

[63] See: Herrera (2010).

[64] Althusser (1995, p. 209).

[65] Strauss (1989, p. 55–74).

7. tends to legitimize, by an ethical guarantee, the practice of capital, as if it were "naturalizing," by allowing it to last beyond the failure of its crisis management;
8. sheds light on the dynamics of capital by preserving what is essential to it, while at the same time, through the backlash of the implementation of neoliberal policies, arranging what is accessory to it;
9. becomes one and the same entity with the State form, unique at the national level (embryonic at the world level?), a State that confers authority and autonomy to it, while bringing to the State the confirmation of its universality and the fiction of a consensus; and
10. produces the illusion that the struggle is limited to the field of ideas and to the framework of academic institutions where "the weapons of criticism" make one forget "the criticism of weapons."

In a passage from an old manuscript spared by the magnanimity of mice, two young men wrote: "The real practical solution of this phraseology, the elimination of these representations in the consciousness of human beings, will be achieved, let us repeat, only by a transformation of circumstances and not by theoretical deductions."[66] As for the very reactionary Ludwig Von Mises, he preferred to declare: "Undoubtedly most human beings are incapable of following a difficult line of reasoning. (...) Only the masses, precisely because they cannot think for themselves, obey the leadership of the so-called educated. If one succeeds in convincing the latter, the game is won."[67]

References

Alleg H. (2006), *Retour sur "La Question,"* Brussels: Aden.

Amin S. (1997), *Critique de l'air du temps*. Paris: L'Harmattan.

Amin S. and R. Herrera (2000), "Le Sud dans le système mondial en transformation," *Recherches internationales*, n°s 60–61, p. 87–99, Paris.

Althusser L. (1995), *Sur la Reproduction*, Paris: Presses Universitaires de France.

Aristotle (1931), *Physique*, Book VI, 239 b, vol. 2, Paris: Les Belles Lettres.

[66] Marx and Engels (1968, p. 41).

[67] Von Mises (1938, p. 11).

BADIOU A. (1998), *D'un Désastre obscur*, La Tour d'Aigues: Éditions de l'Aube.
BLANCHARD O.J. (2008), "Neoclassical Synthesis," *The New Palgrave Dictionary of Economics*, London: Macmillan.
BASTIAT F. (1864 [1855]), *Harmonies économiques, in Œuvres complètes*, Paris: Guillaumin & Cie.
BERNAL M.G. (1996 [1987]), *Black Athena - Les racines afro-asiatiques de la civilisation classique*, Paris: Presses universitaires de France.
BLUM W. (2002), *L'État voyou*, Lyon: Parangon.
BÖHM-BAWERK E. (von) (1959 [1890]), *Capital and Interest*, South Holland: Libertarian Press.
CAMBOIS E., C. LABORDE and J.-M. ROBINE (2008), "La 'double peine' des ouvriers: plus d'années d'incapacité au sein d'une vie plus courte," *Population et Sociétés*, Institut national d'Études démographiques, n° 441, Paris.
CANGUILHEM G. (1977), *Idéologie et rationalité dans l'histoire des sciences*. Paris: Éditions Vrin.
——— (1996), *Vie et mort de Jean Cavaillès*. Paris: Allia.
CHOMSKY A.N. (2005), *Les Dessous de la politique de l'Oncle Sam*, Montreal: Écosociété.
COMMISSION GULBENKIAN (1996), *Ouvrir les sciences sociales* (Rapport pour la restructuration des sciences sociales), Paris: Descartes & Cie.
CRÉDIT SUISSE (2013), *Global Wealth Report 2013*, Research Institute, October, Zurich.
DAHAN- DALMEDICO A. and J. PEIFFER (1986), *Une Histoire des mathématiques*, Paris: Le Seuil.
DIOP C.A. (1979), *Nations nègres et culture*. Paris: Présence africaine.
——— (1981), *Civilisation ou barbarie*. Paris: Présence africaine.
DORNBUSCH R., S. FISCHER and P.A. SAMUELSON (1977), "Comparative Advantage, Trade, and Payments in a Ricardian Model with a Continuum of Goods," *American Economic Review*, vol. 67, n° 5, p. 823–839.
DAUBEN J.W. (1979), *Georg Cantor: His Mathematics and Philosophy of the Infinite*, Princeton: Princeton University Press.
EDGEWORTH F.Y. (1967 [1881]), *Mathematical Psychics*, New York: Augustus M. Kelley.
ENGELS F. (1978), *Anti-Dühring*. Paris: Éditions sociales.
FRIEDMAN M. (1986), *Free to Choose*. London: Penguin Books.
FRYDMAN C. and R.E. SAKS (2008), "Executive Compensation," *National Bureau of Economic Research (NBER) Working Paper*, n° 14145, Cambridge (MA).
GREENSPAN A. (1996), Speech delivered to the *American Enterprise Institute* in Washington DC, 12 May.
HAYEK F.A. (1976), *The Constitution of Liberty*. London: Henley-Routledge & Kegan Paul.

——— (1981), *Droit, législation, liberté*. Paris: Presses universitaires de France.

HERRERA R. (2000), "Critique de l'économie 'apolitique'," *L'Homme et la Société*, n° 135, p. 87–104, Paris.

———(2001), Les Théories du système mondial capitaliste. In J. Bidet & E. Kouvélakis (Eds.), *Dictionnaire Marx contemporain* (pp. 201–221). Paris: Presses Universitaires de France.

——— (2010), *Un Autre Capitalisme n'est pas possible*, Paris: Syllepse.

——— (2012), "Neoclassical Economic Fiction and Neoliberal Political Reality," *International Critical Thought—A Review of the Chinese Academy of Social Sciences*, vol. 3, n° 1, p. 98–107, London: Routledge.

——— (2018), "La colonisation vue par Marx et Engels: évolutions (et limites) d'une réflexion commune," *in Le Colonialisme - Textes de Marx et Engels*, p. 3–73, Paris: Éditions Critiques.

——— (2020), *En Lutte! Les résistances populaires en France de 1981 à nos jours*, Paris: Éditions Critiques.

——— (2022), "Les Métamorphoses de la pensée de Marx sur la colonisation," *Revue de Philosophie économique*, Paris, to be published.

JEVONS W.S. (1957 [1871]), *The Theory of Political Economy*, New York: Kelley and Millman.

KENNEDY S.W. (2008 [1955]), *Introduction à l'Amérique raciste*, Paris: L'Aube.

KRUGMAN P.R. and M. OBSTFELD (2003), *Économie internationale*, Brussels: De Boeck.

KUHN T.S. (1996), *The Structure of Scientific Revolutions*, 3rd ed., Chicago: University of Chicago Press.

MALINVAUD, E. (1993), Regard d'un ancien sur les nouvelles théories de la croissance. *Revue d'économie politique, 44*(2), 171–188.

———, E. (1996), Pourquoi les économistes ne font pas de découvertes. *Revue d'économie politique, 106*(6), 929–942.

MARX, K. (1978), *Le Capital - Critique de l'économie politique*. Paris: Éditions sociales.

MARX K. and F. ENGELS (1968 [1846]), *L'Idéologie allemande*. Paris: Éditions sociales.

MARSHALL A. (1920 [1890]), *Principles of Economics*, 8th ed., London: Macmillan.

MCNAMARA R.S. (1995), *In Retrospect: The Tragedy and Lessons of Vietnam* (with B. Van De *Mark*), New York: Times Books.

MENGER C. (1950 [1871]), *Principles of Economics*, Glencoe: Free Press.

MILL J.S. (1865 [1848]), *Principles of Political Economy with Some of Their Applications to Social Philosophy*, London: Longmans.

MONTCHESTIEN A. (de) (1889 [1615]), *Traicté de l'œconomie politique*, Paris: E. Plon, Nourrit et Cie.

Observatoire des inégalités (2011), "Les inégalités d'espérance de vie dans le monde," April, available on: http://www.inegalites.fr/.

Ortiz I. and M. Cummings (2011), *Global Inequality: Beyond the Bottom Billion*, Social and Economic Policy Working Paper, April, New York: UNICEF.

Oxfam (2014), "Working for the Few: Political Capture and Economic Inequality," *Briefing Paper*, n° 178, January, Oxford.

Pareto V. (1964 [1897]), *Cours d'Economie politique*, Paris: Droz.

Petty W. (1690), *Political Arithmetick* (1690), available on: https://la.utexas.edu/users/hcleaver/368/368PettyPolArithtableedit.pdf.

Preiswerk R. and D. Perrot (1975), *Ethnocentrisme et histoire - L'Afrique, l'Amérique indienne et l'Asie dans les manuels occidentaux*, Paris: Éditions Anthropos.

Ramonet I. (1995), "La Pensée unique," *Le Monde diplomatique*, January.

Said E.W. (2000), *Culture et impérialisme*, Paris: Fayard and Le Monde diplomatique.

Say J.-B. (1803), *Traité d'économie politique*, 1st ed., Paris: Imprimerie de Chapelet.

——— (1852), *Cours complet d'économie politique pratique*. Paris: Guillaumin.

Smith A. (1937 [1776]), *An Inquiry into the Nature and Causes of the Wealth of Nations*, New York: Random House.

Soros G. (1998), *La Crise du capitalisme mondial*, Paris: Plon.

Stiglitz J.E. (2003), *Quand le Capitalisme perd la tête*, Paris: Le Livre de poche.

Strauss L. (1989), *La Persécution et l'art d'écrire*, Paris: Agora.

Tosel A. (1992), "L'Impensable du libéralisme," *in* J. Bidet and G. Labica (eds.), *Libéralisme et État de droit*, Paris: Méridiens Klincksieck.

Tran D.L. (2021), "Imperialism and Transition to Socialism in Vietnam," *in* R. Herrera (ed.), *Imperialism and Transitions to Socialism*, p. 141–156, Bingley (UK): Emerald.

Turgot A.R.J. (1788 [1766]), *Réflections sur la formation et la distribution des richesses*, In.12, R 24520, Bibliothèque nationale de France, Paris.

United Nations Development Programme (1992), *Human Development Report*, Paris: Economica.

Varian H.R. (1984), *Microeconomic Analysis*, 2nd ed., New York and London: W.W. Norton & Co.

Vergara F. (2002), *Les Fondements philosophiques du libéralisme*, Paris: La Découverte and Syros.

Von Mises L. (1938), *Le Socialisme - Étude économique et sociologique*, Paris: Éditions M.-Th. Génin - Librairie de Médicis.

Wallerstein I. (1997), *Impenser la science sociale*, Paris: Presses universitaires de France.

Walras L. (1988 [1874–1877]), *Éléments d'économie politique pure ou théorie de la richesse sociale*, *in Œuvres économiques complètes*, tome 8, Paris: Economica.
World Bank (The) (2000), *World Development Report*, The World Bank: Washington DC.
——— (2013), *World Development Report*, The World Bank: Washington DC.
——— (2014), "Gross National Income per capita Atlas Method and PPP," *World Development Indicators Database 2012*, April, The World Bank: Washington DC.
Zinn H. (1980), *A People's History of the United States*, New York: Harper & Row / HarperCollins.

CHAPTER 2

Growth: A Mainstream Theory (Which is also Itself) in Crisis

Let us continue the exploration of "neoclassicism" by evaluating, in this second chapter, its theory of growth.[1] By "growth theory" we mean the analysis that the authors of this current propose of the processes of capital accumulation and production increase in the long period—as opposed to those dealing with short-term fluctuations and cycles, notably in their version of "real business cycles." Our criticism of these last models (known as "RBC") will be terser, because of the much more limited longevity and scope of their success—and rightly so—compared to their long-run counterparts, which still dominate the discipline to a very large extent, and on which we will concentrate here.

Indeed, the fact is that, for nearly four decades, the so-called "endogenous growth theory," which the neoclassical mainstream simply calls "the new growth theory," had absolutely dazzling success, to the point of conquering a predominant, not to say exclusive position in long-term macro-dynamics. It has given rise to innumerable variants, mathematically more or less sophisticated, and emanating from some of the most prominent neoclassical theorists, in a wide variety of fields, such as innovation,

[1] This chapter summarizes some of the results of a series of works by the author over several years. From: HERRERA (2000a, b, c, 2006) to HERRERA (2010a, b, c, 2011).

R. Herrera, *Confronting Mainstream Economics for Overcoming Capitalism*, Marx, Engels, and Marxisms,
https://doi.org/10.1007/978-3-031-05851-6_2

education, demography, infrastructure, international trade, development, finance, the environment, etc., as will be seen.[2]

Nevertheless, it should be observed that, with very few exceptions, the heterodox authors have remained uncritical of this theory, which is yet clearly neoclassical—not to say even silent, when they have not simply joined themselves the mainstream… It is true that some have thought that this was an opportunity to establish their interventionist theses, and others have perhaps also sought academic recognition. We will show that this is a mistake, and that the radicalization—in our opinion absolutely necessary—of the attacks against these theoretical developments of the mainstream would allow heterodoxies, Marxists in particular, to show themselves more attractive again.

Here we invite the readers to follow us for a moment in examining the most recent growth models of neoclassicism. These will be presented, without too many technical, mathematical, and econometric details, in the line of the old neoclassical formalizations, rather than from the classical perspective, before showing their implications, notably as regards State intervention, and pointing out some of their most problematic and, in our opinion, insurmountable limits. Those of our readers curious and daring who would like to penetrate the "entrails of the monster" to learn more about these technical details—where many secrets of neoclassicism are hidden—are invited, as to them, once strapped and clinging to the parapet for their safety, to a guided tour, to be planned over several days, that we propose in other places.[3] Nonetheless, to properly grasp the fundamental issues of this theoretical debate, we must go back in time, to a fairly distant past, but which should not be forgotten.

2.1 The Classics and Growth

To get an idea of the distance between the old and the "new," let us begin with a brief look at the dynamic vision of the economy as it was given by the classics. In this representation, expounded by David Ricardo[4]

[2] Let us content ourselves for the moment, and before returning later in detail to these models, with quoting well-known authors such as: Romer (1986, 1990), Lucas (1988), Grossman and Helpman (1989), Barro (1990), Becker et al. (1990), Krugman (1993a, 1995)…

[3] For more technical (mathematized) references of the author, see: Herrera (1998, 2010a, 2012).

[4] Ricardo (1951 [1817]).

in particular, long-term growth results from a process of accumulation in which the rate of profit plays a key role in the reinvestment of the surplus. In an extremely simplified system of a uni-sectoral (agricultural) economy, the increase in production is the consequence of a higher rate of capital accumulation, which itself depends on a profit rate considered sufficiently high by the capitalists and ensuring the rise of the wage fund, and therefore the expansion of employment, which ultimately leads to the growth of the product.

With accumulation, however, operates the so-called law of "diminishing returns": as the cost of production of the agricultural good rises with the cultivation of land of diminishing fertility, the relative shares in the total product of rents and wages become more important—because the price of subsistence goods and the nominal natural wage rate increase—which then causes a tendency for the rate of profit to fall. Accumulation stops when the profit rate is reduced to a minimum value that ensures only a simple, identical reproduction of the Ricardian system.

The stationary state, a permanent stable regime with a zero growth rate, where production, capital, and population remain constant, is then reached. Technical progress may postpone the deadline, but it will always remain insufficiently sustained to prevent the exhaustion of growth, which is inevitable according to David Ricardo. The only way out is, therefore, to open up to international trade and to exercise the principle of comparative advantage.[5]

Beyond the pessimism associated with it, classical analysis reveals the complexity and, in many respects, the relevance of the mechanisms mobilized to grasp the profound nature of capitalism as a dynamic system. At the same time as the limits on growth comes up and stumbles, some of the concepts whose enrichment will soon allow the infallibility of the stationary state to be overcome are in fact outlined: the extent of the market, the division of labor, and a broad understanding of capital (including, in particular, the "qualifications of workers") in Adam Smith's work; the acceleration of labor productivity and technical progress *à la* Ricardo; reasoning in terms of external effects or collective consumption for John Stuart Mill; or dynamic misalignments between equilibrium

[5] For a "modeling" of the Ricardian model, see, for instance: HICKS and HOLLANDER (1977); SAMUELSON (1978); or also BHADURI and HARRIS (1987).

demand and "effective demand" according to Thomas Malthus, then J.C.L. Simonde de Sismondi, announcing John Maynard Keynes.[6]

And the fact is that, until J.M. Keynes, as in the main currents of economic thought before him, there is, in filigram, a thread of this idea of a tendency for the rate of profit to fall as the accumulation of capital is pushed forward; thus also that of a fading of the growth process in the long period. This was the case, of course, with Adam Smith, who argued that the profit rate declines as the wealth of nations increases under the pressure of capital competition, but that land rent increases, while real wages vary little; so that the interests of industrialists and merchants are ultimately opposed to the general interest.[7] The same was true for David Ricardo, as we have seen, but also for John Stuart Mill, or for an atypical classic—because he was an opponent of "Say's law"—such as T.R. Malthus, and then, much later, of certain marginalists, like W.S. Jevons.

As far as State intervention is concerned, the determination of the latter most often consists, for classical authors, in deducing the constraints weighing on individuals from their very freedom, and thus in explaining the conditions under which what was soon to be called the "public sector" becomes, despite the limits imposed on individual freedom, an instrument for the realization of such freedom. The important thing here is to dispel the idea that the State was useless for these early liberals. As a matter of fact, according to A. Smith, for example, its action is circumscribed to the strictly necessary (defense, justice, some infrastructure, education of "the youth and the crowd"[8]), but its role is recognized, beyond the "obvious and simple system of natural liberty," as quite essential in the construction and harmonious functioning of a "market society."

However, the essential point remains, as far as the "expenses required for the administration of justice" are concerned, the protection of the rich by the State or, better still, the defense by the latter of the right to property in the face of the recurrent passions of the poor which "lead [them] to invade property," such as "the aversion to work and the love of present enjoyment": "For a very rich man, there must be at least five hundred poor. (…) [The] poor man (…), driven by need and excited by

[6] Here, respectively, Smith (1937 [1776]); Ricardo (1951 [1817]); Mill (1985 [1848]); Malthus (1986 [1798]); Sismondi (1971 [1815]); and Keynes (1985 [1936]).

[7] Smith (1937 [1776], Book V, Chapter 1, Sect. 2, p. 363).

[8] Ibidem, p. 319.

envy, often gives in to the desire to seize the goods of others. Only under the aegis of the civil magistrate can the possessor of valuable property, acquired by the labor of many years or perhaps of several successive generations, sleep a single night with peace; at any moment he is surrounded by a host of unknown enemies whom he cannot appease, even though he has never provoked them, and against whose injustice he can only be protected by the powerful arm of civil authority constantly raised to punish them. Thus, the acquisition of property of a certain price (...) necessarily requires the establishment of a civil government."[9]

Nevertheless, and although they admit market failures, the classics were not yet able to pinpoint with precision the criteria for dividing up what is the domain of the self-regulating market and what can or must be the responsibility of the State. The question of the status of the latter in its relation to the economy thus remained largely open at the time when the marginalist methodology and the edification of the Walrasian-Paretian system were imposed in the last third of the Nineteenth Century.

But it was in the wake of J.M. Keynes's *General Theory of Employment, Interest, and Money*[10] and, essentially, with the efforts undertaken to transpose to the long period the analysis of the short-term functioning of an economy tending toward a stable imbalance or disequilibrium of underemployment, that the founding problematics of the macroeconomic models on which modern growth theory is based were elaborated.

2.2 The Contribution of the Keynesians

The Keynesian interpretation had to be placed in a dynamic perspective of long-term growth paths. This was made possible, on the one hand, by the integration of the supply component of investment (the "accelerator effect") and, on the other hand, thanks to a dynamic interaction with demand (the "multiplier effect"). From then on, Keynesian authors could justify State intervention in the direction of demand-stimulation policies, the aim of which was to guarantee entrepreneurs sufficiently good business prospects to encourage them to invest and mobilize their unused production capacity.

[9] Ibidem, this time Chapter 11.

[10] Keynes (1985 [1936]).

Distinct but similar in their conclusions, the reflections respectively proposed by Roy F. Harrod[11] and Evsey D. Domar[12] question the capability of a capitalist market economy to experience a growth process which is both regular and sustainable. The aim is to construct an aggregated representation of the framework built by J.M. Keynes, whose characteristics and conditions of equilibrium will be sought. The functioning of the "Harrod-Domar model" is based on the investment decisions of entrepreneurs; an investment which can be simultaneously seen as determined and determinant.

According to the traditional Keynesian scheme, equilibrium in the market of goods is considered to have been achieved when the equality between *ex ante* investment and *ex post* savings is verified at a given point in time. This requires a growth in investment and output equal to the quotient of the propensity to save (noted as s) and the capital coefficient (v): this is the guaranteed growth rate (g_w), which transposes the static equilibrium into a dynamic one, in an inspiration very close to Alfred Marshall's. The fixity of s and v makes it possible to obtain regular balanced growth at a constant rate. But the growth path of the product, given by the rate g_w, turns out to be a "highly unstable equilibrium." If a shock occurs, the system does not tend to return to equilibrium, through the possible play of self-correcting mechanisms. Any deviation is cumulative and aggravating, so that growth at the g_w rate is achieved on a "knife's edge."[13] In such a representation, the instability of growth would thus be a major feature of the dynamics of capitalism.

Guaranteed growth ensures full employment if we have: $g_w = s/v = n$. The existence of a path of regular balanced growth, known as the "golden age," requires that output and investment grow together at the "natural" rate of labor power (that is, n). Balanced growth at full employment is, therefore, highly unlikely. Indeed, the parameters s, v, and n refer to behaviors that are independent of each other, because they are, respectively, social, technological, or demographic in nature, and therefore only exceptionally—in fact, fortuitously—satisfy the preceding equality.

This system is then said to be mathematically "overdetermined"; in general, it has no solution. Since the Keynesian model lacks the centripetal

[11] See: Harrod (1939, 1948).

[12] Domar (1946, 1947).

[13] Tobin (1955).

forces allowing to stabilize it, it is up to State intervention to act as an exogenous regulator, in order to avoid oscillatory tendencies and, finally, to bring the guaranteed and natural rates into line and coincide.

The arguments in this regard, especially in its Harrodian version, are articulated around two axes. On the one hand, an opportunity to guide the economy in phases of depression, in periods of underemployment, arises from the multiplier effect, by reducing the propensity to save, which results in an autonomous investment corresponding to public spending. The amount of the latter is subtracted from the saved fraction of income available for guaranteed growth. On the other hand, the interest rate can be used, via the money supply, as an objective for action on the capitalistic intensity of investment, by impacting its cost, and then by influencing on the coefficient of capital. As a consequence, the economic policy that is then advocated aims to modify the guaranteed growth rate to bring it closer to the natural rate, through a counter-cyclical and expansionary fiscal policy—thanks to the widening of the State budget deficit, without raising taxes—and an accompanying monetary policy.

Under these conditions, it is not surprising that the Harrod-Domar model, although initially designed for the study of growth cycles in developed countries, has been so successful in development economics. Its logic inspired numerous (non-Soviet) planners in the post-war period, particularly in India.[14] Its influence was to be further boosted by the dissemination of the analysis of a rather special disciple of J.M. Keynes, Walt Whitman Rostow,[15] who unfortunately also had a definite impact—willingly or unwillingly—on many governments in Southern economies (Appendix B). One even finds extensions of this in the elaboration of the "two-gap" models,[16] built on the hypothesis of an unavailability of foreign currency replacing the insufficiency of savings as a constraint on domestic investment; hence the call for foreign capital in order to accelerate growth—in the spirit of another Marshall, George Catlett, this time a U.S. military officer.

By insisting on the role of capital accumulation, Keynesian-inspired models provided an explanation of "poverty traps," with low labor

[14] For example, MAHALANOBIS (1953).

[15] ROSTOW (1960).

[16] About the "two-gap models:" CHENERY and BRUNO (1962); MCKINNON (1964); CHENERY and STROUT (1966).

productivity, in economies that are insufficiently endowed with capital and where the agricultural sector predominates. They also made it possible to address, to some extent, the complex phenomena of underemployment and/or permanent latent unemployment, which are characteristic of countries in the South with rapid population growth. Finally, the various economic policy recommendations aimed at favoring growth, by acting on savings and on the cost and allocative efficiency of capital, were not to the displeasure of the leaders of newly independent countries, who were willingly interventionist.

Besides, it was against this State voluntarism that the new modelizations of neoclassicism models were deployed in the second half of the 1950s, under the impetus of Robert M. Solow[17] As we shall see, these formalizations proposed a fairly sophisticated mechanism of market self-regulation, capable of bringing balanced growth into the permanent regime of the "golden age," with full employment of factors. Formally, this will involve making the factorial structure of production more flexible, implying an endogenous average productivity of capital.

For, the solution to the mentioned problem of "overdetermination" in the Harrod-Domar model would inevitably entail the endogenization of an additional variable, which would open up several opportunities—at least three—corresponding to different (and very distant) theoretical configurations of the system.

i) First, according to a Malthusian approach, endogenous adjustment was made possible by modifying the natural rate, which could become a function of the level of *per capita* income. This was the path taken by T.M. Haavelmo.[18]
ii) For post-Keynesians, it is rather the flexibility of the propensity to save that ensures internal regulation, which shifts the focus of the problematics to the issue of income distribution, with differentiated saving functions, in the manner of Joan Robinson, Nicholas Kaldor, or Luigi Pasinetti.[19]

17 Solow (1956).

18 See: Haavelmo (1956). Hence, following it, in a certain way of analyzing migrations: Harris and Todaro (1970).

19 Here, respectively, Robinson (1938, 1964); Kaldor (1956, 1957); and Pasinetti (1960).

iii) Finally, in a challenge to the Keynesian rigidities characterizing real remunerations and the factorial structure, the coefficient of capital linked to capitalistic intensity was assumed to be variable, with factor substitutability and flexibility of the capital/output ratio. It is precisely this last solution that neoclassical theorists adopted in response to the dual challenge of unstable growth and the improbability of full employment.

2.3 Neoclassicals, from the Traditional Dynamic Model to Optimal Growth

Robert M. Solow, a former doctoral student of Wassily W. Leontief (as were such different and important theorists as Paul Anthony Samuelson, Vernon L. Smith, and Hyman P. Minsky, among others), sought to demonstrate the possibilities of the existence and stability of balanced growth at full employment by retaining some of the essential assumptions of the axiomatics bequeathed by Walrasian theory, and more particularly: a mode of reasoning in terms of marginal productivity, with perfect functioning of competition, adjustments performed by prices, obligatory non-increasing returns... The aggregate productive system that R.M. Solow provides is technically described by a two-factor production function, giving a composite good. The assumed substitutability between capital and labor, through a variable coefficient of capital, guarantees the availability of an infinite number of productive combinations, while the flexibility of all prices, including wages and interest rates, makes the model tend toward equilibrium. Therefore, the competition generated on the markets provides the automatic mechanisms for adjustment to quantities.

Production is then pushed until the marginal productivities of the factors are equal to their respective prices, and remunerations are distributed according to the factorial productive contributions. An assumption of convexity in the technology leads to the retention of a "well-behaved" functional form, which does not pose major mathematical problems. This implies that the production function is concave, with constant returns to scale, but decreasing marginal returns to capital—hence the assurance of the existence, uniqueness, and stability of the equilibrium.

The process of capital accumulation is guaranteed by the reinvestment of savings, and the question of equilibrium on the goods market is settled by the equalization of investment with these savings, verified at all times. This equilibrium is one of full employment, which is postulated a priori and maintained on all markets by the conditions of price flexibility and factor substitutability according to relative prices. So, at any point, the wage and "profit" rates vary in such a way as to induce entrepreneurs to adjust the coefficient of capital in a manner that the guaranteed and natural rates come to merge.

It is then possible to determine the growth path of capital that ensures full factor employment and—that of labor force being known—the growth trajectory of the output. The problem of the existence of an accumulation path compatible with any natural growth rate is solved *ipso facto*: when the economy has reached this level of *per capita* capital, it is on its equilibrium path, characterized by a growth of output, capital, and labor at the same constant rate—that is, the natural rate. Here, in the absence of technical progress, the coefficient of capital and the product per worker remain constant.

Therefore, this demonstrates, against the Keynesians, the possibility of a permanent regime of balanced growth at the natural rate. The adjustment is made "not by an extraordinary stroke of luck, but as a consequence of the meeting of supply and demand."[20] The malleability of capital allows to select the equilibrium value that ensures a regular growth and maintains full employment. If the system is on the path, it remains there; if it is not, self-correcting mechanisms guarantee stability, whatever the initial state, by convergence toward the path of regular balanced growth and full employment. The steady-state growth rate, given by (exogenous) demographic change, is independent of the savings rate and changes in the latter have an impact only on the level of output—not on its growth. So, State intervention is thus no longer required to ensure balanced growth at full employment.

But then, would all economic policy become useless? The answer to this question only makes sense if we strive to achieve an "optimal" growth path, integrating a normative dimension into the reasoning. This involves seeking the value of the savings rate that corresponds to a balanced path at a constant rate that satisfies a collectively desirable criterion of optimality. This criterion could be, for example, the maximization of *per capita* consumption (that is to say, the "golden rule"). By following a

[20] Solow (2000).

comparative dynamics approach that chooses, from among several systems with the same permanent regime but different savings rates, the one that conforms to this objective criterion of maximization, neoclassical theorists have been able to demonstrate that there exists an optimal savings rate that makes it possible to reach the maximum level of *per capita* consumption, and that corresponds to the rate that makes the marginal productivity of capital tend toward the growth rate.[21] The preceding problem is in fact equivalent to determining a combination of present and future consumptions by an intertemporal choice index—an actualized sum of consumptions over an infinite horizon, in general—that satisfies a given growth program. However, it is no longer certain that the economy can reach such an "optimal" path by itself. If the conditions are not those of the above-mentioned "golden rule," balanced growth may become impossible.

It is precisely in this context that State intervention, reserving the possibility of choosing the trajectory deemed "optimal," may be justified. Nevertheless, the analyses of State action given by neoclassicism have long been more concerned with the topics related to efficient financing of public spending than with its impact on growth; and this has led them to insist on the various crowding-out effects operating to the detriment of private savings.[22] The influence of the State was seen as penalizing through its influences on investment, and aggravated by price distortions and alterations in competition. No positive impact of State intervention on private supply was really accepted until 1986, just three decades after the conception of the Solowian model, when the theory of so-called "endogenous" growth, or self-sustaining growth, appeared.

2.4 Generic Form of Endogenous Growth Theory

It was largely in order to overcome the shortcomings of this very simplistic and reductive interpretation of the role of the State, as well as to overcome some of the disadvantages inherent in the formalization traditionally used by neoclassicism since 1956, that the study of growth was revived, which would finally lead to its "endogenization."

[21] Koopmans (1965). Also: Cass (1966).

[22] For example: Blanchard and Fischer (1989), Tanzi (1985), Friedman (1976). Also: Becker (1985).

For R.M. Solow, in the absence of technical progress, the marginal return on capital was a decreasing function of capital, so that the exhaustion of growth in the long term was caused by the cancelation of the marginal productivity of *per capita* capital as accumulation advanced. Indeed, the decline in the profitability of capital reduced the incentive to invest and the contribution of this factor to growth. Under these conditions, the mechanism that made competitive equilibrium possible—in this case, decreasing factorial marginal productivities—was the same one that inhibited growth. This model was, therefore, inadequate to represent a sustained dynamic over the long period. Taking place at an exogenous pace, growth was independent of the choice of resource allocation by the agents, and first of all of their savings decisions—on which there may possibly be room for maneuver for public action. Even if the growth rate of employment were positive, accumulation could not be maintained because the marginal productivity of capital is canceled out.

Added to this, empirical studies that explored methods of calculating total factor productivity in a Solowian framework led to the unpleasant observation that the increase in the usual factors of production (capital and labor) was not enough to fully "explain" economic growth. Other engines were at work that were not included in the accounting of the production factors of aggregate output increase, but only represented by time. What was called for a long time the "Solow residual," that the econometric works systematically revealed, corresponded to "a measure of our ignorance"[23] (or rather the ignorance of neoclassicism, to be more accurate), but above all suspended any economic policy recommendation. And this was the case from the end of the 1950s until the mid-1980s.[24]

Nonetheless, for several decades, ignorance did not prevent countless mainstream econometricians from pursuing their attempts to dissolve exogenous technology and to put forward the most varied "explanations" of the famous residual. These "explanations" are sometimes far-fetched, but more often than not, they are limpidly ideological. They pretend to have demonstrated so, with "robust" results of econometric tests, and obtained from so-called "qualitative" indicators drawn from statistical databases on the "institutional context" provided by a few hand-picked private agencies or large multilateral organizations such as the World

[23] Abramowitz (1956).

[24] See, for example: Denison (1985).

Bank,[25] that the "quality of institutions"[26] contributes to reporting, in addition to the factors of production considered as traditional, some international divergences in performance in terms of productivity between economies. The countries that would succeed would be those with little "bureaucratic red tape" and, above all, with legal rules that eliminate any risk of "expropriation" or "denunciation of contracts" by the State.

It is in this very particular context that we must return to the theory of endogenous growth, because it moved the lines. The identification of the formal mechanism authorizing its appearance involves, fundamentally, the questioning of one of the key hypotheses of the Solowian model: that of the cancelation of the marginal productivity of capital when the stock of the latter tends toward an infinitely large value. And it is precisely this axiomatic relaxation that will avoid the extinction of growth in the long run.

A huge majority of these endogenous growth models—but not all of them[27]—therefore consider that the elasticity of production to the total stock of all accumulable factors is at least unitary. This assumes that the production function is linear in a single input, in other words, that this function can be characterized by the constancy of its returns to scale and, simultaneously, by that of the marginal return of this aggregated input. The latter, assumed to be homogeneous with the output, is conceived in a sufficiently broad sense to include various elements that are themselves subject to accumulation: knowledge capital, human capital, infrastructural capital, that is, always capital... It is thus an assumption of linearity in the relationship linking capital to the final product that lies at the heart of the generic form of endogenous growth, known as "AK."[28]

In this representation, the production function, with a single factor and constant returns, is written: $Y = AK$, where K is a composite capital and A its apparent productivity, assumed to be an exogenous constant. If we

[25] Let us quote, among others: *International Country Risk Guide* (by the consulting company Frost & Sullivan). For the World Bank: Easterly and Levine (1997).

[26] Olson (1996).

[27] In the last century, and in another life, the author of these lines demonstrated that endogenous growth can be mathematically proven within an augmented Solowian framework, while maintaining a convexity in the technology, and therefore a concave macroeconomic production function, with constant returns to scale on all the factors—whether they are reproducible or not. See: Herrera (1998).

[28] Rebelo (1990).

consider that capital accumulation is given by: $\Delta K = I = AK - C = sY$, then the growth rate of the economy is: $g = \Delta K/K = s\,A$. The resolution of the "AK model" consists of maximizing under constraint a utility function, where σ is the intertemporal elasticity of substitution and ρ is the rate of preference for the present. This finally gives the following growth rate: $g = \Delta c/c = \Delta k/k = \Delta y/y = (A - \rho)/\sigma$. There is an equalization of the rates of return on investment for the firm (A) and of the consumption for the household ($g\sigma + \rho$). So, the growth rate g is determined by the marginal productivity of capital (A) and the savings rate, itself linked to σ and ρ. The growth rate of the economy is thus effectively endogenized.

The interest of this model is to suggest that constant total returns are sufficient to bring about self-sustaining, perpetual growth, without the need to resort to increasing returns, which are known to be particularly problematic in their relationship with imperfect competition. The basic writing will consist in eliminating the fixed factors of production in order to combine all the reproducible or accumulable components into a composite whole, whose marginal productivity no longer cancels out when the production of this aggregate capital increases. The growth rate is determined by the productivity of capital and by the savings rate, the latter being in turn itself related to the parameters of intertemporal elasticity of substitution and of preference for the present. The higher the productivity of capital and/or the greater the inclination of agents (or should we say rather the agent in the singular?) to save—the lower their rate of preference for the present and their aversion to risk—the higher the growth rate will ultimately be.

In the presence of constant global returns, such self-sustaining growth becomes possible, and the savings rate will determine not only the level of the output, but also, and above all, its long-term growth rate—which is thus endogenized. Since the State can act on this savings rate, we understand the importance of explaining the mechanisms of accumulation of the various components of the broad aggregate of capital, as well as of identifying the implications to expect from the permanent nature of this dynamic in terms of public action. Another strong originality of this "AK model" lies in its predictions of the absence of systematic "convergence" between economies. Therefore, State intervention could consist, for example, in modifying the growth path of a country that would be stuck in a "poverty trap," so as to enable it to catch up with the leading country.

At this stage of the reasoning, several limitations of this model can already be encircled. The first relates to the assumption of unitary elasticity of output to capital. The AK model is deliberately placed on the "knife's edge," which is very problematic. At the microeconomic level, the firm's production function exhibits variable returns to scale—increasing, then decreasing, as production increases. It is then necessary to postulate that this function is fixed at equilibrium and that a firm located below the point of reversal of returns will have an interest in growing in size in order to increase its productivity; while, on the contrary, a firm located above this turning point will have an incentive to reduce its size. It is only under these conditions that the macroeconomic function, that is, the supposed aggregation of microeconomic forms, will also be able to have unitary returns to scale. Second, the AK model considers that all factors of production are reproducible. As a consequence, the integration of non-accumulable resources (such as "simple" labor, exhaustible natural resources, land) will lead to increasing returns to scale. The rise in factors will cause a more than proportional increase in the product, hence, extremely serious difficulties in preserving the competitive framework. Third, this model leaves unexplained the determinants of the very heart of growth, because of a much too loose definition of "capital."

It is the exploration of this core that neoclassical theorists will undertake. Their successive models retain the most diverse and varied engines of growth, and their reflections on the endogenization of technical progress lead to a return to the old microeconomic hypotheses of non-convexities, mobilizing, for the occasion, externalities, and increasing returns.

2.5 Canonical Models and Public Policies

Paul Michael Romer's objective, stated in his doctoral dissertation defended at the University of Chicago in 1983,[29] was to provide a solution to the problem of the exogeneity of economic growth, which neoclassical authors had encountered in their vain attempts to enrich the old Solowian model without abandoning the axiom of perfect competition. As a matter of fact, the obligation imposed on them to maintain convexity in technology (i.e., concavity of the production function)

[29] Romer (1983).

required the integration of technical progress as the only exogenous engine of growth in the long run.

This was relevant, insofar as technological activity is economic in nature, but it made technology a public good, not remunerated, since in the presence of constant returns to scale, the remuneration of privately used factors exhausted all income—in accordance with Euler's theorem. And if one were to consider a specific remuneration for this factor, corresponding to the taking into account of the incentive to undertake efforts likely to lead to a technological innovation, conceived as the result of an arbitration choice entirely motivated by a logic of private profit, this would basically amount to questioning the mathematical conditions of endogenization of the term of total productivity of factors.

Paul M. Romer's originality lies in having succeeded in establishing a compatibility between, on the one hand, the increasing returns due to externalities and, on the other hand, the competitive equilibrium necessary for the resolution of the selected optimization program. It was, therefore, needed to build a model with endogenized total factor productivity that integrates an additional factor of technical progress, characterized by externalities that increase returns to scale, and which can itself be accumulated without a decrease in its marginal productivity.

Consequently, the approach should focus on the justification and treatment of the hypothesis of increasing returns. Here, one way of getting around imperfect competition is to consider returns to scale as "external" to the firm. If, for a particular firm, the conditions of production are carried out with non-increasing returns, which safeguards competition, increasing returns can arise from the participation of different firms in a common activity, because the extension of the size of the market can allow each of them to benefit from externalities. It is in this perspective that, in 1986, P.M. Romer proposed a model—considered to be founding to endogenous growth theory[30]—that chose to incorporate the externalities produced by the accretion of a capital factor understood in the broad sense of knowledge, but whose reference remains that of physical capital. Firms have a technology in which labor and this "knowledge capital" enter.[31] "Knowledge capital" intervenes at both the private and

[30] Romer (1986).

[31] In this area, a pioneering model, fundamental for the mainstream, had been that of Arrow (1962).

collective levels. This technology is assumed to have constant returns on private capital and labor, but increasing returns to scale on the whole, also including collective capital. Growth is then explained by the presence of externalities coming from investment in physical capital and leading to increasing returns to scale.

An important problem with this model is that it opens up very (and too) different configurations. Indeed, a sustained and stable growth path is only possible in the long run in one specific case: that of an elasticity of production to the stock of private and collective knowledge that is exactly unitary—that is, again, on the "knife's edge." However, beyond this weakness, which is not negligible, what is finally demonstrated is the possibility of endogenous growth in a competitive economy, described by the dynamics of the stock of capital and of the product evolving at an identical rate—i.e., a constant or increasing rate.

What the author goes so far as to call the "social planner"[32] integrates into its optimization program the fact that the investment of each producer increases the total stock of knowledge from which all benefit. The effect of externalities is to separate the competitive equilibrium from the social optimum. The decentralized equilibrium is no longer Pareto-optimal. Since agents (but should we use the plural?) do not take externalities into account in their decisions, a bias of under-accumulation of capital undermines economic growth. There is, therefore, room for State action, via an incentive scheme of tax-subsidies to encourage the accumulation of knowledge, which would make it possible to equalize the private and social marginal productivities of this factor. A temporary exogenous shock striking the stock of knowledge will see its effects preserved and amplified by hysteresis phenomena affecting the growth path, which will keep lasting traces of this disturbance. The effect of economic policies becomes permanent and is thus integrated into the growth rate.

P.M. Romer will present a second model in which the source of growth is located, this time, in technological knowledge deriving from research and development (R&D).[33] This knowledge is incorporated into capital in the form of capital goods, without, however, resulting from physical investment. They are assimilated to non-rival goods, partially exclusive,

[32] Romer (1986, p. 1020).

[33] Romer (1990a, b).

privately appropriable—and thus quite distinct from a public good. The increase in returns comes here from the widening of the range of inputs in equipment goods available to firms producing the final good.

R&D is thus reintegrated into the heart of resource allocation mechanisms, by answering the question of the remuneration of innovation, which had previously been left open. Technical progress no longer intervenes exogenously, but rather results from decisions guided by market incentives. R&D activity, the work of profit-motivated firms, has increasing dynamic returns. The more human capital devoted to research, the higher the productivity of this sector, and the higher the growth rate of knowledge. It is a hypothesis of linearity of progress of knowledge in the stock of knowledge that ensures self-sustained growth in the long run. In this well-defined context, subsidizing R&D can be recommended.

After having led, as early as the 1970s, the most decisive attack on Keynesianism, through the "new classical" school and its assumption of rational expectations, and then having initiated the upheaval of the dynamic interpretation of the short term, with the real business cycles (RBC), Robert E. Lucas, one of the most inventive and intellectually powerful theoreticians of neoclassicism today, can also be found at the origin of this "renewal" of the analysis of capital accumulation in the long period. Lucas provides the mainstream with a model in which human capital, which grows thanks to the decisions of private agents to invest in their own training, plays the role of an engine of long-term growth.[34] All the inputs of the production function are accumulable. By assuming a constancy of returns to scale, he reaches a formalization *à la* AK, where an enlarged "K" now includes physical capital and human capital. The problem of the appearance of endogenous growth thus lies entirely in the appropriate writing of an incentive to invest in human capital formation that does not decrease with its accumulation.

An externality carried by this capital modifies the production function of the final good without the resulting increasing returns being in themselves necessary for the self-sustained, permanent character of growth. Human capital is here privately accumulable, according to a process that associates non-decreasing returns on this factor with its production function, and such that its marginal productivity is constant. The increase of human capital is proportional to the time that the individual devotes to

[34] LUCAS (1988). It was preceded, in optimal growth, by the model given by UZAWA (1965).

the accumulation of his or her skills. It is the linearity of this accumulation in the level of individual human capital that ultimately authorizes endogenous growth. In addition to the implications for economic policy that it opens up, Lucas' model will help to explain that individuals are more productive in environments (workplaces, cities, regions, or countries, for example) that are abundant in human capital, toward which the flows of skilled workers, carriers of human capital, are directed.

2.6 The Dead Ends of the "New" Theory

In a fairly systematic way, these endogenous growth models are presented today, in the various course manuals and literature reviews devoted to them,[35] as being at once: (1) a macro-dynamization of the Walrasian general equilibrium—because they are said to have got solid microeconomic foundations; (2) a break with the representation once given by R.M. Solow—insofar as the modern engines of technical progress would be identified, and therefore also, much more rigorously than the Solowian framework allowed it, those of economic growth, thanks in particular to the mobilization of the notions of externalities and increasing returns; and (3) the rehabilitation of a discourse favorable to State intervention—reflecting a certain rapprochement of neoclassical theorists with concerns that are quite typically those of "heterodox" programs.

As for us, we will argue, on the contrary, that these positions, on which there is almost total consensus in academic spheres—which says a lot, by the way, about the attention currently paid by a majority of "heterodox" economists to the theme of growth theory (from which, however, the topics of employment, public budgets and debt, among others, partly derive), as well as about their level of combativeness—are completely wrong. Let us explain.

From the point of view of neoclassicism, to proceed with the endogenization of technical progress is equivalent to make it the result of decisions by private agents, reacting to market signals, and motivated by individual profit. It would be more appropriate to say, to return to a recurrent problem: the result of decisions of *the private agent*, insofar as these models formalize an aggregation that indeed always refers to the

[35] Let us quote the most famous: Sala-i-Martín (1990); rossman and Helpman (1991); Barro and Sala-i-Martín (1995); Aghion and Howitt (1998); or also: Aghion and Durlauf (2005).

behavior of the famous Robinson Crusoe. This is the same Robinson Crusoe of whom Frédéric Bastiat had said that he was "both a capitalist and a worker," and in whom "all economic evolution would be accomplished."[36] By the way: Does anyone know where Friday, his slave, might be hidden in these reasonings?

The multiple formalizations of the mainstream more recently elaborated in endogenous growth theory can be analyzed, in one way or another, as constructions with a so-called "representative" but unique agent, both "producer and consumer," as F. Bastiat had specified. As a producer, Crusoe's techniques are described by a production function; as a consumer, his preference relations are given by a utility function.[37] This is the case in the simplistic AK model. In Paul M. Romer's model, it is an assumption of symmetry of firms that brings us back to the single agent. But such absurdity, or "powerful instrument of miseducation" resulting from "sloppy habits of thought"[38] as the best of the Robinsons (Joan!) might have said, can also be discovered in much more sophisticated models, notably those with "overlapping generations."[39] Too bad for the old-fashioned nerds who still have not understood, more than three decades after the fall of the Berlin Wall (and iron curtain), that a boss and his or her worker are both free, that they are equal, that they are even brothers (or sisters): one tells you, boss and worker have exactly the same lives, the same "endowments," the same "conjectures," because they are... identical! And happy, on top of that, say J.F. Helliwell, P.R.G. Layard and J.D. Sachs... So here is the "normalized" economy of Robinson Crusoe, here is the city well-policed by our solitary *polis* man who is also, needless to say, "apolitical."[40]

Strictly speaking, one should still avoid speaking of "market" in these models, since the aggregation in question is only the identical duplication of the same individual, supposed to make a choice of resource allocation between the production of the final good and the formation of a stock of reproducible capital. This just makes absurd any reference to an "exchange" and "prices." Faced with this problem, which

[36] Bastiat (1864 [1855]), Chapter 7, "Capital," tome 6, p. 204 *et s.*

[37] Read: Kirman (1989 and 1992).

[38] Robinson (1953).

[39] De La Croix and Michel (2002).

[40] *Cf*. Herrera (2000a).

is worrying from the point of view of determining the remuneration of capital, neoclassicism experiences great embarrassment and does not know what to answer. Modeling in endogenous growth thus requires abandoning the Walrasian ambition which was the one to solve the problem of coordinating the decisions of a multitude of agents—or that, which is at least important in economics, of defining what a "market" is, whether it is capitalist or not.

The idea, too widely disseminated, that such representations would formalize a "dynamized general equilibrium" is, therefore, purely and simply false. The absence of real microeconomic foundations for this new orthodox macro-dynamics is striking and obvious. The optimal intertemporal choices of our guardian of the *pax œconomica* are supposed to correspond to the *per capita* quantities resulting from the calculation of a "multitude of individuals" in perfectly competitive markets. However, the appeal to the basic concepts of standard microeconomics in order to induce an increase of returns—and of technical progress—no longer has any collective dimension.

Furthermore, endogenous growth brings about a return to a rigid relationship between capital and output, which can be seen in the linearity at the heart of its models. It is in this apparent similarity with a Harrod-Domar representation, from which Robert M. Solow explicitly departed, that lies one of the reasons why many commentators have thought it appropriate to bring the young theory closer to the old Keynesian dynamics. Nevertheless, this was to aggravate the misunderstandings, and to forget the essential point: these are *supply* models—and not demand ones, which are curiously ignored—and the public policies they promote regard investment as a flow that increments different forms of *capital*, that is, always supply factors.

This "new" theory does not in any way revive Keynesian modeling; nor does it suggest besides any desire for "synthesis." It should be seen as a continuation of R.M. Solow, rather than as a break with him. All the more so since, formally, as we have indicated, a production function which is linear in a single reproducible input, characterized by a productivity that does not run out with the increase in its production, is sufficient to generate permanent growth. The nodal point is again located in the elasticity of output with respect to the stock of all the produced factors of production, taken as a whole, at least unitary.

For, if we look closely, Solowian growth and endogenous growth are very similar—even though the emphasis in the literature is frequently placed on the presence of increasing returns in order to obtain an internal source of growth, depending on the accumulation variables intrinsic to the system and mobilizing price mechanisms only. Let us emphasize that increasing returns are a sufficient but not necessary condition for the endogenization of technical progress. Self-sustained growth can be demonstrated by writing a production function where returns to scale are constant on all factors, whether accumulable or not—as in Solow's case—by asymptotic convergence toward a macroscopic functional form with unitary elasticity of the final product to a large and composite capital stock. Indeed, there is continuity—rather than discontinuity—between the old and the new, that is to say, between the ancient Solowian framework and the recent theoretical "innovation."[41] The lack of originality of the theory of endogenous growth was, moreover, stated very early on by Solow himself.[42]

The models of neoclassicism thus seem to persevere in their inability to formalize technical change, so striking are their difficulties in identifying the core of growth. Neither the "AK" model nor the diverse variants of endogenization of total factor productivity are capable of revealing what this "K," supposedly homogeneous[43] and the engine of perpetual growth, might actually be, but which could in reality correspond to any factor subject to accumulation—provided that an appropriate mathematical relation can be written linking it positively to the dynamics of productivity.

These models are said to be "rich"; we should say… *too* rich, because there are several—that is, always too many—candidates for the explanation of this growth. Basically, the discretionary selection of the factor whose accretion will authorize self-sustained growth is only an additional level of "adhocity" superimposed on those that already characterize these formalizations, e.g., the condition of aggregation and symmetry of the agents; the integration of external effects without any serious theoretical reference; knife-edge paths to obtain balanced growth that is both non-exhaustible and non-explosive; linear technology in the accumulation of "capital"; among other serious problems…

41 Further details can be found in: Herrera (2006). For a full mathematical exposure: Herrera (2010a).

42 Solow (1988).

43 On the question of the heterogeneity of capital: Zarembka (1975), Brown, Sato and Zarembka (1976).

Finally, very briefly, and with regard to the attempts at empirical verification of this theory, let us leave the floor to Edmond Malinvaud, whose point of view is unambiguous: "Recently, the so-called 'endogenous growth' has been discovered, whose correct model would explain differences in the long growth rates of countries with access to the same technologies. Is there any empirical evidence that the crucial ingredients justifying the explanation, or more precisely any of the competing explanations, are present in real economies? Very little, apart from some loose proofs, such as saying that investment in human capital is important (and yet this is not a new discovery)."[44] In this regard, let us add that, within an orthodox framework, the expected positive impact of the accumulation of "human capital" on growth has even been questioned quite often, empirically, to the point that it is not excessive to argue that the macroeconometrics of neoclassicism has not so far provided convincing evidence of the validity of endogenous growth models.[45]

2.7 What Reactivation of the State?

The contribution of these "new" models lies above all in the circumvention of the mathematical pitfalls that accompany the macro-dynamic incorporation of non-convexities, such as externalities and increasing returns. The stakes associated with this integration are crucial for neoclassicism, since it leads to an invalidation of the welfare theorems, which in turn leads to the authorization of State interference in the allocation of scarce resources. At the same time, however, the exercise of mainstream methodologies evacuates some of the questions that are of most interest to heterodox thinkers, including those relating to demand, income distribution, and unemployment—not to mention the crisis. Thus, the space restored to State action by the theory of endogenous growth is no longer really heterodox.

In particular, it is the conception of the State given by neoclassical theorists that is problematic, because it is totally contradictory. The State is present, or should we say omnipresent, since various recommendations for public intervention are formulated by these authors in an attempt to

[44] Malinvaud (1994, 1996).

[45] For example, Pritchett (1999). For a technical discussion of the properly econometric problems associated with empirical testing of endogenous growth models driven by human capital, see: Herrera (2010a, p. 189–194).

re-establish the lost "Paretian optimality" of equilibrium, through subsidies and tax exemptions in favor of the identified private sector which has been chosen as the engine of growth. But the State is absent, in fact, as an autonomous institution, because it cannot and will never be anything other than the single agent. The one that neoclassicism will clone according to its will, and which could even be immortal (i.e., living on an "infinite horizon") so that growth becomes eternal. The same agent that Robert J. Barro (Appendix C), an author whose name is also attached to this theory, has been telling us for ages that, "[n]aturally, his [or her] choices are governed by the search for his [or her] individual interest, a postulate of optimal behavior, central to economics."[46]

Robinson Crusoe, again, "thing" walled up in his solipsism and enclosing the economist of neoclassicism in a microcosm, situated beyond the frontiers of Pyrrhonism, on the borders of the radical empirical idealism of Bishop Berkeley that the fight against atheism had led to deny the reality of the existence of the material world. The State entity can only be taken into account through an optimization program in a centralized economy where Crusoe, although unable to spontaneously reach an optimal equilibrium in a competitive situation, would manage to "internalize" all the external effects by transforming himself into a "social planner."[47]

All that remains is to touch the fundamental point—and to touch the bottom, in reality...—that is to say, the ideological function of the "new" theory of neoclassicism, where its contacts with the *politics* of neoliberalism can be discovered. For the objective that animated these recent formalizers was opposed head-on to the traditional conception of technology as a public good. This traditional conception was that of R.M. Solow's conception, which referred not only to a technical progress that had "fallen from the sky," outside the economic sphere, or simply represented as a function of time, but also, above all, to its interpretation as being able to be—or even having to be—driven by the State itself.

Paul M. Romer's original choice to characterize technology as a non-rival good, partially exclusive, and therefore privately appropriable and remunerable, was certainly very "realistic" in our time; but it was far from neutral in such normative modelizations. *De facto*, such a choice

[46] Barro, R.J." (1987, p. 10).

[47] For instance: Barro and Sala-i-Martín (1995).

excluded from the reasoning any direct assumption of responsibility for the production of the technological factor by the State and ultimately reduced the latter's action to indirect interventions on the markets, essentially intended to favor the sole *private* investor. We recall that, as to it, Robert E. Lucas's model preferred to incorporate knowledge into human capital; but the training process it described, typically Beckerian, was based on a *private* allocative decision by the agent, with results that could be appropriated by him or her, and him or her alone.[48]

Let us listen to what Paul M. Romer thinks about this issue: "You have to look between the lines of that paper [Romer's 1986 paper] [to] think about technology (…). Solow said treat it as a public good. There are two variants of that. One is that it comes from the sky (…). The other is that the government could publicly provide it. I think Solow had both of those in mind and it does not really matter which you specify (…). What I wanted was a way to have something where there are some increasing returns but also some private provision. I wanted to capture the fact that private individuals and firms made intentional investments in the production of new technologies. (…) [Between his 1986 model and the 1990 one] I worked hard at the mathematics of this and persuaded myself (…) [that] the public-good assumption of Solow was not right."[49]

The reactivation of the State advocated by neoclassicism thus operates in a very particular state of mind—that of a commodification of knowledge—and through the denial of the nature of public goods, which are free (in both senses of the word: available and gratuitous), as well as common heritage of humanity: knowledge and research, education, social infrastructures… These are always modelized to be assimilated to categories of capital, commodified, and subjected to an exclusive logic of profit maximization. Consequently, the neoclassical State is only mobilized to help their accumulation, with a view to privatized appropriation and individualized remuneration.

Thus neoclassicism has achieved its goal: to model the acceptance of a return to power of the State of capital, but now exclusively oriented to

[48] Becker (1964). For an endogenous growth model by this author: Becker, Murphy and Tamura (1990).

[49] *Cf.* P.M. Romer's interview by B. Snowdon and H. Vane, in: Snowdon and Vane (2005, p. 682–683), available on: http://www.ricardopanza.com.ar/files/macro2/Modern_Macroeconomics_Snowdon_Vane_05.pdf.

perfecting industrial organization, and no longer to discussing the possibilities of income redistribution and better social services within capitalist society.

Although they sometimes tolerate very different interpretations of economic policy and often leave the question of the institutional forms to be adopted wide open, these orthodox models take sides. And we will add that this bias is political. Paul M. Romer's conception of innovation and knowledge dissolves the latter in an economy where its production is strictly fenced off by monopolistic and tradable patents; the conception of education and "human capital" by Robert E. Lucas—who was one of P.M. Romer's professors at the University of Chicago—goes against the development of the public education sector. We could multiply the examples here.

How can we understand, by way of conclusion, that the theory of endogenous growth appeared in a precise space–time—in the United States, in the second half of the 1980s—and in what sense can we grasp its links with the present transformations of capitalism? These analyses of neoclassicism were born of the impulse of committed theorists, within the very intellectual establishment that had once launched the offensive against Keynesian therapies and the Welfare State. Let us not forget here that R.E. Lucas, the brilliant "new classic" of rational expectations and of real cycles, aimed above all to rebuild an economic discipline on anti-Keynesian foundations: "What I am doing," he said clearly, "is returning to a pre-Keynesian research program."[50] And we will see that Robert J. Barro, who revisited in his own way the "Ricardian equivalence" and also contributed to the theory of endogenous growth, has always displayed unabashedly neoliberal positions (Appendix C).

This "renewal" of orthodoxy occurred at the height of the Reaganomics era, at a time when a slowdown in factor productivity was being observed in the deregulated United States and, simultaneously, the Asian "miracle," in which the State, especially in the sectors of R&D, education and infrastructure, had played a decisive role in technological catch-up and the acceleration of economic growth, with great concern in the circles of the U.S. establishment. The most lucid of neoclassical (and neoliberal) authors have, therefore, come to recognize the imperative need to soften their overly obtuse anti-State vision of the past, in

[50] Commentaries by R.E. Lucas, excerpts from: Klamer (1988, p. 83).

order to try to save the capitalist system from the excesses of *ultraliberalism*.[51] Since it is above all for the countries of the South, and not those of the North, that ultraliberalism is reserved; the one that attacks the sovereign functions of the State and ensures that globally dominant capital controls the "game."

The center of gravity of debates among economists has today shifted so far to the right that it is not surprising to hear Robert M. Solow declare, in the same year that Paul M. Romer laid the premises of the theory of endogenous growth in his doctoral dissertation in Chicago: "I think I am a neoclassical economist myself, at least the people who don't like me keep telling me so. But it is also clear that I am a Keynesian economist. When the debate is between Keynesians and neoclassicals, I am almost always on the Keynesian side. However, I do not feel in any way conflicted with my neoclassical self. There are problems for which the neoclassical apparatus seems to be better suited. I think there is no real difficulty in distinguishing which case one is in." In economics, one could thus be "both a capitalist and a worker, a producer and a consumer" (as the other said), but also, as we now know, both a neoclassicist and a Keynesian...

And R.M. Solow added: "In fact, I am also convinced that social and economic institutions, attitudes and motivations, widely accepted norms of equity, and all that sort of thing, are closely related to the observed behavior of advanced economists, even in the context of short-term macroeconomics. Does this make me an institutionalist? I confess that in the theological wrangling between neoclassicals and institutionalists, I tend to feel neoclassical without relinquishing an inch of my belief that institutions matter a great deal."[52] No worries: so the economist will be a neoclassical, a Keynesian... and an institutionalist in the same movement! The important point is that he or she remains well within the economic mainstream...

It is, however, somewhat ironic to observe that the "secret" of the determination of the rate of balanced and permanent growth, generated endogenously by the very process of capital accumulation, was "discovered"—albeit in an ascientific way—at the precise moment when the crisis was worsening, from the center of the capitalist world system, the series

[51] For an overview of the possible damage read: ROTHBARD (1973); or a book written by Milton Friedman's son, David Friedman: FRIEDMAN (D.) (1973).

[52] SOLOW (1983, vol. 11, p. 892).

of so-called "financial" crises (in the United States in 1987, in Mexico in 1994, in "emerging" Asia in 1997, in Russia and Brazil in 1998, then again in the United States in 2000, at the same time as in Argentina and Turkey…). A series which, in 2007–2008, we shall return to shortly, was to degenerate into a global crisis, far removed from the imaginary vision proposed by the theorists of neoclassicism of stable and eternal growth, in a mythified capitalism transformed into a state of nature.

References

ABRAMOWITZ M. (1956), "Resource and Output Trends in the United States Since 1870," *American Economic Review*, vol. 46, n° 2, p. 5–23.

AGHION P.M. and S. DURLAUF (eds.) (2005), *Handbook of Economic Growth*, Amsterdam: Elsevier.

AGHION P.M. and P.W. HOWITT (1992), *Endogenous Growth Theory*. Cambridge MA: The MIT Press.

ARROW K.J. (1962), "The Economic Implications of Learning by Doing," *Review of Economic Studies*, vol. 29, n° 3, p. 155–173.

BARRO R.J. (1987), *La Macroéconomie*. Paris: Colin.

———, "Government Spending in a Simple Model of Endogenous Growth," *Journal of Political Economy*, vol. 98, n° 5, p. S103–S125.

BARRO R.J. and X. SALA-I-MARTÍN (1995). *Economic Growth*. New York: McGraw-Hill.

BASTIAT F. (1864 [1855]), *Harmonies économiques*, *in Œuvres complètes*, Paris: Guillaumin & Cie.

BECKER G.S. (1964), *Human Capital: A Theoretical and Empirical Analysis, with Special Reference to Education*, New York: Columbia University Press.

——— (1985), Capital Income Taxation and Perfect Foresight. *Journal of Public Economics, no, 26*, 147–167.

BECKER G.S., K.M. MURPHY and R. TAMURA (1990), "Human Capital, Fertility, and Economic Growth," *Journal of Political Economy*, vol. 98, n° 5, part II, p. S12–S37.

BHADURI A. and D.J. HARRIS (1987), "The Complex Dynamics of the Simple Ricardian System," *Quarterly Journal of Economics*, vol. 102, n° 4, p. 893–901.

BLANCHARD O. and S. FISCHER (1989), *Lectures on Macroeconomics*, Cambridge MA: MIT Press.

BROWN M., K. SATO and P. ZAREMBKA (1976), *Essays in Modern Capital Theory*, Amsterdam North Holland.

CASS D. (1966), "Optimum Growth in an Aggregative Model of Capital Accumulation: A Turnpike Theorem," *Econometrica*, vol. 34, n° 4, p. 833–850.

CHENERY H.B. and M. BRUNO (1962), "Development Alternatives in an Open Economy: The Case of Israel," *Economic Journal*, vol. 72, n° 285, p. 79–103.
CHENERY H.B. and A.M. STROUT (1966), "Foreign Assistance and Economic Development," *American Economic Review*, vol. 56, n° 4, p. 679–733.
DE LA CROIX D. and P. MICHEL (2002), *A Theory of Economic Growth—Dynamics and Policy in Overlapping Generations*, Cambridge: Cambridge University Press.
DENISON E.F. (1985), *Trends in American Economic Growth: 1929–1982*, Washington DC: Brookings Institution Press.
DOMAR E.D. (1946), "Capital Expansion, Rate of Growth, and Employment," *Econometrica*, vol. 14, n° 4, p. 137–147.
——— (1947), *Essays in the Theory of Economic Growth*, New York: Oxford University Press.
EASTERLY W. and R. LEVINE (1997), "Africa's Growth Tragedy: Policies and Ethnic Divisions," *Quarterly Journal of Economics*, vol. 112, n° 4, p. 1203–1250.
FRIEDMAN D. (1973), *The Machinery of Freedom*, New York: Harper Collophon.
——— (1976), "The Line We Dare Not Cross," *Encounter*, n° 2, p. 2–14.
GROSSMAN G. and E. HELPMAN (1989), "Quality Ladders and Product Cycles," *National Bureau of Economic Research (NBER) Working Paper*, n° 3201, Cambridge (MA).
——— (1991), *Innovation and Growth in the Global Economy*, Cambridge MA: The MIT Press.
HAAVELMO T.M. (1956), *A Study in the Theory of Economic Evolution*, Amsterdam: North Holland.
HARROD R.F. (1939), "An Essay in Dynamic Theory," *Economic Journal*, vol. 49, n° 3, p. 14–33.
——— (1948), *Towards a Dynamic Economics*, London: Macmillan.
HARRIS R.J. and M.P. TODARO (1970), "Migration, Unemployment and Development: A Two-Sector Analysis," *American Economic Review*, vol. 60, n° 1, p. 126–142.
HERRERA R. (1998a), "Dépenses publiques d'éducation et capital humain dans un modèle convexe de croissance endogène," *Revue économique*, vol. 49, n° 3, p. 831–844, Paris.
——— (2000a), "Critique de l'économie 'apolitique'," *L'Homme et la Société*, n° 135, p. 87–104, Paris.
——— (2000b), "Éléments pour une critique de la 'nouvelle théorie' néoclassique de la croissance," *Cahier de la Maison des Sciences économiques de l'Université de Paris 1*, n° 75, Paris.
——— (2000c), "Por uma crítica da nova teoria neoclássica do crescimento," *Revista da Sociedade Brasileira de Economia Política*, n° 7, p. 55–73, Rio de Janeiro.

——— (2006), "The Hidden Face of Endogenous Growth Theory," *Review of Radical Political Economics*, vol. 38, n° 2, p. 243–257, New York.

——— (2010a), *Dépenses publiques et croissance économique - Pour sortir de la science(-fiction) néoclassique*, Paris: L'Harmattan.

——— (2010b), *Un Autre Capitalisme n'est pas possible*, Paris: Syllepse.

——— (2010c), *Estado y crecimiento*, Madrid: Maia Ediciones.

——— (2011), "A Critique of Mainstream Growth Theory," *Research in Political Economy*, vol. 27, n° 1, p. 3–64, London and New York.

——— (2012), "Reflections on the Current Crisis and Its Effects," *Economic and Political Weekly*, vol. XLVII, n° 23, p. 62–71, Mumbai.

Hicks J.R. and S. Hollander (1977), "Mr. Ricardo and the Moderns," *Quarterly Journal of Economics*, vol. 91, n° 3, p. 351–369.

Kaldor N. (1956), "Alternative Theories of Distribution," *Review of Economic Studies*, vol. 23, n° 2, p. 83–100.

——— (1957), "A Model of Economic Growth," *The Economic Journal*, vol. 67, n° 268, p. 591–624.

Kirman A.P. (1989), "The Intrinsic Limits of Modern Economic Theory: The Emperor Has No Clothes," *The Economic Journal*, vol. 99, n° 395, p. 126–139 (Supplement Conference Papers).

——— (1992), "Whom or What Does the Representative Individual Represent?," *Journal of Economic Perspectives*, vol. 6, n° 2, p. 117–126.

Klamer A. (1988), "Conversations with Economists: New Classical Economists and their Opponents Speak Out on the Current Controversy in Macroeconomics," *Rowman & Littlefield Publishers*, New Jersey: Totowa.

Koopmans T. (ed.) (1965), *The Econometric Approach to Development Planning*, Amsterdam: North Holland.

Krugman P.R. (1993a), "Economic Geography: on the Number and Location of Cities," *European Economic Review*, vol. 37, n°s 2–3, p. 293–298.

——— (1995), *Development, Geography, and Economic Theory*, Cambridge (MA): The MIT Press.

Lucas R.E. (1988), On the Mechanisms of Economic Growth. *Journal of Monetary Economics, 22*(1), 3–42.

Mill J.S. (1865 [1848]), *Principles of Political Economy with Some of Their Applications to Social Philosophy*, London: Longmans.

Malinvaud E, (1994). Éducation et développement économique. *Économie et Prévision, no, 116*, 1–15.

——— (1996), "Pourquoi les économistes ne font pas de découvertes," *Revue d'économie politique*, vol. 106, n° 6, p. 929–942.

Mahalanobis P.C. (1953), "Some Observations on the Process of Growth of National Income," *Sankhya—The Indian Journal of Statistics*, vol. 12, n° 4, p. 307–312.

Malthus T.R. (1986 [1798]), *An Essay on the Principle of Population*, London: Pickering.

McKinnon R. (1964), "Foreign Exchange Constraints in Economic Development and Efficient Aid Allocation," *Economic Journal*, vol. 74, n° 293, p. 388–409.

Olson M. (1996), "Distinguished Lecture on Economics in Government—Big Bills Left on the Sidewalk: Why Some Nations Are Rich, and the Other Poor," *Journal of Economic Perspectives*, vol. 10, n° 2, p. 3–24.

Pasinetti L.L. (1960), "A Mathematical Formulation of the Ricardian System," *Review of Economic Studies*, vol. 27, n° 2, p. 78–98.

Pritchett L. (1999), *Where Has All the Education Gone?*, Washington DC: The World Bank.

Rebelo S. (1990), "Long Run Policy Analysis and Long Run Growth," *National Bureau of Economic Research, Working Paper*, n° 3325, Cambridge MA.

Ricardo D. (1951 [1817]), *On the Principles of Political Economy and Taxation*, Cambridge (UK): Cambridge University Press.

Robinson J.V. (1938). The Classification of Inventions. *Review of Economic Studies, 5*(2), 139–142.

——— (1953), "The Production Function and the Theory of Capital," *Review of Economic Studies*, vol. 21, n° 55, p. 81–106.

——— (1964). *Theory of Economic Growth.* London: Macmillan.

Romer P.M. (1983), *Dynamic Competitive Equilibria with Externalities, Increasing Returns and Unbounded Growth*, Ph.D. Dissertation, University of Chicago.

——— (1986), "Increasing Returns and Long-Run Growth," *Journal of Political Economy*, vol. 94, n° 5, p. 1002–1037.

——— (1990a), "Endogenous Technological Change," *Journal of Political Economy*, vol. 98, S71–S10277.

——— (1990b), "Growth Based on Increasing Returns Due to Specialisation," *American Economic Review*, vol. 77, n° 2, p. 56–62.

Rostow W.W. (1960), *The Stages of Economic Growth: A Non-Communist Manifesto*, Cambridge: Cambridge University Press.

Rothbard M. (1973), *For a New Liberty*, New York: Macmillan.

Samuelson P.A. (1978), "The Canonical Classical Model of Political Economy," *Journal of Economic Literature*, vol. 16, n° 2, p. 1415–1434.

Sala-i-Martín X. (1990), "Lectures Notes on Economic Growth," *National Bureau of Economic Research, Working Papers*, n°s 3563 & 3564, Cambridge MA.

Sismondi J.-C. L. (1971 [1815]), *Nouveaux Principes d'économie politique*, Paris: Calmann-Lévy.

SNOWDON B. and H.R. VANE (2005), *Modern Macroeconomics: Its Origin, Development, and Current State*, Cheltenham (UK) and Northampton (MA): Edward Elgar.

SOLOW R.M. (1956), "A Contribution to the Theory of Economic Growth," *Quarterly Journal of Economics*, vol. 70, n° 1, p. 65–94.

——— (1983), "Discussion," *World Development*, vol. 11, p. 892.

——— (1988), "Growth Theory and After," *American Economic Review*, vol. 78, n° 3, p. 307–317.

——— (2000), *Growth Theory: An Exposition*, Oxford: Oxford University Press.

SMITH A. (1937 [1776]), *An Inquiry into the Nature and Causes of the Wealth of Nations*, New York: Random House.

TANZI V. (1985), "Fiscal Management and External Debt Problems," *in* H. Mehran (ed.), *External Debt Management*, p. 65–67, Washington DC: International Monetary Fund.

TOBIN J. (1955), "A Dynamic Aggregative Model," *Journal of Political Economy*, vol. 63, n° 2, p. 103–115.

UZAWA H. (1965), "Optimal Technique Change in an Aggregative Model of Economic Growth," *International Economic Review*, vol. 6, n° 1, p. 18–31.

ZAREMBKA P. (1975), "Capital Heterogeneity, Aggregation, and the Two-Sector Model," *Quarterly Journal of Economics*, vol. 89, n° 1, p. 103–114.

CHAPTER 3

Development: Theoretical Rebirth… Or Smiling Recolonization?

Let us move from growth to development.[1] "When I look at the Murphy et al. representation of the Big Push idea, I find myself wondering whether the long slump in development theory was really necessary. The model is so simple: three pages, two equations, and one diagram."[2] This is how Paul Robin Krugman, one of the most prominent economists of neoclassicism, but also one of those claimed to be the most "critical" of neoliberalism, and incidentally noted *New York Times* columnist, summarizes the "fall and rise of development economics," a nearly half-century of history of development thought that stretches between the "Big Push" formulation by Paul N. Rosenstein-Rodan[3] in the first half of the 1940s and its reformulation—and mathematical formalization—by Kevin M. Murphy, Andrei Shleifer and Robert W. Vishny published in 1989 in the *Journal of Political Economy*. One of the earliest ideas of development economics was indeed that the economies of the less developed countries were mired in a cycle of poverty and needed a "Big Push"

[1] This chapter has been written from the following two articles: Herrera (2004a, 2006a).

[2] Krugman (1993). A "leftist" neoclassical, Krugman, is here complimenting and paying homage to three "right-wing" neoclassicals, authors—"progressive" authors to the point of defining corruption as a "sister activity of taxes"—Murphy et al. (1989).

[3] Rosenstein-Rodan (1943). Also see: Dessus and Herrera (1999, 2000).

R. Herrera, *Confronting Mainstream Economics for Overcoming Capitalism*, Marx, Engels, and Marxisms,
https://doi.org/10.1007/978-3-031-05851-6_3

to develop. Such a push was seen as a large boost in investment, helped by the State's infrastructural and social spending, as well as by private foreign capital spending and aid from the governments of the developed countries.

The "glory days of high-level development theory"[4] would thus have lasted, because of its lack of rigor—in fact, according to P.R. Krugman, for lack of equations—only about fifteen years, ending in 1958 with the publication of Albert O. Hirschman's *The Strategy of Economic Development* and his contribution on "unbalanced growth."[5] According to Paul Krugman, development theory was, from the end of the 1950s onwards and until its rebuilding, no more than an approximate literature, which certainly produced some "wonderful and inspiring writings," but which was unable to mathematically model its basic hypotheses—starting with the concept of economies of scale—and finally led to the "intellectual dead end" of the discipline. It was only in the 1980s and 1990s, when orthodox theorists—and, in the midst of them, Krugman himself—managed to integrate the concepts of "non-convexities" like increasing returns or externalities (which we discussed in Chapter 2) into the neoclassical *corpus*, within a framework of imperfect competition,[6] that development economics experienced a rebirth and, to put it bluntly, achieved scientific status.

The thesis of the disappearance-reappearance of development theory, in its various variants, is now shared by a very large number of specialists in this field. It is defended, of course, by the proponents of hardcore neoclassicism, for whom there is no science out of the mainstream, and therefore no discussion of development without explicit reference to their standard models. But, and it is a more serious phenomenon, this thesis also finds a favorable echo among numerous "heterodox" economists, or at least among those who tend to consider the allegiance of their schools to neoclassicism as a "revival." In this field, as in others, the discipline of economics would now find itself appeased, pacified, and purged of its former theoretical-ideological conflicts. Basically, development economics would have reappeared only to disappear again, this time definitively, swallowed up by neoclassical orthodoxy and reduced to the state of a simple

[4] Krugman (1993, 1995).

[5] Hirschman (1958).

[6] Krugman (1989, 1990).

sub-branch, specializing in a few rather minor problems relating to the so-called "developing" countries—a curious expression that the mainstream chooses to mobilize to designate the countries that are precisely not developing, and that it qualified not long ago as "underdeveloped," and even earlier as "backward."

The present chapter, written against this too consensual position, takes strong issue with the mainstream interpretation of development economics. It intends to show how neoclassicism, which has now absorbed development as one of its components, is prisoner of a very deep crisis, and how mainstream domination in this theoretical field must be interpreted as inseparable from that imposed by neoliberalism and its policies on the practices of development.

3.1 Neoliberalism on the Assault on Development

In its contemporary, autonomous form, development theory had its origins in the 1940s and 1950s from a double differentiation. On the one hand, it separated itself from neoclassicism by the rejection of the dogmas of systematic international trade benefits and of the alleged virtues of capitalist markets, and on the other hand, it also moved away from Keynesianism, which was itself mainstream from 1945 to 1975 approximatively, through its critique of the inadequacy of the Keynesian economics of unemployment and short-term growth in examining the structural problems encountered by non-industrialized developing countries. Thus, there was a heterodox element in development theory from the beginning. Because of this, the new research field encouraged those who were more radically heterodox to analyze development, such as Marxists, and these in turn begat the economics of planning, structuralism, Cephalism, dependency theory, or theories of the capitalist world system, among others.[7]

These evolutions in the history of thought were connected to those occurring in the history of facts: the great revolutions of the Twentieth Century (in Russia, China, Vietnam, Cuba...), national liberation movements and the spirit of Bandung (in India, Indonesia, the Arab or Muslim world, Africa...), and even the needs for rebuilding in the postwar

[7] For an introduction to the capitalist world system theories: Herrera (2001).

period (with the lessons learned from the Marshall Plan in the West or, in the East, the aura of particularly influential authors, such as the Polish Michał Kalecki and Oskar R. Lange).[8] The emergence of economists from the South, such as Raul Prebisch, Celso Furtado or Ruy Mauro Marini in Latin America, P.C. Mahalanobis in Asia, or Samir Amin in Africa,[9] showed that development theory, born in Europe, like political economy before it, is not a monopoly of the North.

Therefore, development economics appeared in the intellectual space opened by the profound social transformations occurring under the pressure of the peoples' struggles worldwide, more or less radical attempts to break away from the laws of the economic and monetary world system. As a consequence, the State was placed at the heart of voluntarist strategies for structural change, endeavoring to make autonomous, to "self-center," as far as possible, the conditions of accumulation: planning and industrialization in the East and the socialist countries of the South, and capitalist developmentalism of the national bourgeoisies elsewhere. One understood it all the better because the only takeoff of a non-European country within the capitalist system, Japan, offered the example of an industrialization thoroughly led by the State—i.e., decided by the emperors of the Meiji era from the second half of the 1860s onwards.

Let us understand that it was under the massive pressure of the countries that were still called "Third World" at the time that the entire discipline was forced to emphasize, more frequently than it would probably have wished, the usefulness of economic planning, particularly because of its positive influence on the behavior of private agents. An economic planning that could be more or less rigid depending on the case, sometimes imperative, sometimes indicative… This "anti-hasard" plan, as Pierre Massé put it, was to play the role of "reducer of uncertainties, instrument of information for agents, but also tool of collective learning about economic development."[10]

And, in the academy, even the most right-wing factions had to politely recognize that one of the functions of the "development plan," considered as a complement to the market, was "to provide elements of

[8] Read, for example, Kalecki (1986, 1993) and Lange (1967).

[9] See, in particular, Prebisch (1973), Furtado (2003), Marini (1969), Mahalanobis (1955), and Amin (1993).

[10] Massé (1965).

information and of decision where they are lacking, because of (...) the imperfections of the market"; in short, that "what makes planning more particularly useful in an underdeveloped economy is rather the need to give the different agents (State, enterprises, peasants...) a view of what the evolution of the economy can or should be in the future," because "in an underdeveloped economy, more than elsewhere, the uncertainties about the future are great, the range of choices and development modalities is open, (...) the information about the future that the market transmits is limited."[11]

All good things come to an end. For it is this space, the product of the histories of facts and ideas, which was reconquered in the 1970s and 1980s, by neoliberalism in practice, and by the new neoclassical mainstream in economic theory. As we saw in Chapter 1, neoliberalism reflected the return to power of high finance, that is, the most powerful owners of capital on a global scale, mainly from U.S. origin. This return took place on the ruins of the world system pillars (e.g., fixed currency exchange rates), built after World War II. It started and was clearly affirmed at the end of the 1970s—precisely since the rise in interest rates wanted and imposed by the leadership of the U.S. Federal Reserve Bank, which decisively precipitated and exacerbated what was then called the "Third World debt crisis."[12]

In a context of such profound and global upheavals, the rebirth-rupture of development theory in the post-World War II years could only be considered, from the point of view of Keynesian-neoclassical orthodoxies, and since the paths followed by its pioneers did not follow those of the mainstreams, and the social forces that supported it were themselves losing ground, as a backwater of unscientific decline, or a brief "ascientific" parenthesis. The failures of development policies effectively applied in many countries of the South, notably through the relatively disappointing results of import substitution industrialization strategies, became obvious in the 1980s—the period of the advent of neoliberalism—and their replacement by export promotion.[13] But immediately, and in the same movement, any idea of an authentic development strategy, to be experimented outside the dogmas of neoliberalism—in fact, outside the

[11] Even a reactionary economist like GUILLAUMONT (1985) admitted this.

[12] Read here: NAKATANI and HERRERA (2007).

[13] See, for example, KRUEGER et al. (1981).

laws of capitalism—is henceforth prohibited, as are the various attempts to make development theory itself autonomous as a discipline distinct from the dominant neoclassical *corpus*.

3.2 Good Governance Versus Good Government?

Since the beginning of the 1990s, the main international institutions, first and foremost the International Monetary Fund (IMF) and the World Bank, have very regularly made recommendations on "good governance" to their member States. Nevertheless, the definitions of this notion, and with them the scope of its content, vary considerably from one organization to another, which makes it impossible to establish precise legal contours—all the more so since governance can also, as we know, refer to "corporate governance," "global governance," "environmental governance," etc.

In the context of its lending and "surveillance" operations, the IMF has sought to promote good governance covering "all aspects of the conduct of public affairs."[14] Applicable by countries receiving its technical assistance, and closely associated with the fight against corruption, its code of good governance aims, among other things, to try to make economic policy decisions more transparent, to gain access to the maximum amount of information on public finances, to standardize control practices and, more recently, to "combat the financing of terrorism."[15]

As to it, the World Bank intends to broaden the scope of this good governance of countries to "go beyond public sector dysfunction [dysfunction that this institution sometimes refers to as a 'symptom'] to help them integrate reforms" aimed at improving mechanisms for allocating public resources and "institutional arrangements of the State, processes of policy formulation, decision-making and implementation, and relations between citizens and government."[16]

[14] International Monetary Fund (2003). Read also the IMF "anti-corruption guide," available on: http://www.imf.org/external/np/gov/guide/eng/index.htm.

[15] Regarding the IMF's mandate to combat money laundering and the financing of terrorism (known as "AML/CFT"), see here: http://www.imf.org/external/pubs/ft/survey/so/2008/POL073108A.htm.

[16] World Bank (1994). See the Worldwild Governance Indicators on: http://data.worldbank.org/data-catalog/worldwide-governance-indicators.

While the United Nations Development Programme (UNDP) frequently links good governance to "sustainable human development" and "democracy," the Asian Development Bank most often emphasizes private sector participation, whereas the Inter-American Development Bank places more emphasis on strengthening civil society, the Organisation for Economic Co-operation and Development (OECD) focuses on accountability, transparency, both efficiency and effectiveness, foresight as well as the rule of law, and the European Bank for Reconstruction and Development (EBRD) rather insists on human rights...[17]

Despite the characteristic indeterminacy of the concept of governance, and the most varied criteria of normative judgment that are attached to it, the objectives formulated by these international institutions are quite clear and convergent: what is aimed at, ultimately, is the inflection of the policies followed by national States—or "client countries," as the World Bank's experts say—in the direction of the establishment of institutional environments that are the most favorable to the opening up of the economies of the South to the globalized financial markets.

However, this strategy, which has been uniformly imposed on these countries since the early 1980s through structural adjustment programs (SAPs), deregulation and privatization programs, and the free movement of capital, among other measures, has proven to be a failure in all areas and on all continents. Reflecting the now hegemonic power of high finance, neoliberalism is not a model of development, but a model of domination and exploitation. Its economic destructions, its social disasters, and its human dramas are too well known to be recalled here.[18]

Faced with the impossible "management of the crisis" of the world system by neoliberalism and the refusal of international institutions to recognize the urgency of an alternative that would add to the dynamics of capital's expansion some limits external to its profit maximization logic, this good governance could only harden the criticism of "State failures." Public servants are no longer just accused of "rent-seeking" behavior, in the manner of the reactionary proponents of the Public Choice school,

[17] Respectively: http://www.undp.org/content/undp/en/home/ourwork/democraticgovernance/overview.html; http://www.adb.org/themes/governance/; http://idbdocs.iadb.org/wsdocs/getdocument.aspx?docnum=1555501; http://www.oecd.org/governance/; and http://www.ebrd.com/pages/about/policies/governance.html.

[18] Gazier and Herrera (2002).

such as Gordon Tullock, James McGill Buchanan, and George Joseph Stigler, all three of whom studied at the University of Chicago, or Anne Osborn Krueger of the International Monetary Fund.[19] What is now being questioned is the capacity of these State agents to manage public affairs, especially in the indebted economies of the South, and to build "good institutions"—not so much in the service of the people, but of capital.

However, the coincidence of moralistic discourses on the responsibility of States that would be solely to blame for (almost) all the problems encountered, and on the irresponsibility of civil servants—when it is not their probity that is at issue—is nothing other than a legitimization of the ultraliberal option of abandoning the major regalian functions of the State, going in some cases as far as the delegation to a foreign power of national defense, the substitution of the national currency by a strong foreign currency or the privatization of the collection of taxes graciously entrusted to a few private companies...

Indissociable from the pursuit of neoliberalism and the societal project that is the objective of its deployment, the new anti-State ideological dogma of good governance can only be seen as the inverted symmetry of good government. The aim is not the development of democratic participation of individuals and peoples in the processes of discussion and decision concerning them, nor the respect of their fundamental right to development, but to push States to deregulate markets, that is to say, to *re*-regulate them by the sole forces of globally dominant capital.

Hence the curious paradox, inherent in this good governance, of repeated appeals launched by various international institutions to national governments in order to "internalize" neoliberal policies imposed from outside, and to "appropriate" them, at the very moment when globalized financial markets are dispossessing them of their sovereignty and penetrating their capital ownership structures by force. To manage the State apparatuses of the South (and of the East...) directly from the center of the capitalist world system, while neutralizing their State power, divesting them of all real prerogatives, constraining their margins of maneuver to the extreme, and recolonizing them, with a smile, would this not be, seen from the North, the secret of ideal governance?

[19] Tullock (1993). Before that, from the same: Tullock (1967). And even before, of course: Buchanan and Tullock (1961). Also: Stigler (1971, 2003). Without forgetting: Krueger (1974).

Nevertheless, in the end, what true democracy could such public authorities claim, when they would limit in this way the expression of the sovereignty of their peoples to the opening and liberalization of local markets, or to the payment of foreign debt and dividends on foreign investments?

Under these conditions, we can only be concerned about these initiatives of "public-private partnership for development" that have been taken by the United Nations General Secretariat, especially with the implementation of the "Global Compact."[20] This "moral convention" between the United Nations and the business circles "community," disguised as "citizen corporates" and now speaking only of "ethics," officially intends to "give the globalized market a human face" by ensuring that a set of "shared values and principles" relating to human rights, respect for labor laws and environmental protection are guaranteed by the major transnational corporations. In reality, this adventurous deal allows the latter to make the U.N. institutions themselves dependent on their funding and to use their public and universal "label" for private purposes.[21]

It makes about as much sense as appointing the "Keynesian" economist Jeffrey D. Sachs to head the Millennium Development Goals (MDGs)[22] global program. J.D. Sachs, the inventor of the "World Happiness Indicators," the doctor whose "shock therapies" applied with the same brutality from the post-Soviet and post-Yugoslav economies to Bolivia during the time of the military dictatorship and to most of the African continent, have produced catastrophies that are to be measured in millions of victims.[23]

3.3 The IMF: A Model of "Bad Governance"?

However, in terms of "good governance," the line has been drawn, at least at the theoretical level, by the IMF "experts"—all of them coming from the ranks of neoclassicism or, when this is not the case, from those

[20] Read on this subject the speech given in Davos in 1999 by the Seventh Secretary-General of the United Nations, Kofi Atta Annan. As well as: http://www.unglobalcompact.org/.

[21] Richter (2003).

[22] Sachs (2005). See: Herrera (2006b).

[23] UNICEF (2001) See: http://www.unicef-irc.org/publications/pdf/monee8/eng/5.pdf.

of the ultraliberals. And the fact is that, for these "experts," good governance consists essentially of "liberalizing the exchange, trade and price systems," "limiting arbitrary decision making and preferential treatment of individuals and organizations," and "eliminating direct credit allocations" by the State. Very clearly, their quest for perfection is confused with the generalization of neoliberal policies.

The insistence of this institution on talking about "good governance," which has become one of the levers of the conditionality of aid to Southern countries and of the agreements to reduce their foreign debt, reveals the increasing politicization of its interventions and the drift of its missions well beyond those initially defined by its mandate. Its monitoring of macroeconomic policies and of the environment for private sector activities, whose confidence would condition the terms of sustained growth, now concerns "all aspects" of State institutions, including the nature of the political regime, which it hopes will be as "transparent" as possible.

The question one might ask here is whether this international organization applies with the same determination the imperatives required by the South (and the East) when it comes to its own operations and functioning. To believe the IMF, the answer, of course, would be yes: a "code of conduct" supposed to ensure ethics and to prevent corruption among its own internal staff has been drafted, a "deontology advisor" has been appointed… But there are many facts that suggest that the IMF has become a model of… "bad governance."

Democratic and impartial institutions, dissemination of public information, transparency of decision-making procedures, participation of different actors, the principle of election, efficient management of scarce resources, expertise skills, accountability obligation, total integrity, and respect for human rights would be some of the conditions of this "good governance." What exactly is the situation at the IMF?

i. In this institution—whose building is located at 700 19th St. N.W. in Washington D.C., just across the street from the World Bank—the weight of the member countries depends on their financial contributions, so much so that the United States alone has the right to veto the most important decisions. Moreover, the IMF's dependence on the U.S. Treasury Department, which is located in another building of Washington D.C.—separation of powers demands!—at 1500 Pennsylvania Avenue, between the White

House (executive power) and the Capitol (legislative power), at a good distance from the Pentagon (say, a few miles, across the Potomac river), is no longer a secret to anyone.

ii. Despite recent but still very limited progress, the availability of documents elaborated within the IMF remains highly restricted.
iii. The negotiations involving it remain opaque and generally surrounded by the greatest mystery.
iv. The range of its interlocutors is extremely limited (ministers of Economy and Finance, governors of Central Banks), although it has been slightly enlarged in recent years (to the main private corporation leaders and businessmen of the country visited), but without ever involving or democratically consulting the peoples or their representatives.
v. Consensus being the traditional method used, programs of measures to be applied are adopted by vote only in exceptional cases.
vi. The policies pursued under structural adjustment programs have proven to be totally ineffective in resolving internal and external imbalances, and have contributed at times to propagating or even causing financial crises.
vii. IMF "experts" are not subject to any evaluation procedure as to the relevance of their recommendations—and *a fortiori* as to their adequacy to the most urgent expectations of the peoples.
viii. The scientific quality of the Fund's work is also questionable, given the research available in the academic literature. We shall have the opportunity to give an example of this in Chapter 8.
ix. Anti-corruption rhetoric does not prevent the IMF from knowingly financing notoriously corrupt regimes. No need to insist, their list would take up several pages.
x. Many of the countries that receive its financial aid are criticized for their systematic violation of human rights.

As a consequence, the need for transformations for development and democracy is obvious. Our purpose here is not only to put the governing body of international organizations on trial—the reform of which is demanded from all sides and required by reason. It is also and above all to emphasize that the malfunctions of the IMF, stubbornly defending the sole interests of creditors and transnational corporations, reflect more generally the failure of the governance imposed by the "G7," under U.S. leadership, in an attempt to pull the capitalist world system out of the crisis. The conditions of "good governance" will be sought in vain as long as the structural obstacles preventing the vast majority of the world's countries from implementing their rights to self-determination are not removed.[24]

3.4 The Absorption of Development Theory by Neoclassicism

We have already pointed out on several occasions and in various ways: for more than four decades now, almost alone, "neoclassicism" has dominated economic theory, including the theory of economic development. Its ambition, as we have also said, is to analyze all socioeconomic facts by starting from the maximizing behaviors of individuals, and only from theses individual behaviors. The heart of this mainstream—as well as the source of its claim to having a scientific status, exclusively for it—is the theory of the Walrasian general equilibrium of markets.

Heavily mathematical, strongly normative, and reliant upon a host of absurdly unrealistic assumptions, general equilibrium theory is the keystone of all standard microeconomics. Its very purpose is to determine the way by which the choices of the many agents (buyers and sellers) can be coordinated within a formalized framework integrating the whole of the interdependences linked to their exchanges. Assumed to be free, rational, and driven solely by personal interest, these individual choices within the orthodox axiomatics depend not only on the agents' characteristics (notably their initial production factor endowments, tastes and preferences, conjectures, production functions, etc.), but also on the forms of the social organization in which their relations operate—that is, what the authors of neoclassicism call "market structures" or "institutions" (see Chapter 4).

The privileged case is a market structure of so-called "perfect" competition which allows the model, under certain precise hypotheses, including those defined in particular by Kenneth Joseph Arrow and Gérard Debreu,[25] both Nobel laureates, to give an equilibrium solution for which

[24] Herrera (2004b, c).

[25] Arrow and Debreu (1954). Also: Debreu (1959).

the coordination of very numerous individual choices is possible, and the allocation of scarce resources itself "optimal" (in the sense described above, given originally by the economist Vilfredo Pareto).[26] This theory of general equilibrium of markets claims to show that when every buyer and seller in the marketplace acts out of self-interest, competition will produce a unique set of prices and quantities that will create a perfect match between the supply and demand of every good and service and every input used in production. What is more, once this set of "equilibrium" prices and quantities is reached, social welfare will be as high as it can possibly be, in the sense that no individual will be able to be better off without making someone else worse off.

While this key model aims at processing information concerning a great number of individuals, the technical difficulties encountered by the neoclassicals often lead them to build the model with a very restricted number of agents, on the assumption that these are "representative" of all agents. In extreme cases, but far from being rare in the orthodox literature—since they allow saving mathematical simplifications—there is only a single agent; it is assumed that the entire analysis can be successfully worked out in the case of one individual, like Robinson Crusoe on his island. Insofar as general equilibrium analysis provides an ultimate theoretical frame of reference for almost all neoclassical modelizations, it is quite clear that a thorough knowledge of it is a crucial challenge for heterodox economists, especially if they want to be critical.

This is all the truer because, from the end of the 1970s, this same theory has been amply applied in the specific field of development, thanks to the expansion of the use of what are known as computable general equilibrium models (CGEMs). The latter attempt to calculate, on the basis of "individual behaviors," the values of certain "equilibrium variables" in the economy under study, starting with, for example, price or quantity effects of variations of the model's parameters linked to economic policy, such as taxes or subsidies.[27]

Relying in particular on the work of authors such as Irma Adelman and Sherman Robinson, Shantayanan Devarajan and Dani Rodrik, or also

[26] See: Guerrien (1996a).

[27] For instance, if a nation establishes a minimum wage for workers, will this lead to an increase in unemployment?

François Bourguignon,[28] the World Bank has made almost systematic use of these models, which, by the same movement, has contributed to the wide dissemination of these tools in academic circles throughout the world—including, of course, and unfortunately, in the South (and the East). Since they could be applied through simulations carried out on the basis of "social data matrices," they came to both theoretically justify and politically give credibility to the extremely harsh measures of structural adjustment programs imposed in peripheral countries in a situation of overindebtedness and/or balance of payments crisis.

Furthermore, we will see later that mainstream authors have also been led to address certain questions relating to development through the study of the role of institutions (such as labor unions, the State, the military, religious organizations and rules, and the like) and particularly their role in growth. We shall notice that, for a long time, according to the standard neoclassical theory, that of so-called "perfect" competition, institutions had the status of exogenous data only, and that their analysis was, so to speak, excluded from economic reasoning. And we shall see that the attempt to endogenize institutions within the Walrasian framework has been one of the priority lines of research of the orthodox current in recent decades, especially in the field of development.

Moreover, it should be remembered that the consideration of "institutional factors" in the explanation of growth played an important role in several of the original works of development economics, such as those of the British-Saint Lucian (Sir) William Arthur Lewis, the Swedish Karl Gunnar Myrdal or the Belarusian-U.S. Simon Smith Kuznets (all three of whom won the Nobel Prize in Economics in 1979, 1974, and 1971, respectively).[29] This is also the case with a less prestigious author, although much closer to the mainstream (and of the establishment: he was director of the Rockefeller Foundation and a member of the Council on Foreign Relations), such as Michael P. Todaro, for whom economic decisions cannot be dissociated from their political, social, institutional, and cultural context.[30]

[28] Adelman and Robinson (1978), Devarajan and Rodrik (1991), and Bourguignon et al. (1983). Later: Bourguignon et al. (2008).

[29] Read: Lewis (1955), Kuznets (1966), and Myrdal (1968).

[30] Todaro (1982).

This did not prevent Theodore W. Schultz, the most orthodox of these "pioneers" of development economics, who was a professor in Chicago with G.S. Becker, from affirming that it cannot be concealed that, when one thinks about institutions, the analytical toolbox is "empty"...[31] Having shared the Nobel Prize in 1979 with W.A. Lewis, this same, T.W. Schultz, proponent and precursor of the "human capital" theory—which is in fact, and in our opinion, mainly a war machine against public education[32]—had defended the broad validity of standard microeconomics and extended its application to areas far from its traditional boundaries (like agriculture, in particular).

Nor does it seem inappropriate to recall here that one of the most active branches of current analytical research in economics, and undoubtedly the most formalized of all, in this case, game theory, also makes frequent use, explicitly or implicitly, of this same notion of "institution." Indeed, how can a "game" be precisely characterized if not by a set of rigorously defined rules, thus constituting the "institutional framework" within which each "player" will be led to make his or her decisions? Such an "institution" is often presupposed, depending on the degree of sophistication of the models considered, whether in the simple case of voluntary exchange between two agents—which presupposes, in the background, a "convention" forbidding any haggling in which the "stronger" actor would manage to impose his or her choice on the "weaker" co-trader, or excluding from the game any opportunistic behavior with "asymmetric information"—as in the far more complex case of perfect competition, a configuration in which the functioning of the market requires the centralized processing of a considerable mass of information. However, whatever model is chosen, the link between individuals and institutions always remains twofold or bi-univocal: institutions condition the decisions made by the various "players," while conversely, it is these individual choices that "produce" these institutions. Hence the ultimate and needed recourse to concepts such as the agents' a priori "beliefs," or even "ideology," intervening upstream as determinants, and thus directly on the institutions.

As regards the field of dynamic macroeconomics now, we mentioned in the previous chapter the impressive success of the "new" neoclassical

[31] Schultz (1968). Also: Becker (1964).

[32] Herrera (2010).

theory of growth, known as "growth theory with endogenous technical progress," since the end of the 1980s. Such an evolution has had a decisive impact on development economics. These models seeking to resolve the problems encountered by Robert Solow and to try to explain the growth of per capita output by the accumulation process itself—i.e., the factors of production, without recourse to an exogenous engine—have placed neoclassicism in a quasi-exclusive position in the theoretical formalization relating to growth. Following the canonical founding representations, hundreds (or thousands) of variants have been proposed in the most diverse fields of investigation of development, where their use has become almost systematic,[33] to the point where this approach has gradually become confused with the macro-dynamic study of the long term.

Even if it too remains within a single-agent framework, the effort to modernize the old Solowian apparatus by endogenous growth theorists has enabled neoclassicists to integrate into their paradigm a broad spectrum of development-related themes that had long been neglected or left to non-mainstream authors—such as, among others, the post-Keynesian Nicholas Kaldor,[34] or the classical-Marxist Richard M. Goodwin,[35] a lifelong Marxist, but quite "rebel."[36] All those, so numerous, who have chosen to give their models more original and sympathetic names than the others—such as the alleged "Schumpeterians" Philippe Aghion and Peter W. Howitt[37]—cannot, however, ignore that the methodological framework of endogenous growth, which is totally and exclusively neoclassical, has rid the discipline of all unorthodox "impurity."

Many "heterodox" economists fed up with the virulence of the prevailing anti-Statism, but powerless to produce an alternative way of thinking about modernity—and perhaps also anxious to live (or to survive) in peace in an academic world under the rule of a scientific looking neoclassicism, that is, of a current that is only scientific in appearance—have succumbed to the charms of this "new" growth theory, with the sweet interventionist flavor of yesteryear.

[33] Azariadis and Drazen (1990).

[34] Kaldor (1961, 1982).

[35] Goodwin (1967).

[36] Goodwin (1983).

[37] Aghion and Howitt (1992, 1998, 2005).

3.5 From the Intellectual Catastrophes of Neoclassical "Development"...

As we shall understand it, heterodoxies, especially those of development economics, are still very much on the defensive. And the attacks launched against them by neoclassicism operate, as we have seen, all-round and in all directions, that is to say: on the fronts of microeconomics (by the theory of general equilibrium of markets), of macroeconomics (with endogenous growth theory), and simultaneously of institutions (with the so-called "neoinstitutionalist" currents). Besides, the present aggressiveness of orthodoxy is reminiscent of two of the attacks conduced concomitantly after Marx, and against him, by what Nikolai Bukharin had called, a little over a century ago, "the theoretical economics of the bourgeoisie,"[38] i.e., on the one hand, the so-called German "historical" school (with, among other authors, Georg Roscher, Friedrich Hildebrand, Gustav von Schmoller...) and, on the other hand, the "Austrian" school (led by Carl Menger, Eugen von Böhm-Bawerk, Friedrich F. von Wieser...).

Today, nevertheless, the theoretical resistance of the heterodox authors to these offensives of neoclassicism seems to us to be all the more imperative since the rise of the mainstream, which is quite impressive in the field of development, cannot conceal the theoretical impasses into which the different approaches of orthodoxy have been sinking for quite some time now.

In the first place, as far as microeconomics is concerned, it is obviously the indeterminacy theorems due to Hugo F. Sonnenschein,[39] then confirmed in their "negativity" by theoreticians such as Rolf R. Mantel,[40] and Gérard Debreu himself,[41] that constitute the most serious and difficult challenge to neoclassicism. Mathematically robust, these discoveries have indeed embarrassed for five decades the supporters of orthodoxy, who have still not found the means to overcome them. In essence, and technically, these theorems (also known as impossibility theorems) establish that the net demand functions that can be derived from the market

[38] Bukharin (1972 [1914]).

[39] Read here: Sonnenschein (1972, 1973).

[40] Mantel (1974).

[41] Debreu (1974). See, before that, by the same: Debreu (1959, 1962).

general equilibrium model of Arrow-Debreu type are likely to take "any form", and, consequently, that the conditions on the shapes of the supply and demand curves are no longer deducible from the maximizing behaviors of the agents—this, in perfect competition as well as in monopolistic or oligopolistic cases. It, therefore, becomes impossible to demonstrate the uniqueness of the equilibrium and the convergence of Walrasian "*tâtonnement*" (or trial-and-error process).

These theoretical problems, which are extremely serious in the sense that they crack the central pillar of the neoclassical "paradigm," are obviously never mentioned in the innumerable applied studies devoted to "developing countries," particularly those using CGEMs (mentioned above); nor, moreover, are the difficulties linked, among other and delicate things, to the formation of prices in exchange and to the contradiction of a reference to perfect competition in ultra-centralized representations of the economy, with a "*commissaire-priseur*" (or an auctioneer) *à la* Walras.

The retreat of most of the formalizations of orthodox authors to the postulate of representative agents, or even of a single agent, which is a producer and a consumer at the same time, is only the inevitable consequence of their inability to solve the crucial problems of aggregation and coordination of the decisions of a "multitude" of agents. The question thus remains as to what sense there would be in speaking of "prices"—and therefore also of a "remuneration of capital"—in processes of cloning strictly identical agents.

This is also the case in the neoclassical macro-dynamic models of the short term proposed by real business cycle analysis.[42] Its adherents choose to deal with cycles by postulating, in particular, an economy with a single agent, without money, with full employment, and in a state of permanent equilibrium; an agent that is obviously "rational" and capable of perfectly predicting the future evolution of the entire economic system thanks to its "rational expectations." And all this, which turns out to be purely and simply absurd,[43] does not prevent "the scientific project [that of neoclassicism to model cycles] in dynamic and stochastic general equilibrium"[44]

[42] Lucas (1981), Kydland and Prescott (1982), and Long and Plosser (1983).

[43] For an internal criticism, but clearly insufficient: Summers (1986).

[44] An example: Naoussi and Tripier (2012).

from extending to the heart of sub-Saharan Africa, thus adding to the scourges that already plague it…

Africanists are well advanced! Could we not push the neoclassical-economist delirium a little further to the point of constructing a "Kenyan" or "Malagasy" version of a growth model with endogenous technical progress in which capital would be bovid? A zebu as an engine of growth, why not after all? Or even a bribe, thanks to the payment of which, as many neoliberals believe, the civil servant would be suddenly awakened, indolently dozing in the tropics? Corruption could be a source of technical progress, if one is not embarrassed to write about the positive effect of a "bakchich" on the productivity of our civil servant's work! Or "symbolic capital," whether it be scholar, cultural, artistic, or religious… It is the clearance sale of neoclassicism, where the customer does not know where to turn! For, in this joyous bazaar, anything will do, according to the goodwill—an arbitrariness in fact—of the modeler. But, underneath his or her "endogenization," it is the commodification that we can catch a glimpse of.

And here, in this recurrence of the fundamental neoclassical impossibility of determining the conceptual bases of "capital," the specter of an old polemic resurfaces, that of "the two Cambridges," which, in the 1920s and 1930s, turned into a berezina for the neoclassicals. By a strange effect, the historical victory of neoclassicism in its efforts to substitute holistic methods for a subjectivist perception of human actions and to reduce them to an individualistic psychology led it to take refuge in the flattest and most sterile holism, that of the single agent. Even if the mainstream had managed to overcome these difficulties, we would still be justified in rejecting its explanation of economic phenomena as the result of the agglomeration of behaviors that only take individual interest into account. The apprentice in neoclassical formalization will thus escape the real difficulty, that of grasping the chains and entanglements of the mechanisms of the functioning of economies in all their complexity; a complexity that a few circumstantial equations, used as tools of alienation (not to say as weapons of terror) and vectors of propaganda, will make disappear, by dissolving it.

By thus excluding from reasoning the real sets, proper to holistic and systemic approaches, the deconstructivism of neoclassicism consciously removes from the field of vision the various social forces and historical structures of economic formations—that is to say, Hayek's "popular abstractions"[45]—as well as their multiform connection with human actions. We shall see, in Chapter 4, that a large majority of neoinstitutionalist studies, beyond their diversity, share this same atomistic conception of institutions and that the servitude of the "new institutional economics" to the model of general equilibrium of markets is clearly voluntary in Armen A. Alchian and Harold Demsetz, who flirt with the Austrians, or in the work of an information theorist with a supposed "critical" eye on development, such as Joseph E. Stiglitz, or in the works of the game theory modelers, in the manner of the allegedly "Keynesian" George A. Akerlof, but also, albeit more discreetly, among the most important authors of neoinstitutionalism, starting with Douglass C. North or Oliver E. Williamson himself.

This results in authentic intellectual catastrophes. The fact that these scientific regressions have been crowned by prestigious Bank of Sweden prizes in economics will help the reader to understand not only the ideological nature of these rewards and their similarity to the Nobel Peace Prizes, which have been awarded to famous "peacemakers" such as Heinz A. Kissinger, Frederik W. de Klerk, Barack H. Obama or the European Union!—much more than to the Fields medals—but also the full extent of the damage from which the discipline of economics is currently suffering. A few illustrations will suffice to measure the severity of the disaster.

The interpretation of feudalism suggested by a D.C. North (Nobel 1993), accompanied for the occasion by Robert P. Thomas, amounts to considering that the lord would offer "collective goods" for which there is no market (e.g., defense), in return for which the remuneration of these "services rendered" must take certain adequate institutional forms, such as the drudgery due by the serfs to the lord and other constraints attached to serfdom, in order to prevent possible "free rider" behaviors on the part of the subjects.[46] What a crazy idea then, if you were a miserable peasant in Eighteenth-Century France, to revolt against the privileges of the *Ancien Régime*![47]

[45] Hayek (1953, p. 34).

[46] North and Thomas (1973).

[47] Such analyses are at the antipodes of the Marxist ones. For example, Soboul (2014). Also: Nicolas (2002).

The explanation of the relationship between the master and the slave is conceived in the same spirit, except that such an "exchange" would reveal this time a contract that remained "implicit," but still reflecting, fortunately, a "rational" choice. On this point, we find again the surreal interpretation that Robert W. Fogel (who shared the Nobel with D.C. North in 1993) thought it appropriate to propose, in association with Stanley L. Engerman in this case, of the economic history of slavery in the South of the United States (Chapter 4).[48] R.W. Fogel thus contributed to scientific knowledge by applying statistical techniques to history (thanks to "cliometry") and by arguing, particularly, that, in the Nineteenth Century, plantation slaves enjoyed much better living and working conditions than wage earners in the industries of the North of this country. Put another way, according to Fogel, Black people were in a way victims of the abolition of slavery...[49]

By moving "from morality to economics," as R.W. Fogel and S.L. Engerman used to say, are we not approaching what Friedrich Nietzsche might have thought on the subject? "The fact that we attach more value to a satisfaction of vanity than to any other advantage (security, pleasure...) is shown to a ridiculous degree in that everyone (...) wishes for the abolition of slavery and repels with horror the idea of putting human beings in that state; while everyone must say to oneself that slaves have in all respects a more secure and happier existence than the modern worker, that servile labor is little compared to the worker's labor. One protests in the name of 'human dignity,' but it is (...) this brave vanity, which regards it as the hardest fate not to be on an equal footing, to be publicly counted as inferior. The cynic thinks differently, because he despises honor."[50] *Kein Kommentar...*

Forgive his very numerous well-intentioned groupies, but a Joseph E. Stiglitz also seems to fit smoothly into this vein (Chapter 4), when he argues that, behind the contemporary resurgence of sharecropping in certain rural regions of the South, we could see appear the freedom of individual agents, the rationality of their choices and, what is more, the efficiency of an institution which would be that for which the "contractual" terms would provide the landowner with a serene "balance"

[48] Fogel (1964). Or: Fogel and Engerman (1971).

[49] Read instead: Bénot (2006 [1992]). And: Dorigny and Zins (2009).

[50] Nietzsche (1899, p. 390).

between the risk of uncertainty linked to variations in farm income and the indispensable "incentive" of a sharecropper tempted by "leisure" rather than by work.[51] This would have nothing to do, of course, with the conditions of overexploitation of fractions of the local peasantry, so degraded in these countries that they cause entire sections of their society to regress to a medieval institution!

3.6 ... To Those, Political, of Neoliberal "Development"

But after all, did not Oliver E. Williamson teach us that at every period of history, private "contracts" resulting from free transactions between rational individuals have been, are, and always will be "efficient"[52]? One of the key postulates of the perfect competition model, that of voluntary exchange as the basis of inter-individual relations, is systematically retained in the arguments of neoclassicism. What is essential for our authors, including and perhaps especially if they call themselves neoinstitutionalists, even the most "moderate" ones, is the preservation of the fiction of a "freedom" in individual choices, intimately linked to that of a "democracy," in the bourgeois sense, which conceals the effects of domination by classes and by nations and the violence of the relations of force between exploiters and exploited—that is to say, basically, the most fundamental contradictions of the capitalist world system—and which braces itself on the defense of what Ludwig von Mises called "the integral recognition of the private property of the means of production" against "the anti-logic, the anti-science, the anti-thought" that would be Marxism, the "opium of the intellectual high class."[53]

We shall be told, not without reason, that Marxism is becoming discreet and that it is not really a danger anymore. However, there is perhaps nowadays only to the left of the political spectrum where people do not know that Marxism, which never ceases to agonize, is in reality "*increvable,*" that is to say, indestructible, unstoppable, as the French philosopher Jacques Bidet once rightly remarked. Neoclassicism, as to it,

51 Stiglitz (1974).

52 Williamson (1975).

53 See the preface to the French edition of: Von Mises (1938).

has understood that it is in its supreme interest to consider Marxism as dead and buried.

The U.S. economist of Spanish origin, Xavier Sala-i-Martín, is a good example of this. He was Jeffrey D. Sachs' collaborator and, at Harvard University, the assistant of Robert J. Barro (with whom he co-authored probably the world's best-known textbook on endogenous growth theory), and also worked at the IMF. X. Sala-i-Martín wrote that the use of "conspiracy theories" to write or rewrite history is "fashionable," and that the technique has been perfected over the years by the intellectual heirs of Marxism. For him, Marx thought that history was nothing other than the permanent class struggle, the continuous fight "between perverse exploiters and innocent exploited" for material or economic benefit. According to Sala-i-Martín, the methodology would consist in finding some relation between those who make decisions and "an evil multinational." Once this "trick" is performed, it would automatically be shown that the policies were carried out with the sole purpose of favoring the clandestine interest of the oligarchy. "No need to be precise." He adds that despite the fact that Marx is "one of the worst analysts in history" (with the argument that his prediction of the collapse of capitalism and the consequent emergence of communism should be considered "one of the most ridiculous of the [penultimate] millennium"), Marx's technique remains alive and well among his successors. So, the "paranoid-conspiracy interpretation of history" seems "indispensable" when studying the current foreign policy of the United States. Sala-i-Martín notes the similarity between Marxist methodology and the "new anti-American trend." "It is too simple a way to analyze our world."[54] This is probably why, according to him, "neoliberalism is not a sin."

We have already mentioned the ideological function of recent developments in neoclassical growth theory (Chapter 2), and its close contact with the policies of neoliberalism (Chapter 1). And also the deep motivations for the reactivation of State intervention carried out in order to commodify the common patrimony of humanity in a logic of profit. As well as the compatibility of such a theory with the neoliberal project. Let us add here, however, that this relentless defense of capitalism against the excesses of ultraliberalism operates in a world where these excesses

[54] Source: extract from the personal page of X. Sala-i-Martín (available at: http://www.columbia.edu/%~23).

are always reserved in practice for the economies of the South, and for them alone—and certainly not for those of the North, and especially not for the United States, where the State under neoliberalism has probably never been so interventionist, powerful and warlike in its entire history.

We are therefore a long way from the "Big Push" *à la* Rosenstein-Rodan. The application of an institutional set provided as a turnkey solution, i.e., an economy opened to globalization and confusing "market" and "capitalism," would henceforth be sufficient to set in motion a development process.[55] And in this game of "convergence,"[56] even "the least developed countries"—as Walt W. Rostow used to say—could catch up with the "best ones," in other words, the United States and its "top" factor productivity. Exactly like the Asian "tigers" and "dragons" a few years ago or with the "good students" that the World Bank successively rewards in the hierarchical rankings of its reports. Such was the case of Botswana at one time, until it was discovered in Washington D.C. that almost a third of the Botswana population was carrying the AIDS virus...

Taking up the old idea—also found, among others, in an author such as Moses Abramovitz[57]—that institutions, whether "political, commercial, industrial or financial" in nature, would partly explain international differences in GDP growth rates over the long term, some orthodox economists of neoclassicism[58] argue that the potential for *per capita* income convergence is not limited to middle-income countries,[59] but can also benefit the poorest economies, if the economic rights of all private agents settled within their borders are firmly guaranteed, starting with property rights.[60] Savings could then be mobilized and allocated more efficiently to productive investments. If we understand correctly, Niger, for example, should end up "taking off" and even "converging" toward the leading country (the United States!)... on the simple condition that its government succeeds in "stabilizing the property rights" of private agents, i.e., in fact, that it does not venture to imagine that the very first

[55] For a demonstration radically opposed to the neoclassical position, see: HERRERA and LONG (2019).

[56] On this issue, see: BARRO and SALA-I-MARTÍN (1992, 1995, 1997).

[57] ABRAMOVITZ (1986). More recently, ACEMOĞLU, JOHNSON and ROBINSON (2005).

[58] KEEFER and KNACK (1995) and KNACK (1996).

[59] This is what suggested, for example, BAUMOL et al. (1989).

[60] DELONG (1989).

step toward the development of this country would be the nationalization of what constitutes its main natural resource, uranium.

The reactionary ideology of some "great" economists, indicated above, is relatively well-known and often denounced. But the basically pro-neoliberal arguments of more moderate Nobel Prize winners, usually viewed as popular critics of the system, like Joseph E. Stiglitz, for example, get far less critical attention. This "in-fashion" author, 2000 prize winner, knows how to "surf" on the wave of protests against wild neoliberalism and on the necessity for market regulation to promote a capitalism "with a human face." However, this is a serious misunderstanding, because he does not recommend rebuilding the Welfare State, modifying the capital ownership structure in favor of the public sector, applying a strong policy of income redistribution, or promoting public services—much less arguing in favor of State-led planned development. In spite of a few nuances, his arguments imply that the State should fully submit to the dominant forces of global capital and help its capital accumulation. Stiglitz was still chief economist in the World Bank when the 1998–1999 report on "*Knowledge for Development*" was published. This report teaches us what "cooperation" with the private sector means in the fields of information and telecommunications: privatization, dismantlement of public research (even the transformation of research institutes into joint-stock companies), and marketization of education (by helping the poor to pay for their studies!). It matches the series of reports previously published by the World Bank on infrastructure, environment, health, or peace dividends, which supported big transnational corporations by: insuring them against any risk of nationalization; having transnationals take charge, at State expense, of building infrastructure for capital accumulation; promoting forest exploitation for export; cutting public budgets and social programs; and opening juicy outlets for their military-industrial complexes (before recommending disarmament in order to continue the refunding of Third World debts).

Nowadays, the undivided dominance of neoclassicism in academia, especially in development theory, is on par with that of high finance's power over development policies and goes hand in hand with the dominance of neoliberal politics in the order of development practice. This does not mean, of course, that all the neoclassicals are neoliberals, far from it. As has been said, a strangeness of the present time, and one of its complexities, is precisely this schizophrenia of many economists, who are inflexible neoclassicals on working days and during office hours, but who are convivial "leftists" or pseudo-populists on weekends, and thus also on voting days. This means that there are significative complementarities—a relationship of correspondence, or, better, of collaboration—between these two forms of ideological domination, which are compatible, mutually reinforcing, and interdependent. Thus, in our opinion, it is not only their lack of scientific foundation and their logical inconsistencies that disqualify these approaches, but the ideological function and antisocial project that their methodologies and conclusions support in the service of globally dominant capital.

References

Abramowitz M. (1986), "Catching Up, Forging Ahead, and Falling Behind," *Journal of Economic History*, vol. 46, n° 2, p. 385–406.

Acemoğlu K.D., S. Johnson and J.A. Robinson (2005), "Institutions as a Fundamental Cause of Long-Run Growth," *in* P. Aghion and S. Durlauf (eds.), *Handbook of Economic Growth*, vol. 1, part A, p. 385–472, Amsterdam: Elsevier.

Adelman I. and S. Robinson (1978), *Income Distribution Policy in Developing Countries: A Case Study of Korea*, A World Bank Research Publication, Oxford: Oxford University Press.

Aghion P.M. and P.W. Howitt (1992), "A Model of Growth Through Creative Destruction," *Econometrica*, vol. 60, n° 2, p. 323–351.

——— (1998), *Endogenous Growth Theory*, Cambridge MA: The MIT Press.

——— (2005), "Neoclassical Models of Endogenous Growth," *in* P. Aghion and S. Durlauf (eds.), *Handbook of Economic Growth*, vol. 1, p. 67–110. Amsterdam: Elsevier.

Amin S. (1993), *Itinéraire intellectuel*, Paris: L'Harmattan.

Arrow K.J. and G. Debreu (1954), "Existence of an Equilibrium for a Competitive Economy," *Econometrica*, vol. 22, n° 3, p. 265–290.

Azariadis C. and A. Drazen (1990), "Threshold Externalities in Economic Development," *Quarterly Journal of Economics*, vol. 105, n° 2, p. 501–526.

Barro R.J. and X. Sala-i-Martín (1992), "Convergence," *Journal of Political Economy*, vol. 100, n° 2, p. 223–251.

——— (1995), *Economic Growth*, New York: McGraw-Hill.

——— (1997), "Technological Diffusion, Convergence, and Growth," *Journal of Economic Growth*, vol. 2, n° 1, p. 1–26.

Baumol W.J., S. Blackman and E. Wolff (1989), *Productivity and American Leadership: The Long View*, Cambridge MA: The MIT Press.

Becker G.S. (1964), *Human Capital: A Theoretical and Empirical Analysis, with Special Reference to Education*, New York: Columbia University Press.

Bénot Y. (2006 [1992]), *La Démence coloniale sous Napoléon*, Paris: La Découverte.

Bourguignon F., M. Bussolo and L.A. Pereira da Silva (2008), *The Impact of Macroeconomic Policies on Poverty and Income Distribution*, Washington DC: The World Bank.

Bourguignon F., G. Michel and D. Miqueu (1983), "Short-Run Rigidities and Long-Run Adjustments in a Computable General Equilibrium Model of Income Distribution and Development," *Journal of Development Economics*, vol. 13, n° 1, p. 21–43.

Buchanan J.M. and G. Tullock (1961), *The Calculus of Consent: Logical Foundations of Constitutional Democracy*, Ann Arbor: The University of Michigan Press.

Bukharin N.I. (1972 [1914]), *L'Économie politique du rentier - critique de l'économie marginaliste*, Paris: Études et Documentations Internationales.

Debreu G. (1959), *Theory of Value*, New York: Wiley.

——— (1962), "New Concepts and Techniques for Equilibrium Analysis," *International Economic Review*, vol. 3, n° 2, p. 257–273.

——— (1974), "Excess Demand Functions," *Journal of Mathematical Economics*, vol. 1, n° 1, p. 15–21.

DeLong J.B. (1989), "The Protestant Ethic Revisited: A Twentieth Century Look," *Fletcher Forum of World Affairs*, n° 13, p. 229–242.

Dessus S. and R. Herrera (1999), "Capital public et croissance: une étude en économétrie de panel," *Revue économique*, vol. 50, n° 1, p. 113–126, Paris.

——— (2000), "Public Capital and Growth: A Panel Data Assessment," *Economic Development and Cultural Change*, vol. 48, n° 2, p. 407–418, Chicago.

Devarajan S. and D. Rodrik (1991), "Pro-competitive Effects of Trade Reform: Results from a CGE Model of Cameroon," *European Economic Review*, n° 35, p. 1157–1184.

Dorigny M. and M.-J. Zins (eds.) (2009), *Les traités négrières coloniales: Histoire d'un crime*, Paris: Cercle d'Art.

Fogel R.W. (1964), *Without Consent or Contract: The Rise and Fall of American Slavery*, New York: W.W. Norton.

Fogel R.W. and S.L. Engerman (eds.) (1971), *The Reinterpretation of American Economic History*, New York: Harper and Row.

Furtado C. (2003), *Raízes do subdesenvolvimento*, Rio de Janeiro: Civilização Brasileira.

Gazier B. and R. Herrera (2002), "Escaping from the Crisis: Structural Adjustment and Social Security in the Republic of Korea," *in* K. Marshall and O. Butzbach (eds.), *New Social Policy Agendas for Europe and Asia—Challenges, Experience, and Lessons*, p. 405–417, Washington DC: The World Bank.

Goodwin R.M. (1967), "A Growth Cycle," *in* C.H. Feinstein (ed.), *Socialism, Capitalism and Economic Growth*, p. 54–58, Cambridge: Cambridge University Press.

——— (1983), *Essays in Linear Economic Systems*, London: Macmillan.

Guerrien B. (1996a), *Dictionnaire d'analyse économique - Microéconomie, macroéconomie, théorie des jeux, etc.*, «Dictionnaires repères», Paris: La Découverte.

Guillaumont P. (1985), *Économie du développement*, tome 2, Thémis, Paris: Presses Universitaires de France.

Hayek F.A. (1953), *Scientisme et sciences sociales: essai sur le mauvais usage de la raison*, Paris: Plon.

Herrera R. (2001b), "Les Théories du système mondial capitaliste," *in* J. Bidet and E. Kouvélakis, *Dictionnaire Marx contemporain*, p. 201–221, Paris: Presses Universitaires de France.

——— (2004a), "Un Renouveau de l'économie du développement?," *Recherches internationales* (Paris), n° 72, p. 51–68, Paris.

——— (2004b), "Good Governance against Good Government?," Joint Written Statement of the Centre Europe Tiers-Monde and the American Association of Jurists for the Human Rights Commission of the United Nations, 60th Session, Point 17, E/CN.4/2004/NGO/124, July, Geneva.

——— (2004c), "IMF: A Bad Governance Model?," *Third World Economics*, n° 324, p. 15–21, Penang.

——— (2006a), "The Hidden Face of Endogenous Growth Theory," *Review of Radical Political Economics*, vol. 38, n° 2, p. 243–257, New York.

——— (2006b), "Objectifs du Millénaire pour le Développement: lutte contre la pauvreté ou guerre contre les pauvres ?," *Alternatives Sud*, vol. 13, n° 1, p. 185–199, Louvain-la-Neuve.

——— (2010). *Dépenses publiques et croissance économique - Pour sortir de la science(-fiction) néoclassique*, Paris: L'Harmattan.

Herrera R. and Z. Long (2019). *La Chine est-elle capitaliste?*, Paris: Éditions Critiques.

Hirschman A.O. (1958), *The Strategy of Economic Development*, New Haven: Yale University Press.

International Monetary Fund (2003), *Good Governance: The IMF Role*, Washington DC: IMF.

Kaldor N. (1961). "Capital Accumulation and Economic Growth," *in* F.A. Lutz and D.C. Hague (eds.), *The Theory of Capital*, p. 177–222, New York: St.Martin Press.

——— (1982), *The Scourge of Monetarism*, New York: Oxford University Press.

Kalecki M. (1986), *Selected Essays on Economic Planning*, Cambridge (UK): The University Press.

——— (1993). *Introduction to the Theory of Growth in a Socialist Economy* (1963). *in* J. Osiatyński and B. Jung (eds.), *Collected Works of Michal Kalecki*, vol. IV, New York: Oxford University Press.

KEEFER P. and S. KNACK (1995), "Institutions and Economic Performance: Cross-Country Tests Using Alternative Institutional Measures," *Economics & Politics*, vol. 7, n° 3, p. 207–227.

KNACK S. (1996), "Institutions and the Convergence Hypothesis: The Cross-national Evidence," *Public Choice*, n° 87, p. 207–228.

KRUEGER A.O. (1974), "The Political Economy of the *Rent-Seeking* Society," *American Economic Review*, vol. 64, n° 3, p. 291–303.

KRUEGER A.O. et al. (1981), *Trade and Employment in Developing Countries*, National Bureau of Economic Research, London: The University of Chicago Press.

KRUGMAN P.R. (1989), *Rethinking International Trade*, Cambridge (MA): The MIT Press.

——— (1990), "Increasing Returns and Economic Geography," *National Bureau of Economics Research Working Papers*, n° 3275, Cambridge MA.

——— (1993), "The Fall and Rise of Development Economics," available on: http://www.wws.princeton.edu/pkrugman/dishpan.html.

——— (1995), *Development, Geography, and Economic Theory*, Cambridge (MA): The MIT Press.

KUZNETS S.S. (1966). *Modern Economic Growth: Rate, Structure, and Spread*, New Haven: Yale University Press.

KYDLAND F.E. and E.C. PRESCOTT (1982), "Time to Build and Aggregate Fluctuations," *Econometrica*, vol. 50, n° 6, p. 1345–1370.

LANGE O.R. (1967), *Essays on Economic Planning*, London: Asia Publishing House.

LEWIS W.A. (1955), *Theory of Economic Growth*, London: Harper & Row.

LONG J.B. and C.I. PLOSSER (1983), "Real Business Cycles," *Journal of Political Economy*, vol. 91, n° 1, p. 39–69.

LUCAS R.E. (1981), *Studies in Business Cycle Theory*, Cambridge MA: The MIT Press.

MAHALANOBIS P.C. (1955). "The Approach of Operational Research to Planning in India," *Sankhya—The Indian Journal of Statistics*, vol. 16, n°s 1–2, p. 3–130.

MANTEL R.R. (1974), "On the Characterization of Aggregate Excess Demand," *Journal of Economic Theory*, vol. 7, n° 3, p. 348–353.

MARINI R.M. (1969), *Subdesarrollo y revolución*, México: Siglo XXI.

MASSÉ P. (1965), *Le Plan ou l'anti-hasard*, Collection Idées, Paris: Gallimard.

MURPHY K.M., A. SHLEIFER and R.W. VISHNY (1989), "Industrialization and the Big Push," *Journal of Political Economy*, vol. 106, n° 2, p. 503–530.

Myrdal G. (1968), *Asian Drama: An Inquiry into the Poverty of Nations*, New York: Twentieth Century Fund.

Nakatani P. and R. Herrera (2007), "What Rich Countries Owe Poor Ones," *Monthly Review*, vol. 59, n° 2, p. 31–36, New York.

Naoussi C.F. and F. Tripier (2012), "La Modélisation en équilibre général dynamique et stochastique des cycles économiques en Afrique subsaharienne," *Revue d'économie politique*, n° 5, p. 657–683.

Nicolas J. (2002), *La Rébellion française - Mouvements populaires et conscience sociale: 1661–1789*, Paris: Le Seuil.

Nietzsche F.W. (1899), *Humain, trop humain*, Paris: Mercure de France.

North D.C. and R.P. Thomas (1973). *The Rise of the Western World—A New Economic History*, Cambridge: Cambridge University Press.

Prebisch R. (1973), *Problemas teóricos y prácticos del crecimiento económico*, New York: Naciones Unidas, Comisión Económica para América Latina.

Richter J. (2003), *Building on Quicksand: The Global Compact, Democratic Governance and Nestlé*, Geneva: Éditions CETIM / IBFAN-GIFA / Déclaration de Berne.

Rosenstein-Rodan P.N. (1943), "Industrialization of Eastern and South Eastern Europe," *Economic Journal*, vol. 53, n° 210, p. 202–211.

Sachs J. (2005), *The End of Poverty*, London: Penguin Press.

Schultz T.W. (1968), "Institutions and the Rising Economic Value of Man," *American Journal of Agricultural Economics*, vol. 50, n° 5, p. 1113–1122.

Soboul A. (2014), "Du Féodalisme au capitalisme: la Révolution française et la problématique des voies de passage," *in* A. Casanova et R. Herrera (eds.), *Penser les crises*, p. 34–58, Paris: Le Temps des Cerises.

Sonnenschein H. (1972), "Market Excess Demand Functions," *Econometrica*, vol. 40, n° 3, p. 549–563.

——— (1973), "Do Walras' Identity and Continuity Characterize the Class of Excess Demand Functions?," *Journal of Economic Theory*, vol. 6, n° 4, p. 345–354.

Stigler G.J. (1971), "The Theory of Economic Regulation," *Bell Journal of Economics*, vol. 2, n° 1, p. 3–21.

——— (2003), *Memoirs of an Unregulated Economist*, Chicago: University of Chicago Press.

Stiglitz J.E. (1974), "Incentives and Risk Sharing in Sharecropping," *Review of Economic Studies*, vol. 41, n° 2, p. 219–256.

Summers L.H. (1986), "Some Skeptical Observations on Real Business Cycle Theory," *Quarterly Review*, Federal Reserve Bank of Minneapolis, vol. 10, n° 4, p. 23–27.

Todaro M.P. (1982), *Economics for a Developing World*, Essex: Longman.

Tullock G. (1967), "The Welfare Costs of Tariffs, Monopolies and Theft," *Western Economic Journal*, n° 5, p. 224–232.

——— (1993), *Rent Seeking*, Brookfield: Edward Elgar.
UNICEF (2001), *A Decade of Transition*, Regional Monitoring Report (MONEE), n° 8, Florence.
Von Mises L. (1938), *Le Socialisme - Étude économique et sociologique*, Paris: Éditions M.-Th. Génin - Librairie de Médicis.
Williamson O.E. (1975), *Markets and Hierarchies: Analysis and Antitrust Implications*, London and New York: Free Press - Macmillan.
World Bank (The) (1994), *Governance: The World Bank's Experience*, Washington DC: The World Bank.

PART II

The Limitations of the "Soft Heterodoxies" in Economics

CHAPTER 4

Markets and Institutions: Economics and the Rough Understanding of Organizations

Mainstream economics has long been concerned with the mechanisms by which institutions or organizations—the two terms being very close, despite the extreme (and to be honest somewhat painful) diversity of definitions used in this specific field of the discipline—would intervene in economic activities, particularly in the interactions between markets and their modes of structuring and functioning, as well as in the dynamic processes of transformation of economies.[1]

This field of research was first and foremost taken up by theoreticians who came from currents that were relatively distrustful of *homo œconomicus* and wished to distance themselves from utilitarianism. For Thorstein B. Veblen, institutions are not only modes of *ex post* coordination of agents' actions, but rather a system of norms that also intervene *ex*

[1] One of the bases used to write this chapter was a long survey elaborated for the Organisation for Economic Co-operation and Development (OECD) in 1996, a few months before I joined the CNRS as a full-time researcher: Herrera (1996). The discreetly critical aspect of its initial content meant that this draft, although self-censored and commissioned as an OECD working paper, did not obtain the internal visa authorizing its publication. It thus remained a *mimeo*. The present, liberated text of this chapter has little to do with the original one, which was too polite—because it was excessively polished.

R. Herrera, *Confronting Mainstream Economics for Overcoming Capitalism*, Marx, Engels, and Marxisms,
https://doi.org/10.1007/978-3-031-05851-6_4

ante, that is, upstream of their decisions and influence their own preferences and values.[2] This author thus considers institutions in a broad sense, as including not only the "habits of doing" (or routines), but also the "established habits of thinking, common to most human beings," which exert an influence on their cognitive processes, and even their perceptions.

The studies of the "American institutionalist school" go in this direction,[3] as well as those of other historicist, evolutionist, or structural economists. Their methodologies, almost always non-formalized, exposed them, however, to frequent criticism from those who, like Carl Menger[4] in particular, were soon to form the new orthodoxy in economics, or "neoclassicism," on the basis of the subjective theory of value-utility and marginalist analysis.

Nevertheless, for the neoclassical theoretical *corpus*, at least in its standard version known as "perfect competition," established from the core of microeconomic hypotheses formulated by Kenneth Joseph Arrow and Gérard Debreu (undoubtedly the two most important mainstream theoreticians, winners of the Nobel Prize in economics in 1972 and 1983, respectively), institutions are generally given only a subordinate status of exogenous data.[5] Their role is most often reduced to that of figuration, and their interpretation is, therefore, excluded from economic reasoning proper, to be referred to other social science subjects dealing with collective categories—above all to history, anthropology, sociology, or political science. Thus, the formal inclusion of "institutionally determined" parameters in a mainstream model meant, at most, the integration of phenomena likely to be influenced—not by "nature," but—by human actors, without their characterization as exogenous values being really modified.

It is in this context, and especially since the contributions of authors such as Oliver E. Williamson and Douglass C. North, that the "endogenization" of institutions within the various analytical frameworks claiming to be "Walrasian" has been able to constitute one of the major developments of the research program of neoclassicism in recent decades. Since its

[2] Veblen (1899a, 1899b, 1900).

[3] For example, Mitchell (1913), Commons (1931), Ayres (1944), and Clark (1957).

[4] Menger (1996 [1833]).

[5] Arrow and Debreu (1954).

proponents consider all of these institutions or organizations as a necessary condition for the emergence and good functioning of markets, it would be their job to analyze the terms of this condition.[6] Even if it means that beyond the ideological discourse, which is always latent, a certain confusion reigns...

4.1 In Search of Definition(s)

A first difficulty arises from the distinction to be made between markets and institutions (or organizations). As a matter of fact, many economists oppose institutions to markets, by considering that the function of the former (institutions) is to coordinate individual actions in situations where the efficiency—or even, in some cases, the very existence—of the latter (markets) is not guaranteed.[7]Institutions thus appear to be efficient modalities that ensure the coordination of the decisions of economic actors and supplement the traditional mechanisms, absent or failing, of markets, to be conceived as their symmetries. Other authors (or sometimes the same ones, for that matter) see the market, on the contrary, as being itself a particular institution, with various norms of individual behavior and a legal framework specifically attached to it.[8]

In the mainstream literature, the market is often described as a mechanism for transferring property rights. It differs from institutions, which would be the rules prior to these transfers. The market can also be distinguished from organizations, whose internal operations are characterized by the absence of such transfers. It should be noted, moreover, that although some authors make a distinction between institutions and organizations, it is only one of degree, and not of kind: an organization could be transformed into an institution as soon as its practice becomes extensive, standardized, and recognized.[9]

Another difficulty encountered by the orthodox economist is still to be found in the theory and is due to the contradictory fact that the institution is frequently considered both as a correction of market imperfections

[6] This was the pioneering position of Coase (1987 [1937]). And also that of Hicks (1969).

[7] Among others: Williamson (1975).

[8] Williamson (1985). Also see authors as different as: Alchian (1977), Hirschman (1986), and Coase (1988).

[9] De Janvry et al. (1993).

and, in itself, as an imperfection, at the source of various distortions. This ambiguity of the concept is very often found, as we shall see, at the heart of neoclassical analyses devoted to the economic role of the State. When the mainstream takes into account imperfections that disrupt the functioning of markets, due to the presence of "transaction costs," the institution—which can be the State, but which is not only the State, of course—sometimes represents a solution to the problem of suboptimal equilibrium.

Much work on the imperfection of markets, in a context of imperfect information in particular, deals with the ways in which the agents' actions are coordinated, as well as with the required nature of the institutional supports for their individual decisions, such as the types of contracts involved. This is the case, for example, of the "new institutional economics," which has completed the neoclassical analysis by elaborating, in particular, a theory of the firm, which until then had been largely neglected by standard theory.[10] The firm is then perceived as an institution alternative to the market, and justified by the importance of the transaction costs encountered in the latter.[11]

Let us say, at this level of reasoning, that one of the major functions of institutions would be to "economize" (in the sense of "to reduce") transaction costs. Such "saving money" can take the form of mitigating risk and/or uncertainty. It could, therefore, be a matter of allowing one or more agents to improve their welfare (in the Pareto sense) without deteriorating that of others, or of allowing them to achieve a higher level of their—not necessarily exclusively economic—objectives, under some constraints.[12]

Such a reduction in transaction costs can be obtained, for example, by taking advantage of deeper specialization or possible economies of scale and/or externalities. Insofar as a large number of different institutions—market institutions (for goods and services as well as for factors of production) or non-market institutions (firms, among others)—are likely to perform functions of this kind, it is logical that individual choices can be determined in a situation of competition between several types of alternative institutional arrangements—in a theoretical perspective in

[10] Williamson (1995).

[11] Coase (1987).

[12] Lin and Nugent (1995).

many respects inspired by the work of the British Nobel Prize winner in economics and professor at the University of Chicago, Ronald H. Coase.[13]

If we attempt to classify studies on institutions schematically, it is possible to identify several—at least three—clearly distinct approaches.[14] A first series tends to assimilate institutions to systems of property rights, established by legal rules. It will then be shown that any system of property rights is likely to lead to a Pareto optimum, provided that it is "complete,"[15] that is to say, if the system is such that all the rights to all the benefits of all the resources are attributable to any individual and can be exchanged on a market. Nevertheless, the "completeness" of a property rights system is never fully assured, because of the existence of transaction costs. Some incomplete systems—i.e., some "institutions"—are, however, relatively more conducive to access to a Pareto-optimal situation than others.

A second approach rather uses the term "institutions" in the sense of norms of economic behavior, or in that of "conventions." As "supplements" to the law, these conventions may even turn out to be more efficient than the law because they have lower transaction costs.

A third body of works considers institutions as related to the categories of contracts in use. These may concern markets as different as, for example, the insurance market, in order to cover a given risk in a context of uncertainty, or the labor market, in order to define the contractual forms of employment.

Information economics, for its part, although distinct in many respects from studies of institutions, as Joseph E. Stiglitz has pointed out on numerous occasions,[16] has some affinities with them. Information economists do not treat institutions as exogenous variables, but as endogenous ones: they would adapt to reflect the system of informational (and of course transactional) costs characterizing the economy. Institutions can then be interpreted as a means of reducing risk and uncertainty—and can explain certain behaviors of agents that are different, or atypical, compared to those of the "competitive" framework.

[13] Bertrand (2003).

[14] For an example of typology: Matthews (1986).

[15] Coase (1960).

[16] Stiglitz (1988, 1995, 2001).

All these institutional elements are relatively stable in time and space—without being temporally immutable or spatially identical. The expression "institution" would, therefore, apply to very diverse collective entities, imposing themselves on agents from the outset and defining the framework of what, sympathetically, one uses to call the "rules of the game" of the economy. A framework that directly influences inter-individual relationships and in which their coordination strategies are deployed. Institutions share this common function of providing economic agents with order and stability, and, therefore, predictability and credibility, in their actions and in the relations they maintain between themselves.

In environments of marked uncertainty and complexity, agents would need to form reciprocal and stable expectations in order to make their choices and decisions—that is, in order to perform their "transactions"—as well as to know each other's respective rights and duties. This is normally what institutions would make possible.[17]

4.2 A (so to Speak) Systematic Connection to the General Equilibrium of Markets

In the end, what should be understood by "institutions"? Some authors answer, in an inevitably (but excessively) vague manner, that they constitute "a set of socio-economic rules, put in place under historical conditions, over which individuals or groups of individuals [would] have very little control in the short and medium term, and which [would] aim to define the conditions under which individual or collective choices about the allocation and use of resources can be made." And also: "Institutions [would] not [be] coordination mechanisms *per se*, [but would rather] contribute to defining the socio-historical conditions in which these mechanisms can be established."[18]

"Socio-economic rules (…) [in] socio-historical conditions" is certainly a better formula than simple "rules of the game." But the fact is that it means, roughly or exactly as one would like to say, the same thing. For this elegant rhetoric is generally applied to arguments which, whether modeled or not, all or almost all claim to be based on the theory of the general equilibrium of markets. However, what we have known about this

[17] Boland (1979).

[18] *Cf.* Ménard (1990).

theory since its inception is that its "purity" does not take into account the historical dimension of the real economy, nor the thickness of the society that is interwoven into this economy and determines it. Consequently, in this domain, there is neither "socio" nor "historico" that holds...

It is clear that the approaches of the "new institutional economy," or similar approaches, are far from forming a monolithic block. What is important, however, is to understand that they share the same individualistic or atomistic conception of the economy. The origin of institutions is still and again interpreted as the result of an aggregation of individual decisions, according to a cost-benefit calculation and on the basis of a voluntary exchange contract between supposedly free agents. This means that the vast majority of these works are, in one way or another, based on the assumptions of methodological individualism; and that the ultimate theoretical reference for such analyses remains, almost systematically, and exclusively, the framework provided by the neoclassical model of perfect competition in its orthodox version due to K.J. Arrow and G. Debreu.

Let us read here one of the leaders of this current, the 1993 Nobel Prize winner in economics Douglass C. North, whose reference to the "Walrasian model" is recurrent: "In a world where there would be perfect and cost-free information (...), the Walrasian system would provide the model of the economy."[19] Or again, elsewhere, from the same author: "Let us begin by considering the neoclassical theoretical reference model, i.e., the Walrasian model..."[20] And another major theorist of institutions, also a Nobel Prize winner (in 2009), Oliver E. Williamson, starts, "for ease of exposition," from the fundamental hypothesis of neoclassicism according to which "in the beginning, there were markets..."[21] Similarly, a "Keynesian" like George A. Akerlof begins one of his most famous articles on the role of institutions with these words: "There is a standard model of economic behavior, the Arrow-Debreu general equilibrium model of perfect competition...".[22]

[19] See, for example, North (1984).

[20] North (1990a). Earlier: North (1987).

[21] Williamson (1975).

[22] Akerlof (1984).

According to D.C. North, the essential difference between the "Walrasian system" and what constitutes the object of study of neoinstitutionalist economists and economic historians lies in "transaction costs."[23] The latter, which we have already mentioned above several times, now play a key role in the axiomatics of neoclassicism. When they are linked to measurement difficulties, these costs would sometimes be explained by a "tendency of human nature," such as opportunism or the "limited rationality" of agents, and sometimes by the uncertainty or opacity of contracts.

It is necessary to recognize that most neoclassical-inspired topics concerning the complex and dynamic links between institutions and growth are mainly formulated from a microeconomic perspective. Macroscopic approaches that openly claim to be "neoinstitutional" are, however, extremely numerous. Although their authors quite often affirm that their demonstrations have solid methodological foundations, in the form of axioms of individual agent behaviors, the least that can be said here is that the theoretical articulation between the micro-institutional and macro-institutional levels is one of the weak points of neoclassicism.

It is not surprising, then, to observe a number of orthodox economists arguing that "institutional innovations" result from the confrontation of supply and demand in a "market of institutions." For example, and in a caricatured way, Yujiro Hayami and Vernon W. Ruttan—the former having been a professor at the University of Tokyo, and the latter at the University of Chicago, where he was able to collaborate with Nobel Prize winner (1979) Theodore W. Schultz—argue that changes in the demand for institutional innovations are influenced by changes in factor endowments, and therefore, by the changes in the relative price structures of the factors of production—which does not deter them from surreptitiously telling the reader that their perspective relating to the sources of the demand for institutional change is… "similar to the traditional Marxian view"![24]

After making short work of K. Marx, the two friends continue to unfold their powerful argument: the quantities offered of new institutions would depend on the costs of mobilizing the resources necessary for such innovations. These costs would be determined, in particular, by

[23] North (1984).

[24] Hayami and Ruttan (1984).

the distribution of power between the different interest groups making up society, the expected gains from institutional changes for each of them, as well as other exogenous factors characteristic of the economy studied, such as the "cultural endowments" of individuals, of which "ideology" would be a part. It is difficult to find a more schematic analysis; all the more so since, in such markets, the possible nature of "public good" or "quasi-public good" of very many institutions has been overlooked.

Although long absent from the theoretical reflections of neoclassicism, the study of institutions, and especially that of their genesis, was from the outset considered by some of the founders of the marginalist current as an essential task incumbent on the economists. Whereas he cannot really be considered an "institutionalist," this was certainly the position of the Austrian Carl Menger,[25] as mentioned above. His "antihistoricist" and "anti-collectivist" method attempted to reconstruct the emergence of social phenomena, including "social institutions," from the analysis of "the simplest elements," namely the behavior of individual agents, striving to satisfy their needs for market goods as best they could. As a consequence, the fact to recognize certain social phenomena as "organisms" would be, according to him, "in no way in contradiction with the desire to have an exact understanding of them," i.e., an "atomistic" understanding of them. Following this author, economic progress would not result, as in the Smithian vision, from a deeper division of labor, but rather from the increase in the knowledge acquired by agents concerning the specific relations linking their needs and market goods. It is thus understandable that the selection of the appropriate institution is no longer made by collective intention.

By the same movement, by excluding from their reasoning the real sets or groups proper to holistic and systemic approaches, the theorists of neoclassicism have consciously dismissed from their field of vision collective forces, socially constructed institutions, historical structures of social formations—in other words, almost everything that another Austrian, F.A. Hayek, had chosen half a century later to call "popular abstractions and collective pseudo-entities"—[26]as well as their multifaceted and complex connections with human beings' actions.

[25] Menger (1996 [1833]).

[26] Hayek (1953).

4.3 The Sacrosanct Private Property Rights

By its very nature, nevertheless, the institution does indeed refer to a "social state" of individuals; or to the representation of an authority in relation to the interests of individual agents. The notion is thus likely to cover a very heterogeneous set of elements with a collective dimension, as diverse as the family, the firm, trade unions, political parties, the State, international institutions, but also the moral values of prohibition or organization (including religious ones), the legal rules (laws, doctrine, jurisprudence, customs…), or even "supports of economic activity," such as money, for example. Nonetheless, of all these elements, property rights occupy by far the most important place in orthodox literature.

Since then, and reading Douglass C. North and Robert P. Thomas, everything would be "very simple": it would be enough to set up the appropriate "institutions"—that is, according to these two authors, those that would strictly ensure the permanence of "property rights," i.e., that would minimize "transaction costs"—to establish the decisive conditions for economic take-off. In fact, if the exclusivity and enforcement of property rights could be clearly guaranteed, i.e., if there were no transaction costs, economic growth would be achieved very simply.[27]

For D.C. North, property rights, like laws, are part of the "formal rules" that, with their informal complements of sanctions, taboos, customs, traditions, and codes of behavior, among others, constitute the so-called institutions, which are defined as "the humanly conceived constraints that structure political, economic, and social interactions (…) [and which] provide an incentive structure in an economy."[28]

Many authors adopt a rather similar conception, where the institution is read as a complex set of constraints that apply to the behaviors of individuals or groups of individuals, as much as to the links between them, whether bilateral or multilateral. Therefore, a formal organization, a contractual relationship, a code of behavior, a rule of cultural order, or even a market will fall into the category of institutions simply because these entities are likely to be able to exert an effective constraint on the actions and relationships of economic agents.[29]

[27] North and Thomas (1973). See also the concentrated and early version: North and Thomas (1970).

[28] North (1991).

[29] Nabli and Nugent (1989).

At the heart of the various neoinstitutionalist currents, and beyond their extreme diversity, can be found this key idea that the efficiency of resource allocation in the economy depends fundamentally on the nature of the institutions that characterize it and, even more so, on the structure of its property rights. Thus, the ambition of these studies is also to compare the relative efficiency of different modes of organization of the economy.

Most of the formulations proposed proceed to an endogenization of institutions by retaining bi-directional relations between them and "development."[30] The appearance of new economic activities, linked to the discovery of natural resources, technical innovation, or the cultivation of unexploited land, for example, could be analyzed as the expression of a demand for better adapted, more sophisticated institutions, which, thanks to the reduction in transaction costs that their creation would entail, would make it possible to promote the growth of such activities.

According to D.C. North, the evolution of institutions would dynamically modify the structure of transaction costs, and it would consequently act on the development process. And in return, technological and demographic dynamics—as well as those of the associated information costs—would cause variations in the relative prices of factors of production, which in turn would be likely to lead to more or less crucial institutional changes, as long as certain actors find a gain in making these changes.[31]

Still following this author, such a theory would be a relevant tool for analyzing economic history, particularly the links between the dynamics of institutional change and economic development. For him, the study of the growth of an economy's gross domestic product (GDP) would be inseparable from an understanding of the genesis and evolution of the "institutional base" that is historically and territorially specific to it. This institutional base is said to endure while changing, through mechanisms of path dependency (or self-reinforcement) and of lock-in, which may be favorable or unfavorable to development.[32]

[30] *Cf.* the articles relating to institutions published in the volumes of *Handbooks of Development Economics* successively coordinated by H. Chenery and T.N. Srinivasan (1988), J. Behrman and the same Srinivasan (1995), T.P. Schultz and J.A. Strauss (2008), then D. Rodrik and M. Rosenzweig (2010).

[31] North (1981).

[32] North (1990a).

The effects of institutions are often considered to be indirect on the behaviors of individual agents. In many studies dealing with so-called "transition countries,"[33] modifications in legal systems, insofar as they strengthen the structure of property rights, and thus also the incentive regime in a market economy, would contribute, if we are to believe experts at the World Bank and elsewhere, "to stimulate profitable investment, provide incentives for careful monitoring and controlling its evolution, encourage effort, and create the conditions necessary for entering into binding contracts... [that] unerringly lead to economic growth and wealth creation."[34]

The idea, of course, is not new. John M. Clark, whose pioneering work occupies a barycentric place between "neoclassicism," the "Keynesian revolution," and the institutional approach, had already emphasized, well before others, that factor productivity is relative to the system of property rights within which the economy in question is embedded.[35] However, this sequence has been restyled to fit in with the theoretical literature which, from R.H. Coase—who won the Nobel Prize in 1991—to Armen A. Alchian—whom F.A. Hayek declared deserving of the same prize—has constantly insisted on the positive dynamic links existing between rigorously defined property rights, efficiently allocated resources, and strong economic growth.

It is this theoretical legacy that forms the cornerstone of the World Bank's *World Development Report* on the State. It claims that property rights are a fundamental element of a market-driven mode of development and the basis for poverty reduction. It is far from sufficient, however. As a matter of fact, businesses need to be able to operate in an environment that encourages them to allocate resources efficiently, increase factor productivity and innovate. And unless they are confident that public policies will remain relatively stable over time, they will not invest and growth will suffer.[36] It is a similar reasoning—consisting in the absolute respect of the sacrosanct private property rights (that is to say, physical property, intellectual property, etc.)—that one will try to apply everywhere: to legal institutions, organization of firms, financial systems, direct foreign

[33] See: SHLEIFER (1995); and, in the same document: BLANCHARD (1995).

[34] BANQUE MONDIALE (1996).

[35] CLARK (1924).

[36] BANQUE MONDIALE (1997).

investments, and international technological diffusion between leading countries and following countries...

R.W. Fogel analyzed, together with S.L. Engerman, the "economic significance of property rights in man." He considered that the—seemingly "bizarre"—extension of the neoclassical use of the concept of "capital" beyond its usual application (machines, buildings, inanimate objects, etc.) to include "the wealth inherent in the capacity of human beings to perform work," i.e., the famous "human capital," was justified. According to him, when there is freedom, each person would hold, more or less, the title (of ownership) to his or her own human capital. The essential difference between a free society and the "peculiar institution" of the slave system would be, in his view, not so much the existence of "property rights in man," but rather the question of who holds the title to such property rights. Fogel added that what makes the application of the concept of human capital to free societies odd is that free people are not traded in well-defined markets, and thus do not determine market prices. Nevertheless, the absence of explicit market prices on human beings does not mean that these free individuals do not actually have capital values, but only that this absence of exchange of human beings generally prevents their capital values from being made explicit. Just to be clear, following him, the legal recognition of the fact that free persons continue to have capital values would be revealed whenever courts award money to a widow whose husband was killed in an industrial accidents.[37]

4.4 The Principle of Rationality in the Face of the "Traditional Societies" Conundrum

A crucial postulate of the perfect competition model, that of voluntary exchange as an elementary form of inter-individual relations, is thus most often present in neoinstitutionalist arguments. However, from the point of view of standard theory, whose validity is subject to an axiomatic of the rationality of agents, there is also much at stake in the analysis of the integration of institutions as supports—or as substitutes[38]—for this rationality. Consequently, it is not surprising to observe a considerable

[37] Fogel and Engerman (1974a, p. 233). Also see: Fogel and Engerman (1974b).

[38] See: Fields (1981), and: Rutherford (1989).

body of works on the subject, from very different perspectives, ranging from the heart of the mainstream empire to its distant frontiers—which we will leave here to the reader to judge whether they are internal or external.[39]

The neoinstitutional theses have been most frequently applied to the history of industrialized countries. Although this history is in no way transposable to the study of societies in the South, a number of authors have taken the plunge and drawn lessons that are supposedly universally valid. This includes so-called "traditional" economies, in the sense that they would be dominated by a "principle of tradition," and where the institutions that characterize them would be understood to be stable and not to deviate from a model of social rules inherited from the ancestors. Social life would be oriented toward a past that agents would have to reproduce and thus to preserve. "Traditional" economy certainly does not exactly mean "inferior"... but almost (backward, one would say, so as not to use the terms "retarded"). The institutions examined will be those that respond to specific needs of individuals, such as security and survival in a hostile natural environment or in an "underdeveloped" economic environment (gradually and more elegantly called "developing," or "in development," and most recently "emerging," with little change in the underlying prejudices).

The traditional institutions of the Southern countries, whether family-based or village-based (associating larger units, linked by actual lineages or imaginary progenies), are often seen as obstacles to development, because they are likely to lock up economic life to the narrow confines of subsistence and self-consumption, to make it difficult for independent individuals to associate for productive operations, to be supported by a regime (patriarchal, gerontocratic, etc.) that would discourage initiative and innovation, but, above all, not to allow, or not sufficiently to allow the individualization of income and/or ownership. This last element, fundamental in a so-called "developed" capitalist system, would be lacking insofar as, in these latitudes and by a curious habit, solidarity can make income belong to the family as a whole,[40] or property to an

[39] Alchian and Demsetz (1972) and Favereau (1989).

[40] Mahieu (1989).

entire community.[41] These would be fragmented universes, too narrow to envisage an advanced division of labor and to encounter sufficiently independent individuals capable of cooperating with the aim of a common economic interest of a certain scope; hence, a tendency that would be observed to limit the potentialities of "development."

This judgment had to tolerate some nuances, however, such as that regarding the persistence of a traditional family framework during Japan's historical takeoff. The Japanese family structure even seems to have been reused and placed at the service of national development. In the post-World War II period, when a great deal of investment was needed, this family system allowed for a relative compression of consumption, favorable to savings, and provided a typical pattern of organization for the large firm, as well as the original financial support for the famous *zaibatsu* trusts, when trust was a problem between partners not related by blood or by law.[42]

Moreover, the leaders of numerous non-governmental organizations (NGOs)—not-for-profit, yet for many of them resolutely pro-systemic—have applied the bulk of their efforts and initiatives directly to the village (or even family) level to implement supposed "participatory development" by "stimulating local energies," stressing the existence of obstacles to strengthening the role of local actors, while at the same time stressing the need to engage in "decentralization reform of the State."[43]

These traditional institutions are associated with systems of values, mentalities, worldviews, and typical cultural and social behaviors, representing their "ideological underpinnings." This would include a principle of conformity (to nature and the established society), as well as a principle of hierarchy, closely related to the former. The attitude toward time, often perceived as cyclical, would also pose problems, and require distinguishing the notion of foresight (which is fully applicable, within the framework of known realities) from that of forecasting (the projection of economic actions on a distant and uncertain future, according to a conception of

[41] On the issue, for example, of communautary ownership of land (and the very powerful attacks on it) in Papua New Guinea, read: Herrera and Tetoe (2011, 2012, 2015).

[42] For an analysis of the Japanese firm, complementary to that of O.E. Williamson: Aoki (1986).

[43] Schneider and Libercier (1995).

open time, being less widespread, as it can be individually problematic). The same applies to the attitude toward money.

Fortunately, neoclassicals are not anthropologists or ethnologists! Rather than "civilizing" savage thinking by inculcating cost-benefit calculation in the natives, they would have been condemned to try to understand exotic "agents" as bizarre as those populating lands described by Claude Lévi-Strauss: "To what extent attitudes so different from those of the Western world can be very deeply rooted, one sees it in a rather pleasant way in an observation recently made in New Guinea among the Gahuku-Gama. These natives have learned from the missionaries to play soccer, but instead of seeking victory for one side, they multiply the number of games until the number of defeats and victories is exactly balanced. The game is over not when there is a winner, but when it is assured that there is no loser."[44] Is this choice, leading to the happiness of the winners not being the misfortune of the losers, not worth another?

We know that the question of the rationality of individual behaviors is a central theme in the neoclassical analysis of institutions. It has long been argued that the decisions of certain agents, for instance peasants, especially in the Southern nations, do not obey the principle of rationality that is the basis of standard microeconomic calculations. For some economists, farmers would face problems of uncertainty and lack of information of such magnitude that they are unable to respond to the signals and incentives conveyed by market price variations. Other authors argued that the social structures of these "traditional" economies place such heavy constraints on farmers that they leave little room for individual choices. Besides, others explained the stubborn refusal of peasants, particularly in Africa, to adopt institutional or technological innovations that are, however, economically profitable by the own logic of these agents, which would obey different rules from those guiding the "normal" *homo œconomicus* maximization program.

Nevertheless, the idea of "irrational" behaviors on the part of "Southern agents" was quickly challenged within neoclassicism.[45] Neoinstitutionalist works, especially in econometrics, carried out by using diverse methodologies, tried very early on to show that the hypothesis of rationality of the decisions of peasant individuals or households could

[44] Lévi-Strauss (1962, p. 44).

[45] Here: Schultz (1968).

not be rejected.[46] Their authors have generally considered that these individuals choose, among several possible forms of institutions, the one that will allow them to minimize transaction costs. Taking into account problems of informational asymmetry, uncertainty, or faulty incentives that prevent the proper functioning of markets in rural areas, or emphasizing the effect of incomplete markets, would not compromise the expression of rational choices on the part of these agents evolving in quite "atypical" environments—and which are frequently used to characterize "stylized facts" specific to the South. The existence of high transaction costs could explain why farmers do not react to opportunities linked to variations in market conditions, i.e., the price and profit systems. Such inertia would be precisely due to a rational calculation on their part, as transaction costs reduce the expected benefits of their activities by too much.[47]

4.5 Legitimizing the "Re-feudalisation of the World"

An abundant literature has thus developed within neoclassicism in an attempt to elucidate the paradox, observed in studies related to land tenure systems in particular, of the survival in the present time of totally archaic institutions. This is the case, among others, of sharecropping. This type of rural lease is a form of organization of agricultural production that takes the concrete form of a "contract" between a landowner (lessor) and a rural worker (sharecropper), under the terms of which part of the income generated by the production carried out by the second "contractor" is paid back to the first one.

This is an institution that is characteristic of the feudal era in Western Europe, but which is still quite widespread in the South—and even, recently, is on the rise in several countries, such as Morocco and Tunisia.[48] This has prompted some orthodox theorists—and not the least, since the French economist ("probably the most active and influential of his generation")[49] Jean-Jacques Laffont, founder of the Institute of Industrial Economics at the University of Toulouse, showed himself intrigued

[46] For example, Barnum and Squire (1979) and Singh et al. (1986).

[47] De Janvry et al. (1991).

[48] Matoussi and Nugent (1989).

[49] See: http://www.universalis.fr/encyclopedie/jean-jacques-laffont/.

by the resurgence, in the case of Tunisia that he studied,[50] of this distant past in the so serene decor of the modernity—to try to find the rationality hidden behind the appearance of anachronism. For, sharecropping seems at first sight to be an economically inefficient type of organization, and inferior, for example, to tenant farming. It leads to balances that are suboptimal, particularly in comparison with wage contracts or fixed annuities.

How could such a category of contract encourage the effort of the person working the land? This is all the truer since the often extremely small size of the land plot hardly allows for any improvement in productivity and, moreover, the landowner is not encouraged to make progress either. Could it be that the economic stagnation of Southern countries is partly explained by the persistence of ancestral institutional forms, which constitute flagrant departures from the conditions of marginal efficiency of the standard model of neoclassicism? The payment of a fraction of the farm income limits the marginal profitability of the sharecropper's work and thus his or her incentive to work. Consequently, from the point of view of the orthodox *corpus*, which has been aware of this for a long time, this contract would be likely to lead to a net loss of product for the economy (because the number of hours worked decreases), compared to more modern contractual forms, foremost among which is, of course, wage employment.[51]

In a series of pioneering contributions, Steven Ng-Sheong Cheung—an U.S. economist from Hong Kong, a supporter of privatization of State-owned enterprises in the People's Republic of China and, incidentally, a multi-millionaire in trouble with the law in Seattle for trafficking in fake antiques—argued that, when transaction costs are taken into account, this choice of sharecropping contract would be neither irrational nor inefficient: it would aim to manage a risk in a context of uncertainty associated with exogenous (climatic) fluctuations in revenue from the product of the land.[52] It is the landowner who would bear the risk in the case of (guaranteed) wage contracts, and the agricultural worker in the case of fixed annuity contracts; but only sharecropping would allow "risk sharing." The behaviors of agents, in rural areas as elsewhere, depends on their

[50] Laffont and Matoussi (1995).

[51] Here: Marshall (1920 [1890]). Also: Johnson (1950).

[52] Cheung (1968, 1969a, b).

"aversion to risk," and those with the best "entrepreneurial qualities" naturally prefer a fixed-rent contract, likely to benefit the most from their "individual endowments."

J.E. Stiglitz, who did not forget to praise S. N.-S. Cheung in his Nobel Prize acceptance speech (as did R.H. Coase in his)[53]—extends this argument by arguing that the supposed objective of the sharecropping contract, i.e., the sharing of risk, could be achieved in an equivalent way from a mixed contractual arrangement between landowner and rural worker, combining both wage and fixed annuity payments. However, the existence of risk would not be sufficient to explain the frequency of sharecropping contracts. Stiglitz's demonstration introduces the idea of the landowner's trade-off between the risk he or she must bear and the (necessary) incentive to work of the farm laborer. The landowner receives an income described as a positive function of the amount of work provided by the peasant. But this work can only be controlled by the lessor indirectly, through the contract's terms. If he or she chooses to increase the share of agricultural income received by the sharecropper, the latter is encouraged to work, but the risk borne by the landowner increases. The sharecropping contract chosen is, therefore, the one whose conditions allow the landowner to balance this risk and the incentive to work very precisely.

We are thus reassured by Dr. Stiglitz: there is no question, in this whole affair, of a hardening of the balance of power in favor of the landowner and against the agricultural producer, nor of a deterioration of the working conditions of the peasant, nor of any kind of exploitation—even when we are faced with cases of sharecropping "by the fifth," where the four-fifths part of the income goes to the former (landowner) and the remaining fifth to the second (sharecropper)!

Clearly, what orthodoxy proposes is a rationalization of social injustice, of the accentuation of a violence in social relations that no longer says its name. What these mainstream economists offer is a legitimization of exploitation, or a justification of the "re-feudalization of the world," to say it with Jean Ziegler.[54] Yet, as Stiglitz suggests, we should only see here "institutions" (those of oppression, we may add) evolving over time according to changes in transaction costs and information asymmetries.

[53] Stiglitz (1974).

[54] Ziegler (2005).

This helps us, by the way, to understand how this author—together with Lyn Squire, one of the promoters of orthodox project analysis,[55] who is not really known for being a "progressive"—was able to occupy the post of chief economist at the World Bank, before being sold today as a "violent critic" of international institutions...

Numerous other theorists of neoclassicism—sometimes disguised, like J.E. Stiglitz, as "neo-Keynesians"—have also studied the impact of constraints associated with some discriminatory customs on individual choices. This is the case, for example, of the analysis on the caste system provided by George A. Akerlof,[56] who shared the 2001 Nobel Prize in economics with Stiglitz and Andrew M. Spence—and who, without going too far into his private life, is also the husband of the "democrat" Janet Yellen (former Chair of the Board of Governors of the U.S. Federal Reserve from 2014 to 2018, then the Secretary of the Treasury from January 2021 onwards). The caste system, as we know, is linked to specific economic activities, intended for members of societies whose organization is extremely rigid. G.A. Akerlof questioned why such a clearly segregationist institution has remained stable over an extremely long period of history, when there are opportunities for institutional change.

According to Akerlof, such a system is very strictly defined by a social classification of agents into groups, closed to each other and mutually exclusive. Within each group, agents would use specific indicators to make their forecasts and transaction decisions. These indicators would correspond to economically useful information, or to "social conventions" (in the sense given by K.J. Arrow[57]) characterizing "culture," as "regularities in the internal and external behavior of the members of society" (excluding those that are hereditary). If the economic environment is affected by costly and/or incomplete information—and this is the case, Akerlof notes, as soon as one departs from the Arrow-Debreu theoretical framework in order to move toward a little more realism—the credibility of such conventional-cultural indicators is likely to render the behaviors of agents predictable and regular, but, at the same time, to fix them arbitrarily by a codified set of discriminating customs.

[55] Squire and Van der Tak (1975).

[56] Akerlof (1976, 1984).

[57] See: Arrow (1972a, b).

In a society divided into castes, if an individual member of caste *A* knows that his or her relations with an individual of caste *B* are governed by precise and intangible rules of behavior, he or she will be able to predict, through this knowledge, how members of all castes, including those other than *A* and *B*, will relate to him or her in the future. These predictions would lead to an equilibrium through which the agents' expectations are all fulfilled and the incentives favor the observance of segregationist codes, and thus the maintenance of the caste system—even if this ultimately leads to a suboptimal equilibrium in the Pareto sense.

G.A. Akerlof defines "caste equilibrium" as the state of society where customs are respected and no agent can individually improve his or her position by disobeying the customs. The originality of this model lies in the fact that it introduces a device of sanctions against any individual who attempts to disobey the rites governing his or her caste, and that this device modifies the attitudes of all the members of society toward the offender. The behavior of one agent toward another is predicted by their respective social status, but also affects the interactive connections between all individuals. The rule breaker is sure to be excluded from society, or placed out of caste, and to remain excluded in the future, the ostracism being borne, on an infinite horizon, by successive generations of descendants. The division of society into three distinct groups (dominant caste, non-dominant caste, and non-caste) is matched by a division of labor into skilled, unskilled, and under-skilled ("scavenging") jobs, so that the punishment suffered consists in receiving the lowest wage.

By showing that agents who choose not to break social rules receive the highest benefits, Akerlof explains that discriminatory type institutions can thus persist. Although economically inefficient, they will remain in place in the long period as suboptimal Nash equilibria, if each individual taking part in the "game" has no rational interest in changing his or her behavior with respect to these rules, lest his or her disobedience bring him or her loss. Again: here, no historical perspective, no social depth, and above all no theory of exploitation in the analysis of this "pure economy."

4.6 The Institution *Par Excellence*: The State

Let us now turn to the institution *par excellence*: the State. The standard approach of neoclassicism to the State is fundamentally derived from the theorems of "welfare economics." The latter establish, in a situation of perfect competition and market completeness, on the one hand, that any Walrasian general equilibrium is a Pareto optimum, and, on the other hand, that there is a price vector such that any Paretian optimum can be associated with an equilibrium. Nevertheless, the results of this referential scheme, of normative scope, are entirely conditioned—with strict respect for the perfect competition axiomatics—by the verification of convexity hypotheses (that is to say, convexity of consumption preferences in the space of utilities as well as convexity of production sets in the space of productions), which explicitly exclude certain phenomena, namely: increasing returns to scale, which are at the origin of the constitution of natural monopolies; indivisibilities, characterizing public goods for which the market price mechanism proves to be inappropriate; and externalities, which may emanate from collective goods.[58]

These three categories of phenomena, economies of scale, public goods, and externalities, are called "non-convexities" by the theorists of neoclassicism.[59] The consequence of their introduction is the impossibility of decentralizing the optimal allocation of resources through a Walrasian-type price system; hence, the invalidation of the equivalence mentioned above between the competitive equilibrium and the Paretian optimum. In other words, as soon as non-convexities are incorporated in the production sets and/or consumer preferences, then the welfare theorems are no longer verified. In the same way, the application of these theorems is limited by the consideration of informational asymmetries, such as moral hazard or anti-selection.

Such are here synthesized, in very brief, the bases of the justifications of neoclassicism for State intervention in a capitalist market economy. In (mainstream) theory, State actions can, therefore, concern extremely important and rather broad areas of economic activity. These are areas in which certain non-convexities can be observed (e.g., externalities from research or infrastructure with economies of scale), and in which recent macro-dynamic models have sought new candidates for explaining the "engines" of growth in the long term—we have already touched on this fundamental point in Chapter 2.

The neoinstitutionalist analyses of the State, in its relations with the market—beyond "perfect competition," which is obviously not very much in evidence in the implementation of economic policies—are very diverse.

[58] Herrera (2010a).

[59] See: Laffont (1982) and Tirole (1988).

The major ambiguity in these works lies in the net effect of the role of the State. Well conducted, public intervention will be able to accelerate the development process; mishandled, it will bring stagnation, or even worse. When it "cooperates with the private sector,"[60] the State is generally recognized as indispensable to the expansion of the market. It is the State that enacts and enforces the rules applicable to all—including to itself—rules that, together with uses, form the institutional framework of the economy and arbitrate individual actions. It is an actor in the economic "game," negotiating markets, making contracts, investing resources, all of which influence transaction costs and the behaviors of agents. It is the (only) institution or "political-judicial structure that ensures the stability of property rights"[61] and, in this way, is likely to have an impact on the final output, by modifying the transaction costs for each agent, and thus also the growth trajectory of the entire economy.

So, the World Bank itself stresses that centuries of history would teach us that the State can promote development in several ways: by creating a macro- and microeconomic framework that would boost efficiency; by putting in place the institutional infrastructure—property rights, peace, law and order, and regulation—that would encourage efficient, long-term investment... Not without adding, in the same reasoning, that history would also teach us that the State could have extremely harmful actions: if the latter are inadequate, the applicable rules could have a dissuasive effect on wealth formation by distorting prices; and even when the rules are "intrinsically good," the administrations, and their employees, could sometimes apply them in a prejudicial way, which would induce very high transaction costs in the form of red tape or bribes; but it would be in creating uncertainty that the State could probably do the most harm. If it keeps changing the rules, businesses and individuals will not be able to know what is profitable and will seek to protect themselves against an uncertain future. And how to do that, says the World Bank experts? They will protect themselves... by placing their capital abroad! So be it. As a consequence, capital flight would almost be self-defense...

[60] The World Bank (1997, p. 53).

[61] North (1987). On the crucial role of the State in maintaining the stability *of property rights:* De Long (1989).

And further on, these experts add that if overnight the State changes its rules, it would lose all credibility and the markets would suffer.[62] The serene perception that private agents have of their State would, therefore, be essential to the strengthening of confidence, to the elaboration of expectations, and *de facto* to the stimulation of savings and investment behaviors. The chain and sequence thus link the credibility of the discourse and action of the State, the predictability of the rules of law in the face of uncertainty, the stability of economic policy, on the one hand, and, on the other, long-term economic growth.

Since the 1970s and the observation of a crisis in so-called "Keynesian" regulation, the (multiple) interventions of the State have increasingly been interpreted as being at the origin of failures. This is because, generally, says D.C. North, governments would not implement "efficient property rights."[63] One of the reasons for this would be the very composition of the State institution, which is also made up of *homines œconomici* seeking to satisfy their personal interests. This would have the effect that its purpose could only be to take advantage of its privileged position as a monopoly—free from the pressure of competition—and to apply policies designed to favor its own constituent elements, to the detriment of the general welfare: bureaucratic heaviness, barriers to entry, prohibitive costs and cumbersome administrative procedures seen as so many obstacles to private initiative…[64]

Such institutional constraints would partly explain the rise of informal sectors, operating at the margins or outside the law—although the system of property rights is not absent from parallel markets: these property rights are themselves informal, but transferable, and frequently higher than in formal markets because of the uncertainty that discourages investment and, hence, growth.

Why, then, does the State implement such ostensibly punitive rules? Would it thus be reasonable to think, in the spirit of the Public Choice school,[65] that all (or a fraction of) the individuals constituting the State could have an interest that diverges from that of the rest of society—that is, technically, that the utility function arguments of public agents

[62] The World Bank (1997, pp. 35–38).

[63] North (1990a).

[64] Cf De Soto (1986).

[65] Buchanan (1975). A little before, in parallel: Niskanen (1971, 1975).

or some of them would be distinct from those of private individuals? Here, answering in the affirmative requires a break with the traditional approach to the State, as with welfare economics, which refers to the concept of general interest, and in which public decisions simply reflect the preferences revealed by private agents.

Such a reconsideration would also mean taking into account differentiated individual behaviors of the governed and the governors: the governed would select, as voters, candidates for public office by seeking to maximize the utility derived from political programs; the governors would choose the presentation of these programs that would be likely to ensure their (re)election by maximizing the number of votes in their favor. And the combination of the two behaviors would lead to suboptimal situations: for electoralist purposes, the politicians would tend to increase non-directly productive public expenditures (operating budgets, sumptuary projects, consumer subsidies, transfers to local authorities, etc.), which penalize economic growth, either directly (because of their inaction on the output) or indirectly (by increasing the budget deficit and through the vicious circle of public indebtedness). D.C. North stated that the opportunity would be offered to individuals with superior coercive power "to impose the implementation of rules to their advantage; and this without any consideration of economic efficiency."[66]

Inscribed, like North's thesis, in a certain British tradition claiming to be the legacies of James E. Meade or Arthur C. Pigou—and, well below, that of John Locke himself—the conception of the State given by Ronald Findlay and John D. Wilson proposed to analyze in a formalized way the argument of institutional failures.[67] The resolution of their model makes it possible to represent by a non-linear relationship the link between the production of the economy and the "service" rendered by the system of property rights, called "public order." For these two authors, the State would basically be nothing more than a "contractual agreement" between equal individuals, an agreement whose purpose would be to provide this service, considered "productive." The "bureaucrats" would be supposed to seek to increase their power or prestige by increasing the number of people they manage. But when the State is insufficiently strong to control the number of civil servants ("when bureaucrats are out of control"),

[66] North (1987).

[67] Findlay and Wilson (1987).

then bureaucratic drift leads to an expanding public workforce, until tax revenues are absorbed by the cost of remunerations, and the supply of services is suboptimal, because of excessive public spending.

4.7 The Neoinstitutionalist State, Guardian of Property Rights

Following and according to Ronald H. Coase, neoinstitutionalist analysis has suggested that a country's growth is—provided that transaction costs are assumed to be zero in the economic and political spheres—independent of the nature of its government. However, as soon as these transaction costs become positive, the distribution of political power within the society in question and the institutional structure of decision-making bodies, especially those responsible for setting the "rules of the game," would turn out to be important factors in development.[68]

The currently dominant neoinstitutionalist views of the State are largely based on the studies D.C. North[69] has devoted to the property rights system and factor productivity. In addition to the analysis in terms of transaction costs, they sometimes incorporate elements of agency theory to articulate them within the framework of rational selections of institutions and political processes. For him, there would be a structural production frontier for each economy that is reached by rational agents choosing from among all feasible organizational forms the property rights structure that minimizes costs and maximize output. This structural frontier of production is clearly distinct from the technical frontier of production, which very (neo)classically describes the upper technical limits accessible in terms of productivity and production in this economy, based on its factor endowments and the level of available knowledge.

This structure of property rights is itself dependent on the political structure characterizing the economy studied. Now, some political structures have the characteristic of generating a series of incentives likely to shift the structural frontier of production until it coincides at the optimum with the technical frontier of production; on the contrary, others tend to make the two representative curves, structural and technical, diverge. Shifts in the structural production frontier necessitate a political shock

[68] Coase (1989 [1937]).

[69] North (1979).

(e.g., a change in the constitutional regime), which in turn requires a cost-benefit analysis of the economic reforms to be promoted, and therefore a comparative evaluation of the costs of the political change and the costs of maintaining the system as it is.

This approach is also formulated in dynamic terms (through the growth rate of the output), describing the rhythms at which the production frontier of the economy can move, depending on the specific features of the selected property rights systems. The rate of investment in new products or manufacturing processes is then generally assumed to be written as an inverse function of the cost of capture (or appropriation) by private agents of the potential benefits of their investments.

Since then, how can we understand the economic role of the State? Douglass C. North answers that modern societies potentially allow access to high levels of productivity and production. These require a specialization of productive activities and the extension of exchange networks between individuals or groups of individuals. In general, technological progress tends to make the transactions to be carried out by agents institutionally more complex, and the transaction costs associated with the use of these technologies higher. It is, therefore, necessary to define structures of property rights capable of reducing the transaction costs linked to these advanced technologies, up to levels accessible to private users.[70] In such a framework, the State would be more precisely the institution with the greatest relative advantage in offering the structure of property rights that is desired by the agents. It would be that organization with a "comparative advantage in violence" and which extends over a geographical area whose boundaries are determined by its power to levy taxes on the governed.[71] The ability of the production factor owners to provide appropriable assets, which is the source of the impetus given to economic growth, would thus depend on the set of social rules, expressed in particular through the exclusive exercise of defense, the efficient organization of justice and the establishment of stable laws that protect property.

D.C. North argues that most of the time in the economic history of the industrialized countries, the State has not provided economic agents with adequate property rights structures, i.e., structures that allow the economy to be placed as close as possible to its technical frontier of

[70] Idem. Also: North (1981).

[71] North (1981, p. 21).

production. For him, there is "little evidence" in the study of the past to suggest that the property rights structures put in place by the State have been "efficient."[72] He even goes so far as to argue that, in several historical cases, such as France with its great revolution—how could it be otherwise?—the "economic decline" would be mainly attributable to institutional failures for which the State would bear the dominating responsibility.[73] In the long period, France's "stagnation" in the Eighteenth Century was essentially explained by the State's inability to adopt the institutional arrangements best suited to fostering economic growth—especially by promoting individual initiative and the accumulation of private wealth. The French long-term path would have diverged from those of the Netherlands and, above all, England, whose governments were able to stimulate the creation of the appropriate institutions and to facilitate transactions that made trade more efficient, by making room for representatives of social categories directly involved in the new activities of trade and industry.

For North, the success of some economies, most notably the United States—surprise!—would be explained largely by the "fact" that property rights are firmly anchored in a legal structure that precludes "confiscation" or "arbitrary modification," and by the relatively small proportion of transactions assumed by the State.[74] This would make it easier for private actors to absorb transaction costs and for the economy taken as a whole to achieve a total efficiency gain. In this framework, State intervention, through the establishment of property rights, but also through the production of certain public goods, would give rise to economies of scale, which would represent a key explanatory factor for a country's take-off—we have previously examined this point in the penultimate chapter, through a critical analysis of the neoclassical theory of growth.

On the contrary, our author reveals nothing to us, unfortunately, about the role that could have been played in the marvelous performance of this economic "model" by the securing of property rights for slave-owning planters in the South of the United States, and this until the heart of the Nineteenth Century—we have seen what a R.W. Fogel thinks of all this. And not much more about the contribution to "social welfare" of the

[72] North (1990a).

[73] North (1990b).

[74] North (1987).

robber barons of high finance at the turn of the Twentieth Century—about which we will also say a few words in Chapter 7. But is "economic freedom" the only condition for sustainable and sustained growth? Does not the latter also require something... democratic?

4.8 Democracy... Or Neoliberalism?

Within neoclassicism, a vast literature, mostly empirical, has also been disseminated on the theme of the dynamic links that might exist between "democracy" and growth. It generally asserts that "economic freedoms"—that is, basically, those of markets operating in competition, without any distortion, but with a "State" whose action would be limited to ensuring the strict respect of all property rights through legal norms—would favor the acceleration of the growth rate of a country's GDP. The question of knowing whether the advances in "political freedoms," as a process of "democratization," would encourage such economic growth or not is, on the contrary, a much more contentious, disputed issue, and far from being settled.

For a long time, leading figures in economics and related disciplines have argued, following an idea already formulated by Milton Friedman,[75] that more political democracy could stimulate growth through the strengthening of economic rights, and that in return, as the U.S. sociologist Seymour M. Lipset,[76] for example, has suggested, the increase in the quantity and quality of goods and services that agents can appropriate would lead, so to speak, "naturally," to a certain democratization.

An orthodox author, such as John F. Helliwell, even believed that he had demonstrated, by means of econometrics, the existence of a positive and statistically significant relationship going from the level of income toward "indicators of democracy"[77]—and this was shortly before he discovered, through contact with the master thinker Jeffrey D. Sachs and the British baron Peter R.G. Layard, a faith in the classification and ranking of countries according to their "level of happiness." The main finding of their famous (and smoky) "World Happiness Reports" was that happiness on earth would be greatest in North America—surprise?—with

[75] Friedman (1962).

[76] See: Lipset (1959).

[77] Read: Helliwell (1994).

a score of 7.133 out of 10 for the region. Blessed Israel even got 7.301 out of 10, and the blissful United Arab Emirates 7.144, both of them being congratulated by the jury for their respective democratic innovations. And the Colombians, also very lucky—even if, curiously, not all of them seem to have understood it, after more than half a century of civil war—are declared happier than the Spanish, the Italians or the Japanese...[78] In other words: a lot of nonsense, or pure ideology, but we did not expect anything else with the thinkers of neoclassicism.

Nonetheless, other authors, as orthodox as the previous ones, but in a different way, insist on the contrary on the "handicaps" that would represent in their eyes democratic institutions. In particular, the latter would allow incongruous income redistribution reforms and intensified actions by "collective interest groups," starting with workers' unions and various citizens' associations or "pressure groups." These handicaps could, however, "correct" some of the shortcomings of an authoritarian regime, but only on the condition that it very strictly respects private initiative and guarantees property rights.[79] Did not Taiwan and South Korea succeed in their economic take-off under "strong" governments—in other words, without democracy?

This is probably why so many theorists of neoclassicism, from Arnold C. Harberger to Gary S. Becker and even more recently Robert J. Barro (Appendix C), have so delicately declared their love for General Augusto Pinochet. In addition, R.J. Barro has also studied econometrically the interactions between democracy and growth.[80] In a sample of a hundred countries and over the period 1960–1990, he examined the effects of different "types of freedom" on GDP growth: while the maintenance of the rule of law and the competitive functioning of markets have a positive influence, the impact of "political democracy" is slightly negative. This last variable is approximated by indicators of political rights, such as "the right of every adult to participate fully in the political process," developed by Raymond D. Gastil for Freedom House.[81]

Is this U.S. non-governmental organization (funded by the U.S. government) not the "champion of the rights of democratic activists,

[78] Helliwell, et al. (2013).

[79] In particular: Schwarz (1992).

[80] Barro (1996).

[81] See: Gastil (various years).

believers, (...) journalists, and free market actors"[82]? Is it not a NGO whose board was chaired until 2005 by the director of the Central Intelligence Agency in person? And whose irreproachable objectivity authorized it to "vigorously oppose the invasion of Afghanistan by the Soviet, the genocide in Bosnia, (...) the brutal violations of human rights in Cuba, in the People's Republic of China and in Iraq"[83] (let us specify, for the last country on the list: before its destruction by the United States, with consequences that are so obviously beneficial today...).

To explain such a result, deduced from the rigorous empirical methods of his science, R.J. Barro argues that there is a "non-linear relationship" between political and economic variables. Thus, deepening the democratic process would accelerate growth as long as the level of political freedom is low, but would slow it down as soon as a certain modest but "sufficient" level of democracy is reached. Conversely, higher GDP *per capita*, higher school enrollment, and lower infant mortality rates would increase the likelihood that a country's political institutions would move toward more democracy—which would have some of the characteristics of a "luxury good," according to the author.

The conclusion that R.J. Barro draws from his experiments (performed on the world as seen by the CIA)[84] is that if the so-called "developed" countries of the North want to "export" their "successful" and "efficient" institutions, it is better to start with those of an economic nature, in this case "property rights and free markets," which are the most beneficial in terms of growth, rather than those of a political nature, namely their "democracy," understood in the (limited) sense of a "plurality" of political parties and a representation of citizens through "free" elections by universal suffrage. One imagines that the *USAus homo œconomicus* will consider here that, for there to be "plurality," two parties are enough, without the shadow of an alternative, and that "freedom" of elections means that the alternation in power between donkey and elephant can be manipulated as they please by the powers of money, the financial oligopolies of high finance, their lobbying networks, their "information" media, and a few confetti wholesalers. We are no longer really in the case

82 Here: http://fr.wikipedia.org/wiki/Freedom_House.

83 Consult the website www.freedomhouse.org, and immediately afterward, consult a doctor in case of prolonged exposure to this ideological irradiation.

84 Cf. Kojm (2012). Available on: http://fr.scribd.com/doc/115962650/Global-Trends-2030-Alternative-Worlds.

of suboptimality due to excessive operating expenses, as in R. Findlay and J.D. Wilson: the "bell curve" drawn by Barro is not about the weight of the State, but about the excessive participation of citizens in decision-making concerning their common future.

Should we then understand that non-democratic institutions, to say the least, would constitute a "lesser evil" from the point of view of economic growth? Some authors of neoclassicism have replied that not all non-democratic regimes are equal, because they do not produce the same effects on the rate of growth in the long period. The reference in this regard goes back to the typology proposed by Anne O. Krueger[85]—former first deputy managing director at the IMF, chief economist at the World Bank, and a muse of the rent-seeking current—who classified political regimes into three categories: "predatory," "authoritarian bureaucrat" and "benevolent dictator" (or guardian State). Following her, they could be distinguished according to the economic policy objectives pursued by their governments, that is, according to the forms taken by the utility functions that characterize them and the "social welfare maximization" programs they seek to solve.

In this somewhat special, entirely neoclassical universe, the "benevolent dictator" would know how to abstain from any intervention that alter the incentives for private initiative of the agents (in fact, of the single agent!) and to maximize utility by weighting that of each agent (always very representative!) by its importance in the population; as to it, the "authoritarian bureaucrat" would define its policy by maximizing a utility that depends on the size of the government's budget, and therefore on its revenues; and the "predator" would only be concerned with its own utility, linked to the level of government consumption. This "model" would make it possible to establish a hierarchy between political regimes according to their respective equilibrium growth rates, such that the rate of a "benevolent dictator" would be higher than that of an "authoritarian bureaucrat," which in turn would be better than that of a "predator." Proponents of Public Choice have succeeded one another in "verifying" this "unambiguous relationship," here in theory, there in empirical terms.[86]

[85] See: KRUEGER (1974, 1990, 1993).

[86] Among other examples: BHAGWATI (1982), WELLISZ and FINDLAY (1986), SCULLY and SLOTTJE (1991), and SCULLY (2002).

All in all, however, we are plunged into confusion and even thrown into arbitrariness. Firstly, at the analytical level, the delimitation between democracy and "benevolent dictatorship" is quite uncertain, since the determination of the respective policies by maximizing social welfare leads to mathematical expressions very close for the equilibrium growth rates in these two regimes. Secondly, interpretations are quite tricky for those who want to translate such imaginative views into practical recommendations, because econometrically, we frequently observe "benevolent dictatorial" type States with much better GDP growth performance than "democracies." Finally, from a scientific point of view, what can be thought of the objectivity of statistical databases provided on a turnkey basis by private sources such as the International Country Risk Guide and the Business Environment Risk Intelligence, for example, or "public" sources such as the *World Factbooks* of another intelligence, that of the CIA?[87]

What about the reliability of "political indicators," sometimes composite, sometimes "hedonic," built by experts supposedly free of partiality and bias, purged of subjectivity and dishonesty, and whose skills go so far as to judge the nature of the political or economic regime of a given country? Who would dare to dispute that, like Papua New Guinea or the Dominican Republic, Colombia is "obviously" a "political democracy"—as the student economist is taught from his first textbooks[88]—? Would there be any bad spirits to question the fact, "proven," that Saudi Arabia and Gabon, among others, are to be classified as "benevolent dictators" and not as "predatory" regimes? Has not it been "demonstrated" that Venezuela was a democracy until early December 1998, when it inadvertently fell into dictatorship soon after Hugo Chavez Frías won the presidential elections and transformed it into a Bolivarian Republic?

References

Akerlof G.A. (1976), "The Economics of Caste and of the Rat Race and other Woeful Tales," *Quarterly Journal of Economics*, vol. 90, n° 4, p. 599–617.

——— (1984), *An Economic Theorist's Book of Tale—Essays That Entertain the Consequences of New Assumptions in Economic Theory*, New York: Cambridge University Press.

87 Central Intelligence Agency(various years).

88 Gillis et al. (1990, p. 267). For a very different perspective: Herrera (2010b, 2017a).

Alchian A.A. (1977), *Economic Forces at Work*, Minneapolis: Liberty Press.

Alchian A.A. and H. Demsetz (1972), "Production, Information Costs and Economic Costs, and Economic Organization," *American Economic Review*, vol. 62, n° 2, p. 92–101.

Aoki M. (1986), "Horizontal vs. Vertical Information Structure of the Firm," *American Economic Review*, vol. 76, n° 5, p. 971–983.

Arrow K.J. (1972a), "Models of Job Discrimination," *in* A.H. Pascal (ed.), *Racial Discrimination in Economic Life*, p. 83–102, Lexington MA: Lexington Books.

——— (1972b), "Some Mathematical Models of Race in the Labor Market," *in* A.H. Pascal (ed.), *Racial Discrimination in Economic Life*, p. 187–204, Lexington MA.: Lexington Books.

Arrow K.J. and G. Debreu (1954), "Existence of an Equilibrium for a Competitive Economy," *Econometrica*, vol. 22, n° 3, p. 265–290.

Ayres C.E. (1944), *The Theory of Economic Progress*, Chapel Hill: University of North Carolina Press.

Banque mondiale (1996), "De l'Économie planifiée à l'économie de marché," *Rapport sur le développement dans le monde* de la Banque mondiale, Washington DC: The World Bank.

——— (1997), "L'État dans un monde en mutation," *Rapport sur le développement dans le monde* de la Banque mondiale, Washington DC: The World Bank.

Barnum H.N. and L. Squire (1979), "An Econometric Application of the Theory of the Farm Household," *Journal of Development Economics*, n° 6, p. 79–102.

Barro R.J. (1996), "Democracy and Growth," *Journal of Economic Growth*, vol. 1, n° 1, p. 1–27.

Bertrand É. (2003), "Les 'Théorèmes de Coase:' énoncés et critiques microéconomiques," Ph.D. Dissertation, University of Paris 1 Panthéon-Sorbonne, Paris.

Bhagwati J.N. (1982), "Directly Unproductive Profit Seeking Activities," *Journal of Political Economy*, vol. 90, n° 5, p. 988–1002.

Blanchard O.J. (1995), "Comment on 'Establishing Property Rights' by Shleifer," *Proceedings of the World Bank Annual Conference on Development Economics 1994*, p. 118–121, Washington DC: The World Bank.

Boland L. (1979), "Knowledge and the Role of Institutions in Economic Theory," *Journal of Economic Issues*, vol. 13, n° 4, p. 957–972.

Buchanan J.M. (1975), *The Limits of Liberty—Between Anarchy and Leviathan*, Chicago: University of Chicago Press.

Central Intelligence Agency (various years), *The World Factbook*, Public Affairs, Washington DC.

CHENERY H.B. and T.N. SRINIVASAN (eds.) (1988), *Handbooks of Development Economics*, Amsterdam: Elsevier.

CHEUNG S.N.-S. (1968), "Private Property Rights and Sharecropping," *Journal of Political Economy*, vol. 76, n° 6, p. 1107–1122.

——— (1969a), *Theory of Share Tenancy*, Chicago: University of Chicago Press.

——— (1969b), "Transaction Costs, Risk Aversion, and the Choice of Contractual Arrangements," *Journal of Law and Economics*, vol. 13, p. 49–70.

CLARK J.M. (1924), "The Socializing of Theoretical Economics," *in* R.G. Tugwell (ed.), *The Trend of Economics*, p. 73–105, New York: Alfred A. Knopf.

——— (1957), *Economic Institutions and Human Welfare*, New York: A.A. Knopf.

COASE R. (1960), "The Problem of Social Cost," *Journal of Law and Economics*, n° 3, p. 1–44, October.

COASE R.H. (1988), *The Firm, the Market and the Law*, Chicago: University of Chicago Press.

——— (1989 [1937]), "La Nature de la firme," *Revue française d'Économie*, vol. 2, n° 1.

COMMONS J.R. (1931), "Institutional Economics," *American Economic Review*, vol. 21, n° 4, p. 648–657.

DE JANVRY A., M. FAFCHAMPS and E. SADOULET (1991), "Peasant Household Behavior with Missing Markets: Some Paradoxes Explained," *Economic Journal*, vol. 101, n° 409, p. 1400–1417.

DE JANVRY A., E. SADOULET and E. THORBECKE (1993), "Introduction," *World Development*, vol. 21, n° 4, p. 565–575.

DE LONG J.B. (1989), "The Protestant Ethic Revisited: A Twentieth Century Look," *Fletcher Forum of World Affairs*, n° 13, p. 229–242.

DE SOTO H. (1986), *El Otro Sendero*, El Barranco, Lima: Institute for Liberty and Democraty.

FAVEREAU O. (1989), "Marchés internes, marchés externes," *Revue économique*, vol. 40, n° 2, p. 273–328.

FIELDS A. (1981), "The Problem with Neoclassical Institutional Economics: A Critique with Special Reference to the North/Thomas Model of pre-1500 Europe," *Explorations in Economic History*, n° 18, p. 174–198.

FINDLAY R. and J.D. WILSON (1987), "The Political Economy of the Leviathan," *in* A. Razin and E. Sadka (eds.), *Economic Policy in Theory and Practice*, London: Macmillan.

FOGEL R.W. and S.L. ENGERMAN (eds.) (1974a), *Time on the Cross: The Economics of American Negro Slavery*, New York: W.W. Norton and Co.

——— (1974b), *Time on the Cross: Evidence and Methods—A Supplement*, Boston: Little, Brown and Co.

FRIEDMAN M. (1962), *Capitalism and Freedom*, Chicago: The University of Chicago Press.

GASTIL R.D. (various years), *Freedom in the World: Political Rights and Civil Liberties*, Westport (CT): Greenwood Press.

GILLIS M., D.H. PERKINS, M. ROEMER and D.R. SNODGRASS (1990), *Économie du développement*, Brussels: De Boeck.

HAYAMI Y. and V.W. RUTTAN (1984), "Toward a Theory of Induced Institutional Innovation," *Journal of Development Studies*, vol. 20, n° 4, p. 203–223.

HAYEK F.A. (1953), *Scientisme et sciences sociales: essai sur le mauvais usage de la raison*, Paris: Plon.

HELLIWELL J.F. (1994), "Empirical Linkages Between Democracy *and Economic* Growth," *British Journal of Political Science*, n° 24, p. 225–248.

HELLIWELL J.F., P.R. LAYARD and J.D. SACHS (2013), *World Happiness Report 2013*, New York: Sustainable Development Solutions Network.

HERRERA R. (1996), "Institutions et croissance: une étude appliquée aux pays en développement," *mimeo*, Paris: OECD Development Centre.

——— (2010a), *Dépenses publiques et croissance économique - Pour sortir de la science(-fiction) néoclassique*, Paris: L'Harmattan.

——— (2010b), *Un Autre Capitalisme n'est pas possible*, Paris: Syllepse.

——— (2017), "La Colombie telle que l'a vécue Marulanda," *in* R. Herrera, *Figures révolutionnaires de l'Amérique latine*, p. 65–72, Paris: Éditions Delga.

HERRERA R. and P. TETOE (2011), "Le Capital étranger dans le secteur des mines en Papouasie Nouvelle-Guinée," *Économies et Sociétés*, série F, tome XLV, n° 2, p. 321–336, Paris.

——— (2012), "Le Paradoxe *Papua Niugini*: archaïsme de la propriété de la terre, modernité des résistances paysannes?," *Revue française de Socio-économie*, n° 9, 2012/1, p. 133–152, Paris.

——— (2015), "The *Papua Niugini* Paradox," *in* R. Herrera and K.-C. Lau (eds.) *The Struggle for Food Sovereignty—Alternative Development and the Renewal of Peasant Societies Today*, p. 119–135, London: Pluto Press.

HICKS J.R. (1969). *A Theory of Economic History*, Oxford: Oxford University Press.

HIRSCHMAN A.O. (1986). *Vers une Économie politique élargie*, Paris: Éditions de Minuit.

JOHNSON D.G. (1950), "Resource Allocation Under Share Contracts," *Journal of Political Economy*, vol. 58, n° 1, p. 111–123.

KOJM C. (2012), *Global Trends 2030: Alternative Worlds*, Washington DC: National Intelligence Council.

KRUEGER A.O. (1974), "The Political Economy of the *Rent-Seeking* Society," *American Economic Review*, vol. 64, n° 3, p. 291–303.

——— (1990), "Government Failures in Development," *National Bureau of Economic Research (NBER) Working Paper*, n° 3340, Cambridge (MA).

——— (1993), *Political Economy of Policy Reform in Developing Countries*, Cambridge MA: MIT Press.

LAFFONT J.-J. (1982), *Cours d'analyse microéconomique - Tome 1: Fondements de l'économie publique*, Paris: Economica.

LAFFONT J.-J. and M.S. MATOUSSI (1995), "Moral Hazard, Financial Constraints and Sharecropping in El Oulja," *Review of Economic Studies*, vol. 62, n° 3, p. 381–399.

LÉVI-STRAUSS C. (1962), *La Pensée sauvage*, Paris: Plon.

LIN J.Y. and J.B. NUGENT (1995), "Institutions and Economic Development," *in* J. Behrman and T.N. Srinivasan (eds.), *Handbook of Development Economics*, vol. III, Chapter 38, p. 2302–2369, Amsterdam: Elsevier.

LIPSET S.M. (1959), "Some Social Requisites of Democracy: Economic Development and Political Legitimacy," *American Political Science Review*, vol. 53, n° 1, p. 69–105.

MAHIEU F.R. (1989), "Transferts et communauté africaine," *Stateco*, n°s 58–59, p. 107–136.

MARSHALL A. (1920 [1890]), *Principles of Economics*, 8th ed., London: Macmillan.

MATOUSSI M.S. and J.B. NUGENT (1989), "The Switch to Sharecropping in Medjez-el-Bab," *in* M. Nabli and J.B. Nugent (eds.), *The New Institutional Economics and Development*, p. 140–157, Amsterdam: North Holland.

MATTHEWS R.C.O. (1986), "The Economics of Institutions and the Sources of Growth," *The Economic Journal*, vol. 96, n° 384, p. 903–918.

MÉNARD C. (1990), *L'Économie des organisations*, collection «Repères», n° 86, Paris: La Découverte.

MENGER C. (1996 [1833]), *Investigations into the Method of the Social Sciences*, Grove City: Libertarian Press.

MITCHELL W.C. (1913), *Business Cycles*, Berkeley: University of California Press.

NABLI M.K. and J.B. NUGENT (eds.) (1989), *The New Institutional Economics and Development*, Amsterdam: North Holland.

NISKANEN W.A. (1971), *Bureaucracy and Representative Government*, Chicago: Aldine.

——— (1975), "Bureaucrats and Politicians," *Journal of Law and Economics*, vol. 18, n° 3, p. 617–643.

NORTH D.C. (1979), "A Framework for Analyzing the State in Economic History," *Explorations in Economic History*, vol. 16, n° 3, p. 249–259.

——— (1981), *Structure and Change in Economic History*, New York: W.W. Norton.

——— (1984), "Government and the Cost of Exchange in History," *Journal of Economic History*, vol. XLIV, n° 2, p. 255–264.

——— (1987), "Institutions, Transaction Cost and Economic Growth," *Economic Inquiry*, vol. 25, n° 3, p. 419–428.

——— (1990a), *Institutions, Institutional Change and Economic Performance*, Political Economy of Institutions and Decisions, Cambridge (UK): Cambridge University Press.

——— (1990b), "Institutions and a Transaction-Cost Theory *of* Exchange," *in* J.E. Alt and K.A. Shepsle (eds.), *Perspectives on Positive Political Economy*, Cambridge: Cambridge University Press.

——— (1991), "Institutions," *Journal of Economic Perspectives*, vol. 5, n° 1, p. 97–112.

North D.C. and R.P. Thomas (1970), "An Economic Theory of the Growth in the Western World," *Economic History Review*, vol. 23, n° 1, p. 1–17.

——— (1973), *The Rise of the Western World—A New Economic History*, Cambridge: Cambridge University Press.

Rodrik D. and M. Rosenzweig (2010), *Handbooks of Development Economics*, Amsterdam: Elsevier - North Holland.

Rutherford M. (1989), "What Is Wrong with the New Institutional Economics (and What Is Still Wrong with the Old)?," *Review of Political Economy*, vol. 1, n° 3, p. 299–318.

Schneider H. and M.H. Libercier (1995), *Mettre en œuvre le développement participatif*, Centre de Développement de l'OCDE, Séminaires du Centre de Développement, Paris.

Schultz T.P. and J. Strauss (2008), *Handbooks of Development Economics*, Amsterdam: Elsevier - North Holland.

Schultz T.W. (1968), "Institutions and the Rising Economic Value of Man," *American Journal of Agricultural Economics*, vol. 50, n° 5, p. 1113–1122.

Schwarz G. (1992), "Democracy and Market-Oriented Reform: A Love-Hate Relationship?," *Economic Education Bulletin*, vol. 32, n° 5, p. 13–128.

Scully G.W. (2002), "Economic Freedom, Government Policy and the Trade-Off Between Equity and Economic Growth," *Public Choice*, vol. 113, n°s 1–2, p. 77–96.

Scully G.W. and D.J. Slottje (1991), "Ranking Economic Liberty Across Countries," *Public Choice*, vol. 69, n° 2, p. 121–152.

Shleifer A. (1995), "Establishing Property Rights," *Proceedings of the World Bank Annual Conference on Development Economics 1994*, p. 93–107, Washington DC: The World Bank.

Singh I.J., L.Squire et J. Strauss (dir.) (1986), *Agricultural Household Models: Extension, Application and Policy*, Baltimore: Johns Hopkins University Press.

Squire L. and H.B. Van der Tak (1975), *Economic Analvsis of Projects*, Baltimore and London: Johns Hopkins University Press (for The World Bank).

Stiglitz J.E. (1974), "Incentives and Risk Sharing in Sharecropping," *Review of Economic Studies*, vol. 41, n° 2, p. 219–256.

——— (1988), *Economics of the Public Sector*, New York: W.W. Norton & Co.

——— (1995), "Economic Organization, Information, and Development," *in* H. Chenery and T.N. Srinivasan (eds.), *Handbook of Development Economics*, vol. I, Chapter 5, p. 94–160, Amsterdam: Elsevier.

——— (2001), "Information and the Change in the Paradigm in Economics," *Prize Lecture at Columbia Business School*, Columbia University, December 8.

TIROLE (J. (1988), *The Theory of Industrial Organization*, Cambridge MA: The MIT Press.

VEBLEN T.B. (1899a), "Preconceptions of Economic Science (I)," *Quarterly Journal of Economics*, vol. 13, p. 121–150, January.

——— (1899b), "Preconceptions of Economic Science (II)," *Quarterly Journal of Economics*, vol. 13, p. 396–426, July.

——— (1900), "Preconceptions of Economic Science (III)," *Quarterly Journal of Economics*, vol. 14, p. 240–269, February.

WELLISZ S. and R. FINDLAY (1986), "Central Planning and the Second Economy in Soviet-Type Systems," *Economic Journal*, vol. 96, n° 383, p. 646–658.

WILLIAMSON O.E. (1975), *Markets and Hierarchies: Analysis and Antitrust Implications*, London and New York: Free Press - Macmillan.

——— (1985), *The Economic Institutions of Capitalism: Firms, Markets, Relational Contracting*, New York: Free Press.

——— (1995), "The Institutions and Governance of Economic Development and Reform," *Proceedings of the World Bank Annual Conference on Development Economics 1994*, p. 171–205, Washington DC.

WORLD BANK (THE) (1997), *World Development Report*, The World Bank: Washington DC.

ZIEGLER J. (2005), *L'Empire de la honte*, Paris: Fayard.

CHAPTER 5

Some Serious Limits of John Maynard Keynes on Money, the Crisis, and the State

There is no lack of motives, faced with such and such a character trait, such behavior or idea of John Maynard Keynes, which could grieve progressive minds like him concerned with "justice and good sense"—all the more so if they are Marxists. It is probably his contradictions that best portray Keynes.[1] Known for having admonished the rentiers, he was nonetheless intimately linked to the financial oligarchy of the time, moving from the services of Her Majesty's Treasury or the Bank of England to the boards of directors of insurance companies—in addition to having exercised his talents as a stock market speculator. The content and purpose of the *General Theory of Employment, Interest, and Money*, judged "moderately conservative" by its own author,[2] nevertheless shocked his contemporaries and was even going to be and was even declared "revolutionary" by many of his disciples.

[1] This chapter owes much to two articles jointly written with Paulo Nakatani: Herrera and Nakatani (2010) and Nakatani and Herrera (2013).

[2] Robinson (1971, p. 131).

R. Herrera, *Confronting Mainstream Economics for Overcoming Capitalism*, Marx, Engels, and Marxisms,
https://doi.org/10.1007/978-3-031-05851-6_5

A leading figure of the left in politics, he did not hide his deep aversion to revolutions: that of 1789, of course, accentuating a certain Francophobia that was not devoid of humor,[3] but above all that of October 1917, which aroused in him anxiety and hatred.[4] This fear of the masses in revolt, turned toward socialism and threatening to throw down "the determined era of civilization,"[5] comes certainly from the elitism of a first baron (of Tilton) in the House of Lords, but also from a class option: "I can be influenced by what seems to me to be justice and good sense; but the class war will find me on the side of the educated bourgeoisie."[6]

The freedom of tone and the courage he sometimes showed, for example, when he resigned from the British delegation led by Lloyd George during the peace negotiations on German reparations at Versailles in 1919, coexisted, a little later, with calls for an increase in the military budget and the apology of the arms race.[7] His reluctance to see Great Britain, at the end of the First World War, give up control of its monetary policy to the Federal Reserve System of the United States did not prevent him, at the time of the signing of the agreements on the British debt in 1945, from accepting the submission of his country's sovereignty and from blissfully believing in the "generosity of the Americans."[8] Let us not dwell on what saddens many commentators; let us rather place the debate on the theoretical level—and in relation to Karl Marx. Even if "his ideas were not always clear and coherent,"[9] Keynes, an immense intellectual, was obviously an economist of genius. Here we offer the reader some notes for a critical evaluation of the contributions of Keynes's theories of money, the crisis, and the State, and of their relationship, also full of contradictions, with Marx.

[3] J.M. Keynes liked to say that the French are incompetent… just when the Popular Front was nationalizing. Or that the English preferred to deprive a sovereign of his power than of his head… See: Keynes (1971, p. 199).

[4] At the Second Congress of the International, Lenin, in the midst of praising Keynes for advising not to pay the debt, called him "a well-known bourgeois and (…) implacable enemy of Bolshevism" (Lenin [1965], pp. 213–263).

[5] Harrod (1951, p. 224).

[6] Keynes (1933, p. 233).

[7] Keynes (1920).

[8] *Proposals for an International Currency Union* of November 1941, in Keynes (1987, vol. XXV, pp. 42–66). Also: Keynes (1951).

[9] Robinson (1971, p. 128). Also: Robinson (1972, p. 124 *et s*).

5.1 Keynes and the Dominant Economics

To begin with, note that J.M. Keynes' criticisms of the dominant economics of his time, which he curiously called "classical" and not "neoclassical" as one would expect, are amply disseminated in the literature, beginning with macroeconomic textbooks. His proposed use of the term "classical school" to refer to "the successors of Ricardo, that is, the economists who adopted and improved his theory, including in particular Stuart Mill, Marshall, Edgeworth and Professor Pigou,"[10] was, however, equivocal and, since he mentions very few major differences between classical and neoclassical economics, his arguments are in fact exposed to objections when it comes to showing against whom they were directed. On this subject, A. Kicillof writes: "In the opinion of many economists, Keynes' criticism was directed against a non-existent theory, which he himself had invented, but which did not correspond adequately to the state of orthodox economics of his time."[11] So, this lack of precision allowed the neoclassicals, at least at that time, not to be deeply affected by Keynes' attacks and challenges. Neoclassical theory emerged intact, so to speak, taking refuge in microeconomics. Worse, the neoclassical authors managed to absorb some of Keynes' critical principles into their paradigm and ended up dominating macroeconomics as well, after the second synthesis (illustrated by the IS-LM model).[12]

Keynes thus begins the *General Theory* with a critique of the postulates of so-called "classical" economics: (*i*) the wage is equal to the marginal product of labor; and (*ii*) the utility of the wage, when a given volume of labor is employed, is equal to the marginal disutility of that volume of employment.[13] The first postulate would determine the supply of labor by entrepreneurs, as a condition for the equilibrium of production that maximizes their short-term profit in a competitive market. According to the law of diminishing returns, as the volume of employment increases, the marginal product of labor decreases and real wages fall so that the supply of new jobs increases. The second one would determine, as for it, the demand for labor by workers through the balance of utility (i.e., the

[10] Keynes (1936, p. 29, introduction, note 1).

[11] Kicillof (2007, p. 154).

[12] This model was presented by Hicks (1937).

[13] Keynes (1936, p. 31).

level of satisfaction corresponding to the wages) and disutility (or effort performed to work).

These postulates would ensure that the equilibrium obtained in the labor market is full employment; in other words, that the unemployment that remains is voluntary, since the decision to work or not would result from the rational choice of the individual worker to be employed or not. Consequently, this situation would not really be unemployment, since it would be the workers themselves who would not want to be employed for a wage objectively determined by the marginal productivity of labor. For most neoclassicals, there is no unemployment if workers accept a fall in real wages, without interference in the negotiations between them and employers. J.M. Keynes challenges this foundation of neoclassical theory, according to which real wages are determined by a negotiation between workers and employers.[14]

Keynes' critics reverse the cause-and-effect relationship. In the neoclassical model, the real wage is an independent variable that balances labor supply and demand. Keynes argues that workers can oppose a reduction in nominal wages, but that they have no means of counteracting a reduction in real wages, which also determine the evolutions of the market for goods and services. It is from this point that a new category is introduced: involuntary unemployment.[15] The reasoning is, however, very different from K. Marx, for whom the demand for labor power depends on the rate of accumulation and the organic and technical compositions of capital.[16] For, Keynes' conception does not go so far as to recognize the class condition of the wage worker, free but alienated, and whose only solution for survival is to sell his or her labor power as a commodity. Nowhere does Keynes speak of exploitation.

The third assumption on which Keynes fires is Jean-Baptiste Say's "law," which assures that the full-employment equilibrium between the supply and demand for labor would also determine the equilibrium between the aggregate supply and demand for goods and services. This "law," expounded by Say in chapter XV of his *Treatise on Political Economy* (1803) and popularized by the expression that "every supply creates its own demand," is based on the author's conception of the

[14] Ibidem, pp. 37–39.

[15] See: *The Collected Writings of John Maynard Keynes*, p. 23, *in* KEYNES (1987).

[16] MARX (1978, p. 199).

nature and functions of money.[17] It was defended by economists such as John Stuart Mill and David Ricardo,[18] as well as by the founders of marginalism and neoclassical theory, who never really moved away from it in order to establish their "automatic market equilibrium."[19] Léon Walras[20] does not deal directly with the question, but comes to the same conclusion: the goods offered by the seller necessarily find a buyer, since supply equals demand on all markets. Say's "law" defends the idea that any income that is not consumed becomes savings, used by other agents or invested. The standard neoclassical model formalizes this idea, according to which the equilibrium between savings (by households) and investment (by firms) is obtained by varying the interest rate. If the latter rises, then households prefer to receive interest rather than consume, but entrepreneurs are discouraged from borrowing to invest, as the rate of profit falls. A high demand for resources to be invested pushes up the interest rate, which stimulates household savings, and vice versa.

For Keynes, the interest rate does not constitute the variable that achieves the balance between the desire of households to save and the demand for resources that entrepreneurs wish to invest. It is the rate that encourages savers not to hoard. As a matter of fact, in order to realize fully his or her psychological time preferences, an individual would have two kinds of decisions to make. The first has to do with that aspect of time preference which Keynes has called the propensity to consume, a force which determines for each individual what part of his or her income he or she consumes, and what part he or she reserves in the form of any right to future consumption. But, once this decision has been taken, another decision remains to be made. He or she must choose the form in which he or she will retain the right to future consumption that he or she has reserved either in his or her current income or in his or her previous savings.[21] This difference between Keynes and the neoclassicals is related to their respective conceptions of money. While the neoclassicals separate the real and monetary spheres, Keynes defends the idea that such a separation makes no sense. Neoclassical authors considered that

[17] Say (1996, p. 138).

[18] Mill (1865 [1848]) and Ricardo (1951 [1817], p. 197).

[19] Jevons (1957 [1871], p. 126).

[20] Walras (2009, p. 179).

[21] Keynes (1936, p. 177).

the production of real wealth takes place in the real sphere and, based on quantitative theory, that money only affects prices—variations in its quantity pushing them up or down. This is what is known today as the "neutrality of money."

Keynes gradually moved away from the quantitative theory of money to defend the idea that, before influencing prices through a derivative effect, variations in the quantity of money primarily affect investment. Money is no longer perceived solely as a medium of exchange, but also functions, in Keynes' view, as a reserve of value.[22] But beyond the conception of money, these differences refer to the very vision of the foundation of capitalist production. Therefore, according to him, if "human nature" had no taste for risk, if it did not feel any satisfaction (other than pecuniary) in building a factory or a railroad, in exploiting a mine or a farm, the investments alone, aroused by a coldly established calculation, would probably not take on a great extension.[23] Keynes' analysis of the origin of capital at the foundation of capitalist production comes close to the abstinence thesis. Indeed, a part of the purchases from other entrepreneurs would be balanced by the value of the current investment made in equipment, and the surplus would represent the sacrifice which the production of the wealth sold has cost, over and above the total sum paid to the factors of production.[24] Nevertheless, pushed to the extreme, this thesis leads to absurdity, since it is only valid if it applies to money-capital,[25] which is not the case considered by Keynes. We will come back to this point.

One of the fundamental concepts put forward by Keynes, which differentiates him very clearly from the neoclassicals of his time, is that of "uncertainty." Let us try to follow him on this subject: a necessary condition must be fulfilled for there to be a preference for liquidity as a means of holding wealth; this necessary condition would be the existence of uncertainty about the future of the interest rate. So, if all future values of the rate of interest were known with certainty in advance, they could be deduced from present values of interest rates at different terms, which

[22] Ibidem, pp. 178–179.

[23] Ibidem, pp. 162–163.

[24] Ibidem, p. 86.

[25] Mandel (1985, p. 224).

would be adjusted to the known values of future interest rates. We shall come back to this soon.[26]

The history of thought has shown, however, as we know, that this did not prevent neoclassical theorists, in successive waves, from absorbing, digesting, and formalizing without major difficulties the bulk of the criticisms formulated by Keynes, whose theoretical contributions—indisputable, such as the one linked to the consideration of uncertainty—remained to a large extent compatible with the economic mainstream of neoclassicism.

5.2 On the Theory of the Crisis

Keynes pretended to ignore Marx; and when he spoke of him—rarely—it was always with a contempt that did little to conceal his irritation and aggressiveness. According to him, Marx would have based his theories—considered to be illogical, old-fashioned, scientifically erroneous, of no interest or practical use to the modern world—on the acceptance of classical assumptions, not on its abolition.[27] After having tried "once more to read that old Karl Marx"—in fact the correspondence with Engels—Keynes claimed not to have found more than outdated quibbles.[28] He is even said to have crossed out all bibliographic references to Marx on the list of works suggested by his Oxford colleagues for his students at Cambridge University, recommending instead the reading of his "opponents" Alfred Marshall and Arthur C. Pigou.[29] To Joan Robinson, who had tried to bring him closer to the author of *Capital* in an essay published in 1942, Keynes had retorted that it was futile to try to give meaning to what has no meaning.[30]

To understand his state of mind, note that in a letter dated January 1, 1935, addressed to Bernard Shaw, Keynes wrote, with reference to the *General Theory*, in which he had been encountering persistent difficulties

[26] Keynes (1936, p. 180).

[27] Keynes (1926, p. 48).

[28] Quoted by Mattick (1972, p. 33).

[29] See: Bloumine (1952, p. 185).

[30] Robinson writes, in particular: "Many refinements and complications (...), neglected by Marx, are elaborated in the Keynesian theory, but the main outline is clearly to be seen in Marx's analysis of investment as 'purchases without sales,' and saving as 'sales without purchases'." See: Robinson (1971, pp. 66–67).

for months (in particular with the measurement of the value of capital): "I believe myself to be writing a book on economic theory which will largely revolutionize (…) the way the world thinks about economic problems. When my new theory has been duly assimilated and mixed with politics and feelings and passions, I can't predict what the final upshot will be in its effect on actions and affairs. But there will be a great change, and, in particular, the Ricardian foundations of Marxism will be knocked away."[31] In Keynes's eyes, Marx was clearly an enemy. Or, if one prefers, he never wished to make an ally of him.

Nevertheless, it must be said that Keynes, in his very attempt to radicalize the criticisms directed against the neoclassical mainstream of the time, drew some of his ideas and strengths from a conceptual, methodological, and theoretical background shared with Marx. The two authors find themselves of course in a rejection of Say's law of outlets.[32] Without bringing it to the fore, nor making explicit reference to the exploitation of workers, Keynes returns to a large extent to a classical theory of labor value. As Kicillof rightly points out: "For Keynes, the normal price of any commodity is equal to the cost of labor which, measured in units of wages [i.e., in the monetary wage of the unit of labor (or 'wage unit')], makes it possible to establish the quantity of units of labor used to measure the volume of employment [or 'labor unit'], i.e., the quantity of 'simple' labor required to produce each commodity."[33]

In the *Treatise on Money* (1930), he was to take up the Marxist reproduction schemes of Book II of *Capital*, relying on the distinction between sectors of production of capital goods and sectors of production of consumer goods, in order to approach the problem of the depression from a monetary angle—in the manner of most business cycle theorists of the time, and thus very different from Marx, for whom the emphasis must be on the character of production as capital production—and to conclude that it is the insufficiency of investment (and not of savings) that causes the depression. But as with Marx, he saw an evolution of

[31] Harrod (1951, p. 462).

[32] See, for example, Marx (1974, pp. 121–122): "Nothing more silly than the dogma according to which circulation necessarily implies the balance of purchases and sales, since all sale is purchase, and vice versa. (…) [T]hese two acts, circulation separates them (…) [and] if the split (…) is accentuated, their intimate connection is affirmed – by a crisis."

[33] Kicillof (2007, p. 443).

capitalism leading to a collapse, the causes of which were inherent in the very functioning of this system.

And if we look closely, the ultimate cause of the depression that Keynes identifies goes to the heart of the Marxian interpretation: what explains the "depression," upstream of the insufficiency of investment, due to the decrease in the marginal efficiency of capital (itself linked to the obsolescence of capital and accentuated, possibly, by a rise in interest rates), is indeed, in the last instance, "capitalist competition," that is to say, what Marx calls the internal contradictions of capitalism. At the starting point of the Keynesian monetary circuit, there is the demand for additional money that is created to meet the need for the means of financing necessary for investment of enterprises.[34] Keynes's selected definition of profit as the income from the enterprise's capital (normally higher than the interest rate) is closer to that of Marx than to that of the neoclassical theorists. A key concept in the Keynesian scheme is that of the incentive to invest, which depends on the difference (expected to be positive and not zero) between two variables that bring distinct mechanisms into play: the marginal efficiency of capital (or return on capital) and the interest rate.

The expected profit (or income of entrepreneurs) controls and orders effective demand (i.e., the aggregate demand anticipated by these entrepreneurs) and thus expectations of net investment (the net addition to the value of equipment of all kinds, taking into account the changes in the value of old equipment which enter into the calculation of net income).[35] Furthermore, Keynes maintains that it is effective demand that will determine the volume of employment provided by enterprises, a volume on which aggregate income will depend itself—in the short term—and from which consumption will also ultimately flow. In sum, when profit tends to fall, the resulting deterioration in expectations leads to a decline in investment, then the economy enters a depression, characterized by an equilibrium "without full employment" (or lasting underemployment) and the absence of spontaneous adjustment mechanisms by the market. Paul Mattick was quite right when he said that Keynes's theory, adopting Marx's analyses without his conclusions, was in its essence a kind of bastardized repetition of the Marxian critique and

[34] See: POULON (2000).

[35] KEYNES (1936, p. 96).

aimed at cutting short the decline of capitalism, at warding off its eventual collapse.[36]

Besides, Keynes does not provide a "general" or completed theory of the crisis, but rather a great many partial, scattered and sometimes conflicting elements of theoretical analysis, which have often given rise to confusion or misunderstanding on the part of commentators, as well as on the part of some of his own disciples—starting with the highly complex concept of "effective demand."[37] For Keynes rarely referred to the crisis by its name, preferring to speak of its manifestations, or of "depression," "deflation," "inflation," or of what he considered to be the most shocking aspects of capitalism[38]: unemployment, first and foremost, but also income and wealth inequalities... However, the search for strategies to get out of the crisis, with the ultimate goal of "safeguarding capitalism" or finding the secret of a "crisis-free capitalism," because it would be "regulated," occupies most of his reflections, from his most theoretical works to his practical commitments and political struggles.

Like Joseph Aloïs Schumpeter,[39] Keynes understood that the course of history was moving in the direction of the overcoming of capitalism by socialism, and he was fully aware of the exacerbation of the class struggle in his time. One of the tasks he set himself was to deepen the theory in order to find the means to ensure the permanence of capitalist society for as long as possible. It was to better "reason out" the anti-capitalist temptations that he found himself forced to conduct a radical critique of neoclassical theory, according to which it proved impossible that the crisis was inherent in the capitalist mode of production. He, therefore, defended the idea that the crisis was the result of weak aggregate demand (and insufficient investment, linked to the fall in the marginal efficiency of capital) and proposed as a solution the creation of "effective demand" through an exogenous factor: State intervention through public spending.

Keynes showed that, since capitalism did not automatically generate an equilibrium of full employment, contrary to what was generally asserted by neoclassicism, the State could be justified in stimulating investment

36 Mattick (1972, p. 39).

37 As shown by Lavoie (1985), effective demand, as the anticipated value of sales, must in reality be interpreted as... supply.

38 Keynes (1936, p. 228).

39 Schumpeter (1951).

and, consequently, in encouraging the creation of new jobs. As a consequence, this allowed for the building of the institutions and instruments necessary for the implementation of monetary and fiscal policies that would rationalize State action in the expansionary and contractionary phases of economic cycles, as well as minimize the impacts of the crisis on output and employment.

Although the importance of the role attributed to monetary factors varied in the course of his work, the place occupied by money in Keynes's work is such that he was unwise to venture to explain the rise and fall of the great civilizations of the past by the monetary flows of entry or exit of precious metals. Thereby, Keynes wrote in his *Treatise on Money*: "It would be a fascinating task to re-write Economic History, in light of these ideas, from its remote beginnings; – to conjecture whether the civilizations of Sumeria and Egypt drew their stimulus from the gold of Arabia and the copper of Africa, which, being monetary metals, left a trail of profit behind them in the course of their distribution through the lands between the Mediterranean and the Persian Gulf, and, probably, farther afield; in what degree the greatness of Athens depended on the silver mines of Laudrium – not because the monetary metals are a more truly wealth than other things, but because by their effect on prices they supply the spur of profit; how far the dispersal by Alexander of the bank reserves of Persia, which represented the accumulated withdrawals into the treasure of successive empires during many preceding centuries, was responsible for the outburst of economic progress in the Mediterranean basin, of which Carthage attempted and Rome ultimately succeded to reap the fruits; whether it was a coincidence that the decline and fall of Rome was contemporaneous with the most prolonged and drastic deflation yet recorded; if the long stagnation of the Middle Ages may not have been more surely and inevitably caused by Europe's meagre supply of the monetary metals than by monasticism or Gothic frenzy...".[40]

[40] Keynes (1930, vol. 2, pp. 150–151). We do not include here the author's notes, but we respected his original punctuation. Eleven years earlier, he wrote in *The Economic Consequences of the Peace*: "Lenin is said to have declared that the best way to destroy the capitalist system was to debauch the currency. (...) [He] was certainly right. There is no subtler, no surer means of overturning the existing basis of society than to debauch the currency. The process engages all the hidden forces of economic law on the side of destruction, and does it in a manner which not one man in a million is able to diagnose" (Keynes [1920], pp. 219–220). Fine, but even if Lenin said that, he did not say—and did—only that....

Others had ventured into this field long before J.M. Keynes, beginning with representatives of the Salamanca School, such as Luis Saravia de la Calle and Martín de Azpilcueta—in addition to defending private property, usury, and a quantitativist theory of scarcity-value. In his 1859 *Contribution to the Critique of Political Economy*, Marx also reproached the Eighteenth-Century Humean empiricists: "Quite inappropriate are references – in vogue among Hume's disciples – to rising prices in ancient Rome brought about by the conquest of Macedonia, Egypt, and Asia Minor. For a detailed analysis of the circulation of money, Hume, like all other Eighteenth-Century writers, lacked the necessary material, i.e., on the one hand, a reliable history of commodity-prices, and on the other hand, official and continuous statistics regarding the expansion and contraction of the medium of circulation, the influx or withdrawal of precious metals, etc., in other words material which on the whole only becomes accessible when banking is fully developed."[41] The analysis of money depends fundamentally on those of "all economic life" (values, prices, wages, population, working time, etc.) and of "the whole social complex" in which it is inserted.[42] On the basis of a reformulation of the theory of labor value leading to exploitation, Marx makes money emerge as the necessary result of the unfolding of the internal contradictions of the commodity form.[43] As we shall see, Keynes proceeded quite differently.

5.3 Money, Credit, and the Financial System

The theory of money proposed by J.M. Keynes constitutes a major advance in the interpretation of capitalist societies, compared to neoclassical thought. He succeeded (only in part)[44] in breaking out of the mainstream of the time, for whom money was essentially reduced to a means of exchange, and introduced it into the circuit of the reproduction of capital. The fundamental consequence of this is that the overcoming of the orthodox vision of an automatic equilibrium, which prohibited

[41] Marx (1972 [1859], pp. 122–123). Available on: https://www.marxists.org/archive/marx/works/download/Marx_Contribution_to_the_Critique_of_Political_Economy.pdf.

[42] Vilar (1974, p. 35).

[43] See, for more details: Nakatani and Gomes (2010).

[44] Lavoie (1985). Also on this subject: Barrère (1979).

crises in the theory, by construction, is achieved by placing money at the heart of the capitalist dynamic and by reformulating a theory of interest that gives the latter a key—but excessive, as we have said—role in determining investments in a capitalist economy. This theory of money reaches its climax in the *General Theory of Employment, Interest, and Money*, more precisely in chapter 17 of Book IV entitled "The Essential Properties of Interest and Money."[45]

From his earliest work (entitled *Indian Currency and Finance* and dating from 1913) to his proposals for the reorganization of the monetary system and the creation of an international clearing union (during WWII), Keynes has – almost – always criticized the gold standard as attached to a "barbarous relic."[46] In the *General Theory*, he came to consider money as paper money with forced course or inconvertibility. The supply of money is posed as exogenous and carried out by the Central Bank—but it is possible to reformulate this hypothesis of exogenous supply on the basis of endogenous monetary creation by the banking system—while the demand for money is determined by the "tendency to hoard" or the preference for liquidity, which itself varies as a function of the interest rate. Liquidity is defined as the possibility available at any time to an agent holding claims to convert them, without loss of capital, into money, "liquidity *par excellence*."[47] He writes, in Chapter 15: "There is, however, a necessary condition failing which the existence of a liquidity preference for money as a means of holding wealth could not exist. This necessary condition is the existence of uncertainty as to the future rate of interest, i.e., as to the complex of rates of interest for varying maturities which will rule at future dates. For if the rates of interest ruling at all future times could be foreseen with certainty, all future rates of interest could be inferred from the present rates of interest for debts of different maturities, which would be adjusted to the knowledge of the future rates."[48]

For him, money is a very singular asset, whose nature derives from its function as a store of value. Having the capacity to store wealth and transfer it into the future, it can be converted by its holder into any

[45] Keynes (1936, p. 229 *et s*). Available on: https://www.files.ethz.ch/isn/125515/1366_KeynesTheoryofEmployment.pdf.

[46] Keynes (1971 [1920], p. 198).

[47] Keynes (1936, Chapter 13).

[48] Ibidem, Chapter 15, Section II, pp. 179–180.

other available capital asset. But not being alone in this power, money is confronted with other yielding liquid capital assets, such as stocks, bonds, debt securities, etc. One of the crucial characteristics of these assets is their scarcity, from which comes precisely the fact that they serve a yield. "Thus the rate of interest at any time, being the reward for parting with liquidity, is a measure of the unwillingness of those who possess money to part with their liquid control over it. The rate of interest is not the 'price' which brings into equilibrium the demand for resources to invest with the readiness to abstain from present consumption. It is the 'price' which equilibrates the desire to hold wealth in the form of cash with the available quantity of cash."[49] Like money, each of these durable forms of wealth bears a specific rate of interest (i.e., its "own rate of interest"), which is measured in units of itself and expresses the difference between its current price and its future price. It is this rate that makes it possible to define, over a given period of time, the total expected return on the asset in question; a return from which must be subtracted a "cost of conservation," but also a "liquidity premium" (which is an approximation of the "cost of negotiation").

In Keynes's view, what distinguishes money from other liquid assets is a higher liquidity premium for the latter than for the former (for which it tends toward zero). And in addition to its zero return, since it does not in itself yield a remuneration,[50] money is characterized by a very low cost of conservation and a fairly high liquidity premium (the latter being much higher than the former in the case of State money, whereas it is the reverse for other durable wealth). The specific rate of interest of money would be the highest of all, because "we have been tacitly assuming that the kind of money to which we are accustomed has some special characteristics which lead to its own-rate of interest in terms of itself as standard being more reluctant to fall as the stock of assets in general increases than the own-rates of interest of any other assets in terms of themselves."[51] The solution adopted by Keynes is, therefore, very different from that of Marx, who considers money to be money-capital.

[49] Keynes (1936, Chapter 15, Section II, pp. 178–179).

[50] "Except in an insane asylum, who would want money as a store of value?" Read: Szmreczanyi (1978).

[51] Keynes (1936, Chapter 17, Section III, pp. 236–237).

According to J.M. Keynes, the properties of money would be: "1° (...) [to have] both in the long and in the short period, a zero, or at any rate a very small, elasticity of production (...). Money (...) cannot be readily produced; labour cannot be turned on at will by entrepreneurs to produce money in increasing quantities as its price rises in terms of the wage-unit. (...) 2° The second *differentia* of money is that it has an elasticity of substitution equal, or nearly equal, to zero which means that as the exchange value of money rises there is no tendency to substitute some other factor for it (...). 3° [W]e we must consider whether these conclusions are upset by the fact that, even though the quantity of money cannot be increased by diverting labour into producing it, nevertheless an assumption that its effective supply is rigidly fixed would be inaccurate."[52] In connection with this last characteristic, Keynes argues that changes in (nominal or real) wages would alter the quantity of money available to meet the demand for liquidity, which would affect the interest rate.

We could perhaps accept, at least in theory, that money, as a commodity money, presents an elasticity of production equal to or close to zero in countries that can produce a "commodity currency"; but this is no longer the case when it is an inconvertible State currency with a forced course—unless we consider this money to be totally independent of the market. And even if the supply of money were exogenously fixed by the Central Bank, we would still run into a problem arising from the divergence between the theoretical conception and the practical functioning of monetary creation. In theory, the nature of contemporary money as paper money of forced course and free of any attachment to a monetary standard based on commodity money gives Central Banks, in the present era, the possibility of creating money apparently without limit. We know, however, that in practice the accentuation of capitalist contradictions, especially those between the production of wealth and its ownership, which have manifested themselves throughout the last decades of the last century by inflationary tensions leading to the devalorization of this wealth in monetary form, has pushed Central Banks to take on the task of controlling the monetary supply in a much stricter way, according to the dogmas of the theoretical quantitativist line.

Nevertheless, the creation of unconvertible money by the Central Bank does not take place all at once, nor even periodically, but permanently, in

[52] Ibidem, pp. 237–238.

the very course of the functioning of the mechanisms of the monetary and financial market. This process operates continuously, through flows of money creation and destruction. Strictly speaking, one is dealing here with a supply of money in flows, and not in stocks—even if, for statistical convenience, the total amount of money created at a given moment is frequently presented in "stocks." In addition to this "primary" process of incrementing the monetary base with Central Bank money, the banking system can also increase the money supply through "secondary" monetary creation. The growth of the banking system allows for the expansion of credit money—that is to say, private money—which replaces State money with forced course in most buying and selling transactions, both between firms and between the latter and consumers, and is canceled, after being created, when each contract expires.

Given this monetary supply, a certain amount of money is demanded for each interest rate, so that it becomes possible to draw a net demand curve that would determine the specific interest rate of money—leading to the supply–demand equilibrium. The demand for money is determined by what Keynes chose to call the "income-motive" ("to bridge the interval between the receipt of income and its disbursement"), the "business-motive" ("to bridge the interval between the time of incurring business costs and that of the receipt of the sale-proceeds"), the "precautionary-motive" (e.g., "to provide for contingencies requiring sudden expenditure"), and the "speculative-motive" (much more complex to grasp and consisting in anticipating the "psychological state" of the financial market).[53]

Keynes represents this demand by the following equation: $M = M1 + M2 = L1(R) + L2(r)$, with $L1(R) = R/V = M1$ and $L2(r) = M2$, and where M corresponds to the total demand for money, $M1$ to the demand for money related to the income, business, and precautionary motives, $M2$ to the demand for money arising from the speculation motive, R to income and V to the income velocity of money (i.e., the classical concept approximated by the ratio of income to quantity of money). Of course, the equation $L2(r) = M2$ is not the only one that describes the interest rate (r), insofar as income, money demand, and the interest rate are

[53] Keynes (1936, Chapter 15, Section I, points (i), (ii) and (iii), respectively, p. 203 *et s*).

economically correlated.[54] Thus we understand that while Marx's determination of the interest rate refers to money-capital, Keynes formulates it on the basis of money: the preference for liquidity, or the propensity to hoard, determines the interest rate.

Keynes argues—curiously in a simple but crucial note—that money can be defined as follows: the line of separation between "money" and "claims and receivables" may be drawn at the point which best suits the study of each particular problem. For instance, any right to general purchasing power that has not been disposed of for a period longer than three months may be considered money, and rights disposed of for a longer period may be considered claims and receivables. Instead of three months, one may as well choose one month, three days, three hours, or any period of time; or one may exclude from money any wealth that does not have immediate liberating power. According to him, it is often convenient in practice to extend the name of money to time deposits in banks and even sometimes to certain instruments of credit, such as Treasury bills.[55]

This means, in his view, that the important thing is not the difference between money that does not earn interest and deposits or interest-bearing securities, but rather their common basis, which lies in their liquidity.[56] The assets in question, deposits and securities, may be considered money because economic actors have confidence in their fundamental property of being—not so much universal instruments of exchange, but—quite highly liquid, i.e., relatively easily convertible into money, without loss of capital. In any case, in Keynes's reasoning, it is the comparisons made by capitalists of the expected rates of return on each of the durable assets as well as of the specific interest rate of money in relation to the marginal efficiency of capital that would make it possible to determine the investments that would be, respectively, carried out in each of these assets and, consequently, the aggregate investment. Considering that the total volume of employment is determined by the amount of this aggregate investment, the "way out of the crisis" by reviving production and employment would then depend—under the condition that the state of the economy is not such that the marginal efficiency of capital does

[54] Ibidem, p. 209.

[55] Ibidem, p. 178.

[56] On this subject: Kicillof (2007, p. 457), where the author rightly links Keynes's analysis of money (presented in Chapter 17 of the *General Theory*) to his conception of capital (explained previously, in Chapter 16).

not fall faster than the interest rate—on a monetary policy involving a reduction in the interest rate and a stimulation of investment.

5.4 Keynes, Yesterday and Today

For some time now, renowned neoclassical theorists have been distancing themselves from the vision of a self-regulating adjustment of capitalism and challenging the neoliberal line. Most of them have done so not so much to convert to "Keynesianism" (which remains one of the surest ways to lose all academic consideration) as to accelerate the siphoning off of Keynes's legacy by the dominant paradigm and to continue the work of "Keynesian-neoclassical synthesis" begun in the late 1930s by the efforts of eminent authors such as Sir John R. Hicks or Paul A. Samuelson. Their descendants, who remained faithful to the standard orthodox theory (at the cost of a few adaptations on price adjustments, expectations, or imperfect competition...), are currently Joseph Stiglitz, Nobel laureate and former vice-president of the World Bank, or Paul Krugman, winner of the same prize, who ends one of his latest books with this affirmation: Keynes would be now, more than ever, on the agenda.[57] It is not unreasonable to argue that the monetary policy recently pursued by the world's major Central Banks has some proximity to Keynes' monetary theory. Nonetheless, it can be observed that the effects of the so-called "Keynesian" monetary policy measures, applied in the United States in particular, disappeared in what Keynes himself called the "liquidity trap": the interest rate cuts granted (prime rates were sometimes even reduced to zero) did not succeed, in general, in increasing the marginal efficiency of capital, nor in moving significant masses of capital out of the financial sphere and into the productive sphere. In fact, it is the dogmas of neoliberalism that the governments of Northern countries have continued to follow, despite the crisis, notably through the reduction of public spending on operations and investment, the elimination of civil service jobs, and the stagnation of the purchasing power of the workers, but also the "rationalization" of management and the "reorganization" of social security accounts, as well as the reduction of retirement benefits and the extension of contribution periods. Is this the path indicated by Keynes? In short, and once again, all these measures are the opposite of what Keynes suggested.

[57] Krugman (2009). Also: Hicks (1974).

In any case, as we have just suggested to the reader by way of a retrospective comparison with the interpretations given by Marx, we find ourselves confronted, in Keynes's *General Theory*, with important theoretical difficulties and shortcomings relating to the treatment of money, in general, and the financial system, in particular. Although an analogy can be drawn with Keynes's idea of locating one of the causes of depression in the insufficiency of effective demand, let us recall it, for Marx, the potentiality of the occurrence of a crisis of overproduction is already contained in the commodity-money-commodity cycle itself, where the contradiction internal to the commodity as use value and exchange value is permanently expressed and resolved, and where money functions as a means of circulation; or more precisely, and above all, in the separation of this cycle into two stages or "metamorphoses" opening up the possibility for any seller to sell his or her merchandises without having to immediately buy others.[58] Moreover, the fundamental property of money to function as capital, analyzed by Marx, does not appear in a developed or even clear way in Keynes's theory of money—and even less, obviously, in the quantitative theory of money due to neoclassicism. However, the function of money as a means of payment—which is the basis of the origin of credit money—becomes more ideal[59] as the financing systems of economies develop and modernize.

Consequently, the limited analysis that is given of the credit system in the *General Theory* as well as the lack of differentiation between State money and credit money[60] logically—but improperly—leads Keynes to attribute a completely excessive responsibility to the State in determining the interest rate, through the creation of exogenous money by the Central Bank. The latter could indeed push the interest rate down through the expansion of the money supply, with the aim of stimulating investment in capital assets where the marginal efficiency of capital is higher. The limit of such a mechanism would be reached when the accumulation of capital in all sectors of economic activity came to the point where the demand for goods and services of the society in question would reach its maximum and gradually eliminate what Keynes considered to be shocking effects

[58] Marx (1974, Book I, vol. 1, pp. 113–114).

[59] Ibidem, p. 140.

[60] For a detailed discussion of this issue: Macedo e Silva (2008, pp. 241–265).

of capitalism[61]—foremost among which are unemployment and income inequality.

We know, however, that the monetary policy currently implemented by the Central Banks of the main capitalist countries has completely reversed the process by which the interest rate is determined by the market. As a matter of fact, with the priority objectives of fighting inflation and stabilizing the currency, Central Banks use the interest rate as the main instrument, and as a tool independent of monetary control, in an institutional context reorganized accordingly. Instead of regulating the quantity of money supplied, the core of monetary policy now consists of setting and manipulating a base interest rate, from which all other interest rates are structured by type of credits and maturities and which would allow—according to what is claimed—both to distribute the total supply of money following the different "motives" of monetary demand and to control the latter as a fundamental variable in price determination. But we also know that this base interest rate of the Central Bank is itself strongly influenced by various rates fixed by the big banking and financial oligopolies on each of the segments of the financial markets (and especially the derivatives futures markets) on which they impose themselves in a dominant position. Would not the Keynesian State be, in fact, a fiction?[62]

If the main orientations of the policies followed by capitalist governments continue to be faithful to the neoliberal dogmas—although it has been shattered, and for a very long time—the violence of the crisis triggered in the United States in 2007–2008 has brought Keynesian theses back to the forefront, including those of certain "forgotten" authors, recovered for the occasion, such as Hyman Minsky. In one of his major works, recently republished in the United States,[63] H. Minsky showed that the capitalist economy has, by its very nature, an instability inherent to its functioning. An instability to which he proposes to bring solutions through important reforms, among which a strong government (in size, expenditures, and taxes), a strategy for employment, and financial reform.[64] That is, more or less the opposite of what is being done today...

[61] Keynes (1936, p. 228).

[62] Herrera (2001, 2003).

[63] Minsky (2008).

[64] Papadimitriou and Wray (2008).

For all that, what can be reproached to the majority of Minsky's recently convinced "disciples" is that they see in the current "moment" only a financial crisis requiring, to be overcome, the deepening of existing banking regulation exclusively.[65] Some go further, opposing budget cuts, like Paul Krugman and Richard Layard, two authors of a *Manifesto for Economic Sense*, signed by thousands of economists.[66] Others, some of whom claim to be "structural Keynesians,"[67] do not accept this merely financial reading of the crisis and radicalize the critique against neoliberal policies that have aggravated inequalities in the United States and world imbalances; this would require, according to them, more profound changes than a new banking regulation, in this case the end of neoliberalism—but not the end of capitalism, of which neoliberalism is only a form.[68] In one way or another, everyone argues that the State would have the means to resolve the crisis in order to hope to return to a regulated economy similar to that of the "golden years" of the post-war period. Without having learned the lessons of its limitations, they then fall back on the belief in a benevolent State, combined with the good will of capitalists, as in many passages of the *General Theory*.[69]

According to Keynes, capitalist society could well end up reaching a level of accumulation for which the marginal efficiency of capital would be so low that the increase of capital would become impossible, as we saw, even if the interest rate were kept extremely low. He thus writes, in Chapter 16, that, under such conditions, a well-governed community, equipped with modern technical resources, and whose population is not rapidly increasing, should be able within a single generation to lower the marginal efficiency of capital to an equilibrium level close to zero. The conditions that characterize a stationary economy would then be realized.[70] But can we not ask ourselves whether the most developed capitalist societies in the world nowadays, the United States, Europe, or Japan,

65 Are we experiencing a "Minsky moment"? See, among many others, an answer sketched out by KREGEL (2010).

66 http://www.manifestoforeconomicsense.org/.

67 PALLEY (2010). Available at: http://monthlyreview.org/author/thomasipalley.

68 A Marxist critique against such arguments is due to FOSTER and MCCHESNEY (2010).

69 KEYNES (1936, Chapter 16, p. 227).

70 Ibidem, pp. 228–229.

have not already reached this quasi-stationary stage where there is no longer any economic space for the productive accumulation of capital—and this would have been the case for several years—? Contrary to what Keynes and some of his followers imagined, for whom the contradictions of the capitalist system could be solved by the State, we are today, at the beginning of the Twenty-first Century, confronted with a situation of over-accumulation of capital and an even higher degree of complexity of the contradictions of capitalism than in the previous century. We shall elaborate on this point later (Chapter 7).

Keynes wrote that if we are right in believing that it is relatively easy to multiply capital goods until their marginal efficiency is zero, this is probably the most reasonable way of gradually eliminating most of the "shocking features" of capitalism. Now, it seems quite clear that these negative characteristics (inequalities and unemployment) have not disappeared anywhere, neither obviously in the Southern societies, nor even in most of those of the North, where poverty tends to massify and misery to reappear. The measures set out by Keynes and many of those who claim to be his followers today—often not very faithful to his teachings because they still remain prisoners of neoclassicism—are no longer capable of solving the problems posed by the over-accumulation of capital, which we eventually have to recognize collectively as approaching sheer madness.

Nonetheless, it would be delusional to persist in believing in the possibility of a new "Keynesian compromise." The previous one—and it was the only one—sealed after World War II—was not conceded by the capitalists, but wrested from them by multiple, convergent popular struggles—including, certainly, those in the East and the South. At the present time, however, high finance, which has regained power, does not seem to be willing to make any concessions. Keynesianism—which, of course, we can hope for—has neither reality nor future. From now on, it is the financial oligopolies that dictate their law to the States, whether to fix interest rates, to create money, or, if necessary, to nationalize... None of the currents of thought, from the neoclassicals to the Keynesians, suggest that we should think in depth about the conditions for overcoming capital as a social relation of domination and exploitation. Consequently, it is the deepening of the destructive line of neoliberalism that continues to be followed...

It is for all these reasons that we maintain that a return to Marx is necessary, both in theory and in practice. The analysis of money must be inserted into the analysis of the contradictions of commodity production that Marx contributed to unveil in *Capital*, from Chapter 3 of Book I, about gold as a measure of value, a means of circulation, and a currency, to Sections 4 and 5 of Book III, about the historical process of development of money and the credit system, before arriving at the concept of "fictitious capital," which we shall discuss later (Chapter 7).[71] Marx opened the theoretical way which we think it would be fruitful to pursue. In practice, such a return to Marxism(s), responding to the interests of the workers' world, is all the more necessary since the contradictions of the expansion of capital require a new mode of production and, more broadly, a new form of society.

References

Barrère A. (1979), *Déséquilibres économiques et contre-révolution keynésienne*, Paris: Economica.

Bloumine I. (1952), "L'économie politique de Keynes," *La Pensée*, n° 42–43, p. 182–186, Paris.

Foster J.B. and F. McChesney (2010), "Listen Keynesians, It's the System! Response to Palley," available on: http://monthlyreview.org/2010/04/01/listen-keynesians-its-thesystem-response-to-palley#.UIWcxm-HWU.

Harrod R.F. (1951), *The Life of John Maynard Keynes*, London: Macmillan.

Herrera R. (2001), "Brève introduction à la Théorie de l'État chez Marx et Engels," *Cahier de la Maison des Sciences économiques de l'Université de Paris 1*, n° 1, Paris, available on: https://vimeo.com/144550507.

——— (2003), "L'État contre le service public?", *Actuel Marx*, n° 34, p. 147–160, Paris.

Herrera R. and P. Nakatani (2008), "La Crise financière: racines, raisons, perspectives," *La Pensée*, n° 353, p. 109–113, Paris.

——— (2010), "Keynes (et Marx), la monnaie et la crise," *La Pensée*, n° 364, p. 57–68, Paris.

Hicks J.R. (1937), "Mr. Keynes and the Classics: A Suggested Interpretation," *Econometrica*, vol. 5, n° 2, p. 147–159.

——— (1974), *The Crisis in Keynesian Economics*, New York: Basic Books.

Jevons W.S. (1957 [1871]), *The Theory of Political Economy*, New York: Kelley and Millman.

Keynes J.M. (1920), *The Economic Consequences of the Peace*, London: Macmillan.

——— (1926), *Laissez-faire and Communism*, New York: New Republic Inc.

[71] Read: Herrera and Nakatani (2008), and Nakatani and Herrera (2009).

——— (1930), *Treatise on Money*, 2 volumes, London: Macmillan.
——— (1933), *Essais de persuasion*, Paris: Gallimard.
——— (1936), *The General Theory of Employment, Interest and* Money, Cambridge (UK): Macmillan Cambridge University Press (for Royal Economic Society).
——— (1951), *Essays in Bibliography* (first edition in 1933), Rupert Hart-Davis, Londres.
——— (1971 [1920]), *A Tract on Monetary Reform*, The Collected Writings of J.M. Keynes, vol. IV, London: Macmillan.
——— (1987), *The Collected Writings of John Maynard Keynes*, London: Cambridge University Press, Macmillan.
Kicillof A. (2007), *Fundamentos de la Teoria General: las consecuencias teoricas de Lord Keynes*, Buenos Aires: Eudeba.
Kregel J. (2010), "Minsky Moments and Minsky's Proposals for Regulation of an Unstable Financial System," Draft of Opening Remarks for the 19th Annual H.P. Minsky Conference, available on: http://www.levyinstitute.org/pubs/conf_april10/19th_Minsky_Kregel_drt.pdf.
Krugman P.R. (2009), *The Return of Depression Economics and the Crisis of 2008*, New York: W.W. Norton & Co.
Lavoie M. (1985), "La Théorie générale et l'inflation de sous-emploi," *in* F. Poulon (ed.), *Les Écrits de Keynes*, p. 131–152, Paris: Dunod.
Lenin V.I. (1965 [1920]), *Collected Works*, 4th ed., vol. 31, Moscow: Progress Publishers.
Macedo e Silva A.C. (2008), "Do Treatise à General Theory: o extravio dos 'detalhes monetários'," *in* J. Sicsú and C. Vidotto (eds.), *Economia do desenvolvimento: Teoria e políticas keynesianas*, p. 241–265, Rio de Janeiro: Elsevier.
Mandel E. (1985), *La Crise*, Paris: Flammarion.
Marx K. (1972 [1859]), *Contribution à la critique de l'économie politique*, Paris: Éditions sociales.
——— (1974), *Théories sur la plus-value*, vol. 1, Paris: Éditions sociales.
——— (1978), *Le Capital - Critique de l'économie politique*, Paris: Éditions sociales.
Mattick P. (1972), *Marx et Keynes: les limites de l'économie mixte*, Paris: Gallimard.
Mill J.S. (1865 [1848]), *Principles of Political Economy with some of their Applications to Social Philosophy*, London: Mongmans.
Minsky H. (2008), *Stabilizing an Unstable Economy*, New York: MacGraw Hill.
Nakatani P. and R. Herrera (2009), "Critique des politiques anticrise orthodoxes," *La Pensée*, n° 360, p. 31–42, Paris.
——— (2013), "Keynes et la crise: hier et aujourd'hui," *Actuel Marx*, n° 53, p. 153–168, Paris.

NAKATANI P. and H. GOMES (2010), "Dinheiro: natureza e funções", *mimeo*, Vitoria: Federal University of Espirito Santo.

PALLEY T. (2010), "The Limits of Minsky's Financial Instability Hypothesis as an Explanation of the Crisis," available on: http://monthlyreview.org/2010/04/01/thelimits-of-minskys-financial-instability-hypothesis-as-an-explanation-ofthecrisis#.UIWZv2–_HWU.

PAPADIMITRIOU D.B. and L.R. WRAY (2008), "Minsky's Stabilizing an Unstable Economy: Two Decades Later," in H. Minsky (ed.), *Stabilizing an Unstable Economy*, p. xxv et s., New York: MacGraw Hill.

POULON F. (2000), *La Pensée économique de Keynes*, Paris: Dunod.

RICARDO D. (1951 [1817]), *On the Principles of Political Economy and Taxation*, Cambridge (UK): Cambridge University Press.

ROBINSON J.V. (1971), *Essai sur l'économie de Marx*, Paris: Dunod.

——— (1972), *Hérésies économiques*, Paris: Calmann-Lévy.

SAY J.-B. (1996), *Cours d'économie politique et autres essais*, Paris: Flammarion.

SCHUMPETER J.A. (1951), *Ten Great Economists*, London: George Allen & Unwin Ldt.

SZMRECZANYI T. (ed.) (1978), *John Maynard Keynes*, São Paulo: Ática.

VILAR P. (1974), *Or et monnaie dans l'histoire*, Paris: Éditions Flammarion.

WALRAS L. (2009), *Œuvres économiques complètes*, Paris: Economica.

CHAPTER 6

Thomas Piketty's Regulation of Capitalism Through a "Tax Revolution"

In 2013, Thomas Piketty published, with the success that we know, a thick volume entitled *Le Capital au XXe siècle* (Capital in the Twenty-first Century).[1] A success in any case deserved, because the book represents a rather rare effort among economists to trace the history of a number of economic variables, including the growth rate of the economy (that is to say, GDP) and the rate of return on "capital," as well as that of inequality, over three centuries (with even a retropolation attempted up to the year zero, which is a bit of an overstatement). It also draws comparisons between the major rich countries of the North (but also, with less data, between them and emerging countries). This is an impressive piece of work, carried out with a concern for clarity and pedagogy that must be commended. It is an indisputably useful work, in which the reader will find a wealth of information, which sometimes goes against received ideas.

For example, we learn that a GDP growth rate of 1%, which seems quite modest, however, is not sustainable in the long term, because it would correspond to an exorbitant multiplication of this indicator after a

[1] This chapter takes up to a large extent the developments of an article co-written with Tony Andréani, see: ANDRÉANI and HERRERA (2015a). Also read: ANDRÉANI and HERRERA (2015b).

R. Herrera, *Confronting Mainstream Economics for Overcoming Capitalism*, Marx, Engels, and Marxisms,
https://doi.org/10.1007/978-3-031-05851-6_6

few centuries, which makes us think about such an evolution.[2] We learn that the United States was for a long time, and until the end of the Nineteenth Century, much less unequal than European countries, and that it did not want to be like them in this respect; or that social mobility is lower there nowadays than it is in Europe. We also learn that patrimonial capitalism would be more developed today in France and Germany than in the United States. We also discover, for those who had not thought of it, that public assets in France, despite their importance in the eyes of investors, are almost nil (public debts being of about the same amount). And so on.

But this book does not simply compile series of statistical data. It defines a problematic, states a thesis, confronts it with the facts, exposes a trend for the Twenty-first Century, and tries to seek solutions. According to the author, without (fiscal) regulation, "capitalism"—if it does not lead to the apocalypse, as Karl Marx is supposed to have thought—nevertheless becomes incompatible with democracy, because the latter is antinomic with plutocracy and can only be based on meritocracy. Before going into detail, it is necessary to begin by stating the central thesis of *Le Capital au XXe siècle.*

6.1 The Fundamental Contradiction of Capitalism According to Piketty

Thomas Piketty's thesis can be summarized very briefly, as he does repeatedly in his book, as follows: if the return on capital is higher than the rate of growth of the economy, this capital snowballs, because "the assets resulting from the past are recapitalized faster than the rhythm of production and wages [...]. The past devours the future."[3]

It should be made clear from the outset that, for this author, capital is assimilated to what would be better called "capital goods," encompassing in fact everything that brings in money, and thus not only capital engaged in production, but also residential real estate (which is approximately equal in volume to productive capital), land, works of art, etc.

[2] This could comfort the supporters of the degrowth thesis (see Chapter 9). But we are also entitled to think that, in the decades to come, growth (not just any growth, of course) is desirable to lift most of humanity out of poverty, which is possible if it is true that world demography is going to stabilize.

[3] Piketty (2013, p. 942).

As a consequence, the "return on capital" considered is by no means limited to corporate profit. We will return to this point later. By deliberate choice, therefore, Piketty takes up the notion of capital found in everyday language, but also and above all the conception retained by mainstream neoclassical economists of a capital seen as any asset, which would be remunerated at its marginal productivity (the price of the last useful unit of a good). Capital is, therefore, "*le patrimoine*," as we say in French, or patrimonial wealth.[4]

As for the growth rate of the economy, Piketty logically breaks it down into population growth and growth of *per capita* production, which is more relevant than growth as such, because it takes into account the evolution of the population—the demographic factor being too often neglected, whereas the changes in its structures, fairly predictable, have crucial consequences for the economy.[5] It will thus appear that the growth rate of the U.S. economy is only higher than that of most European countries because the demography is relatively more dynamic.

Let us return here to the "fundamental law" of capitalism to add a clarification: the value of patrimonial wealth (in relation to national income) is all the higher the stronger the savings rate and the lower the GDP growth rate. And let us see how this "law" would play out. If the rate of return on capital were lower than the GDP growth of the economy (e.g., a return of 1% for a GDP growth of 2%), this would "kill the engine of accumulation,"[6] because capitalists would see their profit constantly diminishing and would no longer invest enough. If the rate of return on capital were equal to the growth rate of the economy, these capitalists would have to invest all their income (which would correspond to savings of 100%, reinvested in full) so that their capital would grow at the same rhythm as the economy, and thus consume nothing, in order to maintain their social position. This could happen if the capital already accumulated represented such a considerable mass (20 to 30 years of national income) that it would no longer yield much.[7] However, what would prevent capital from yielding 2% rather than 5%? Would it be the fact that the marginal productivity of the latter would decrease because of

[4] LONG and HERRERA (2018).

[5] PIKETTY (2013, p. 127).

[6] Ibidem, p. 943.

[7] Ibidem, p. 925.

its overabundance, as Piketty maintains, or would it be the fact that the share of labor would continue to decrease? We will come back to this.

Piketty's conclusion is that the rate of return on capital must remain above the GDP growth rate of the economy if capitalists are to continue to invest without ceasing to consume. Is there, therefore, an optimal volume of accumulated capital, such that the rate of return is sufficient to promote growth? The fundamental problem for Piketty seems to be to reduce the concentration of this capital by dispersing it through progressive taxation on the income it brings in and a tax on wealth, thus widening the field of private investors,[8] which, according to Piketty, is much more effective than a public power that would have destroyed most of the private patrimonial assets, as in the Soviet system. These taxes should not make the after-tax return on capital too low, because this would discourage investors. This would be called "regulating capitalism."

One must now ask whether Piketty's thesis allows one to account for the movements of capital (its rate of return and its rate of accumulation relative to the rate of growth), and whether it is possible to regulate capitalism *post festum*.

6.2 Capitalism and Its History According to Piketty

Piketty warned us in his introduction: "I am not interested in denouncing inequality or capitalism as such [...]. What interests me is to try to contribute, modestly, to determining the most appropriate modes of social organization, institutions and public policies that would allow for the real and effective implementation of a just society."[9] Nevertheless, what kind of capitalism are we talking about? Indeed, let us note that the selected definition of capital as "synonymous with patrimony," or with wealth, can be applied to any patrimonial social system, as well as to the "*Ancien Régime*" society and its privative holding of land in the hands of the aristocracy and the Church, as to other private forms of possession of the means of production. The regulation—by taxation—would apply

[8] There was indeed in the Twentieth Century a certain dispersion, with the constitution of a patrimonial middle class. However, "it only snatched a few crumbs: hardly more than a third of the patrimony in Europe, and barely a quarter in the United States" (Piketty [2013], p. 411).

[9] Piketty (2013, p. 62).

equally to any system of private or even public ownership. That said, it was capitalism itself that implemented such a regulation from the end of the Nineteenth Century.

However, capitalism has undergone a second political regulation, which will also affect the accumulation of capital. This is, as we have seen, a "mechanical" phenomenon that leads to growing inequality. This is the effect of the divergence between the rate of return on capital and the rate of growth of the economy. It would be even greater, says Piketty, if there were not a "force of convergence," namely the diffusion of knowledge and the rise in qualifications, which play in favor of wages.

This is where regulation by the social State comes into play, because for Piketty it is this State that best promotes education. Nonetheless, this force of convergence is not sufficient to compensate for the dynamics of wealth, reinforced by inheritance, contrary to what some rather optimistic economic historians, such as Simon S. Kuznets,[10] have believed. The double political regulation, both fiscal and social, only moderated the pace of accumulation and the worsening of inequalities.

But this does not explain the fall in patrimonial wealth after 1920 (when it represented six to seven times the national income). According to the author, it was major historical accidents that slowed down the phenomenon of accumulation to such an extent, namely: world wars, revolutions, and decolonization destroyed large quantities of capital, private savings were drained by the warring States and eaten away by inflation, and finally, the "new political context of mixed and regulated property in the post-war period" caused the price of assets to fall.[11] The movement then resumed its course, with patrimonial wealth rising again from 1950 onwards to reach five to six years of national income today.

As we can see, the author is careful not to underestimate institutional and political factors—although he did not completely break away from neoclassicism, T. Piketty claims to be a "political economist," against the economism of most economists—but these factors modify the mechanism of accumulation in some way. However, it is this mechanism itself that must be questioned. What is it that makes capital accumulate, that gives it a return that is generally higher than the rate of growth, and that takes the lion's share of value added? This cannot be understood by

[10] Read: KUZNETS (1955, 1971).

[11] PIKETTY (2013, p. 233).

reasoning from the marginal productivity of production factors, because this productivity, if it can be calculated at all, is not independent of the mode of ownership of these factors, and of the resulting balance of power. Doubtless more a philosopher than an economist, a classical thinker like Adam Smith already knew this.[12] We must recognize that the Marxist analysis has a much greater explanatory power, and that it sheds more light on the contemporary history of capitalism.[13] And this is why.

6.3 So What Is Capital and Its Dynamics?

If Thomas Piketty had carefully read Marx's *Capital* (but has he even read it?), he would not have made him say that capital can "accumulate without limit."[14] On the contrary, capital sees its rate of profit decrease even as it accumulates, and this slows down accumulation itself. This is the famous Marxian law of the tendency of the rate of profit to fall, which Piketty does not ignore, but which he believes is based on an error: the rate of profit would actually fall if capital only increased in volume, whereas "it is the permanent growth of productivity and of the population that makes it possible to balance the permanent addition of new units of capital (…) Otherwise capitalists are effectively digging their own grave."[15]

Nevertheless, not only does Marx not ignore the growth of productivity, but it is on it that he bases a large part of his analysis. Before explaining this, however, it is necessary to return to the very concept of capital. If we want to understand the dynamics of the capitalist economy in depth, we must, following Marx, think of capital not as a mass of goods, but as everything that sets labor in motion, in industry as in other economic sectors, and which thereby produces new wealth, i.e., added value.

Examples. The tenant of an accommodation does not create any new use value or any value at all, he or she merely consumes a good, paying a price for the use of this good. The owner of a piece of land can only valorize it if he or she works on it, or if he or she uses the labor of a tenant to extort a rent from him or her, or pays a wage to a farm worker

[12] Diatkine (2021).

[13] Here: Casanova and Herrera (2014), Presentation.

[14] Piketty (2013, p. 27).

[15] Ibidem, p. 362.

to cultivate it (he or she then becomes an agrarian capitalist). The owner of money can only draw an income from it if he or she lends it (through credit or bonds) to an entrepreneur or puts it at the latter's disposal (by subscription to a share). The owner of a work of art does not modify it by any work, he or she only consumes its use, or resells it, according to its rarity, on which he or she can also speculate.

In short, all these goods are not productive capital, and if they bring in money, it is because value has been produced elsewhere; these rents correspond only to the redistribution of surplus value realized in production. This redistribution is hidden, because the equalization of profits between the productive sector and the various non-productive sectors, through the movement of the capital market, lowers the pure corporate profit. As a consequence, and fundamentally, the dynamics of capitalism are located in the productive process (of goods or services), and only there.

A rather similar argument was developed by David Harvey in *Afterthoughts on Piketty's Capital*,[16] but in a circumstantial way. As a matter of fact, Harvey argues that money, land, real estate, and equipment that are not used productively are not capital. If the rate of return on capital that has been practiced is high, it is because some capital is being taken out of circulation and is on strike. Restricting the supply of capital for new investments (a phenomenon that we are currently observing) ensures a high level of return on this capital that is in circulation. This would be the creation of an "artificial scarcity," which would raise the rate of profit, as the capitalist would do by saving constant capital. However, the fundamental process here is the displacement of capital into the unproductive sector, which is simply the work of the market in capital goods.

Nonetheless, and to return to our own critical study of Piketty, it is precisely because technical progress increases the productivity of labor in the strict sense (i.e., for the same duration and intensity of labor) that capital logically sees its profit decrease; not because it employs more machines and a corresponding number of additional workers, but because it decreases the labor necessary for production (in Marxian terms, constant capital increases with respect to variable capital) and, consequently, decreases the new value produced, and therefore also—if the wages remain constant—the share of the profit. Moreover, competition

[16] See Harvey's *Afterthoughts on Piketty's Capital* (May 17, 2014): http://davidharvey.org/2014/05/afterthoughts-pikettys-capital/.

between capitalists accelerates this substitution of capital for labor. The great law of capitalist accumulation does not mean that capital tends to grow infinitely, as Piketty's interpretation of Marx claims, but that this capital is concentrated in fewer and fewer hands. If it seems to accumulate globally, it is because it seizes new sectors belonging to other modes of production (notably in peasant agriculture or in crafts) or that it exploits new sectors, hitherto neglected.

This, then, is more precisely the fundamental "mechanism" of the capitalist economy proper, according to Marx. This mechanism is doubly hidden. On the one hand, because capital, as if "by magic," seems to generate its own income—which is what neoclassicism maintains without being able to demonstrate it, or even to measure capital (Chapter 2)—whereas it draws its energy from labor. And, on the other hand, because the surplus, which Marx calls surplus value, is redistributed by the market among all capital goods, whether or not they produce real wealth. It is because it is hidden that Marx opposes his "esoteric" economy to the "exoteric" or vulgar economics.

Nonetheless, this mechanism, which should lead to a tendency for the rate of profit to fall, does not seem to be verified in practice, since the "rate of return on capital," to use Piketty's words—and neglecting here the confusion he introduces between capital and capital goods or patrimony—would not, according to him, decrease over a long period. This is where we must find the whole of the Marxian analysis, which is not limited to this mechanism, the latter functioning "like" a law of nature. And we shall see that it allows us to explain the contemporary history of capitalism much better than Piketty does: the great air gap of capital during most of the Twentieth Century and its strong comeback or return in force since the 1970s and 1980s.

6.4 Understanding the Strong Comeback of Capital

Economic growth has always been weak, says Piketty, based on the data collected, "apart from exceptional periods and catching-up phenomena."[17] After the so-called "*Trente Glorieuses*" (or the "Glorious Thirty" period, stretching from 1945 to 1974 approximately), it returned

[17] Piketty (2013, p. 125).

to its normal rhythm. Nevertheless, it is not very convincing that the 5% GDP growth rate of this period can be explained solely by post-World War II reconstruction and the catching up of the United States by the European countries. It was also a period of dynamic demographics and a period in which the balance of power was in favor of labor for reasons linked to the historical situation—something that Piketty does not deny in fact.

What about the rate of return on capital, which should not be confused with the rate of profit in the productive sectors, but which can provide an approximation of its evolution? It was high in France and Great Britain (the two cases detailed in the study) around 1950, before declining sharply, and then rising again a little after the year 1980, and falling again twenty years later.[18] However, as growth has weakened, wealth is soaring again despite this average return.

So what happened? The growth rate is indeed high during the "Glorious Thirty" period because labor productivity is high: it puts a lot of capital into motion. The Marxist analysis would have it that the rate of profit decreases, precisely because the productivity of labor is high: it takes less labor to put the same quantity of capital into motion, which reduces the source of surplus value.

How then can we explain that the rate of profit is high during this period, which seems to invalidate the law of the tendency of the rate of profit to fall? By the fact that "the cause that thwarts the law" invoked by Marx intervenes: capital tends to decrease in value, not only because it experiences material wear and tear and obsolescence (rapid if technical progress accelerates), but also because high productivity, especially in the equipment goods sector, reduces the quantity of capital necessary for production. This is what Marx calls "economizing constant capital." To this must be added the high intensity of labor linked to Taylorism and Fordism, which, contrary to productivity, increases the quantity of labor used, and consequently the profit—if the wage does not follow.

Why did the GDP growth rate and the rate of profit fall from the mid-1970s onwards? Because of two basic movements. The first one was the crisis of the Taylorist-Fordist model, which has been too often forgotten today: workers were increasingly unhappy with commanded work or work in pieces, and were less motivated by the search for an improvement in a

[18] Ibidem, p. 318.

standard of living, which was higher. This led to a fall in their productivity, which "participative management" tried to rise, without much success. The second movement is that technical progress has slowed down. As a result, the share of labor in the value added decreases along with its productivity, so that the source of profit is reduced. "The cause counteracting the law"—that is, economizing capital—no longer acts with the same intensity.

Finally, how is it that the rate of profit rises sharply from the first third of the 1980s, before falling slightly, and then stabilizing? Here again, a Marxist analysis appears relevant, and there is nothing "mechanical" about it. It is very consciously that capitalists engage in a series of policies to increase the quantity of work supplied: the duration of work starts to increase again, as does its intensity, as many indicators show. They are also making strong capital savings through just-in-time (Kanban-type, for example) and total quality methods. They seek to combat passive resistance from workers through "participative management."

Nonetheless, all this only works if wages are contained; it is already wage austerity. And the capitalists achieve this all the more easily when structural unemployment is high—another "cause" invoked by Marx to counteract the fall in the rate of profit: "relative overpopulation," which weighs on the wages of those who have a job. To impose this wage austerity, they still need the help of the State. Neoliberal policies were then put in place: making the labor market more flexible against the various existing regulations perceived as so many rigidities to be eliminated, reducing the "cost of labor" by reducing wages, including social security contributions which are in fact indirect salary (reimbursement of medical expenses, payment of unemployment benefits, etc.) or deferred salary (retirement pensions).[19]

These are the policies that are being pursued today and with even greater vigor. For globalization has weighed on corporate profits, so that pressure on wages has had to be re-emphasized through relocations and/or the threat of them. For, also, the hypertrophy of the financial sector, driven by the rise of the credit system and the overaccumulation of fictitious capital,[20] has amputated the real economy of a share of its profits. A hypertrophy that can be explained in part by the decline in

[19] Read: ANDRÉANI (1999).

[20] See: HERRERA (2015a, b).

demand from the working classes following wage deflation, a decline that could only be contained by an unrestrained expansion of credit.

The Marxist analysis provides, as can be seen from this brief synthesis, a more refined explanation of the movements of GDP growth and the return on capital. It directly reintroduces the class struggle into these movements insofar as managerial policies are anything but "mechanical" phenomena. It also reintroduces it indirectly, because the ruling class has had to storm the State and take control of it in order to weaken the institutions of the Welfare State and the means of resistance of wage earners.

This neoliberal offensive is not about to stop, because globalization is still unchecked (especially in a European Union open to all winds), and the financial sector remains largely unregulated. However, there are other reasons as well. Labor productivity remains lower than in the era of the "Glorious Thirty," which slows down growth, and which means that capital accumulates without yielding as much. Many economists wonder about the mystery of this decline in productivity, aware that the revolution in new information and communication technologies (NICTs) has not had as beneficial an impact on GDP growth rate as previous technological revolutions. Even if one admits that these new technologies will take a long time to produce their positive effects, it is likely that, for the next few years, they will not greatly increase labor productivity. Finally, it is the mode of growth itself that is in crisis, because of the multiplicity of its negative externalities. And the reconversion of the growth mode, if there is the political will to carry it out, will require considerable amounts of capital, which will tend to drive the rate of profit down, and will thus lead to increasingly aggressive policies against labor.[21]

6.5 The Difficulty and Limits of a "Tax Revolution"

The success of T. Piketty's book is due, in particular, to the relentless highlighting of the rise in inequality.[22] This is not surprising for Marxist economists: the long trend of capitalism—as Marx showed in a way that

[21] Observatoire international de la Crise (2019).

[22] Also read: Piketty (1995, 2003), Piketty and Saez (2003), Piketty and Qian (2011), Piketty and Zucman (2014), Piketty et al. (2017).

no one can deny anymore[23]—is, on the one hand, the centralization of capital (to the detriment of other systems of production) and, on the other hand, its concentration (in fewer and fewer hands). Of course, pre-capitalist societies also had impressive inequalities, but with means of coercion that were much more extra-economic (i.e., political).

Similarly, it appears that today's inequalities are proportionally higher than in the "*Belle Époque*" (a period marked by technological, economic, and social progress, in Western Europe, and going from the end of the Nineteenth Century to the eve of World War I in 1914), but the current level of inequality is unprecedented, because it is now global in scale. Therefore, 4.5 million people own about 20% of the world's wealth. And even more dramatically, the wealth of the world's 85 richest billionaires equals that of half of humanity—the approximately 3.5 billion poorer people.

Addressing this through taxation, however, is an extremely difficult path, given the tax competition that exists between different countries, including with and through tax havens. The Organisation for Economic Co-operation and Development (OECD) is aware of this and is urging its members to agree to practice the automatic exchange of information on individuals' financial accounts in order to counter tax evasion. Assuming that recalcitrant countries can be brought to heel by various means of retaliation, this would not prevent States from tax dumping and transnational corporations from performing tax optimization, which would so allow the wealthiest to continue to enrich themselves—legally. And even if tax optimization were itself curbed, the countries with the lowest taxes would continue to enrich their own owners.

Piketty knows all this very well and would like to see a global wealth tax; but he has to fall back on its generalization at the regional level and especially at the European level. As this tax competition is written into the European treaties, then it would be necessary to review them—and to obtain the agreement of the (currently) 27 countries that make up the Union. Would it be possible to harmonize the taxation of capital (on income and patrimonial wealth) at least at the level of the euro zone? The governments of this zone would first have to agree on this. Unless a parliament of the euro zone is set up, where a majority of deputies would adopt this harmonization, which is Piketty's proposal. This would be a

[23] Herrera (2018).

"small revolution," but it would not put an end to the tax dumping practiced by countries outside the euro zone and in the rest of the world. In fact, the only way to combat it would be to return to a kind of protectionism, by taxing imports from such competitors. But, by the same way, this would also undermine one of the foundations of the current European Union…[24]

It is above all the taxation of high incomes and wealth that would meet with fierce resistance from their holders, who believe that high inequalities are conducive to development and that the happiness they enjoy cannot be touched.[25] Besides, the most senior executives of transnational corporations convince themselves and try to make people believe that they deserve their high remuneration and their fortune by the exceptionality of their talents, which would make them the true creators of wealth. This claim is not only unverifiable (Piketty himself acknowledges that it would be impossible to determine their "marginal productivity," because they are in exceptional situations within companies), but also unfounded.

In reality, the only merit that can be attributed to these "entrepreneurs" who have been so "successful" is that they have taken on managerial responsibilities, generally with borrowed money, and that they have had a flair for discovering market opportunities a little before others. For real innovators very often remain in the shadows. It was not Bill Gates who discovered computing… However, it will be rather difficult to make these very rich people admit that they are not so "great" and even to the less rich that they do not quite deserve their remuneration. The income tax, which rose to confiscatory levels in the United States during the presidency of Franklin D. Roosevelt (in an exceptional situation of extremely serious crisis and then of world war), would have the advantage, Piketty assures us, that it would discourage top executives from being granted exorbitant salaries, since the latter would be greatly eroded. But this is doubtful: it is also a matter of prestige for them.

As for the big holders of capital—that is, the so-called "investors"—they can always boast that they have made the right investments, but the

[24] Here: Herrera (2022).

[25] It is surprising that Piketty does not refer to an important book, supported by solid statistics: *Pourquoi l'égalité est meilleure pour tous* (why equality is better for everyone) by Wilkinson and Picket (2013). Equality for everyone and all, therefore, including the richest, especially in terms of physical and mental health….

credit for this usually goes to specialized agents whom they pay (handsomely) to do so. They still believe they have the legitimate right to collect their rents. Another measure to reduce wealth inequality would be a heavy tax on inheritance, which would limit the concentration of patrimonial wealth. Nevertheless, this measure meets with even greater resistance than the income tax, because it touches on the desire to perpetuate oneself through one's children. This opposition to tax redistribution is mitigated in egalitarian societies, such as those of Scandinavia, and particularly in Denmark, where high tax rates are accepted as a counterpart to a very protective social model, especially since the deduction is made at source through "withholding tax."

In reality, in tax matters, the only really effective way to significantly reduce inequality is to act on the primary (pre-tax) distribution of income. Reducing earnings in the form of salaries and other benefits (such as stock options, "golden pensions," bonuses on arrival) would very probably not break the motivation of real entrepreneurs, because what drives them is first of all the taste for action and power. To which we must add that there is no real "market" for business leaders—we are dealing rather with a system of co-optations—a market which would cause their remuneration to fall (Marx would have thought that they would be paid in this case according to the value of their labor power). Nevertheless, fixing ceilings for remuneration, as has been done for the managers of public enterprises in particular, or instituting a salary scale, as is the case in the civil service, or any other method, turns out to be impossible in a capitalist market economy where private property dominates. In the same way, one can want to "regulate" high finance as much as one wants, but one cannot, in a "neoliberal" economy, limit before tax the income of investors (dividends, interests, capital gains, etc.). Indeed, this would require a profound change in the economic system.

6.6 Democracy Is Not Meritocracy…

Changing the economic system. Piketty only alludes to this very briefly at the end of his book, when he speaks of "new forms of shared ownership, intermediate between public and private property, which is one of the great challenges of the future."[26] This can mean many things: shareholder ownership with powers conceded to "others," new forms of public ownership, cooperatives, and so on. And that is precisely the root of the matter...

This leads us to the issue of democracy, again. One of the problems is here that of "meritocracy"—which etymologically means the government by the best. Meritocracy as a principle of social justice is questionable. Apart from the fact that it is impossible to distinguish between involuntary talent and effort, it is based on competition between individuals, where the success of some is also the failure of others. But here the problem posed is political: in order to ensure the effectiveness of public action, should it be entrusted to the competent? Would not meritocracy only be a new form of aristocracy? This, whereas the ideal of democracy, its *omega* point, is the power of all citizens, which does not only consist in being represented and directed by the most capable and competent[27] or presumed to be so.

First of all, it would be necessary that these most capable and competent can easily emerge from the people. However, as we know, these elites tend to transmit their cultural and relational inheritance to each other, that is, to "reproduce themselves," so that equality of opportunity, even in a world where material inheritance would have disappeared or would have been reduced to little by heavy inheritance taxes, is impossible to achieve, whatever the efforts of the public educational system. Here, we must not forget social endogamy either. All this means that the "competent elites" tend to live in a closed circle and cut themselves off from the concerns and needs of the people. This is especially noticeable today in the countries of the North, where the globalized elites, living in large metropolises, with an entourage of service workers and domestic staff, have lost contact with the workers, employees, farmers, and even small entrepreneurs relegated to the periphery, that of small and medium-sized towns and villages in the countryside.[28] If the elites no longer owed their status to the size of their financial wealth, this would not profoundly alter this social divide. If executives were no longer the "super-cadres" of today's society that Piketty

[26] PIKETTY (2013, p. 945).

[27] Also see: BIDET (2022).

[28] Cf. the study by GUILLUY (2014).

talks about, they would still be jealous of their interests and centered on themselves.

Then, it is not enough to be able to regularly elect "good representatives" (or even to be able to revoke bad ones) who would become, through the functioning of the political parties, professionals in politics. It would also be necessary for the voters themselves to have sufficient background and to be sufficiently well-informed to designate them with full knowledge of the facts and to judge their actions adequately. Ideally, this should be the role of the educational system and news media. However, it is the deep development of *economic* democracy that would help most powerfully.

Finally, it remains that it is up to each individual to appreciate the effects of political choices on his or her concrete life. One more time, we find the question of democracy, and even here of *direct* democracy. It is not obvious that the drawing of lots for officials, as practiced by the ancient Greeks, is the solution, because of the technical skills that are required. On the contrary, more referendum procedures, under certain conditions, and on the most important subjects for the collective future of citizens, would surely prove necessary. And, on a daily basis, the processes of *participatory* democracy are the means for citizens to always have their say. Again, we are therefore a long way off the mark with meritocratic democracy.

To conclude, T. Piketty's book, which will become a reference for the richness of its data, confirms in fact what we already knew, but without as much precision; in other words, that capitalism produces cumulative inequalities, and that they end up being completely antinomic with a real functioning of democracy. Its empirical value seems indisputable to us, but its explanatory value is very limited.

One issue is how the growth rate of the economy interacts with the rate of return on capital. The growth rate depends, among other things, on population growth, as well as labor productivity. But, on the one hand, labor productivity only affects growth in the productive sector, in the real economy, and, on the other hand, the rise in productivity tends to reduce the return on capital: this is what we wanted to point out by following Marx. Then, in order to raise it, it will be necessary not only to save capital, but also, for the capitalists, thanks to the power conferred on them by their ownership, to take resolute action to both increase the quantity of work supplied and to slow down wages. Piketty wanted to do a political economy, but his economics is basically not very political, in a broad sense of the term.

Another question is what links the savings rate to the rate of return on capital, without simply saying that the former determines the latter. However, the right level of return on capital is the one that favors investment, but, on the one hand, the rich consume a significant part of their income in lavish spending instead of investing, and, on the other hand, at the same time, they save much more than the others, that is to say, than the middle classes and, even more so, the working classes, which limits consumption, and therefore growth. Here again, Piketty's economics is not political enough. A highly unequal society is not conducive to rapid growth—good or bad, that is another question...

Variations in the GDP growth rate of the economy depend on technological factors and political events, of course, but also on the policies carried out and the nature of the political system itself. The strong growth of the "*Trente Glorieuses*" period was linked to a process of catching up, but also to a deliberate and interventionist State policy, all the more effective and efficient because the State had the levers of control in its hands. The same can probably be said of China today: if its GDP growth rate is so high, higher than that of other emerging countries, and even higher than that of the Northern countries, it is because the State is "pulling out all the stops."[29] Thus, Thomas Piketty's economics is decidedly not very political.

Consequently, the fiscal policy he advocates not only runs the risk of coming up against strong political blockages, but also leaves unchanged the basis of a system—let us talk very frankly: the capitalist system—that produces, through the power of domination conferred by private ownership of capital, inequalities that constantly restrain economic growth (and, therefore, the added value to be shared), that even produces negative growth—if one deducts all the costs of social and environmental destruction, as we shall see in Chapter 9—and that, finally, distorts democracy in the service of the powerful.

[29] On the Chinese economy and society, read: ANDRÉANI et al. (2021). Also, in connection with Piketty's analysis: HERRERA and LONG (2017, 2018, 2021) and LONG and HERRERA (2018, 2021, 2022).

References

Andréani T. (1999), "Une Explication marxiste. Quelques éléments d'interprétation de la crise des économies capitalistes développées," Tony Andréani's personal blog.

Andréani T. and R. Herrera (2015a), "Piketty: Réguler le capitalisme par la fiscalité ?," *La Pensée*, n° 381, p. 105–117, Paris.

——— (2015b), "Which Economic Model for China?," *International Critical Thought—A Journal of the China's Academy of Social Sciences*, vol. 5, n° 1, p. 105–117, 111–125, Beijing.

Andréani T., R. Herrera and Z. Long (2021), "Is China Transforming the World?," *Monthly Review*, vol. 73, n° 3, p. 21–30, New York.

Bidet J. (2022), *L'écologie politique du commun du peuple*, Fontainebleau: *Éditions du Croquant*.

Casanova A. and R. Herrera (eds.) (2014), *Penser les crises*, Paris: Le Temps des Cerises.

Diatkine D. (2021), *Adam Smith, the Discovery of Capitalism and of Its Limits*, London: Palgrave Macmillan.

Guilluy C. (2014), *La France périphérique - Comment on a sacrifié les classes populaires*, Paris: Éditions Flammarion.

Herrera R. (2015a), *La Maladie dégénérative de l'économie: le "néoclassicisme"*, Paris: Éditions Delga.

——— (2015b), "Defense and Security (Economics of)," *International Encyclopedia of Social and Behavioral Sciences*, 2nd ed., Amsterdam and London: Elsevier.

——— (2018), "La colonisation vue par Marx et Engels: évolutions (et limites) d'une réflexion commune," *in Le Colonialisme - Textes de Marx et Engels*, p. 3–73, Paris: Éditions Critiques.

——— (2022), *La Monnaie: du pouvoir de la finance à la souveraineté des peuples*, Geneva: Éditions du Centre Europe - Tiers Monde (CETIM).

Herrera R. and Z. Long (2017), "Las Leyes del Capital en el Siglo XXI de Piketty en China," *Economía y Desarrollo*, año XLVIII, vol. 158, n° 2, p. 6–21, Havana.

——— (2018), "The Enigma of China's Economic Growth," *Monthly Review*, vol. 70, n° 7, p. 52–62, New York.

——— (2021), *Dynamique de l'économie chinoise: croissance, cycles et crises de 1949 à nos jours*, Paris: Éditions Critiques.

Kuznets S.S. (1955), "Economic Growth and Income Inequality," *American Economic Review*, vol. 45, n° 1, p. 1–28.

——— (1971), *Economic Growth of Nations: Total Output and Production Structure*, Cambridge (MA): Harvard University Press.

LONG Z. and R. HERRERA (2018), "The Laws of Capital in the Twenty-First Century in China. Piketty in Beijing," *China Economic Review*, online on March 11, Columbus (OH).

——— (2021), "'21世纪资本论'在中国:皮凯蒂的资本定律在中国成立吗?," *政治经济学报* (*zhèngzhì jīngjì xuébào, Tsinghua University Review of Political Economics*), vol. 21, n° 4, p. 94–116, Beijing.

——— (2022), *Dynamics of China's Economy: Growth, Cycles and Crises from 1949 to the Present Day*, Amsterdam and Chicago: Brill and Haymarket, to be published.

PIKETTY T. (1995), "On the Long-Run Evolution of Inheritance: France 1820–2050," *Quarterly Journal of Economics*, vol. CXXVI, n° 3, p. 1071–1131.

——— (2003), "Income Inequality in France, 1901–1998," *Journal of Political Economy*, vol. 111, n° 5, p. 1004–1042.

——— (2013), *Le Capital au XX*^{e} *siècle*, Paris: Éditions du Seuil.

PIKETTY T. and N. QIAN (2011), "Income Inequality and Progressive Income Taxation in China and India, 1986–2015," *in* A.B. Atkinson and T. Piketty (eds.), *Top Incomes: A Global Perspective*, p. 40–75, New York: Oxford University Press.

PIKETTY T. and E. SAEZ (2003), "Income Inequality in the United States, 1913–1998," *Quarterly Journal of Economics*, vol. 118, n° 1, p. 1–39.

PIKETTY T. and G. ZUCMAN (2014), "Capital Is Back: Wealth-Income Ratios in Rich Countries 1700–2010," *Quarterly Journal of Economics*, vol. 129, n° 3, p. 1255–1310.

PIKETTY T., Y. LI and G. ZUCMAN (2017), "Capital Accumulation, Private Property and Rising Inequality in China, 1978–2015," *National Bureau of Economic Research (NBER) Working Paper*, n° 23368, Cambridge (MA).

OBSERVATOIRE INTERNATIONAL DE LA CRISE (2019), *Le Capitalisme face à son déclin*, Paris: Éditions Critiques.

WILKINSON R. and K. PICKET (2013), *Pourquoi l'égalité est meilleure pour tous*, Paris: Éditions Les Petits Matins.

PART III

Toward a Marxist Analysis of Contemporary Capitalism

CHAPTER 7

From the Domination of High Finance to the Systemic Crisis of Capital: A Marxist Interpretation

We could certainly have supplemented the critical arguments presented above to the readers with an evolutionary analysis of the theoretical *corpus* that the orthodoxies or mainstreams—first classical, then marginalist-neoclassical, after that Keynesian-neoclassical, and finally, at present, neoclassical-neoliberal—have devoted to international trade and monetary relations. This body of work represents a considerable volume of literature, ranging from the seemingly irrefutable logic of Ricardian comparative advantage to the various recent, more sophisticated modelizations of imperfect competition, or to the convoluted nuances of the non-formalized babble that neoclassicism knows how to make room for when it wants to consolidate its ideological positions.

We would then have meandered between distrust of State intervention, denunciation of the dangers of protectionism, and rejection of any voluntary, interventionist development strategy; but, from start to finish, we would have remained as close as possible to the dotted lines drawn along the same ideological-political line: that of openness to free trade, to floating capital in search of profitable investments, to foreign direct or portfolio investments, and finally to a globalization that is beneficial—with slight nuances—to all the "partners" of the exchanges.

R. Herrera, *Confronting Mainstream Economics for Overcoming Capitalism*, Marx, Engels, and Marxisms,
https://doi.org/10.1007/978-3-031-05851-6_7

Instead, we would like to end by drawing attention to an essential problem, if not the essential problem: the crisis. What about the theoretical and political interpretations of the current crisis, within neoclassicism, but also, and finally, outside of it? In this Chapter , we shall examine successively, after having noted the staggering theoretical vacuum produced by the mainstream on this subject: the domination of finance, from its controversial origins in the United States, then outside of it, to the present era of neoliberalism; the different aspects of the recent entry into systemic crisis of capital, in its causes as well as in its effects; and the need to move from the false orthodox anti-crisis policies presently being implemented to real solutions to be defined in terms of possible counterpowers and controls of this predatory high finance.[1]

7.1 The Absence (and Impossibility) of a Neoclassical Theory of the Crisis

The fact is—quite incredible, but true—that, today, within neoclassicism, there is no, or very little, coherent theoretical analysis of the crisis. And this at the very moment of the emergence of the most serious capitalist crisis since the Great Depression of the 1930s. Worse still: in the vast majority of the works of neoclassicism, the crisis *does not exist*—the crisis *cannot exist*—in the element of theory. Besides, it is revealing to observe that most orthodox economic encyclopedias, at the research top level, do not have, contrary to any introductory high school textbook or basic dictionary intended for the general public, a single chapter relating to the capitalist crisis or crises as such—nor even an index entry on the subject—while references to the economics of charity, sports, auctions, marriage, drugs, cinema, monarchy, parking, chaos, religions, postage stamp pricing, sex, second-hand cars, superheroes, happiness, crime, arrogating, the market of pollution rights, housing (including with Scarf algorithm!), etc., abound in these voluminous works.[2]

[1] This chapter is based on various articles: Herrera (2012, 2013a, 2014). Its main conclusions are similar to those of two press articles of the same author, published in *L'Humanité* (n° 21,354, p. 12, February 7-8-9, 2014) and in the monthly journal *Afrique Asie* (n° 102, p. 14–15, May 2014).

[2] To take another example, concerning France, in the original version of the *Dictionnaire d'analyse économique*—one of the most solid and useful books in the French language for systematizing the critique of neoclassicism—his author, Bernard Guerrien,

The theme of the crisis or crises is taboo, repressed, and hidden. Even that of pre-capitalist crises—all the more so as the theorists of neoclassicism are too busy to waste their time trying to find out why "market" and "capitalism" are not synonymous. Or that of "mixed" crises, in the midst of which the old order and the modern one are intertwined—as, very late in the Nineteenth Century, in the United States, still partially slaveholding, or in Russia, not yet rid of serfdom.[3] It must, therefore, be recognized that the "scientific ideology" of capitalism does not take the crisis as its object of study, and is not at all capable of explaining in depth the crisis of actually existing capitalism.

Some neoclassical theorists, aware of this aberration, have nevertheless the "extravagance" to take an interest—if not in the subject of the crisis(es) in itself, at least—in the possible reversals of the conjuncture, fluctuations, or cycles. But when they do so, they usually choose to build mathematical models in which money is absent and the behavior of the economy[4] is reduced to the wanderings of Robinson, whose first names can also be Adam, in a "game of life,"[5] or Bob, once he is established in life.[6]

These assumptions, such as that of rational expectations—according to which the forecasts of the agent, who is supposed to know all the characteristics of the economic structure, are "perfect" —are also those of real business cycles (RBC). Robinson-Adam-Bob Crusoe, in his delirium and repeated frenzies, will take himself in turn to be a businessman or a cleaning man, just as others may think they are Napoleon Bonaparte or ceiling painters. All this, of course, without a dollar in his pocket, since in this world money does not exist! Such a "theory," if we dare call it that, symptomatically rewarded in recent years by several Nobel prizes

did not even need to devote a single article to it (GUERRIEN [1996a])—nor in the numerous books he wrote for the student public (e.g., GUERRIEN [1989, 1996b]). At the other end of the spectrum, and in a completely different genre (low-end product), Gérard Horny, author of *La Bourse pour les nuls* (The Stock Market for Dummies), "fortunately" devotes three and a half pages (out of 392) to it, before attempting for the umpteenth time to convince us to invest even a small part of our savings in securities (HORNY [2012])...

[3] CASANOVA and HERRERA (2014), Presentation.

[4] On money: HERRERA (2022), Introduction.

[5] Here: BINMORE (2005).

[6] See: AUMANN (1996).

(examples: the awards given to Finn Erling Kydland and Edward Christian Prescott in 2004),[7] is supposed to integrate short-term fluctuations into a framework of Walrasian analysis and to provide an explanation of cyclical phenomena on the basis of "real shocks"... but concluding that markets are spontaneously self-regulating and that economic policy is definitively useless!

In the long run, the theory of endogenous growth does not do much better—even if the role of the State is treated more intelligently. The creativity of neoclassicism was pushed by the talent of Marco Pagano to the point of "enriching" the AK model (that we discussed in Chapter 2) by endowing it with a "qualitative" parameter corresponding to the efficiency of the financial system, which is supposed to have a positive influence on the rate of growth of the economy. M. Pagano posits that output (Y) is proportional to a stock of reproducible factors, called as "capital" (K), and incremented by investment (I) equal to a constant fraction of savings (S) effectively allocated by the financial system. If: $Y = AK$, $\Delta K = I$, $I = \theta\ S$ and $S = sY$, then the long-term growth rate g is written: $g = \theta\ sA$. Growth would thus, according to him, be a function of the financial system's efficiency (noted θ); and this directly because the cost of intermediation increases with the degree of inefficiency of financial institutions and the imperfection of competition, and indirectly, because the productivity of investments depends on the quality of the projects selected.[8]

As we can see, human knowledge has made a quantum leap forward thanks to this discovery by the ingenious Mr. Pagano. Adding a θ, it was necessary to think about it! A miraculous θ to give us all access to eternal growth, by the divine intervention of high finance! The science of neoclassicism, it is that witchcraft! Famed novelist J.K. Rowling's heroes, starting with Harry Potter and his fellow wizards, could not do any better.

Other neoclassical economists, of the same sect as Pagano,[9] also reducing mathematics to the role of a screen to hide the indigence of a reasoning whose ideological content is obvious, affirm that institutions "interfere" with the growth process and lead to the appearance of "multiple equilibria"—one "low" in the form of a "poverty trap" associating

[7] Kydland and Prescott (1977, 1982).

[8] Pagano (1993).

[9] Also: Levine (2005).

underdeveloped financial institutions with weak growth, and the other "high," characterizing "advanced economies" in which the beneficial action of financial markets and the guarantee provided for the sustainability of investments and the serenity of investors reinforce each other, and ultimately contribute to alleged growth performance. These formalized entertainments of charlatans of "modernity" demonstrate nothing more than an idolatrous panegyric of the current form of domination of finance capital.

For, let us repeat, neither in theory—which means, for neoclassicism, modeling, and only this—nor in empirics—for the same mainstream, equivalent to econometrics—is the theme of the crisis treated head-on. Very few neoclassical academic works venture to tackle it, even at its "neo-Keynesian" (internal) borders. Let us insist, once again, on the fact that, for current orthodoxy, money is not integrated into the economic circuit, and still less into a dynamic of capital reproduction. This means that, for it, value simply equals price, and profit rate equals interest rate. In microeconomics, there is no money in the general equilibrium *à la* Arrow-Debreu. In macroeconomics, money is "a veil"; it is "neutral," "transparent," so that equilibrium becomes automatic; and crisis is "forbidden." Jean-Baptiste Say made emulators right up to the beginning of the Twenty-first Century (Appendix A)!

Nevertheless, since the crisis is a fact that is very difficult to deny in practice, those among the followers of neoclassicism who speak of it almost always do so by evoking phenomena which are "external" to the markets, and more precisely factors that disrupt the functioning of the automatic correction mechanisms of the price system. Such are the cases of the "inappropriate intervention" of the State; of accidental computer bugs (stock market transaction orders being pre-programmed on computers whose reaction time is measured in nanoseconds); of morally and/or legally reprehensible behaviors of "bad individuals," sometimes corrupt, incompetent or imprudent, but always isolated, from Ponzi frauds *à la* Bernard Madoff to the holes dug on the over-the-counter markets by traders of the type of Jerôme Kerviel; not to mention the well-known "rigidity" and "archaism" of the workers unions' claims—trade unions whose existence cannot be denied, unlike that of a class struggle that is only evoked in the hallucinations of a few survivors of the Marxist dinosaurs' extinction...

On the contrary, neoclassicism does not regard the logic of immediate maximum profit and the super-concentration of private property as problems in themselves. And the orthodox vision of the State remains that of an entity separate from the economic sphere and not dominated by the interests of capital.[10] But basically, since 2007–2008, very little has really changed in the mentality of mainstream economists: the old textbooks on finance are slightly altered to take into account the demands of its "whims,"[11] and the conclusions of the new ones are shamelessly completed by recalling the fundamental importance of the "rational expectations revolution"[12]... It is thus appropriate to move away from such interpretations, which turn their backs on reality and are ascientific. For, as we shall see, crises are an integral part of the contradictory dynamics of the expanded reproduction of capital.

7.2 At the Origins of High Finance: From the "Robber Barons"...

The origins of U.S. high finance are controversial, to say the least. In his famous book *A People's History of the United States*—which is said to be a "totally false" version of history or bordering on "Manicheanism"[13]—the critical intellectual Howard Zinn—who is claimed to be "not a real historian, but merely a Marxist propagandist"—has unabashedly described the actions of its "American notable financiers," especially those he calls the "robber barons," i.e., "who control the people with the people's money."[14] The same ones that the mainstream media and so many academic textbooks present as philanthropists...[15]

Let us read instead what he writes about John Pierpont Morgan (1837, Hartford CT.—1913, Rome). H. Zinn explains that, during the Civil War, J.P. Morgan bought from a military arsenal five thousand rifles at 3.5 dollars each, which he sold to a general at 22 dollars each—these defective rifles would have torn off the thumb of any soldier who used them. He adds that the fact was reported to U.S. Congress, but also that

[10] Herrera (2003a).

[11] For example: Bourguinat (1999).

[12] Mishkin (2010).

[13] Here: http://fr.wikipedia.org/wiki/Howard_Zinn.

[14] Zinn (1980).

[15] This is obviously the case for the articles devoted to major bankers, businessmen, billionaires by the famous "free encyclopedia" Wikipedia...

a federal judge objected that the deal was based on a legally valid contract. Besides, Morgan had escaped service during the war by paying himself a substitute for barely 300 dollars. John Davison Rockefeller (1839, Richford NY.—1937, Ormond Beach FL.), Andrew Carnegie (1835, Dunfermline, Scotland - 1919, Lenox MA.), Philip Danforth Armour (1832, Stockbridge NY.—1901, Chicago IL.), Jason Jay Gould (1836, Roxbury NY.—1892, New York NY.), and James Ross Mellon (1846, Pittsburgh PA.—1934, Pittsburgh PA.) did the same.[16]

Zinn goes on to say that the U.S. government entrusted the bank Drexel, Morgan & Co. with the task of issuing 260 million dollars in Treasury bills—even if it could have done this itself, but it apparently preferred to pay the bankers 5 million dollars in commissions—and that in 1895, the government's gold reserve was at a low ebb, while 26 New York banks had nearly 129 million dollars in gold in their vaults. A pool of bankers led by J.P. Morgan & Co. offered the government gold in exchange for Treasury bills and immediately after the bankers sold these bonds at a higher price, pocketing a capital gain of 18 million dollars.[17] And also this: in 1900, Andrew Carnegie, at a dinner, agreed to sell his steel mills to J.P. Morgan; he scribbled the price on a piece of paper: 492 million dollars. As for John D. Rockefeller, the founder of the Rockefeller empire, after buying his first oil refinery and creating the Standard Oil Company of Ohio in 1870, Zinn says that he got rid of the competition, in his own way. In Buffalo, a competing refinery was destroyed in an explosion organized by Standard Oil officials. And soon, the Rockefeller fortune reached two billion dollars.[18]

At the time when the empires of these magnates and other moguls of high finance were born, it was already known that the collusion between public and private business, completing the use of often illegitimate and sometimes illegal methods, had to somewhat nuance the traditional thesis of an opposition between law and force, making people believe in the neutrality of a State which, situated above the conflicts of society, would have embodied universal political rationality—whereas in reality, it subordinates fictitiously "free and equal" citizens to the interests of those who

[16] ZINN (1980, p. 296).

[17] *Ibidem*, p. 297.

[18] *Ibidem*, p. 298.

have finally taken possession of it, in the very logic of the generalization of private property of the means of production.[19]

This "acquisition" of the State by the most powerful owners of capital, that is to say, the "elites" of high finance, is carried out essentially through economic mechanisms, and in particular the public debt, which has fallen into the hands of financial oligopolies. This high finance was able to organize itself into a dominant power over society in the form of the modern State, after the fusion of its activities of banking and industry. The State, whose repressive character was accentuated in the face of multiple popular rebellions, and which also managed money by ensuring its reproduction as a general equivalent in circulation, was placed under the tight control of an aristocracy of rentiers speculating on government's convertible securities. And "real" historians will be able to tell beautiful stories in which J.P. Morgan came to the rescue of the municipality of New York, the government of the United States and the pool of great bankers to save them all, and several times, from bankruptcy…[20]

It was this control of State financing that played, at the time, a role in accelerating accumulation by transforming unproductive money into productive, reproducible capital. In this way, and to speak in the manner of Marx, the public debt served as an impetus to joint-stock companies, to the trade in negotiable securities, and to the various stock market games. Acting independently of individual capitalists and sometimes even against their immediate particular interests, the State was thus able to preserve the general conditions of reproduction and the stability of the system as a whole, while resolving the oppositions between dominant fractions in the name of their superior class interest.

7.3 … To the "War-Mongers"

It was also under the leadership of high finance that the United States set out to conquer the world market. We shall argue here that this expansion movement only really began to gain momentum with their intervention

[19] Marx and Engels (1968 [1846]) (e.g., p. 105); from the same authors: (1965 [1848]). Also: Marx (1984 [1850]); and Engels (1975) (where we find the formula: '*zwischen gleichen Rechten entscheidet die Gewalt*,' to be translated by "between equal rights, it is force that decides"). For a synthesis, *cf*. Herrera (2001).

[20] See, for example, http://www.next-finance.net/JP-Morgan.

in the Cuban War of Independence from the year 1898.[21] Let us stop for a moment to understand the importance of this event and its main lines. For, under Spanish colonial rule, this Caribbean island had very early entered into the close economic dependence of the United States. On the eve of the war, in fact of the Second War of Independence, which began in February 1895, Cuba, the world's largest exporter of sugar, was the second largest foreign market for U.S. goods. It was thus a step, but a very decisive one, on the way of the United States to hegemony in the world system.

The war between the United States and Spain, by which Washington took away the supremacy over Cuba (plus Puerto Rico and the Philippines), revealed their will to power, which had already projected its armies more than a hundred times beyond its borders since independence in 1776. Examples. In Asia: Japan (1853), China (1859); in Africa itself: Angola (1860); but above all in Latin America—to retain only the U.S. military interventions of the second half of the Nineteenth Century, of a certain size and prior to 1895—Nicaragua (1850), Argentina (1852–1853), Nicaragua (1853–1855), Uruguay (1855), Panama (1856), Nicaragua (1856–1858), Uruguay (1858), Paraguay (1859), Mexico (1859), Colombia (1860–1861), Panama (1860–1861, 1865), Mexico (1866), Nicaragua (1867), Colombia (1868), Nicaragua (1869), Mexico (1870, 1873), Colombia (1873), Panama (1873), Mexico (1876), Panama (1885), Nicaragua (1885), Haiti (1888), Argentina (1890), Haiti (1891), Chile (1891–1892), Nicaragua (1894), Brazil (1894–1895), Colombia (1895), Panama (1895), etc. Without forgetting that there were also, before the year 1850, the Dominican Republic, Puerto Rico, Costa Rica, Peru... and, of course, Cuba (1814–1821, 1822, 1823, 1824, 1825, etc.). This list, although not exhaustive, is long, but it reveals a historical reality.[22]

The war of 1898 had been engaged less than a decade after the closure of the "interior frontier" (in 1890, date of the last massacre of the Native Americans at Wounded Knee). For, if Louisiana and Florida had been acquired by "peaceful purchases," such was not the case for the South and the West, which were taken by force. The war against Spain was certainly

[21] Herrera (2003c, 2006, 2021).

[22] Herrera (2010b) and more precisely: Appendix 2, p. 147–148.

led by agents of State power: Theodore "T.R." Roosevelt Jr. in the executive branch, Alfred T. Mahan in the army, Henri Cabot "Slim" Lodge and Joseph Benson Foraker in Congress… Thirteen years after the Berlin Conference and its "division of the world" between great powers, its aim was to get hold of strategic points weighing on the U.S. zone of influence declared since the Monroe doctrine.

However, the truly new aspect, which distinguished this war from those of the past, was that it was the effect of the push of U.S. finance capital, and the condition for its penetration abroad. The interests of high finance had already acquired their fabulous power within the United States and were on the verge of global domination. It is in this sense that it could be interpreted, particularly by Lenin,[23] as the first "imperialist" war in the history of the United States, whose capitalism, before the turn of the Twentieth Century, had completed its oligopolistic mutation. At that time, despite its small size and hyperspecialization (in the sugar sector), Cuba offered significant opportunities for the export of capital, productive investments, but also portfolio investments, including in the public debt, where criminal financial logics and the total subordination of the country by corrupt local elites were then crystallized.

Thus, the Platt Amendment authorized the United States to intervene militarily and ceded to it a part of Cuban territory, Guantánamo—which has still not been returned. This amendment, to which the senator from Connecticut, Orville H. Platt, associated his name, was drafted by Elihu Root, the Secretary of War (and Nobel Peace Prize winner!), who was also the lawyer of the banker Sir (and First Baronet!) Edgar Speyer, himself a personal friend of President Theodore Roosevelt, who commanded the military operations during the war. Besides, it was a loan from this Speyer bank that financed the disarmament of the Cuban liberation army, which was soon replaced by a professional army trained and supervised by Washington. In December 1901, a Commercial Reciprocity Treaty guaranteed the United States exclusive access to the Cuban market.

In this context, in 1900, the first U.S.-owned company was established on the island, the Cuba Co., whose board of directors included agents of the two main financial groups that would soon dominate the country's economy: Morgan and Rockefeller. Let us be clear: this conquest was carried out under military occupation and according to the methods

[23] For example, the Chapter IX (criticism of imperialism) in: Lenin (1969 [1916]). Also: Lenin (1970 [1916]).

known as "primitive" or "original accumulation." The various mining concessions were distributed to competing U.S. capitalists by order of General Leonard Wood—who was successively governor of Cuba, chief of staff of the U.S. army, and then governor-general of the Philippines.

Between 1914 and 1924, high finance, led by the expansion of the empire that J.P. Morgan had built, took over the Cuban sugar sector. Joint-stock companies took off, and by 1915, when the Cuba Cane Sugar Co. arrived, funds were being raised on the most modern stock markets in the United States. The Cuba Cane Corp. was the first company in Cuba to be run directly by U.S. finance, especially Morgan's, and it acquired sugar plantations and mills that gradually gave it control over the bulk of the local sugar crop. This very rapid evolution of the capital ownership structure concentrated Cuban plants in the portfolios of U.S. holding companies, most of the time operating by agreements.

The expansion was driven by big financial groups whose investment plans had ceased to be sectorally targeted and were now integrated into a global scheme, operating in all directions. So, in 1925, high finance had a strangle hold on the mines, under the control of the Bethlehem Steel Corp. and American Metal, both of them controlled by the J.P. Morgan group, as the U.S. Steel Corp. The electricity monopoly was held by General Electric, controlled by Morgan, and the telephone monopoly by Cuba Telephone, whose capital was almost entirely owned by the International Telephone & Telegraph, allied with American Telephone & Telegraph and Western Union, both owned by Morgan. A large part of the railroads sector was held by the Cuba Railway, a subsidiary of the Cuba Co. in which Morgan, by direct holdings, and the Rockefellers' Chase Manhattan, through intermediaries, could be found. In 1920, the law of liquidation of the banking system marked the bankruptcy of the local establishments, which were quickly absorbed, like the National City Bank, by the Stillman-Rockefellers.

In fact, it was the U.S. high finance that managed the Cuban Treasury's accounts, and the State itself became dependent on the public debt.[24] The J.P. Morgan group soon dominated the pool of creditors, along with the Rockefellers, through Chase Manhattan. The finance corporation was in the picture and operated as it had earlier at home: without the slightest scruples. The road that led to its control of the entire Cuban

[24] See: Herrera (2005).

economy, from 1920 onwards, is littered with financial scandals, political corruption, and military pressure, along with the purchase of latifundiary plantations and giant sugar mills at good prices… Just before the Great Depression, in 1925, Cuba was the third largest recipient of U.S. capital exports in the world.

7.4 The Return of the Domination of High Finance in the Era of Neoliberalism

Shortly after the U.S. fiasco of the attempted invasion of Playa Girón (in Cuba in April 1961), the imperial heir David Rockefeller, in close liaison with the White House and the C.I.A., founded a "business organization" (read: a lobby), the Business Group for Latin America, which became in the early 1970s the Council of the Americas. The latter brought together some of the country's most influential businessmen in order to "promote free trade and democracy," but also "the rule of law in the Western Hemisphere," that is to say, the American continent taken as a whole, from Alaska to Tierra del Fuego, including the Caribbean—and the largest of these islands…

Among the "like-minded business people" of this Council of the Americas are currently some 200 leaders of the transnational firms that invest most in Latin America: the financial groups JPMorgan Chase and Citigroup, the insurer American International Group, the oil and gas companies ExxonMobil Corp. and Chevron, the conglomerate General Electric Co., the car manufacturers General Motors Corp. and Ford Motor Co, the computer companies International Business Machines and Microsoft Corp., the soda companies Coca-Cola and PepsiCo, the restaurant chain McDonalds, the retail company Wal-Mart Stores Inc., the media company Time Warner Inc., the (very diversified) tobacco company Altria-Philip Morris, the pharmaceutical companies Pfizer and Johnson & Johnson, the law firm Sullivan & Cromwell LLP, etc.

This same Council of the Americas strengthened its activities when Thomas F. "Mack" McLarty—who heads the consulting firm Kissinger McLarty Associates—became White House Chief of Staff to President William J. Clinton. It was this Mack McLarty who played a key role in the implementation of the North American Free Trade Agreement (NAFTA-TLCAN), at a time when the blockade against Cuba was still being tightened,[25] as well as in the elaboration of the Free Trade Area of the Americas (FTAA-ALCA) project.[26] As a bonus, the "belief in private property and free markets" still offers the opportunity for a unique crusade "against communism."

But what is important to understand is that the global expansion of high finance had come to a halt, a long parenthesis that lasted from the Great Depression of the 1930s until the beginning of the neoliberal era in the 1970s. We have proposed to define "neoliberalism" as the doctrinal system on which the global strategy of domination of modern high finance, with the institutional and ideological superstructure it commands, is developed.[27] Composed of the most powerful banking and financial oligopolies that largely control the dominant world capital, this high finance still has today its center of gravity located at the very heart of the hegemony of the world system, i.e., in the United States. It has imposed itself since the 1970s, when the institutional framework of the so-called "Bretton Woods" gold exchange standard, which had been set up after World War II, was dismantled. The decline in profit rates that had been recorded in the main countries of the center since the end of the 1960s deepened in the following decade and turned out into a generalized crisis, characterized by a swing of the whole system into monetary-financial chaos, exploding inequalities, and mass unemployment.

The turning point in this return to the control of high finance—as we have seen, born at the end of the Nineteenth Century and then placed under supervision after the 1929 crisis—occurred, above all, when in 1979 the Federal Reserve Bank of the United States, lender of last resort of the international monetary system, decided to raise its interest rates unilaterally and brutally. This sudden increase, which was an attempt to solve the problem of the declining rate of profit observed over the past decade, can be interpreted as a "financial coup d'Etat" by which U.S. high finance succeeded in regaining the power—which it had lost during the Great Depression—over the hierarchy of the world system. The consequences of this strategic reorientation, which launched the modern *reconquista* of high finance, were global, affecting both the economies of the North, whose policies buckled under the external

[25] On the U.S. blockade against Cuba: HERRERA (2003b, 2004b , 2013b).

[26] HERRERA (2004a).

[27] Read: HERRERA (2010a), Chapter 5.

constraint weighing on the external and internal components of their monetary policy (exchange rates and money supply, respectively), and those of the South, by setting up the conditions for the outbreak of the debt crisis that was to come.[28]

A general idea of how the "global network" of high finance would be structured at the end of the 2000s was provided in a well-known study by Stefania Vitali, James B. Glattfelder, and Stefano Battiston. These authors tried to show that a rather limited number (just over 750) of companies would secure control of 80% of the world's transnational firms. More than 40% of the total would even be controlled by 147 of them, called "super-entity." Half of these companies are United States, with the UK far behind, followed by other Northern countries, like Japan, France, Switzerland, the Netherlands, Germany, Canada, etc.[29] And the fundamental point is that of the 25 institutions in this "super-entity" with the densest connections, twelve belong to high finance, namely: Barclays, JPMorgan Chase, Morgan Stanley, Goldman Sachs, U.B.S., Merrill Lynch, Deutsche Bank, Crédit Suisse, Bank of New York Mellon, Mitsubishi Financial, Société Générale and Bank of America, i.e., some of the most powerful banking and financial oligopolies in Wall Street or the City of London.

These same oligopolies are the most decisive players in the chain of powers and hierarchies of the international economy. They hold in their respective portfolios, intertwined, the essential part of the ownership structure of the capital of most transnational corporations in the capitalist countries of the North as well as of the South, either by majority control, or by minority participation ensuring them a key influence among the shareholders because of special prerogatives, or even via various establishments on which depends a whole cascade of enterprises held by the credit system. They are also the ones which have subordinated the States of a considerable number of peripheral economies, and even those at the center of the world system. This is reflected, moreover, by the importance of the current forms of public debt, not only in the destabilization of States, which have nationalized considerable amounts of private debt

[28] Nakatani and Herrera (2007).

[29] Vitali, Glattfelder, and Battiston (2009).

(in order to pass on the cost to their own people), but also in the destabilization of local governments, whose public finance problems will in future put many budgets with a social purpose in danger.

In this chain of events, by which this global financial network captures a large part of the real productive wealth, notably thanks to the joint strategic efforts of these oligopolies, neither the European Union nor even the United States are spared. It is these banking and financial entities that Wilhelmus Dierckxsens has called "private States without borders," which operate unaccountably, in the absolute secrecy of a "capitalism without citizenship," for the control of transnational capital.[30] It is this high finance that—sometimes supported by irresponsible leaders of government—sponsored enterprises—has seen its strategy of global domination lead most of the world's economies to catastrophe recently.

It has certainly been known for a long time, as some specialists in "criminal finance" and money laundering by organized crime have shown, that "financial markets are increasingly suspected of playing an important role in recycling the masses of dirty money that pollute the world economy."[31] Of course, we also know that speculation is causing havoc, that the 2000s were marred by multiple financial scandals (such as the Enron bankruptcy at the end of 2001, which led to the bankruptcy of prestigious auditing firms) and that commonplace banking frauds are more and more spectacular.

Every day, the nauseating effluvia of the activities of high finance is spread, and the quidam, powerless, or passive, is not finished being offended. One example will suffice. JPMorgan Chase, an oligopoly whose assets could correspond to nearly 15% of the GDP of the United States (i.e., almost that of France!), wisely paid what was necessary to avoid the lawsuits that the financial group has been facing since its involvement in the "Madoff affair." It had the delicate attention of addressing a detailed apology to the African-American community when it bought several banking establishments that had owned slaves as guarantors of loans in the Nineteenth Century. And it was still able to choose which of its executives would represent it at the ultra-select meetings of the Bilderberg Group and the Trilateral Commission—a group and a commission

[30] Dierckxsens (2000).

[31] Dupuis (1997, p. 90).

created by former JPMorgan Chase chairman and founder, the "banker and philanthropist" named David Rockefeller.

Yet, to turn away for a moment from the racy headlines of the mainstream media, speculation, whether legal or not, does not reveal the excesses or errors of "corporate governance." Much more fundamentally, the speculative operation is a "magic potion" against the structural evil of capitalism, a remedy to counteract the falling tendency of the profit rate—the latter being the key variable, one that is nevertheless generally "forgotten" by the theorists of neoclassicism, but obviously not by capitalist decision-makers and entrepreneurs—and thus a solution to offer new outlets to the masses of capital that no longer find a profitable place to invest in the productive sphere. As a consequence, the bursting of speculative "bubbles" is the price to pay (to be paid by the people). Let us take a closer look.

7.5 Overaccumulation and Fictitious Capital

The current crisis is not only or even primarily a financial phenomenon, through which the "real" or "productive" sphere of the economy would be "contaminated" by disturbances in the "financial sphere." It is, in reality, the aggravation of a structural crisis of capital, one of the most visible—and mediatized—manifestations of which has been revealed in the financial sector, due to the extreme financialization of contemporary capitalism. We are dealing with a multidimensional and global crisis; a crisis that now affects the core of the capitalist system; namely, the center of power of high finance that has controlled accumulation for more than four decades.

This translates into an excess of saleable production, not because of a lack of people with the desire to consume, but because of the concentration of wealth which is so unequal that it tends to exclude a growing proportion of the population from the possibility of buying goods. However, instead of being confronted with a standard overproduction of goods, we can observe here that the rise of credit and financial markets now allows capital to accumulate in ever more complex, and "fictitious" forms of money-capital.

The Marxian concept of "fictitious capital"[32] seems to us to be very important for analyzing this crisis. Its essential principle is the capitalization of an income derived from a future surplus value. Its places of formation are the intersections between capitalist corporations and States, in this case: banking credits, stock market shares, pension funds, speculative investment funds (hedge funds, with their discrete "tax havens" at the beach or in the mountains, as the case may be), but also public debts (bonds, etc.). At present, privileged vectors of this fictitious capital are securitization (that is to say, the transformation of assets into securities) and the resulting exchanges of derivatives—which can set in motion several degrees of fictitious capital, by piling up and combining such products. In a context where money is changing its form to become increasingly immaterial, this concept allows us to apprehend the fictitious movements of capital,[33] which include the credit system and monetary capital.

The analysis of expanded reproduction must, therefore, be carried out in connection with the exorbitant expansion of increasingly "ideal," unreal, or abstract forms of capital, as autonomous sources of valorization, seemingly separated from surplus value and appropriated without labor—as if "by magic." This fictitious capital is contradictory, dialectical in nature, simultaneously unreal and real, because although it is partly parasitic, it benefits from a distribution of surplus value, since its liquidity gives its owner the power to convert it, without any loss of capital, into money, the "liquidity *par excellence*." And, by doing so, it can then feed an accumulation of additional fictitious capital as a means of its own remuneration.

The crisis that broke out in the subprime segment of the U.S. housing market had been prepared by several decades of overaccumulation of fictitious capital. It must be understood in the long-term perspective of an aggravation of the dysfunctional mechanisms of regulation of the world

[32] Karl Marx uses this concept, along with those of interest-bearing capital and the credit system, in Sect. 5 of Book III of *Capital*, and especially from Chapter XXV, above all in Chapter XXIX ("Components of bank capital"), until Chapter XXXIII. See: MARX (1978), Book III, (vol. II). In German: MARX (1964).

[33] See: CARCANHOLO and NAKATANI (1999); NAKATANI and CARCANHOLO (2001); HERRERA and NAKATANI (2008); NAKATANI and HERRERA (2009); MARQUES and NAKATANI (2009), CARCANHOLO and SABADINI (2009), GOMES (2015), PIQUERAS (2017), NAKATANI and MARQUES (2020). Earlier, from a different but complementary perspective: HARVEY (1982).

system, since at least the 1960s and the overaccumulation of capital-money linked to U.S. deficits, to tensions on the dollar, and to the multiplication of eurodollars, and then petrodollars, on the interbank markets. In this process, certain events played a decisive role, including, as we have seen, the decision by the United States, starting in 1971, to demonetize gold, to make exchange rate regimes more flexible and to deregulate the monetary and financial markets, with the concomitant "liberalization" of exchange rates and interest rates at the end of the 1970s.

At the root of the current crisis are these waves of deregulation, *re*-regulation by oligopolies, and integration of financial markets into a globalized network, clearly shifting the center of gravity of world power toward high finance, and allowing the latter to impose its dictates on economies. Above all, it is important to understand the present crisis at the very articulation of the financial and productive spheres, because some of its major factors are of a "real" nature, and due to austerity policies. The so-called "subprime crisis," through which so many poor (or less poor) families have found themselves in default, can also be explained by the neoliberal "reforms" implemented for more than forty years and pushing for austerity, which have curbed wages, made employment more flexible, massively increased unemployment, and degraded living conditions; all policies that have broken demand and activated springs making it artificial, and, therefore, unsustainable. As a consequence, growth could only be maintained during the neoliberal era by doping private consumption demand and by pulling hard on credit lines—and this extraordinary credit boom ended up revealing the crisis of overaccumulation itself, in its modern version.

During this new "regime" of neoliberalism—which remains an empty word if it is not linked to the power exercised by the oligopolies of high finance—financial markets have been modernized, notably through the introduction of hedging instruments. Derivatives, that is to say, contracts that support transactions by fixing future financial flows according to variations in the price of underlying assets, are precisely these hedging tools, made necessary by the very flexibilization of exchange rates and interest rates; but these financial products are most often mobilized for speculative strategies, playing on their hybridization and the "leverage effect" by taking on risk from a limited investment—especially when they give rise to short sales. As a result, the amounts corresponding to this creation of fictitious capital (among other things, the exchanges of over-the-counter contracts negotiated with very few prudential rules and recorded off-balance sheet) rapidly and largely exceeded those intended for the reproduction of productive capital.

It has thus been possible to estimate the exchanges of derivative products at 600,000 billion dollars, i.e., ten times more than real production.[34] The amounts in question, measured daily in teradollars (or millions of millions), are exchanged by a very small number of banking and financial oligopolies, essentially the primary dealers, which the U.S. Federal Reserve Bank calls the "G15," namely: Morgan Stanley, Goldman Sachs, and thirteen others... It is above all credit derivatives that have posed—and continue to pose—problems, with extremely complex synthetic arrangements, for example, asset-backed debt (collateralized debt obligation, CDO) and default hedges or credit event derivatives (credit default swaps, CDS). These instruments transform the vision of credit, by bringing into play several degrees or "powers" of fictitious capital, such as CDO^2 or, as a recent innovation, CDO^3 (i.e., CDOs of CDO^2).

The collapse of these modern-day pyramids was, therefore, inevitable, as was the case with the bankruptcy of American International Group Inc. (AIG), whose interpretation of its business as an insurer went so far as to juggle hundreds of millions of dollars of CDOs, which were themselves composed of CDS on pools of loan-backed bonds (or RMBS for Residential Mortgage-Backed Securities), out of control.

It has been measured that the wealthiest "1 per cent" of U.S. households have managed to capture almost 95% of the growth income since 2009, while the "99 per cent" have become poorer.[35] The COVID-19 pandemic has further considerably increased these already abysmal, glaring inequalities.[36] In such a society—the United States, today—where ever greater masses of individuals are excluded and kept without rights, the expansion of the outlets offered to the owners of dominant capital could delay for a time the devalorization of the surplus capital placed on the financial markets; but by no means avoid it.

[34] Estimate at the end of December 2010. *Cf.* the Bank for International Settlements (BIS) report dated June 2011.

[35] Saez (2013) and The World Top Incomes Database (http://topincomes.g-mond.parisschoolofeconomics.eu/).

[36] Oxfam (2022).

In a Marxist framework, it would also be necessary to decipher the movements of increase of unproductive labor and devalorization of labor, and then to grasp the tendency to this accumulation "without labor," in connection with the financialization of capitalism and the rise of fictitious capital which is at the root of the great contemporary crisis. We are also witnessing a process of separation of labor and money, as illustrated by crypto-currencies (bitcoin, etc.), which are new forms of fictitious money and, above all, new social relations of power inscribed in the contradictions operating within great financial empires; contradictions between the different fractions of high finance that are at stake—particularly, in the United States, between "Globalists," whose epicenter is the Democratic Party, and "Continentalists," gravitating around former President D. Trump at a certain time around.[37]

7.6 A *Systemic* Crisis of Capital and the Inevitable Failure of Orthodox Anti-crisis Policies

One of the immediate manifestations of this crisis was, therefore, a massive destruction of fictitious capital: in 2008, the total capitalization of the world's stock markets fell from 48.3 to 26.1 trillion dollars. This downward spiral in asset values was thus accompanied by a loss of confidence and a situation of illiquidity in the interbank market—in a world that is, however, over-liquid, the most likely hypothesis being that of the insolvency of a significant number of banking institutions. As a consequence, knowing that the prices of composite securities and the risks associated with them were very poorly assessed (because they could not be assessed, even by the best rating agencies), the problems moved from the subprime segment to that of real estate credit, then to that of creditworthy loans, before the implosion of the "bubble" of instruments backed by real estate mortgages affected the other sections of the financial markets and, from there, the money market proper (i.e., interbank market). The whole system of financing economies then came to a standstill.

The devalorization of capital has of course had a real dimension, notably through the contraction of credit, and first of all consumer loans.

[37] See: Dierckxsens and Formento (2016), and Observatoire international de la Crise (2019).

In a more or less pronounced way and each according to their specificities, the economies of the capitalist world system entered into depression in the course of 2008, conjuncturally—but, structurally, while a peak had already been reached for the exploitation of strategic natural resources (especially oil) and while the search for new sources of energy poses objective limitations to economic growth. We shall come back to this important point in Chapter 9.

As a result, most of the fundamental economic indicators went haywire: drops in GDP growth rates, consumption, and trade; operating deficits of industrial companies; losses of jobs, housing, and savings accounts... We know, nevertheless, that the worst consequences of this crisis have been and are still being borne by the poorest individuals or households among the working classes, where the damage is enormous—including, of course, in the United States, the world's leading economy, but with very poor social indicators compared to most other industrialized countries (in terms of life expectancy, infant mortality rate, right to health, access to education, or even security).[38] The multiple damages observed as a result of the crisis also include, in the Northern economies (but not only), the worsening of a generalized malaise, a pain in life, or bad feelings, especially in the workplace (for those who have a job), and even phenomena—noted by occupational medicine consultations—of individual psychological collapse.[39]

It is in this context and according to this chain of events—which, of course, did not begin with the accentuation of the crisis in 2008, but

[38] Herrera (2011). Also see: Herrera, Dierckxsens and Nakatani (2014).

[39] We are thinking here of the combined effects of tension and stress caused by the threat of unemployment and the pressure exerted by individual evaluation methods, leading to heightened competition between workers within the same production unit. This leads to a rupture in the bonds of conviviality, respect, loyalty, and solidarity between colleagues. Hence, the appearance of distrust among them, fear at work, self-control, reciprocal surveillance, as well as that of pathologies of loneliness, accompanied by feelings of moral betrayal of oneself, awareness of a "lie" in the face of the requirements of total quality and certification by the market (e.g., Dejours [2010]). Hence also, in a universe where the mobilization of energies is permanent, where flexibility and instability tend to become normalized and, at the same time, where collective spaces for thinking and acting together are reduced, a loss of moral reference points, of the sense of responsibility and of motivation to regain the instruments of a transformation of human relationships at work. Not to mention the hardening of labor conflicts, and forms of repression against workers who resist and against those who defend them (in the case of France: Herrera [2019, 2020]).

which have been aggravated by the new episode of a structural crisis of capital, the conditions for which have been in place, as we have said, for decades—that, in the Northern countries, cases of suicide at work by wage earners (as well as, here and there, by unemployed workers) have multiplied over the last few years, including within socio-professional categories that were previously little affected (such as farmers, for example). All this has been terribly aggravated since 2020 and the outbreak of the COVID-19 pandemic.

Since 2011, in the United States, a very worrying problem, at the macroeconomic level this time, has been that of State indebtedness, that is to say, debts contracted by the Treasury, the federal government, but also the federated States and local governments. By the end of 2010, then Fed Chairman had warned the U.S. Secretary of the Treasury and Congress that he would not continue to finance government deficits and that it was time to tighten fiscal and budgetary adjustment plans.[40] It was necessary, he said, to raise interest rates and reduce imbalances by raising taxes and cutting spending, including by reducing the number of civil servants and their salaries. The burden of austerity would be shifted onto workers—at the expense of their health and pensions, where the cuts were to be concentrated. Consequently, we understand that, in reality, there is no return to "Keynesianism" either in the United States or in Europe, where the dominant conception of the State remains that of an institution largely placed at the service of capital—i.e., in a neoliberal perspective.

What are the main effects of the crisis in the Southern countries? First, there is the acceleration of transfers from the South to the North, via various well-known channels: repatriation of profits from direct or portfolio investments, repayment of external debt, transformation of foreign exchange reserves into credits (immediately granted to the United States), but also corruption, capital flight, unequal exchange…[41] These transfers of income toward the North will have to be further intensified in the near future in an attempt to finance the rescue operations of central capitalism—knowing that the U.S. hegemony has the key currency, and the military arsenal that goes with it, as we shall see in next chapter, to carry out this enormous drain of long-term capital from the rest of the world.

[40] Bernanke (2010).

[41] For a Marxist alternative, based on the theory of unequal exchange, opposed to the neoclassical analysis of international trade, see: Long, Feng, Li, and Herrera (2020), and Herrera, Long, Feng, and Li (2021).

The United States has so far been able to impose this on everyone, from its partners in the North to its potential rivals in the East and South, including Russia and China; but for how long?

We defend the idea that the current crisis of capitalism, whose gravity exceeds those of the past, even during the 1930s, is *systemic*. What exactly is meant by *systemic* crisis? It means that the capitalist system does not find and, in our opinion, will no longer find internal solutions to the contradictory dynamics that it deploys. This is one of the fundamental reasons why the most extreme form of devalorization of capital, war—military, not just economic—is more and more frequently (not to say permanently) used by this high finance in power. We shall talk about that in Chapter 8. Nevertheless, the continuation of this destructive trajectory sharpens the contradictions of the capitalist system.

In the United States, it is probably thought that a depreciating dollar will help to reduce the trade deficit and stimulate domestic production. This is a mistake, because for several years now we have seen that these variables react little, and less and less, to declines in the dollar. The result is that U.S. GDP growth remains very weak on trend—despite recent slight upward shifts (before the COVID-19 pandemic). To be sure, the economic growth rate of the neoliberal regime was already low and for a long time. But this sluggishness has worsened since 2007, because the causes of the deterioration of the situation are now more related to the extremely serious problems of the entire system of financing the economy.

It should be remembered that the anti-crisis policies had consisted, above all, of coordinating the actions of the various Central Banks to allow massive injections of liquidity into the interbank market through the creation of primary money, offering generous credit lines to banking oligopolies, and sharply reducing interest rates. The objective was to avoid the outright collapse of the system, but also to limit the devalorization of fictitious capital by slowing down the fall of the markets so that derivatives would be paid as close as possible to their face value.

Let us not forget: in mid-September 2008, in the United States, the center of the superpower of the most powerful owners of globally dominant capital, the financial section of capitalism—that is to say, of this horizon that is said to be "unsurpassable," "eternal," "natural"—came very close to collapsing, like a house of cards or a stack of casino chips; something that the general public, dramatically misinformed, disoriented, and robbed on top of it, has obviously not yet really realized...

The decisive turning point was the non-intervention of the U.S. public authorities during the bankruptcy of the investment bank Lehman Brothers Holdings Inc. on September 15, 2008. The fact is that the risks of destabilization of the entire system had not been measured. In a few hours, however, a 180 degrees change of course was decided, jointly by the Central Bank and the Treasury: nationalization of endangered financial institutions; temporary suspension of short sales; opening by the Fed of special credit lines to primary dealers at almost zero interest rates; government assistance for the buyout and recapitalization of financial giants; creation of a public hive-off structure to guarantee "toxic" "securities; unlimited" extension (in October 2008) of the device of the Federal Reserve Bank's temporary reciprocal currency arrangements, or "swap lines," to the Central Banks of the North and some key countries of the South; support plans for the flagships of national industry (without, however, preventing waves of layoffs); and with, in passing, occasional recapitalizations of a Fed that was out of breath…

The result of this astonishing series of measures, quite exceptional—because they were ultra-interventionist—has been a hypercentralization of the monstrous power of the banking and financial oligopolies in ever more concentrated capital ownership structures. Nonetheless, if we look closely, none of the deep contradictions of the system have been resolved to date. The concerns raised by the extent and duration of the crisis are strong. Should not we, therefore, move from false orthodox "solutions" to real alternatives? We have seen in Chapter 5 that, according to Paul Krugman, Keynes is back in the spotlight.[42] Joseph Stiglitz also shares this opinion[43] and, with him, a fairly large number of authors who, like them, can be qualified as followers of neoclassicism in theory, but with an ideological sensitivity oriented to the left.[44] But, in the particularly tormented context of the beginning of the Twenty-first Century, to get out of the crisis, Keynesianism will not be enough. The recipes he enunciated are no longer capable of solving the extremely grave problems posed by this overaccumulation, driven by a high finance whose quest for profit borders on madness.

[42] Krugman (2009).

[43] Stiglitz (2003).

[44] Morin (2006).

The probability of a worsening of the crisis, as a systemic crisis of capital, is indeed high today. All the conditions are there for this to happen. Capitalism is in danger, including at the center of the system. Since the Great Depression of the 1930s, capital has been able to forge the institutions and instruments of public intervention that allowed it to "manage" the crises it went through and to cushion their devastating effects, at least in the North; without, however, these various reorganizations of capital's domination ever suppressing the profound contradictions that characterize it.

The present situation resembles, not the "beginning of the end of the crisis," but rather the beginning of a long, slow, gradual process of collapse of the present stage of the capitalist system, both financialized and oligopolistic. For, we believe that another capitalism, that is, a reformed capitalism, "with a human face," is not possible. We have said it over and over again: in order to restart a cycle of expansion in the Northern countries, the current crisis would have to destroy even more colossal amounts of fictitious capital; but the contradictions of capitalism have become so deep and difficult to resolve that such a devalorization would risk pushing it toward a collapse. This system, become essentially destructive, is doomed, and sentenced. However, it will only fall under the pressure of mass, progressive, anti-systemic, and convergent struggles. This process, therefore, opens up very broad perspectives for post-capitalist transitions and forces us to reconsider alternatives for social transformation. Should not we, to begin with, stop the infernal machine operated by high finance which regulates the world by means of war?

References

Aumann R.J.Y. (1996), "A Reply to Binmore," *Games and Economic Behavior*, vol. 17, n° 1, p. 138–146.

Bernanke B. (2010), "Fiscal Sustainability and Fiscal Rules," *Annual Meeting of the Rhode Island Public Expenditure Council*, Providence, October 4.

Binmore K.G. (2005), *Natural Justice*, New York: Oxford University Press.

Bourguinat H. (1999), *Finance internationale - Après l'euro et les crises*, 4th ed., Paris: Presses Universitaires de France.

Carcanholo R.A. and P. Nakatani (1999), "O Capital especulativo parasitário," *Revista Ensaios*, vol. 20, n° 1, p. 284–304.

Carcanholo R.A. and M. Sabadini (2009), "Capital fictício e lucros fictícios," *Revista da Sociedade Brasileira de Economia Política*, n° 24, p. 66–84.

Casanova A. and R. Herrera (eds.) (2014), *Penser les crises*, Paris: Le Temps des Cerises.
Dejours C. (2010), *Observations cliniques en psychopathologie du travail*, Paris: Presses Universitaires de France.
Dierckxsens W. (2000), *The Limits of Capitalism*, London: Zed Books.
Dierckxsens W. and W. Formento (2016), *Geopolítica de la crisis económica mundial - Globalismo vs. Universalismo*, Buenos Aires: Ediciones Fabro.
Dupuis M.-C. (1997), *Finance criminelle*, Paris: Presses Universitaires de France.
Engels F. (1975), *Sur Le Capital de Marx*, Moscow: Éditions du Progrès.
Gomes H. (eds.) (2015), *Especulação e lucros fictícios: formas parasitárias da acumulação contemporânea*, São Paulo: Outras Expressões.
Guerrien B. (1989), *La Théorie néo-classique - Bilan et perspectives du modèle d'équilibre général*, Paris: Economica.
——— (1996a), *Dictionnaire d'analyse économique - Microéconomie, macroéconomie, théorie des jeux, etc.*, «Dictionnaires repères», Paris: La Découverte.
——— (1996b), *L'Économie néo-classique*, Paris: La Découverte.
Harvey D. (1982), *The Limits to Capital*, London: Basil Blackwell.
Herrera R. (2001), "Brève introduction à la Théorie de l'État chez Marx et Engels," *Cahier de la Maison des Sciences économiques de l'Université de Paris 1*, n° 1, Paris, available on: https://vimeo.com/144550507.
——— (2010a), *Un Autre Capitalisme n'est pas possible*, Paris: Syllepse.
——— (2010b), *Les Avancées révolutionnaires en Amérique latine - Des transitions socialistes au XXIe siècle?*, Lyon: Parangon.
——— (2003a), "L'État contre le service public?", *Actuel Marx*, n° 34, p. 147–160, Paris.
——— (2003b), "Why Israel Should Vote to Lift the Embargo of the United States Against Cuba?," *Haaretz*, (in English and Hebrew), heshvan 7, 5764, vol. 85, n° 25662, Tel Aviv.
——— (ed.) (2003c), *Cuba révolutionnaire: Histoire et culture*, Tome 1, Paris: Éditions L'Harmattan.
——— (2004a), "On the Free Trade Area of the Americas (FTAA)," Joint Written Statement of the Centre Europe Tiers-Monde and the American Association of Jurists for the Human Rights Commission of the United Nations, Geneva.
——— (2004b), "Cuba: Why Lift the Embargo?," *Monthly Review*, vol. 55, n° 8, p. 49–54, New York.
——— (2005), "When the Names of the Emperors were Morgan and Rockefeller," *International Journal of Political Economy*, vol. 34, n° 4, p. 25–49, New York.
——— (ed.) (2006), *Cuba révolutionnaire: Économie et planification*, Tome 2, Paris: Éditions L'Harmattan.

——— (2011), "Tendances de l'économie étasunienne sous la mandature de Barack H. Obama," *Recherches internationales*, n° 91, p. 151–169, Paris.

——— (2012), "Reflections on the Current Crisis and Its Effects," *Economic and Political Weekly*, vol. XLVII, n° 23, p. 62–71, Mumbai.

——— (2013a), "La Domination de la haute finance états-unienne: origines, mécanismes, alternatives," *Marché & Organisations*, n° 19, p. 127–146, Paris.

——— (2013b), "On the Lifting of the Embargo Against Cuba," Joint Written Statement of the Centre Europe Tiers-Monde, the International Association of Democratic Lawyers and the American Association of Jurists for the Human Rights Council of the United Nations, Geneva.

——— (2014), "A Marxist Interpretation of the Crisis," *World Review of Political Economy*, vol. 5, n° 2, p. 128–148, Shanghai.

——— (2019), "Pushback on Human Rights in France: The Republic on the Move, in Reverse Gear," *Social Justice—A Journal of Crime, Conflict & World Order*, digital version, San Francisco.

——— (2020), *En Lutte! Les résistances populaires en France de 1981 à nos jours*, Paris: Éditions Critiques.

——— (2021), "De los ciclos de no-especialización a la era del azúcar: Elementos de historia de Cuba en un largo período (1492–1958)," *International Journal of Cuban Studies*, vol. 12, n° 2, p. 182–212, London.

——— (2022), *La Monnaie: du pouvoir de la finance à la souveraineté des peuples*, Geneva: Éditions du Centre Europe - Tiers Monde (CETIM).

HERRERA R., W. DIERCKXSENS and P. NAKATANI (2014), *Beyond the Systemic Crisis and Capital-led Chaos—Theoretical and Applied Studies*, Brussels and Berlin: P.I.E. Peter Lang.

HERRERA R., Z. LONG, Z. FENG and B. LI (2021), "¿El que pierde gana? La guerra comercial sino-estadunidense en perspectiva," *El Trimester Económico*, vol. LXXXVIII, n° 4, n° 352, p. 1073–1097, Mexico.

HERRERA R. and P. NAKATANI (2008), "La Crise financière: racines, raisons, perspectives," *La Pensée*, n° 353, p. 109–113, Paris.

HORNY G. (2012), *La Bourse pour les nuls*, 2nd ed., Paris: Éditions First-Gründ.

KRUGMAN P.R. (2009), *The Return of Depression Economics and the Crisis of 2008*, New York: W.W. Norton & Co.

LENIN V.I. (1969 [1916]), *L'Impérialisme, stade suprême du capitalisme*, Moscow: Éditions du Progrès.

——— (1970 [1916]), *Œuvres - tome 39: Cahiers de l'impérialisme*, Paris and Moscow: Éditions sociales and Éditions du Progrès.

LEVINE R. (2005), "Finance and Growth: Theory and Evidence," *in* P. Aghion and S. Durlauf (eds.), *Handbook of Economic Growth*, vol. 1, p. 865–934. Amsterdam: Elsevier.

Long Z., Z. Feng, B. Li and R. Herrera (2020), "U.S.-China Trade War: Has the Real 'Thief' Finally Been Unmasked?," *Monthly Review*, vol. 72, n° 5, p. 32–43, New York.

Kydland F.E. and E.C. Prescott (1977), "Rules Rather than Discretion: The Inconsistency of Optimal Plans," *Journal of Political Economy*, vol. 85, n° 3, p. 473–492.

——— (1982), "Time to Build and Aggregate Fluctuations," *Econometrica*, vol. 50, n° 6, p. 1345–1370.

Marques R.M. and P. Nakatani (2009), *O que é capital fictício e sua crise*, São Paulo: Ed. Brasiliense.

Marx K. (1964), *Das Kapital - Kritik der politischen Ökonomie*, *Buch* III: *Der Gesamtprozeß der kapitalistischen Produktion* (*Band* 25), Institut für Marxismus-Leninismus, Berlin: Dietz Verlag.

——— (1978), *Le Capital - Critique de l'économie politique*, Paris: Éditions sociales.

——— (1984 [1850]), *Les Luttes de classes en France 1848–1850*, Paris: Messidor - Éditions sociales.

Marx K. and F. Engels (1968 [1846]), *L'Idéologie allemande*, Paris: Éditions sociales.

Marx K. and F. Engels (1965 [1848]), *Le Manifeste du Parti communiste*, *in* Économie I, La Pléiade, Paris: Gallimard.

Mishkin F.S. (2010), *Monnaie, banque et marchés financiers*, Chapter 27, 9th ed., Paris: Pearson Education.

Morin F. (2006), Le Nouveau *Mur de l'argent - Essai sur la finance globalisée*, Paris: Le Seuil.

Nakatani P. and R. Herrera (2009), "Critique des politiques anticrise orthodoxes," *La Pensée*, n° 360, p. 31–42, Paris.

Nakatani, P. et R. Carcanholo (2001), "Capital especulativo parasitário versus capital financier," *Problemas del Desarrollo*, vol. 32, n° 124, p. 9–31.

Nakatani P. and R. Herrera (2007), "What Rich Countries Owe Poor Ones," *Monthly Review*, vol. 59, n° 2, p. 31–36, New York.

Nakatani, P. and R.M. Marques (2020), *O Capitalismo em crise*, São Paulo: Expressão Popular.

Observatoire international de la Crise (2019), *Le Capitalisme face à son déclin*, Paris: Éditions Critiques.

Oxfam. (2022), *Inequality Kills: The Unparalleled Action Needed to Combat Unprecedented Inequality in the Wake of COVID-19*, available on: https://www.oxfam.org/en/research/inequality-kills.

Pagano M. (1993), "Financial Markets and Growth: An Overview," *European Economic Review*, vol. 37, n°s 2–3, p. 613–622.

PIQUERAS A. (2017), "El Capital ficticio especulativo-parasitario se pone al mando del capitalismo," *Áreas - Revista Internacional de Ciencias Sociales*, n° 36, p. 11–23.

SAEZ E. (2013), "Striking It Richer: The Evolution of Top Incomes in the United States," Department of Economics, University of California, Berkeley, available on: http://elsa.berkeley.edu/~saez/saez-UStopincomes-2012.

STIGLITZ J.E. (2003), *Quand le Capitalisme perd la tête*, Paris: Le Livre de poche.

VITALI S., J.B. GLATTFELDER and S. BATTISTON (2009), *The Network of Global Corporate Control*, Zurick: ETH.

ZINN H. (1980), *A People's History of the United States*, New York: Harper & Row / HarperCollins.

CHAPTER 8

For a Political Economy of Defense: Imperialist Wars and Their Links to the Crisis of Capital

The study of war is very rarely addressed by the mainstream economists of neoclassicism, who turn away from it and leave it to specialists in polemology in other disciplines, especially in political science, international relations, or geostrategy.[1] An exception to be underlined is game theory, which is mainly purely mathematical exercises and often leads to indeterminate results—indeterminate results which constitute a positive contribution in itself, given the fact that the works of orthodox authors very generally highlight dogmatic postulates, restrictive methods, and allegedly unequivocal conclusions. Quite distinctly, the field of "economics of defense" has been the subject of innumerable works, including by leading theoreticians,[2] or less important authors but who have played in one way or another, at one time or another, the role of "pioneers" in this sub-discipline.[3] Furthermore, these studies have become increasingly

[1] This chapter is a brief synthesis of several works carried out by the author on the subject, in particular: Herrera (1994, 1998, 2000, 2001, 2007, 2010a, 2013a, b, c, 2015, 2021).

[2] Among others: Leontief (1941), Schelling (1960), Samuelson (1983 [1947]), Arrow (1992), Arrow and Li (1993), Tinbergen (1990), Barro (1991), and Sen (1992).

[3] See: Boulding (1962), Benoit and Boulding (1963), Benoit (1972), Isard (1988), and Intriligator (1990).

R. Herrera, *Confronting Mainstream Economics for Overcoming Capitalism*, Marx, Engels, and Marxisms,
https://doi.org/10.1007/978-3-031-05851-6_8

technicalized as they have been integrated into the nebula of neoclassicism, or some of its satellites.[4] Nevertheless, the paradox is that, until now, taken as a whole, these researches have failed to reach clear, secured advances. It is interesting to note that neoclassical economists have begun in earnest to develop a defense economics, but so far they have been unsuccessful. One reason for this failure is the inability of neoclassicism to deal with conflict. But building a defense economics without conflict—a pale replica of mainstream economics without politics—is a big problem in an analysis of war... We shall see—once again—that it is necessary to leave neoclassicism and its dependencies to analyze the contemporary imperialist wars and their links with the crisis of capital.

8.1 A Needed Contextualization of the Debate

First of all, the theoretical and empirical debate on the role of defense in the economy must be put in context. The first and most important element to highlight is the extension, in successive waves, of the network of U.S. military bases on a planetary scale.[5] We shall come back to this point. Secondly, at a worldwide scale, military spending grew almost exponentially throughout the Twentieth Century, at least until the beginning of its last decade. After a decline until the second half of the 1990s, these expenses began to grow strongly again at the beginning of the Twenty-first Century, until the crisis of the end of the 2000s—when they exceeded the level they reached in 1990. Since the mid-2010s, they have started to increase again, clearly. They were approaching two trillion dollars in 2020. And if one includes the interests and amortization of associated debts, that is, a form of fictitious capital, the burden is much higher.[6]

At this same date (2020), Washington D.C. was responsible for almost 40% of world military expenditure. U.S. spending of 778 billion dollars, up 4.4% from a year earlier, was more than three times the level of spending by second-place China, with the latter country recording an

[4] For surveys: Hartley and Sandler (2007) and Anderton and Carter (2007).

[5] Herrera and Cicchini (2013). Original sources are from: U.S. Department of Defense (various years).

[6] Stiglitz and Bilmes (2008).

increase less than half as fast as that of the United States.[7] U.S. arms spending is more than twelve times greater than Russia's—which is about the same as Britain's, a key member of NATO under the Pentagon command. This said to keep in mind who threatens whom in "normal" times—that is, in times of "peace," i.e., of relentless expansion of the network of U.S. and/or NATO military bases toward Russia as well as toward China—and, possibly—that is to say, when war finally breaks out—what is the share of responsibility of each other between the different protagonists.

Now, the renewed interest in these issues of defense economics on the part of the neoclassical mainstream was decisively driven from the beginning of the 1990s by the concerted research programs led by international organizations: the World Bank, Organization for Economic Co-operation and Development (OECD), International Monetary Fund (IMF)... Mainly focused on the economic effects of the reallocations of resources generated by the so-called "peace dividends" at the end of the Cold War,[8] these various programs coincided—not by chance—with the closing of a cycle of work previously devoted to the problem of the external debt of developing countries, whose major political conclusions had been to explain this debt, not so much by the dysfunctions of international relations, but by a "mismanagement" of the public finances of these economies, thereby opening up the toward the imperative of "good governance." This concept was initially elaborated by the IMF and then applied to "all aspects of the conduct of public affairs"—including, moreover, after the attacks of September 11, 2001, in the "fight against the financing of terrorism,"[9] as we have seen (Chapter 3).

The pressures then exerted on the public budgets of the countries of the South—and the East, following the collapse of the Soviet bloc, the end of the "arms race" against the United States and the launch of "transitions to capitalism" (in the form of shock therapy)—were to justify a series of recommendations to reduce defense spending and reconversion of military industries. In this group of countries, these new changes

[7] Data published by the Stockholm International Peace Research Institute (SIPRI). See: https://www.sipri.org/media/press-release/2021/world-military-spending-rises-almost-2-trillion-2020. For further study, read the SIPRI yearbooks (Stockholm International Peace Research Institute [various years]).

[8] For example, Knight et al. (1995).

[9] International Monetary Fund (2003).

have most often led to intrabudgetary trade-offs which have resulted in cuts in public spending, especially those for social purposes, in order to ultimately constitute the surpluses essential to ensure continuity of reimbursement of the external debt service.[10] So, the combined logics of unbalanced disarmament (maintaining the United States' advance in armaments) and accelerated liberalization (with the privatization of State-owned enterprises and generalized flexibility of capitalist economies) have accumulated their negative impacts and brought, in many cases, more human insecurity.[11]

The scissors effect marked by a drop in defense spending and a simultaneous increase in police spending (i.e., the "internal security and public order" posts, turned toward an enemy who is no longer outside), very frequently observed in the South under structural adjustment programs, is no stranger to this problem. Thus, the demanded reductions in military spending made it possible not only to free up some budgetary leeway guaranteeing the non-interruption of debt-related transfers to creditors (financial oligopolies of the Northern countries and international institutions), but also simultaneously to offer the opportunity for the disarmament of emerging Southern regional powers (foremost among them China), at a time when the capitalist world system fell entirely under the unipolar hegemony of the United States.

8.2 About Some Methodological Difficulties

Generally regarded as the sovereign function *par excellence*, defense is a very peculiar category of public spending. The real complexity of this field, which is strengthened by the opacity and scarcity of information on defense, is partly due to the fact that its analyses involve a political-strategic dimension. Therefore, the economist who investigates into this area uses to face several serious difficulties, such as: (i) a lack of statistical data related to military spending, that hampers the econometrician in the attempts of empirical verification; (ii) a problem of identification of the differentiated effects of such expenditures, whose multifaceted role within the economy is difficult to disentangle for the mathematical formalization;

[10] Nakatani and Herrera (2007).

[11] Read: Mushakoji (2008).

and (iii) the need to combine in the analysis both economic and strategic considerations, in order to contribute to more sophisticated modeling.

A study whose purpose is evaluating military spending in an economy, that is to say, the set of material and human resources devoted to defense, has to clarify the issues of definition and measurement of these expenditures—referring to the concepts of the State, security, etc.—and the contours of the different phenomena to grasp. Among the most delicate problems to solve is the determination of the conditions of their international comparability, regarding structural elements, deflators, or conversion factors, etc. The methodological difficulties are many here, and they reveal the fundamentally secret nature of these budgets, but also some complexities which are specifically statistical, for example, double accounting, removing costs from the central budget, foreign exchange manipulations, calculations of debts associated to military spending, aggregation methods...[12]

A thorough review of the main statistical data sources—which are of less poor quality and are other than "primary", i.e., issued by the central authorities of the country—highlights a series of shortcomings. Among the latter, we can mention in particular those related to the retention of information by the governments (is it not legitimate?)—hence, the widespread opacity existing in this area—as well as those linked to a balance of power operating to the detriment of the Southern countries in the international relations. Indeed, the Northern countries occupy dominant positions within the international statistical administrations, like the United Nations or the (IMF).[13] Frequently, their intelligence services even directly support the collection and treatment of such indicators, like in the cases of the Central Intelligence Agency (CIA) or the United States Arms Control and Disarmament Agency (USACDA) for the United States, or, for the UK, the International Institute of Strategic Studies (IISS).[14] Despite the well-known experience and excellence of

[12] For an overview on the concepts, methodological problems, and statistical sources related to military spending, read: HERRERA (1994).

[13] UNITED NATIONS (1991) and INTERNATIONAL MONETARY FUND (various years).

[14] Here: CENTRAL INTELLIGENCE AGENCY (various years), U.S. ARMS CONTROL and DISARMAMENT AGENCY (various years), INTERNATIONAL INSTITUTE for STRATEGIC STUDIES (various years).

their researchers, the few independent observatories, especially the Stockholm International Peace Research Institute (SIPRI),[15] have neither the financial resources nor the institutional power to constitute a reliable and comprehensive alternative source of information.

Therefore, these limits, which are more or less marked depending on the institution considered, prevent to rely on a specific statistical database exclusively. Military spending, as they appear in the national budget documents or in the reports elaborated by specialized international organizations,[16] concern areas of responsibility of the State apparatuses of variable extent, and they include accounting lines which are destined to different purposes. Consequently, the defense budget is not necessarily the most appropriate indicator of the real effort of the State in the matters of security.

All these methodological and statistical problems are certainly difficult to untangle. However, they cannot be used as a pretext to hide the incoherence, defects, and inconsistencies of the arguments of neoclassicism. There is nothing really surprising about this: How would the supporters of the mainstream manage to build a "war economy," those who mobilize a methodology that disregards power, conflict, and politics? Basically, orthodox economics does not grasp conflict and fails to take into account power relations; except—as we have noted before—in game theory, but in a quite limited way. Consequently, the condition for thinking about war is, again, as for analyzing the crisis, to extract oneself from the dominant economic thought. Before that, we need to dwell on it for a moment, to fully understand the issues that this subject entails.

8.3 The Terms of the Problematics Within Neoclassicism

Like the economic theory taken as a whole, defense economics is currently dominated by the neoclassical mainstream.[17] Its basic ambition is to analyze all social phenomena exclusively from the behaviors of individual agents. In the theoretical *corpus* of neoclassicism, defense represents the

[15] Stockholm International Peace Research Institute (various years).

[16] For example, United Nations Institute for Disarmament Research (1992).

[17] For general critical surveys on mainstream economics, see: Herrera (2006a, b, 2011).

typical example of a "public good," the characteristics of which would justify State intervention. Goods produced by the market are, by definition, for private use and the interdependencies between individuals are usually mediated by the price system. Public goods are distinguished by the fact that they are the object of collective consumption, which is not shared, but equal for all and benefiting all simultaneously—without excluding access through prices.

By nature, therefore, these goods cannot be produced and allocated by the market, since price mechanisms no longer ensure their rationing. Neoclassical theory admits under these conditions that their production can be entrusted to the State, which supplies these goods to the community by levying a tax to finance the associated public expenditure. Consequently, the justification for the production by the public sector of such collective goods lies in the inability of the market to provide them.[18]

Two explanations are generally advanced on this subject. First, if the consumption of these goods is not divisible, and if their market price is considered zero, no private sector company will have an interest in producing them.[19] Second, the impossibility of exclusion will lead agents not to reveal their preferences, in order to try to reduce their contributions to be paid. Knowing that the State will levy a tax and that the announcement of their needs would lead them to pay more, the agents could thus be encouraged to behave as free riders to benefit from the collective goods revealed (and therefore paid) by others.[20] An underestimation bias then risks being introduced into the supply of the public good.[21]

The main characteristics of defense clearly place it in the category of public goods. Its supply is indivisible, as is, legally, the "nation" to which it applies. This indivisibility of supply—which refers to the key notion of "increasing returns" and leads to monopoly market structures that can justify State interference—is coupled with an indivisibility of use. As a matter of fact, it is not possible to reserve the exclusive use of this good to certain agents, insofar as any citizen, benefiting from a free right of

[18] The neoclassical methodology has been adopted by a very large majority of authors. By instance, and among a crowd of others: Alexander (1990), Ward et al. (1991), Antonakis (1999), Batchelor et al. (2000), and Yildirim et al. (2005), etc.

[19] Tirole (1988).

[20] See: Samuelson (1983) and Stiglitz (1988).

[21] Stiglitz (1988).

access, cannot be denied such protection. Each individual has a vocation to consume this good, not that providing it is a matter of his or her own decision, but rather because the defense is available to the whole community—with, moreover, an obligation of use. Added to this, the addition of a supplementary agent does not modify the cost of national defense, nor the consumption of other agents, as all individuals consume the good in its entirety, and without rivalry.[22]

So, generally, most authors of neoclassicism admit the intervention of the State in matters of defense for reasons less political—which would refer in particular to the concept of "sovereign function"—than economic. For, in the presence of such a public good that the markets are incapable of producing and allocating by the price system, the State would be the only one capable of ensuring the optimization of the equilibrium of the markets for the whole of society. These are, briefly stated, the general terms of the academic consensus existing today on this issue within the mainstream.

8.4 Effects of Defense in the Neoclassical Mainstream

Nevertheless, the debate on the external effects of military research and development (R&D) remains very controversial among neoclassicals. A number of modeled or empirical studies evaluating the impact of military R&D show that this diversion of resources to defense is costly in terms of production. Several justifications are put forward: military and civilian R&D use similar resources, hence the eviction of one over the other; or the inelastic supply of human capital puts upward pressure on the prices of R&D inputs; the negative price elasticity of demand for inputs in this sector disincentives private investment in R&D… But these arguments are contested; some authors go so far as to say that the technical progress incorporated into military equipment has a stimulating effect on investment in private R&D. Arbitration is, therefore, not convincingly demonstrated.

A relative consensus is however emerging within the neoclassical mainstream around the idea that the contribution of military R&D to total factor productivity is tending to decline. Sometimes assimilated

[22] Samuelson (1983).

to externalities, technological spin-offs from defense to civilian sectors (through transfers, commercial applications, product or process innovations, organizational and/or informational effects, etc.), characteristics of the post-World War II period, could be less significant today. Some even think that the net flow of scientific knowledge has reversed and that it is currently mainly directed from civilian R&D to the defense sector.[23] The diversion of resources intended for the strategic security of a country could in these conditions lead to degrading its "economic security," by slowing down the technical progress of the exporting sectors, and therefore also the gains in productivity and the competitiveness of the economy. These questions are thus difficult to decide and answer for neoclassicism; especially since the effects of military R&D on the economy are contradictory depending on the data, samples, methodologies, or specifications used.

Consequently, finer analyzes, on a case-by-case basis, intra-sectoral and inter-sectoral, of dual technologies would no doubt be recommended. The conclusions of econometric studies considering defense as a public good are also divided. The impact of military spending on total factor productivity or on GDP growth rate turns out to be insignificant in Aschauer[24] or Barro,[25] for example, but negative for many others, directly or indirectly—through effects on investment, the accumulation of human capital or international trade (due to the opacity of import procedures and trade restrictions). Some authors, such as Landau,[26] have tested a hypothesis of non-linearity of the influence of defense on growth, by combining positive effects (reinforcement of security or incentive for the effectiveness of public policies in the face of the external threat) and negative effects (diversion of resources from productive uses) and by resorting to a quadratic functional form linking growth and defense. The estimates confirm this non-linearity: the coefficients of the "military burden" (indicator of military spending as a percentage of GDP) appear, respectively, positive for its simple value and negative for that squared—increases in military budgets being associated with faster growth up to an optimum, and slower beyond this point. Saadet Deger argued that the sign and size

[23] For an ancient study: KENNEDY (1987).

[24] ASCHAUER (1989a, b).

[25] See: BARRO (1981, 1990, 1991).

[26] LANDAU (1983, 1986, 1993). Also: CRESPO CUARESMA and REITSCHULER (2003).

of the impact of defense would depend on *per capita* income: in poor countries, military spending would promote growth through its modernizing influence; for middle-income countries, the relationship would be reversed and investment crowding out would dominate; and the impact would again be positive when *per capita* income rises, thanks to technological spillovers.[27] However, here again, the debate remains quite open.

Derived from multi-sector formalizations of factorial contributions to GDP growth, neoclassical supply models with externalities specify the transmission channels of the effects of military spending on the economy. The most commonly used, inspired by Feder and by Ram, is due to Biswas and Ram.[28] The sources of growth are analyzed within a framework allowing the impact of military spending to be decomposed and estimated separately into two related but distinct effects: one measures inter-sectoral differentials in marginal factor productivity; the other captures the external effects of defense spreading to the private sector. This methodology has been taken up by many authors, in different variants. Most of the econometric estimates carried out, however, give quite disappointing conclusions, very frequently revealing no significant impact of military spending on growth. These inconclusive results could be explained by the persistence of unresolved technical difficulties at the end of the exercise, due in particular to multicollinearity between the variables tested.[29]

Typically neoclassical, with an alleged microscopic approach, CGEMs or computable general equilibrium models have also been mobilized. Their simulations often show investment and GDP gains following a reduction in military spending. Nonetheless, this type of formalization is open to criticism, as we saw.[30] The study of multifaceted effects of defense requires analyzing more specifically the effects of the accretion of various forms of capital. Extending the problematic to long-term growth has made it possible to use more sophisticated models than econometric specifications and to capture the dynamic implications of these expenditures. Thus, endogenous growth theory, with a macroeconomic approach, has

[27] Deger (1985, 1986a, b).

[28] See: Feder (1983) and Ram (1985). Also: Biswas and Ram (1986).

[29] Here: Herrera (1997).

[30] Also: Herrera and Gentilucci (2013).

placed emphasis on the role of human and/or infrastructural capital accumulation in determining the long-run growth rate.

Here, economic policy choices relating to the structure of public budgets may be of some interest in explaining the growth performance of economies, via the trade-offs between military spending and new engines of growth. Among the positive effects, let us mention the increase in total factor productivity (i.e., among production function arguments) caused by the influence of the capital component of defense budget on technical progress (externalities, organization, etc.), or a strengthening security, and therefore an improving well-being (in the social utility function). Negative effects include the mobilization of qualified workers in defense, which reduces the human capital available for the productive sectors, or intrabudgetary arbitration operating at the expense of other public expenditures (education, infrastructure, etc.).[31]

A deficiency of many orthodox models is the absence of consideration of security indicators, which prevents any reflection in strategic terms. The analysis of the links between growth and security, resulting particularly in deepened interactions existing between Pareto-optimality and Nash equilibrium,[32] can then lead to the field of game theory—a field of mathematical expression *par excellence*.[33] All in all, the fact remains that attempts to incorporate military variables into neoclassical works, which have certainly brought interesting intuitions, are very often contradictory, contingent, or fruitless.

8.5 Ultraliberal Currents and the Privatization of the Army

One of the main difficulties in applying public economics of neoclassicism to defense, however, is that it mixes up several types of market imperfections. In order for the expenditure deemed "optimal" that the State devotes to this good to correspond to a level enabling the willingness to pay of individuals to equal the cost of its provision, it is also necessary that the size and composition of public budgets are known by all consumers, as

[31] Herrera (2010a, 2012).

[32] Nash (1950, 1951).

[33] Herrera (1998b, 2010a, 2012). In these works, we attempted to combine—in a critical approach—analyzes in terms of endogenous growth theory and game theory.

well as the technical characteristics and budgetary charges associated with defense and other public services. But, agents obviously come up against obstacles in accessing the information that would be needed for them to measure the precise impact of military spending, especially on their individual well-being or on the level of security of the national territory which determines, between others, the social utility of defense. This problem of information asymmetry, linked to the confidential nature of statistical data relating to military budgets and activities, therefore, disrupts public choices and intrabudgetary resource allocation procedures.

An additional difficulty stems from the atypical and dichotomous nature of the public good of defense, which is very different from civilian infrastructures. For example, defense increases the security—and the level of social utility—of the country which is its instigator; but, it is at the same time intended to reduce internationally the security level of the foreign countries which are viewed as potential enemies in a non-cooperative strategic framework. As a result, it is understandable that, globally, the positive consequences generated by a country's military spending for its national security can be offset, and even beyond, by the negative externalities they cause on agents of foreign countries.

Furthermore, some ultraliberal economists have come to dispute and challenge the public good character of defense.[34] Faced with market failures, underscored by neoclassical theory itself, proponents of the Public Choices school—coming, politically, from the right of the mainstream and most frequently maintaining a utilitarist approach—did not cease to assert that the functioning of market mechanisms, even imperfect ones, remains systematically preferable to the defects of the intervention of the State, which masks individual preferences under the discourse of the general interest.[35]

The adverse and perverse effects denounced by these authors are mostly related to pricing practices deemed sub-optimal, inefficient behaviors of government or public administrations which do not have the information necessary for effective control of natural monopolies, the non-appropriability of profits which hinders the managerial motivation

[34] Goff and Tollison (1990).

[35] Buchanan and Tullock (1961). More recently, Buchanan and Musgrave (1999).

and incentive, or the risks of bureaucratic drift or abuse of a dominant position.[36]

Under these conditions, they wonder why a U.S. citizen, or what they call the "consumer-taxpayer," in Seattle or Washington D.C., for example, would agree to pay a tax intended to finance the protection of the border of the United States with Mexico? According to them, the corresponding tax burden should be borne only by the inhabitants of the States concerned, stretching from Texas to California.

On the basis of extreme anti-State positions clearly in favor of private property and free trade, some "libertarian" theorists have gone so far as to recommend a privatization of national defense.[37] The latter should be, following these authors, submitted to competition laws, like any private good, in a market where enterprises (i.e., private military companies) offer the goods and services provided until then by the public authorities, and that economic agents would have to "freely" select according to their security needs and to a rational quality-price calculus, by performing a standard cost–benefit program.[38]

Although these (quite provocative) analyses represent a minority within the theoretical debates, they have nevertheless ended up influencing significantly political practice in the United States—even if their supporters are frequently firmly opposed to war, according to the argument that war is still a State affair.[39] It comes that while, in theory, defense is most often conceived as a public good, the fact remains that, in practice, it is widely privatized. Since the early 1980s, did not the neoliberal waves of the Reaganomics period prompt the U.S. government to "outsource" many defense-related activities (for consulting, training, logistical support, etc.)? We shall come back to that in a moment.

8.6 Some Heterodox Interpretations

Economic theory has nevertheless undergone quite interesting developments outside or on the fringes of neoclassicism. This was the case, for example, with the models of interindustrial exchanges, inspired by

[36] See: Buchanan (1975).

[37] Such is the case of David Friedman, Milton Friedman's son. See: Friedman (1973).

[38] Squire and Van Der Tak (1975).

[39] Rothbart (1973).

the work of Wassily W. Leontief.[40] Distinct from the neoclassical trend, these studies, carried out using input-output analysis, provide a relevant and original analytical framework for measuring the macroscopic effects of variations in military spending at the national, regional and international levels, taking into account in a disaggregated way the allocations of resources between the civilian and military sectors. Such a methodology, operating by projection over the short, medium, and long terms, turns out to be particularly suitable for evaluating the effects of budgetary choices performed in connection with various disarmament plans. These input–output analyzes have been used on numerous occasions by W.W. Leontief and his teams, in order to study the consequences of military budget cuts on the United States economy, or to simulate regional and international disarmament scenarios.[41] Located at the (external) margins of the mainstream, this current remains still relatively active today.[42]

Note that typically neoclassical simulation macroeconomic models also exist in the literature. For example, according to IMF experts,[43] the short-term impact of a uniform reduction in the world military expenditures would be a slight decrease in the GDP growth rates; but beneficial effects are perceptible in medium run, on consumption, investment, and employment. However, these IMF models present serious shortcomings, resulting from their weak assumptions, such as: absence of investment component in the military sector (which includes only operational costs), of quantified effects on security or of a sufficient data disaggregation (e.g., to know if a country is a producer or an importer of weapons), or also the use of a confusing hypothesis of rational expectations. Such models should thus be treated with suspicion. In the core of the neoclassical mainstream, "microeconomic" CGEMs incorporating military spending have also been mobilized,[44] but we have previously seen that this type of modeling is questionable (see Chapter 3).

[40] Leontief (1941).

[41] Leontief and Hoffenberg (1961), Leontief et al. (1965), Leontief and Petri (1971), and Leontief and Duchin (1983), for example. For a survey on Leontief-inspired works applied to defense economics, see: Gentilucci (2010).

[42] Turner (2004), and Günlük-Enesen (2007) for one of the most recent studies.

[43] Like Bayoumi et al. (1993) and (1995).

[44] Among others: Athanassiou et al. (2002).

As for them, the macroeconomic models of demand, reasoning on the basis of a Keynesian-inspired national income balance equation, postulate a negative impact of the military burden on demand, via the multiplier, by distinguishing between differentiated influences on non-military public expenditure and components of private sector absorption.[45] This approach has the advantage of providing a framework that identifies crowding-out effects resulting from defense spending shocks occurring to the detriment of private investment, consumption or exports, and adversely affecting the activity in the short term, particularly through underemployment.

Nevertheless, these models also have limits. They do not capture the impact of the military sector on the dynamics of accumulation; they do not distinguish with precision the effects operating in the long term compared to those of the short or medium period; nor do they differentiate the contractions of (productive) investment from those of (unproductive) consumption; and finally, they do not really clarify the atypical nature of defense, which has complex relations with the rest of the economy, quite distinct from those associated with other public expenditure. In addition, empirical studies based on such specifications leave uncertainty as to the category of demand likely to suffer the most from these evictions.

Under these conditions, a path followed by certain authors—those of the "Keynesian-neoclassical synthesis"—consisted in taking into consideration, from a long-term perspective, a supply component, with an almost non-existent role in many Keynesian models. Formally, this integration of the supply results in the use of a standard production function. Taking into account military spending in a multisectoral framework, with differentiated production functions, could consider a final good of the private sector obtained from a technology combining the traditional factors (capital and labor), to which is added a military public good—sometimes interpreted as an externality.[46] However, it can also go through a disaggregation of the capital stock into civilian and military components, in order to seek to econometrically estimate the elasticity of the output to military capital and the specific contribution of this stock to growth.

[45] Smith (1977, 1980).

[46] Biswas and Ram (1986).

The economically unproductive (or "not directly productive") nature of defense nonetheless makes this kind of specification quite difficult to support. Other authors have, therefore, been led to incorporate simultaneously, and in dynamic writing, the supply and demand aspects, which allows to deduce from the equilibrium of national income an expression of capital accumulation and a production function in which effectively used capital and efficient labor are integrated—with an efficiency parameter characterizing the underutilization of capital. Growth being given at the stationary state by demographic and technological changes, supposedly exogenous, military spending has no long-term influence on it—except to pose a possible effect of these expenditures on technical progress. The impact is, however, perceptible on the transitional path leading to the steady state.

Such a model, therefore, makes possible the direct effects of military spending: (i) negative on the supply side, on the formation of private capital, via the savings rate, by crowding-out investment; but (ii) positive on the demand side, on the rate of use of capital, through the solicitation of productive capacities in the short term.[47] More indirect influences can also be highlighted, particularly on the propensity to save of the private sector, the share of civilian public expenditure, the capital-output ratio or the balance of payments. The adverse effects can be magnified if, for example, the increased military burden is covered by cuts in social budgets, affecting the educational sector in particular.[48]

From a completely different perspective, the theme of defense is fundamental for theoreticians of Marxist currents. Here, the problems related to war are treated in a broader and deeper way, and have given rise to multiple, important reflections. To begin with, these issues permanently attracted the attention of Marx—and, even more so, of Engels.[49] Marx interpreted war as the means by which the division and distribution of markets between capitalists operate on a global scale, namely "the struggle of competition through war," as that of acquiring "property" originally. However, war is also viewed in its relationships to classes—even if the

[47] Deger and Sen (1995). Also: Broude et al. (2013). About the supply–demand relationships, see: Shieh et al. (2002), Galvin (2003), and Klein (2004).

[48] Deger (1985).

[49] Marx and Engels (1973), *Band* 17. By instance, among many examples, see: "Über den Krieg" by F. Engels. Available on: http://www.mlwerke.de/me/me17/me17_udk.htm.

military terminology is amply transposed to the terrain of social struggles, when saying that the ruling classes use the State, specifically its repressive functions (army and police) "as the national war machine of Capital against Labor."[50] For example, what is expected from the events of 1848 is the chain of events linking a proletarian uprising (in France) to a wider war (in Europe), then to a generalized one (worldwide), and finally to the victory of the revolution. Nevertheless, this logic did not happen, notably because of the impotence of workers' movements to stop the dramatic spiral of imperialist wars (as in 1914) and the unleashing of chauvinism—or the "bad side" of nationalism—pushing peoples to fight first for their existence "as such." Faced with the rise of imperialism, the most prominent Marxists, from Lenin to Rosa Luxemburg,[51] will never cease to emphasize that war, linked to the class struggle and always situated in a given historical context, only serves the interests of capitalists and only makes victims among the working classes; this, while the "reformists," as for them, will call for the renunciation of the class struggle during the war to defend the "fatherland" as a priority. Much more recently, since the Cold War and the "arms race" between the two superpowers which accompanied it, concerns have focused on the risks associated with nuclear weapons.[52]

8.7 Toward Alternative Interpretations Within Marxism

For our part, we propose to question the nature of the contemporary or recent wars undertaken by the United States and its allies—wars which remain a "taboo" of the present times, and whom the mainstream media refuses to call "imperialist"—as well as the links that they could maintain, beyond the simple thesis of the control of strategic natural resources, with the systemic crisis we are currently going through. On this occasion, we join the theories of imperialism, for which militarization is seen as a modality of existence of capitalism, and the use of armed force as a strategy imposed by the dominant fractions of the dominant classes—that is to say, nowadays, high finance, or the most powerful financial

[50] For these three quotations, see, respectively, Marx (1980, 1972, 1978).

[51] From the perspective of studying the revolutionary war, read: Mao (1968).

[52] Here, e.g., Rubel (1997).

oligopolies, mainly U.S. ones—to allow the reproduction of the conditions of their retention in power over the capitalist world system. We will also wonder about the opportunities military expenditures open to big owners of globally dominant capital to transform the very forms of capital; about the eventual possibilities they offer to revitalize accumulation at the center of the capitalist world system; but also and above all about the major risks of aggravation of the internal contradictions of capitalism that they feed.

The war we will discuss is the one generated by imperialist capitalism, currently neoliberalized. As we have seen, the distant origin of the wars that imperialism has launched goes back to the end of the Nineteenth Century, when high finance was formed in the United States, through the formation of financial oligopolies, immediately after their takeover of the U.S. economy itself (Chapter 7). The phenomenon that matters to us here is their departure from national borders, as these giant oligopolies went to war and took on the world. After a parenthesis that lasted from the crisis of the 1930s (the Great Depression) to that of the 1970s (the beginning of the neoliberal era), the expansion of globalized finance resumed by a "financial coup d'Etat": the year 1979 was the turning point in the return of financial oligopolies, when the U.S. Fed decided to raise its interest rates in an attempt to address the decline in the rate of profit since the end of the 1960s and to establish the global dominance of high finance by giving power back to the rentiers.

From the time of the U.S. aggression in Vietnam, private companies had been integrated into the imperialist war effort: Pacific Architects and Engineers for infrastructure works, DynCorp for freight transport, Halliburton and Vinnell for logistical support, Lockheed Martin and General Dynamics for the production of weapons, etc. The weight of private corporations of the military-industrial complex in the manufacture of military equipment was already considerable at the end of World War II—to the point of worrying U.S. President Dwight D. Eisenhower, who warned his fellow citizens against the increasing threat posed by the collusion of interests of this industry, big business and the army: "A vital element in keeping the peace is our military establishment. (…) [N]ow we can no longer risk emergency improvisation of national defense; we have been compelled to create a permanent armaments industry of vast proportions. (…) This conjunction of an immense military establishment and a large arms industry is new in the American experience. (…) We recognize the imperative need for this development. Yet we must not fail to comprehend its grave implications. Our toil, resources and livelihood are all involved; so is the very structure of our society. (…) In the councils of government, we must guard against the acquisition of unwarranted influence (…) by the military-industrial complex. The potential for the disastrous rise of misplaced power exists and will persist. (…) We must never let the weight of this combination endanger our liberties or democratic processes. (…) We should take nothing for granted only an alert and knowledgeable citizenry can compel the proper meshing of huge industrial and military machinery of defense with our peaceful methods and goals, so that security and liberty may prosper together."[53]

Extremely powerful pressure groups have been established at some meeting points, bringing together senior army officials, congressmen from the defense committees, and influent leaders of armament companies, whose interactions converge to obtain contracts from the government agencies. The main suppliers to the U.S. Department of Defense are today giant transnational corporations, operating in the aeronautical and space sectors, shipbuilding, computer services, etc., and whose military contracts with the Pentagon bring in astronomical amounts representing an often dominant part of their turnover. This was recently the case for Lockheed Corp. (with tens of billions dollars in contracts, notably for the U-2 bomber and F-117 Nighthawk fighter), Boeing Co. (for similar amounts, supplying the army in planes, helicopters, and satellites), General Dynamics (at the origin of the F-16 Fighting Falcon), but also Northrop Grumman Corp., Raytheon, BAE Systems, United Technologies Corp., Computer Sciences Corp., etc.

Private military companies have gradually managed to establish themselves as key players in the military sector in the United States. Present in all major conflict areas around the world, they have now become the main client of the U.S. government itself. Hundreds of companies in the sector together currently achieve an annual turnover of more than 100 billion dollars, more than half of which coming from Pentagon

[53] Cf. D.D. Eisenhower's Farewell Address to the Nation on January 17, 1961. Excerpts from Paragraph IV of this speech. See: https://www.ourdocuments.gov/doc.php?flash=false&doc=90&page=transcript. Twenty years later, R. Reagan's position was quite different, who said in 1981: "Government is not a solution to our problem; government is the problem." Read: https://www.reaganfoundation.org/ronald-reagan/reagan-quotes-speeches/.

contracts. To name only the most important companies of U.S. nationality: MPRI, KBR, Blackwater, Control Risks, DynCorp, Vinnell, etc. Thereby, they increasingly provide private entities, as well as international institutions, States, non-governmental organizations, with a wide range of technical services relating to defense and intended to assist or supplement the regular governmental armed forces; in particular: construction and maintenance of military installations; surveillance and protection of strategic sites (military bases, hydrocarbon deposits, mines, lines of communication, etc.); logistics and organization of the supply of food, fuel, equipment or ammunition; troop training, combat simulations, and training; intelligence; public relations, etc. These services go as far as providing specialized security personnel, such as: military consultants and advisers, bodyguards, interrogators, and interpreters, or even battalions of mercenary commandos who participate directly in the fighting…[54] For example, by 2008, the number of U.S. military personnel in Iraq had been exceeded by that of private military companies. The paramilitary troops (75,000 persons employed by some 300 firms which are integrated into the "total force") formed the second largest contingent in 2007, exceeding the allied troops combined. Their main customer is the State, which has turned Afghanistan and Iraq into a market in the "War on Terror" crusade.

But the key thing is that, today, we are dealing with a takeover of the military sector by high finance. The military-industrial complex continues to play a fundamental role, but being placed under the control of high finance.[55] As a matter of fact, as the U.S. government outsources a larger part of its defense logistics support activities, an ever greater share of private military companies falls under the control of the biggest and most powerful financial oligopolies. Indeed, the share of the ownership structure of military capital held by transnational corporations owned by institutional investors which are themselves controlled by high finance is growing. In the early 2000s, it had already reached approximately 95% of the total assets of Lockheed Martin, 75% of General Dynamics, 65% of Boeing… The same evolution occurred for the private military

[54] See: Cicchini and Herrera (2008).

[55] Mampaey (2010).

companies, with an ever larger share of them passing under the thumb of high finance: MPRI was bought out by L-3 Communications, Vinnell by Carlyle, DynCorp by Veritas, etc.[56]

8.8 Links Between Imperialist Wars and the Systemic Crisis of Capital

The links between capital crisis and imperialist wars characterize the destructive spiral in which the world system is trapped today by the strategy of military domination of the United States. First, what are the causal relations operating in the direction going from wars toward the crisis? We have seen that the crisis results from a process of capital overaccumulation (Chapter 7). Historically, after World War II, imperialist wars (particularly in Korea, and then in Vietnam) caused profound imbalances in the U.S. economy throughout the 1960s; imbalances that are at the root of the crisis we are currently experiencing—the same one, systemic, since the 1970s. However, these wars gradually made the mechanisms of regulation of the world system by the U.S. hegemony dysfunctional, since the latter's internal and external deficits increased its foreign debt, multiplied the number of eurodollars, then that of petrodollars on the interbank markets, and caused strong tensions on the dollar. These tensions finally proved unsustainable and contributed to the oil crises of the 1970s, as well as to the world's tipping into monetary and financial chaos, in connection with the demonetization of gold, the deregulation of markets, and the flexibilization of exchange rates, among others. It is on this terrain that, since the 1960s, fictitious capital has developed in Wall Street, Chicago, London's City, and elsewhere.

But there is also a second channel of transmission from wars to the crisis. During the Cold War, the expansion of the productive forces in the United States has been partly driven by military spending and the investments of the military-industrial complex in the "arms race," and the associated technical progress, like complex computerized systems, computer-controlled robots, the ancestors of the Internet, etc. So, the current structural crisis of capitalism has its origins in the exhaustion of the engines of the post-war boom, including the lesser impact of technical progress induced by the military sector. Thus, the modes of organizing

[56] See: Herrera (2010b).

production and extracting surplus value have reached their limits, and have had to be replaced by new methods that have upset the social foundations by substituting more and more capital for living labor. Nevertheless, a question immediately arises: If human beings are replaced by machines, do not the latter risk in the long run leaving no space for labor and employment? This is a major contradiction where the evils of capitalism and recurrent crises are concentrated.

Conversely, we note other causal links acting in the direction going from the crisis toward wars. On the one hand, economically, wars are integrated into the capital cycle, as a form of destruction of capital. Since military spending is considered unproductive, it is a means of destroying surplus capital. This is the reason why the extreme form of devalorization of capital, in this case military war, is increasingly used by the dominant financial fractions of capital—notwithstanding the "democratic peace" theorists, who claim that democratic countries are by nature peaceful.[57] Instead of having economic growth in the United States driven by an active production-oriented strategy, these fractions of the ruling classes, at least as far as the "Globalists" are concerned,[58] have rather chosen to promote both financial and military fictitious capital accumulation. And politically, on the other hand, because it is indeed the State that maked the country wage war on behalf of capital, imperialist wars are there for the reproduction of the conditions for maintaining the command of the ruling classes' dominant fractions, i.e., high finance, over the global system. Such fractions keep their power only through their investments in the military-industrial complex in order to offer capital new outlets and enlarged opportunities for speculation. The capitalist world system seems to function more and more directly through the use of U.S. armed force—the basis of this visible violence being the invisible violence of capitalist relations of production. Militarization is genuinely a modality of existence of the capital of these financial oligopolies. The name of globalization is imperialism—an imperialism more and more openly enforced by war. Finance is at war against whoever tries to carry out or affirm autonomous development, and such development is the basic cause of the imperialist wars supporting finance. Backed by the U.S. military, high finance capital tries to keep control of the petrodollar—even if this means

[57] Babst (1964).

[58] Observatoire international de la Crise (2019).

new wars. Hence, the armed conflicts in the Middle East, an oil-rich and de facto, dollarized and coveted region.

War and the crisis are, under these conditions, embedded phenomena. The two are intrinsically intertwined. The decade 2000 opened with the September 11 (2001) attack and ended with the so-called "subprime crisis" (in 2008). In both cases, there was an intensification of wars in the Middle East. The wars in Afghanistan and Iraq were launched at specific times (2001 and 2003), in times of changes in monetary policy—because of the very need for dealing with the crisis (as in 1913 or 1938) and for financing of the war effort. In 2001, the "new economy" bubble burst. Faced with slowing growth, the Fed reduced the interest rate (from 6.5% in 2000 to 1.7% in 2001, then to 1% in 2003) and military spending started to rise again, after the decline of the post-Soviet era and the "peace dividends." Why, if not also to wage war? The U.S. interest rate remained low until 2004 (and even negative in real terms in 2003), before rising again to over 5% in mid-2005, because of the need to finance these wars. But this gave a boost to the real estate market. The mechanisms of the "subprime" crisis were put in place, with perilous risk-taking. After the military engagement in Iraq, the war effort pushed the Fed to raise the interest rate again (to 5.25% in mid-2006) to attract new capital to the United States.

A few months later, mortgage loan schedules began to be interrupted by defaulting debtors. The Fed kept this rate above 5% until mid-2007, when the crisis was already here. It was not until late, after August 2007, that it granted banks huge amounts of zero interest loans, but this did not prevent a panic. In the meantime, the economy had fallen into a depression—even though financial profits recovered in 2009. The 2008 crisis occurred at the same time as the external and internal imbalances were deteriorating in the United States: external imbalances can be seen in the balance of payments, partly due to industrial relocation (to Mexico and, above all, to China); and internal imbalances (budget deficits and public debt) had several causes, the most decisive of which is the pressure exerted by the increased need for financing to continue the imperialist wars that Washington was undertaking in an attempt to extend its military control of the planet.[59]

[59] Herrera (2015).

8.9 A Global System with Growing Contradictions

Among the options for getting out of the crisis that are being considered by the dominant fractions of neoliberal globalist capital, there is, unfortunately, that of the generalization of a project of warlike destruction. Over-accumulation is a chronic disease of capitalism, from which it cannot escape and which marks its long-term structural tendency to enter into crisis—and even into decadence. To avoid this overaccumulation, a drastic, dramatic solution exists: the devalorization of capital through its massive destruction. This is the terrain of war. Even if, in the end, imperialist wars further aggravate the imbalances. In order to restart a cycle of long accumulation at the center of the capitalist system, the current crisis would have to destroy gigantic additional amounts of fictitious capital—including by means of wars. Nevertheless, as we have already said in the previous chapter, the contradictions of capitalism have now become so deep and serious that such a devalorization would risk pushing it toward collapse. The reorganizations of the domination of capital have not, however, eliminated its contradictions. We will thus continue to suffer for a long time from the evils of this declining capitalism.

The question is whether the U.S. government could revitalize capital accumulation at the center of the capitalist global system through war. We answer no, insofar as the destruction of capital (constant and variable) caused by these armed conflicts—certainly considerable for the countries which suffer from them—are insufficient to stimulate a renewed long cycle of capital expansion in the United States, as it was the case after World War II with the Marshall Plan. They are also insufficient to revive growth when considering the effective demand effects associated with such wars, which mainly concern the short term, or the technological spin-offs, which are positive only for the military-industrial sector. Unless these imperialist wars are extended and become permanent in a context of systemic crisis, accompanied by a drain of capital toward the United States and an aggravation of the North–South confrontation—as well as the NATO-East confrontation.[60]

What about capital accumulation? If a high interest rate tends to inhibit credit and growth, one solution consists in creating billions of dollars of new money out of thin air and buy sovereign securities to reduce that

[60] Foster and Magdoff (2009).

rate—to zero. If the contraction in demand is likely to lead to deflation, money will be issued in the form of State securities with which weapons mega-projects will be financed. However, the ripple effect on the domestic economy will only be guaranteed if there are more wars and/or more arms sales to foreign customers. Since the fall of the USSR, the majority of U.S. military spending has been carried out through indebtedness in U.S. dollars, which is achieved by issuing Treasury bills, thus resorting to fictitious capital, with an associated burden transferred on third countries. Now, military spending thus becomes a major source of profitability for capitalists because it can massively transform unproductive capital—notably when it is financed by public debt—into additional fictitious capital. Faced with the possible tendency of the rate of profit in civilian production to fall, the war economy constitutes "the alternative"—always from the point of view of capitalists.

The work done in this sector, which programs no more and no less than the destruction of human lives, but also of material and natural wealth on a large scale, is unproductive: weapons are said to be unproductive "by its content," in the sense that they do not favor the expansive economic cycle of capital.[61] Since military commodities count as real wealth, the sale of these means of destruction nevertheless allows for the realization of additional profits in a cycle. Yet, even when sold without being "consumed" or without causing destruction in a war, they are retained in the cycle, but do not contribute to the expanded reproduction of total capital, nor do they appear in the next cycle as means of production to increase capital and hire labor power. Then, the capital generated becomes an obstacle to the next cycle. As a consequence, the growth of military capital limits the reproduction of total capital and affects economic growth. And to transfer the burden of this expenditure, it will, therefore, be necessary to fabricate more and more threats, based on real or invented arguments, and even to launch or provoke new wars.

The contradictions of the capitalist world system are then exacerbated and taken to a higher level. Defense is now outsourced by the U.S. government, which often wages war "vicariously." The possibility for the State to authorize private companies to train armed forces abroad or offer them security services opens up the prospects of "foreign policy by proxy." The wars waged in Iraq and Afghanistan were striking examples of

[61] Observatoire international de la Crise (2019).

the growth of the activities of these private companies, where their use by the U.S. administration is widespread. These countries have been transformed into privileged areas of action for the "new war market," above all for mercenaries in charge of tactical missions... before the rout of the United States is total.[62]

In fact, the result is that this privatization of wars was proving to fail. The failure of the "public-private system" is complete, bringing multiple problems and contradictions: inefficiency in winning conflicts, recruitment difficulties, extra costs for the taxpayer, etc. And their share of scandals: eviction from tenders by secret agreements, payments of not-made services, dubious cohabitation of shareholders (e.g., of the Bush and Bin Laden families at Carlyle), tensions between regular soldiers and private mercenaries, exactions abuses of all kinds, etc.[63]

It is the very hegemony of the United States that has entered into crisis, not only at the points of imperialist attacks—in Afghanistan as well as in Iraq where, for it, the difficulties were insurmountable—but also globally.[64] It means that the militarization of finance neoliberalism has no way out. Its strategy of war has reached a dead end. Especially when, recently, it comes up against a power like Russia, which is particularly determined not to let itself be surrounded too closely... And it is very likely that China will not intend to let it go either.

A relatively little-known contradiction is the rise of antiwar resistance within the U.S. army itself. In the 1970s, the change from conscription to professionalization in the United States was a response to technical and economic requirements, but also to political ones, linked to the need for the military command to regain control over the contingents of unruly conscripts in the post-1968 period of defeat in Vietnam. Let us remember the "Resisting Inside The Army" (RITA) movement, which was born in 1967 and had arisen on the initiative of U.S. soldiers opposed to the Vietnam war. Much more recently, the spirit of protest of these "RITAs" yet blew through the "IVAW" or Iraq Veterans Against the War.[65]

[62] Avant (2005).

[63] Schumacher (2006).

[64] Johnson (2010).

[65] Catalinotto (2017). See as well the website: http://ivaw.org/. And: http://appealforredress.org./index.php.

In the early 2010s, we calculated that there would have been 935,700 U.S. military personnel abroad, including the private paramilitary employees paid by the Pentagon, that is, more than the historical record of the post-World War II era (at 927,851), spread over some 1,150 bases worldwide.[66] It is because over a long period, since the 1980s, high finance repatriates more and more flows of profits from the rest of the world that the U.S. army bombards or threatens so many peoples of the South, from its global network of military bases. But the global system cannot continue to operate in this way; it will have to change. However, we cannot exclude a modification of the trajectory of the system toward an even more destructive militarization of hegemony. The U.S. hegemony is now in crisis and its difficulties seem insurmountable. Its very capacity to support its armies is running out. And it would be even worse if the anchor of the petrodollar were to escape it. Indeed, the destabilization of the dollar, the pillar of this hegemony, could unbalance the other pillar, the military pillar, which depends on the country's capacity to incur debt. As soon as Treasury bonds are no longer in demand, the source of financing for the giant military-industrial complex will dry up, revealing its unproductive—and fictitious—character. And if the United States could no longer maintain its network of military bases, its unipolar world would be called into question.

Will the future spare us a cataclysm? The "peaceful coexistence" between the United States and the Soviet Union had led to a substitution of military warfare—apart from localized conflicts—by economic warfare between the two superpowers. Now, the new "Cold War" is rather between Washington and Beijing plus Moscow.[67] However, the pressures exerted by NATO (and, therefore, by the United States, which is in command) against Russia—a country which has also been under Western economic sanctions since 2014—have very recently shown that a spark can rekindle military war, including on the European continent.

Caught in the trap of a global systemic crisis, capital no longer finds solutions within the logic of maximizing immediate profits and becomes more and more dangerous. All the conditions are met for the contradictions of the system to become even more pronounced. Decisively, the urgency remains to stop the "regulation" of the world system under U.S.

[66] Herrera and Cicchini (2013).

[67] Herrera (2021).

hegemony by war. The defense of peace is now a priority. Therefore, it is necessary to unplug the infernal machine of imperialist wars operated by the financial oligopolies through a democratic control on them. Especially since, in the capitalist logic of valorization for valorization's sake, the climate crisis multiplies the risks of ecological disasters, but also of wars for access to water, natural resources, hydrocarbons—with, among many other tragic consequences, massive forced migrations to be expected.

References

Alexander W.R. (1990), "The Impact of Defence Spending on Economic Growth," *Defence Economics*, vol. 2, n° 1, p. 39–55.

Anderton C.H. and J.R. Carter (2007), "A Survey of Peace Economics," *in* K. Hartley and T. Sandler (eds.), *Handbook of Defense Economics*, vol. 2, p. 1211–1258, Amsterdam: Elsevier.

Antonakis N. (1999), "Guns vs. Butter: A Multisectoral Approach to Military Expenditure and Growth with Evidence from Greece," *Journal of Conflict Resolution*, vol. 43, n° 4, p. 501–520.

Arrow K.J. (1992), "The Basic Economics of Arms Reduction," *in* W. Isard and C.H. Anderton (eds.), *Economics of Arms Reduction and the Peace Process*, p. 57–67, Amsterdam: North Holland.

Arrow, K.J. and J.E. Li (1993), "A Note on the Peace Dividend and Reallocation of Knowledge Skills," *in* J. Brauer and M. Chatterji (eds.), *Economic Issues of Disarmament*, p. 26–32, London: Macmillan.

Aschauer D.A. (1989a), "Public Investment and Productivity Growth in the Group of Seven," *Economic Perspectives*, vol. 13, n° 5, p. 17–25.

——— (1989b), "Is Public Expenditure Productive?," *Journal of Monetary Economics*, vol. 23, n° 1, p. 77–200.

Athanassiou E., C. Kollias and A. Zografakis (2002), "The Effects of Defence Spending Reductions: A CGE Estimation of the Foregone Peace Dividend in the Case of Greece," *Defence and Peace Economics*, vol. 13, n° 2, p. 417–427.

Avant D.D. (2005), *The Market for Force: The Consequences of Privatizing Security*, Cambridge (UK): Cambridge University Press.

Babst D.V. (1964), "Elective Governments: A Force For Peace," *The Wisconsin Sociologist*, vol. 3, n° 1, p. 9–14.

Barro R.J. (1981), "Output Effects of Government Purchases," *Journal of Political Economy*, vol. 89, n° 6, p. 1086–1121.

——— (1990), "Government Spending in a Simple Model of Endogenous Growth," *Journal of Political Economy*, vol. 98, n° 5, p. S103–S125.

——— (1991), "Economic Growth in a Cross Section of Countries," *Quarterly Journal of Economics*, vol. 106, n° 2, p. 407–443.
BATCHELOR P., J.P. DUNNE and D.S. SAAL (2000), "Military Spending and Economic Growth in South Africa," *Defence and Peace Economics*, vol. 11, n° 4, p. 553–571.
BAYOUMI T., D.P. HEWITT and J. SCHIFF (1995), "Economic Consequences of Lower Military Spending," *in* L.R. Klein, F.C. Lo and W.J. McKibbin (eds.), *Arms Reduction*, p. 172–219, Tokyo: United Nations University Press.
BAYOUMI T., D.P. HEWITT and S. SZYMANSKY (1993), "The Impact of Worldwide Military Spending Cuts on Developing Countries," *IMF Working Paper*, p. 93–86, Washington DC: International Monetary Fund.
BENOIT E. and K.E. BOULDING (1963), *Disarmament and the Economy*, New York: Harper and Row Publishers.
BISWAS B. and R. RAM (1986), "Military Expenditure and Economic Growth in Less Developed Countries," *Economic Development and Cultural Change*, vol. 34, n° 2, p. 361–372.
BOULDING K.E. (1962), *Conflict and Defense*, New York: Harper and Row Publisher.
BROUDE M., S. DEGER and S. SEN (2013), "Defence, Innovation and Development: the Case of Israel," *Journal of Innovation Economics and Management*, n° 2013/2, n° 12, p. 37–57.
BUCHANAN J.M. (1975), *The Limits of Liberty—Between Anarchy and Leviathan*, Chicago: University of Chicago Press.
BUCHANAN J.M. and R.A. MUSGRAVE (1999), *Public Finance and Public Choice: Two Contrasting Views of the State*, Cambridge MA: The MIT Press.
BUCHANAN J.M. and G. TULLOCK (1961), *The Calculus of Consent: Logical Foundations of Constitutional Democracy*, Ann Arbor: The University of Michigan Press.
CATALINOTTO J. (2017), *Turn the Guns Around*, New York: World View Forum.
CENTRAL INTELLIGENCE AGENCY (various years), *The World Factbook*, Public Affairs, Washington DC.
CICCHINI J. and R. HERRERA (2008), "Sociétés militaires privées: la guerre par procuration ? Le cas de la guerre d'Irak," *Recherches internationales*, n° 82, p. 9–26, Paris.
CRESPO CUARESMA J. and G. REITSCHULER (2003), "A Non-Linear Defence-Growth Nexus? Evidence from US Economy," *Defence and Peace Economics*, vol. 15, n° 1, p. 71–82.
DEGER S. (1985), "Human Resources, Government Education Expenditure, and the Military Burden in Less Developed Countries," *Journal of Developing Areas*, vol. 20, n° 1, p. 37–48.
——— (1986a), *Military Expenditure in the Third World Countries: The Economic Effects*, London, Routledge & Kegan Paul.

——— (1986b), "Economic Development and Defense Expenditure," *Economic Development and Cultural Change*, vol. 35, n° 1, p. 180–196.

DEGER S. and S. SEN (1995), "Military Security and Developing Countries," *in* K. Hartley and T. Sandler (eds.), *Handbook of Defense Economics*, vol. 1, p. 275–307, Amsterdam: North Holland.

FEDER G. (1983), "On Exports and Economic Growth," *Journal of Development Economics*, vol. 12, n°s 1–2, p. 59–73.

FOSTER J.B. and F. MAGDOFF (2009), *The Great Financial Crisis*, New York: Monthly Review Press.

FRIEDMAN D. (1973), *The Machinery of Freedom*, New York: Harper Collophon.

GALVIN H. (2003), "The Impact of Defence Spending on the Economic Growth of Developing Countries: A Cross-Section Study," *Defence and Peace Economics*, vol. 14, n° 1, p. 51–59.

GENTILUCCI E. (2010), "La Spesa militare nell'analisi degli economisti contemporanei," Ph.D. Dissertation, Université de Paris 1 and Università di Macerata, Paris and Macerata.

GOFF B.L. and R.D. TOLLISON (1990), "Is National Defense a Pure Public Good?," *Defense Economics*, vol. 1, n°. 2, p. 141–147.

GÜNLÜK-ENESEN G. (2007), "Accounting for Arms in Input-Output and National Income Accounts," *in* W. Elsner (ed.), *Arms, War and Terrorism in the Global Economy Today*, p. 50–68, Berlin: LIT Verlag.

HARTLEY K. and T. SANDLER (eds.) (2007), *Handbook of Defense Economics*, Amsterdam: Elsevier.

HERRERA R. (1994), *Statistics on Military Expenditure in Developing Countries: Concepts, Methodological Problems, and Sources*, Paris: OECD Development Centre.

——— (1997), "Productivités et externalités des dépenses publiques: une étude économétrique sur séries temporelles," *Économie & Prévision*, vol. 5, n° 131, p. 145–153, Paris.

——— (1998), "Dépenses militaires: quels effets sur les finances publiques et la croissance économique?," *Revue d'économie politique*, vol. 108, n° 4, p. 503–530, Paris.

——— (2000), "Le Rôle des dépenses militaires dans les pays en développement: une analyse critique théorique et empirique," *Mondes en développement*, n° 112, p. 39–58, Brussels.

——— (ed.) (2001), *L'Empire en guerre - Le Monde après le 11 septembre*, Paris and Brussels: Le Temps des Cerises and EPO.

——— (2006a), "The Hidden Face of Endogenous Growth Theory," *Review of Radical Political Economics*, vol. 38, n° 2, p. 243–257, New York.

——— (2006b), "The 'New' Development Economics: A Neoliberal *Con*?," *Monthly Review*, vol. 58, n° 1, p. 38–50, New York.

——— (2007), "War and Crisis," *Political Affairs*, vol. 86, n° 4, p. 34–38, New York.

——— (2010a), *Dépenses publiques et croissance économique - Pour sortir de la science(-fiction) néoclassique*, Paris: L'Harmattan.

——— (2010b), *Un Autre Capitalisme n'est pas possible*, Paris: Syllepse.

——— (2011), "A Critique of Mainstream Growth Theory," *Research in Political Economy*, vol. 27, n° 1, p. 3–64, London and New York.

——— (2012), *Gastos públicos y crecimiento económico*, Caracas: Banco Central de Venezuela.

——— (2013a), "Defense and the Economy," *Journal of Innovation Economics and Management*, n° 2013/2, p. 3–11, Brussels.

——— (2013b), "Between Crisis and Wars—Where Is the United States Heading?," *Journal of Innovation Economics and Management*, n° 2013/2, p. 151–174, Brussels.

——— (2013c), "Crise et guerre sont-elles liées?," *Innovations - Cahiers d'Économie et de Management de l'Innovation*, vol. 2013/3, n° 42, p. 175–194, Brussels.

——— (2015), "Defense and Security (Economics of)," *International Encyclopedia of Social and Behavioral Sciences*, 2nd ed., Amsterdam and London: Elsevier.

——— (2021), "Guerre(s) et crise(s) globales: sur leurs relations systémiques," *Marchés & Organisations*, vol. 2021/2, n° 41, p. 139–155, Paris.

Herrera R. and J. Cicchini (2013), "Notes sur les bases et les effectifs militaires étasuniens à l'étranger," *Innovations - Revue d'économie et de management de l'innovation*, vol. 3, n° 42, p. 147–173.

Herrera R. and E. Gentilucci (2013), "Military Spending, Technical Progress, and Economic Growth," *Journal of Innovation Economics and Management*, n° 2013/2, n° 12, p. 13–35, Brussels.

International Monetary Fund (2003), *Good Governance: The IMF Role*, Washington DC: IMF.

Intriligator M.D. (1990), "On the Nature and Scope of Defence Economics," *Defence and Peace Economics*, vol. 1, n° 1, p. 3–11.

Isard W. (1988), *Arms Races, Arms Control and Conflict Analysis*, New York: Cambridge University Press.

Johnson C. (2010), *Dismantling the Empire—America's Last Best Hope*, New York: Metropolitan Books Henry Holt and Co.

Kennedy P. (1987), *The Rise and Fall of Great Powers: Economic Change and Military Conflict from 1500 to 2000*, New York: Random House.

Klein T. (2004), "Military Expenditure and Economic Growth: Peru, 1970–1996," *Defence and Peace Economics*, vol. 15, n° 3, p. 275–288.

Knight M., N. Loayza and D. Villanueva (1995), "The Peace Dividend: Military Spending Cuts and Economic Growth," *IMF Working Paper*, n° 53,

IMF Middle Eastern Department, International Monetary Fund, Washington DC.

LANDAU D. (1983), "Government Expenditure and Economic Growth: A Cross-Country Study," *Southern Economic Journal*, vol. 49, n° 3, p. 783–792.

——— (1986). Government Expenditure and Economic Growth in Less Developed Countries: An Empirical Study for 1960–1980. *Economic Development and Cultural Change, 35*(1), 35–75.

——— (1993), "The Economic Impact of Military Expenditure Best," *World Bank Policy Research Working Paper*, n° 1138, Washington DC: The World Bank.

LEONTIEF W.W. (1941), *The Structure of the American Economy: 1919–1929*, Cambridge (MA): Harvard University Press.

LEONTIEF W.W. and F. DUCHIN (1983), *Military Spending—Facts and Figures, Worldwide Implications and Future Outlook*, New York: Oxford University Press.

LEONTIEF W.W. and M. HOFFENBERG (1961), "The Economic Effects of Disarmament," *Scientific American*, vol. 204, n° 4, p. 47–55.

LEONTIEF W.W., A. MORGAN, K. POLENSKE, D. SIMPSON and E. TURNER (1965), "The Economic Impact (Industrial and Regional) of an Arms Cut," *Review of Economics and Statistics*, vol. 47, n° 3, p. 217–241.

LEONTIEF W.W. and P.A. PETRI (1971), *Impact of Disarmament on Strategic Raw Materials Demand*, United Nations Department of Political and Security Council Affairs, New York: United Nations.

MAMPAEY L. (2010), *Finance, technologie et production d'armements aux États-Unis: une lecture institutionnaliste*, Saarbrücken: Éditions universitaires européennes.

MAO Z. (1968), *Écrits militaires de Mao Tsé-Toung*, Beijing: Éditions en langues étrangères.

MARX K. (1972 [1859]), *Contribution à la critique de l'économie politique*, Paris: Éditions sociales.

——— (1978), *Le Capital - Critique de l'économie politique*, Paris: Éditions sociales.

——— (1980), *Manuscrits de 1857–1858*, Paris: Éditions sociales.

MARX K. and F. ENGELS (1973), *Werke*, Band 17, 5th ed., Berlin (GDR): Dietz Verlag.

MUSHAKOJI K. (ed.) (2008), *Human (In)Security in the Networks of Global Cities*, Center for Human Security Studies, Chubu University, January, Nagoya.

NAKATANI P. and R. HERRERA (2007), "What Rich Countries Owe Poor Ones," *Monthly Review*, vol. 59, n° 2, p. 31–36, New York.

NASH J. (1950), "Equilibrium Points in N-Person Games," *Proceedings of the National Academy of Sciences*, vol. 36, n° 1, p. 48–49.

——— (1951), "Non-Cooperative Games," *Annals of Mathematics*, vol. 54, n° 2, p. 286–295.

Observatoire international de la Crise (2019), *Le Capitalisme face à son déclin*, Paris: Éditions Critiques.

Ram R. (1985), "Exports and Economic Growth: Some Additional Evidence," *Economic Development and Cultural Change*, vol. 33, n° 1, p. 415–425.

Rothbard M. (1973), *For a New Liberty*, New York: Macmillan.

Rubel M. (1997), *Guerre et paix nucléaires*, Paris: Paris Méditerranée.

Samuelson P.A. (1983 [1947]), *Foundations of Economic Analysis*, Cambridge MA: Harvard Economic Studies.

Schelling T.C. (1960), *The Strategy of Conflict*, Cambridge MA: Harvard University Press.

Schumacher G. (2006), *A Bloody Business: America's War Zone Contractors and the Occupation of Iraq*, London: Zenith Press.

Sen A.K. (1992), "Wars and Famines: On Divisions and Incentives," *in* W. Isard and C.H. Anderton (eds.), *Economics of Arms Reduction and Peace Process*, p. 219–234, Amsterdam: North Holland.

Shieh J.-Y., C.-C. Lai and W.-Y. Chang (2002), "The Impact of Military Burden on Long-Run Growth and Welfare," *Journal of Development Economics*, vol. 68, n° 2, p. 443–454.

Smith R. (1977), "Military Expenditure and Capitalism," *Cambridge Journal of Economics*, vol. 1, n° 1, p. 61–76.

——— (1980), "Military Expenditure and Investment in OECD Countries: 1954–1973," *Journal of Comparative Economics*, vol. 4, n° 1, p. 19–32.

Squire L. and H.B. Van der Tak (1975), *Economic Analvsis of Projects*, Baltimore and London: Johns Hopkins University Press (for The World Bank).

Stiglitz J. E. (1988). *Economics of the Public Sector*. W.W. Norton & Co.

Stiglitz J.E. and L. Bilmes (2008), *The Three Trillion Dollar War*, New York: W.W. Norton & Co.

Stockholm International Peace Research Institute (various years), *SIPRI Yearbook*, Oxford: Oxford University Press.

Tinbergen J. (1990), "Conventional and New Thinking in Defence Economics," *Defence and Peace Economics*, vol. 1, n° 2, p. 121–128.

Tirole J. (1988), *The Theory of Industrial Organization*, Cambridge MA: The MIT Press.

Turner A. (2004), "Estimated U.K. Employment Dependent of Ministry of Defence Expenditure and Defence Exports," *Defence and Peace Economics*, vol. 15, n° 4, p. 331–342.

United Nations (1991), *The U.N. Disarmament Yearbook*, Department of Disarmament Affairs, vol. 15, New York.

United Nations Institute for Disarmament Research (1992), *Aspects économiques du désarmement: le désarmement en tant qu'investissement*, UNIDIR, A/47/346, August, Geneva.

U.S. Arms Control and Disarmament Agency (various years), *World Military Expenditures and Arms Transfers*, U.S.A.C.D.A., Library of Congress, Washington DC.

U.S. Department of Defense (various years), *Active Duty Military Personnel Strengths by Regional*, Area and by Country (309A), Washington DC.

Ward M.D., M. Cochran, D.R. Davis, M. Penubarti and S. Rajmaira (1991), "Military Spending in India: Country Survey," *Defence and Peace Economics*, n° 3, p. 41–64.

Yildirim J., S. Sezgine and N. Ocal (2005), "Military Expenditure and Economic Growth in Middle Eastern Countries," *Defence and Peace Economics*, vol. 16, n° 4, p. 283–295.

CHAPTER 9

Overcoming Capitalism to Protect Humanity and the Environment: Revitalizing Marxism for Modern Socialist Transitions

Since its earliest origins, Western thought on the relationships between mankind and nature, placed under the sign of conflict, has traditionally been oscillating between two opposite poles. On the one hand, nature is seen as the supreme power, spontaneous and creative, at the origin of all life and things, which gives birth and death, imposing its laws on human contingency. And, on the other hand, it is conceived as a set of phenomena that are themselves subject to laws that the sciences have the vocation of piercing and mastering, in order to take control of them. In both cases, however, the key words of these relations are those of constraint and domination. In the interval which separates these two extreme poles, the problem still remains to find the conditions of a harmony between the human beings and the nature. To progress in the reasoning, it is perhaps preferable to speak here of human beings in the plural, rather than of mankind with a singular—a concept which refers to an inaccessible "human nature"—by adding at once that certain "classes" of human beings seem to be in a position to dominate and to order the others, by the means of the system of production and the institutions with which they endowed the society.[1]

[1] The writing of this chapter was partly based on several previous texts by the author, and more particularly: HERRERA (2008, 2010).

R. Herrera, *Confronting Mainstream Economics for Overcoming Capitalism*, Marx, Engels, and Marxisms,
https://doi.org/10.1007/978-3-031-05851-6_9

Besides, it should be observed that, if one intends to situate the analysis within the framework of really existing capitalism, one must resolve to take into account the now essentially destructive tendencies of this system, whether it be the effects suffered by the environment or those that destructure social formations as well as individuals themselves (Chapter 7). For, capitalism has set itself the goal of subjecting all aspects of social life, almost without exception, to the status of merchandises. This merchandization, with the all-round privatization that supports it, has unprecedented devastating consequences: the annihilation of peasant societies expelled from their lands,[2] vital goods (such as water) rendered inaccessible, the waste of natural resources, local environmental disasters, etc. As soon as the global aspects of the ecological crisis are considered, like the "greenhouse effect" or the attacks on biodiversity, in particular, it becomes even more difficult to see the serene horizon of a livable, or even simply living world on earth.

This final chapter will attempt to show that: (1) capitalism as a system—and not just its current neoliberal form—has become a direct threat on a global scale not only to humanity, but also to life itself on our planet; (2) dominant economic theory is incapable of helping to understand and solve these major problems posed to humanity; (3) proposals for "reforms"—especially those that promote the market of "rights to pollute"—or for "degrowth" are proving to be false alternatives; (4) the outline of an effective democratic control of the world's natural resources and environmental protection must be urgently drawn up in an alternative of progress.[3]

9.1 Capitalism, a Threat to Humanity and Life

The general public is nowadays widely aware of the deterioration of the state of the planet, as well as the global risks that result from it. This is the case of the "greenhouse effect" and the main expected manifestations of global warming linked to anthropogenic gas emissions, and particularly: the rise in water levels (notably by additional supply due to the melting of ice floes and glaciers), the accentuation of the geographical polarization of precipitation (with an increase in temperate latitudes and

[2] Herrera and Lau (2015, 2021).

[3] World Forum of Alternatives (2006).

a decrease in subtropical zones), the intensification of floods and cyclones, the displacement of animal and plant distribution areas, shifts in agricultural harvesting calendars, etc. Some consequences of climate change are already noticeable, such as the destruction of natural biodiversity, the degradation of natural sites, the depletion of soils, or the appearance of pure water shortages. The indeterminacy surrounding the exact magnitude of most of these global phenomena—a definition that is extremely difficult to pin down—is now increasingly giving way to the near certainty of their occurrence. Without being overly alarmist, there is every reason to believe that such evolutions, which are so fundamental for human beings, their societies, and their environment, will exacerbate numerous conflicts at the local, regional, and international levels, linked to the appropriation of land or energy resources (oil, gas, minerals, etc.), access to drinking water, or so-called "ecological migrations" through the forced mass displacement of populations as a result of climatic disturbances.

We have sketched out the idea; let us complete it: it is not mankind in general, but ruling classes and dominant nations that direct the march of capitalism, and therefore also the devastating relationships it maintains with the environment. In the majority of the most serious "ecological scandals," those responsible for the damage caused are identifiable. Unfortunately, there is no lack of examples: radioactive effluent discharges (left by nuclear power generation); highly toxic special wastes from industry (due to acids, chemical solvents...) or from agriculture (pesticides...); oil spills (unloading of supertankers at sea); uncontrolled deforestation (leading to the disappearance of primary forests); patenting of life (from local natural biodiversity to the genes of human body); commercialization of genetically modified organisms (transgenic seeds, crops, and animals); or even the use of unconventional weapons (chemical weapons such as "Agent Orange," a dioxin-based defoliant with long-term teratogenic and carcinogenic effects, which was bombed by the U.S. military during the Vietnam War), etc.[4]

Problems related to the environment and natural resources, especially those regarding global ecological crises, cannot be understood without referring to a theory that takes as its object and proposes as its concept the world as a concrete socio-historical entity which makes a "system." The latter, structured by complex relations of interdependence, forms

[4] For example, the transnational Monsanto is on trial for scandals falling under several of these categories.

an assembly of elements of a reality in a coherent totality that positions them and gives them meaning. For, if the national structures of capitalism reproduce themselves first of all locally, at the articulation of a domestic market—on which capital and labor are mobile—and of a set of State apparatuses corresponding to it, what we choose to name, with, and after others,[5] the "capitalist world system," is defined on the contrary by a fundamental dichotomy; that which is established between the existence of a global market integrated in all its dimensions—with the exception of labor, constrained to a restricted mobility—and the absence of a unique political order on a world scale, which would be more than a plurality of State entities and authorities regulated by international public law and/or the violence of the balance of power.

The unit of analysis that is necessary for the understanding of the links between really existing capitalism and the environment, as well as for that of the problems of society, is, especially from a Marxist point of view, the world system—a possible object of a coherent scientific study on this scale—and not only the local situations and the specific social formations that compose it. Explaining the history of capitalist expansion and its relation to nature can, in our opinion, be integrated in the terms of historical materialism, striving at the same time to combine theory and history and to hold together the economic, political, and ideological fields. The main question of the transformation of the world is no longer that of a "catching up" (that is to say, of a priority development of the productive forces reproducing the characters inherent to capitalism), but rather that of the construction of "another world," a world "beyond capitalism," in rupture with this mode of production and its deep nature, the market alienation which subjects the whole of the life: economy, society, politics, and ideology, but also environment and natural resources... Thus the ecological issues are posed with a particular acuteness and urgency to the progressives of our time, whoever they are.

And the fact that many experiences claiming to be socialist (starting with the Soviet Union) have hardly cared about their relationship with the environment, seeking rather to push capital accumulation to its maximum, does not erase the problem, that is: capitalism, more and more destructive, has become a threat to humanity. Its neoliberal form only aggravates the effects of the logic of this system.

[5] Among the most prominent ones: Amin (1974), Frank (1979), Arrighi (1994), Wallerstein (2011). On the concept of "system," see: Herrera (2001).

These reflections on the environment, therefore, force us to re-situate the problematics of growth within the framework of new constraints—in particular, that of the ecological crisis: depletion of natural resources, inflection of the stocks of energy reserves, ambiguity of technical progress (e.g., nuclear power), implementation of programs to combat pollution...

Let us return to theory, one last time and in a renewed light, to examine the way in which economists of neoclassicism have attempted to apply their paradigm to these questions.

9.2 The Failure of Neoclassicism to Integrate the Environment and the Ecological Crisis

Mainstream economists' efforts initially consisted of integrating these themes through CGEMs (computable general equilibrium models). As we have seen previously, such modelizations seek to calculate the values of certain equilibrium variables in the economy (say, for instance, the effects on prices and quantities resulting from variations in policy parameters) on the basis of individual "microeconomic" behavior. Between the 1970s and the 1990s, the center of gravity of these CGE models applied to environmental policies gradually shifted from issues related to the management of energy supply to problems linked to the internalization of the external effects associated with the use of diverse energy sources. It is on the basis of such formalizations that the impact in terms of social costs of climate change resulting from greenhouse gas emissions (carbon dioxide CO^2 and methane CH^4, in particular) has been evaluated. As an example, let us mention the so-called "GREEN models," for General Equilibrium Environmental Models, elaborated by the OECD.[6] These constructions can be distinguished following various criteria, and especially, according to whether they are static or dynamic, with differentiated energy sources (electricity, oil, natural gas, coal, etc.) and polluting emissions (CO^2, CH^4, etc.), with one or more countries or regions, etc.

Other mainstream models have been adapted to local environmental problems (e.g., site pollution, air quality degradation, nuisances, etc.), based on case studies, in order to evaluate the costs for producers and

[6] These are dynamic, multi-sectoral, and multi-regional general equilibrium models. For example, Burniaux, Martin, Nicoletti, and Oliveira Martins (1992).

consumers.[7] As we have pointed out (Chapter 3), it is the "impossibility theorems" that constitute the most serious challenge in the field of microeconomics for such models. Needless to say, these problems, which embarrass the orthodox authors of neoclassicism—unable to find ways to overcome them—and undermine the pillars of their paradigm, are never mentioned in the studies devoted to the environment. Again, should the neoclassical theorists succeed in overcoming these difficulties, we would still reject its vision of environmental facts as the result of the agglomeration of individual choices in a logic exclusively focused on profit maximization.

As far as macroeconomics is concerned, the environment has also been one of the numerous fields where the use of endogenous growth models has been most frequent.[8] Thanks to their "new growth theory," mainstream theorists found themselves in a position—almost exclusive—of being able to integrate environmental topics into a long-term macrodynamic perspective. The concerns associated with global public goods, or "global commons," in particular the depletion of natural resources or global ecological threats, inevitably lead to a risk of slowing down growth—which is already, in practice, and since a long time, very low under the pressure of neoliberal policies. But, as one might have guessed, the mainspring of the incorporation of the environment into the orthodox theory of growth consists precisely in getting rid of a conception of natural resources as a common heritage of humanity. Neoclassicism thus denies their character as "free" goods, without an owner and available free of charge, in order to consider them as singular categories of "capital" (e.g., "natural capital," "energy resources," "environmental factor," etc.) and to subject them to a process of capitalist appropriation, remuneration, and accumulation.

In a framework that authorizes substitution between factors of production, it then becomes possible to circumvent the constraint of non-reproducibility of certain elements taken into account, since it is conceivable to replace exhaustible natural resources by new accumulable forms of capital (such as knowledge), and thus to generate "sustainable" growth.[9]

[7] Bergman (2005).

[8] Brock and Taylor (2005).

[9] Xepapadeas (2005).

We believe that we have sufficiently informed the reader of the insurmountable problems of this "new theory" of growth—although it is supposed to solve the problem of the depletion of natural resources on an infinite horizon by propelling technical progress—to add to it. The essence of our previously developed criticisms remains, especially those directed against the points of contact between neoclassical theory and neoliberal politics. Indeed, the neoclassical reactivation of public intervention operates by denying the status of "public goods" to environmental and natural components. And the capitalist State once again comes to the aid of the transnational corporations—even in the markets for "rights to pollute," as we shall see.

9.3 From One Consensus (that of Washington) to Another (the Copenhagen One)

The reactionary background of the current economic mainstream—the depth of which we probed on several occasions in the previous chapters—is also evident in the conclusions of the so-called "Copenhagen Consensus," which is a sort of extension of the Washington Consensus, but applied to the effects of climate change. The initiative was convened and launched in 2003 by the anti-environmentalist named Bjørn Lomborg, author of the very controversial but quite famous book *The Skeptical Environmentalist*[10]—with the backing of Denmark's National Environmental Assessment Institute. Indeed, Lomborg's perception of the "true state of the world" consisted in asserting that most of the alarmist warnings formulated by the environmentalists (about global warming, depletion of energy resources, deforestation, extinction of species, lack of water, etc.) are unfounded, because they contradict the main results of a cost–benefit analysis in line with the tools of orthodox welfare theory and the reasoning of neoclassicism.

The recommendations of the group of prestigious "experts" that B. Lomborg asked to evaluate the United Nations Millennium Development Goals opposed to the introduction of a "carbon tax" and suggested that: (1) the United Nations give a lower global priority to the goals directed at the incentives to reduce greenhouse gas emissions; (2) the U.N. promote

[10] Lomborg (2001). Also: Lomborg (2004).

more liberalization and the most thorough free trade; (3) greater protection be given to corporate patents of AIDS medicines; and (4) genetically modified organisms be promoted to fight against malnutrition in the South. It is true that this Copenhagen group brought together "the most important actors" in the field of climate change, such as the World Bank sustainable development experts, as well as the cream of conservatism in economics, notably the winners of the Bank of Sweden's Nobel Memorial Prize in economic sciences Douglass C. North, Robert W. Fogel, Thomas C. Schelling, and Vernon L. Smith. The team also included well-known personalities, such as Jagdish N. Bhagwati and Nancy L. Stokey, among others...

A few quick words to situate these "experts," politically. We have already spoken of D.C. North and R.W. Fogel (Chapter 3). Let us rather focus here on the other authors. First, T.C. Schelling. The latter was able to harmoniously combine consulting activities for the CIA with teaching at the University. He was a collaborator of the Rand Corporation, a think tank founded by the U.S. Air Force and working under contract with the Douglas Aircraft Co. armament firm (which later became McDonnell Douglas, then merged with Boeing).[11] And he too was awarded the Nobel Prize in 2005, with Robert J.Y. Aumann, for his "discoveries" in game theory, which "improved the understanding of conflict mechanisms." Schelling's work influenced Secretary of Defense Robert S. McNamara (former Ford executive and future president of the World Bank) in decisions made during the long military escalation of the Vietnam War. Here, it should be remembered that Schelling's thesis, known as the "graduated response," favored the use of the hardest military strikes from the very beginning of the war, in order to give credibility to the threat exerted, including against civilians.[12] He also contributed to science by elaborating complex "segregation models" with spatial division of races (but without equilibrium!).[13] Will it really surprise us to know that his positions on global warming supported the decision of the U.S. government not to ratify the Kyoto Protocol?

[11] Other famous Rand Corporation collaborators have been: Francis Fukuyama, Frank Carlucci, Paul O'Neill, Condoleezza Rice, Donald Rumsfeld or... Pascal Lamy (a member of the French Socialist Party).

[12] See: SCHELLING (1960).

[13] SCHELLING (1969).

And what about V.L. Smith now? Nobel laureate in 2002, he is one of the leading authors of "experimental economics," a branch of the discipline that hopes to understand society and intends to interpret economic phenomena (and in particular the efficiency of stock markets, thanks to the lights of "behavioral finance"!) by testing its hypotheses on individual guinea pigs isolated in laboratory boxes![14] This was well worth the honorary doctorate of the wealthy and private *Universidad Francisco-Marroquin* of Guatemala, created in 1971 by the very reactionary Manuel F. Ayau Cordón, an enthusiastic ultraliberal disciple of Ludwig von Mises, former president of the Mont Pèlerin Society… and of the Guatemala City Stock Exchange.

Finally, let us move on to the last two economists mentioned above. A native of Mumbai, from a family originally from Gujarat, educated at Sydenham College (one of the most prestigious management schools in Asia), then at Saint John's College (Cambridge, UK) and at the Massachusetts Institute of Technology (Cambridge MA), later naturalized as a U.S. citizen and advisor to the Director General of the World Trade Organization, Jagdish N. Bhagwati is known as a champion of free trade. But a "humanized" free trade of course! His book *In Defense of Globalization* strives throughout to make globalization look "nicer."[15] And this is probably why one of his former students, Paul Krugman, has so frequently praised his work as "Nobel-worthy."[16] In return, the master's compliments about his "star pupil" have been rather commensurate, with Bhagwati calling the Nobelist Krugman "the Mike Moore of the economics profession"[17]…

For her part, Nancy Laura Stokey[18] also deserves a paragraph. Professor at the University of Chicago, former doctoral student of Kenneth J. Arrow, former vice-president of the American Economic Association (for which she received the 2011 Ethics Committee Award), she is or has been co-editor of several of the "jet set" journals of economists (the "JET," or *Journal of Economic Theory*, but also *Econometrica*, the *Journal*

[14] SMITH (2000).

[15] BHAGWATI (2004). For a radical criticism: SHAIKH A. (2007), or TANDON (2015).

[16] Read: https://www.imf.org/external/pubs/ft/fandd/2005/09/people.htm.

[17] Now, see: https://www.imf.org/external/pubs/ft/fandd/2006/06/people.htm.

[18] STOKEY (1991).

of Economic Growth, *Games and Economic Behavior*, the *Journal of Political Economy*...)—and, for the sake of the gossip, married to endogenous growth theorist R.E. Lucas. Stokey believes that, "since the fall of the Soviet Union and the communist countries, we are all 'Chicagoans'."[19] So, we could scream loudly with her: Chicago Boys... and Girls, unite! Well, let us stop there with these experts.

9.4 Against Some False Alternatives

Faced with the extremely serious environmental threats of the present and the future, many proposals for "reformist" solutions have been formulated—without, however, ever calling into question the foundations of the capitalist system, or even, more often than not, the orientations of the neoliberal strategy. This is very generally the case with the conclusions of the major conferences on the environment (such as the "Earth Summits" of 1992 in Rio de Janeiro, of 2002 in Johannesburg, and so on), as well as with the theoretical backgrounds of the major international treaties on the climate, first and foremost among which are the indispensable (but too limited) U.N. Framework Convention on Climate Change of 1992 and one of its direct extensions, the Kyoto Protocol. The latter was multilaterally negotiated in December 1997, opened for ratification in March 1998, and entered into force in February 2005. The stated aim is to achieve a schedule of preventive actions intended to predict, measure, and attempt to mitigate the anthropogenic disturbances whose effects are considered the most dangerous on climate change.

It seems a priori impossible not to adhere to the objectives of this agreement—unless one is an "expert of the Copenhagen Consensus." How can one not be in favor of reducing greenhouse gas emissions, considered as the major cause of global warming—unless one is a member of the U.S. government? Nevertheless, it was difficult for a progressive, to be satisfied with the modest "target" set by this Protocol at—5.2% of global carbon dioxide reduction by 2012 (calculated from 1990) for industrialized countries, when a very large majority of scientific researchers of the Intergovernmental Panel on Climate Change (IPCC) argued that an immediate decrease of at least 50% would have then been

[19] And finally: http://www.minneapolisfed.org/publications_papers/pub_display.cfm?id=3459&.

necessary to maintain pollution at current levels.[20] Given the magnitude of the challenges facing humanity, the measures proposed by the Protocol were full of good will, but derisory.

All the more so since the so-called "flexibility" mechanisms that it promoted present quite worrying dangers, in particular that of the "rights to pollute" market. This scheme attempts to attribute a "price" to the negative externality (or external diseconomy) that pollution represents on a market that is administratively organized on behalf of transnational corporations, which are allocated "carbon credits." Basically, these market mechanisms turn nature—starting with the earth's atmosphere—into a merchandise and participates in the launch of a gigantic movement of modern "enclosures." As a matter of fact, pollution becomes a "right," as the expression "pollution right" proclaims it. Pollution will thus be the object of a trade, that is, "emission trading scheme." This is, in our view, definitely a false and dangerous alternative. From the start, the direction that was taken was the wrong one.

The richest agents can buy tradable emission permits on the market that will allow them to remain the biggest polluters, without changing their environmentally destructive behavior. Conversely, the poorest agents are encouraged to sell their "rights," without trying to implement development policies likely to improve their living conditions. In addition, there is a risk of "carbon sink versus water sink" crowding-out effects when "clean development" programs (in the South) replace official development assistance (from the North). The implementation by transnational firms of some of these projects, thanks to which they earn new credits, has sometimes led to the expulsion of peasant communities from their own land, in order to impose "anti-CO^2 crops." Countless fiscal-ecological scandals have been reported, where companies have been able to benefit from the scheme and receive public subsidies by increasing both their profits and... their greenhouse gas emissions.[21]

Without a regulatory and control body other than the transnational corporations themselves,[22] multiple cases of fraud in the declaration of

[20] Let us remember that the Intergovernmental Panel on Climate Change (IPCC) was created by the U.N. in 1988.

[21] Bachram (2004).

[22] During "Green Week" in June 2005, a group of transnational corporations (Ford, Toyota, BP, etc.) formed at the Davos Economic Forum insisted on "market solutions in the fight against climate change.".

pollution levels or usurpation of the "carbon neutral" label—sometimes an ethical pretext for opening up new markets—will continue to be recorded. For the role of the State is not to submit to the power of the markets, in the name of "reformism" and the quest for an untraceable "capitalism with a human face"; it is to impose external limits on capital and its logic of expansion, in order to succeed in protecting humanity as well as the environment against capital's destructive tendencies. Remaining within the framework of profit maximization and based on a State-supported commodification of natural resources, the strategy chosen by the Kyoto Protocol to achieve its objectives is the surest way… to never achieve them. It differs only in degree, not in kind, from the strategy advocated by the Copenhagen Consensus. Since the experimentation of the first local emission permit markets in the United States, the activity that has developed mainly on these new environmental exchanges,[23] from the Chicago Climate Exchange to the European Powernext, is carbon speculation. And the latter remained very active even after the 2008 crisis.

Many other false alternatives exist, which do not place politics at the heart of ecology, nor the structures of capitalism at the center of the problems of the climate crisis. One of them is the thesis of "degrowth." It has had some success among the "alterglobalist" movements of recent times. We should rather speak of degrowth theses, in the plural, since the heterogeneity of these works—and their quality—is extreme[24]; to the point of often being able to rally the approval of activists sincerely devoted to the struggle for a more livable world on this or that specific suggestion presenting a real relevance.

Such is the case, for example, of the call to save resources and to avoid waste, but also to control the passions of consumer society. The rejection of consumerist delusions is no longer only highly desirable; it has simply become indispensable—provided that we do not fall into the opposite excess, i.e., the "praise of poverty." The latter, advocated by some Northern activists, is indeed undoubtedly difficult to hear by the

[23] The Chicago Climate Exchange platform, launched in 2003, was the first "carbon stock exchange" in the world. And the European Union Emission Trading Scheme, opened in 2005, was the European tradable permits market.

[24] Among numerous other analyzes, see: Georgescu-Roegen (1971, 2006), or Latouche (2006). Also: Kallis, Kerschner and Martinez-Alier (2012).

one billion human beings of the South currently living in slums of the urban areas, not to mention the poor peasants in the rural zones.

But the criticisms that can be formulated against these theses must be made taking into account this fact: many of the proponents of degrowth are authentic progressives, who should be brought together with the other militants who fight for a better world, rather than divided. Everyone should agree on the fact that it is up to the ultra-rich, who are also the biggest polluters and wasters, with the most powerful transnational corporations they own, to make the most substantial efforts; and not to the poorest—whether in terms of classes or nations.[25]

This temporary infatuation linked to "degrowth," in the air of time, can be explained to a large extent by the disarray caused by a double failure: on the one hand, the proven impotence or extreme difficulty of the party and trade union organizations of the traditional left to integrate the now absolute imperative of environmental protection into the heart of their programs, and on the other hand, the inability of the huge majority of the "green" movements to admit that, if ecology is indeed political, their salvation will not come through an ever more docile submission to the power of neoliberalized social-democracy. They must realize that democracy—including in the "management" of the planet's natural resources—is inseparable from social progress, which itself is totally irreconcilable with the pursuit of neoliberal capitalism.

Nonetheless, a certain number of supporters of degrowth get lost in confusions that harm the credibility of the project they intend to promote. This is the case when they tend to confuse "growth"—a quantitative indicator (admittedly questionable) of increased production—with "development"—a concept with a qualitative and above all strategic dimension, which makes it much more complex to define.[26] The authors of degrowth also often slip from the criticism of economism, justified and sometimes very relevant, to that of economics in general, and therefore of economic policy—that is, one of the essential instruments of any project of social transformation. Given the asymmetries and inequalities that characterize the capitalist world system, "degrowing" would very probably run the risk of accentuating the most worrying current problems at the

[25] Herrera (2022).

[26] Herrera (2014), Presentation.

social level (imbalances in the labor markets, dismantling of social protection, etc.) as well as at the environmental level (worsening of pollution due to a decrease in energy efficiency, for example).

The heart of the problem resides in the fact that, in their vast majority, the partisans of degrowth do not consider that the very responsible for the environmental catastrophe that is looming is the capitalist system, which they do not call into question as such. Unacceptably there still remains in their speeches, as in those of many ecological activists, a frequently tolerated equivalence between the term "capitalism"—obviously still taboo for some—and those of "progress" or "modernity." In this way, as soon as the alterglobalism of degrowth evacuates from its discussions the inescapable question of the structure of ownership of capital and that of democratic popular participation in economic decisions, it will condemn itself to being only the illusion of "another" capitalism. But such other capitalism than the one that today threatens all of humanity with death is not possible. Definitively. And it should be understood as soon as possible. Before it is too late.

As long as no consistent solutions to the global problems which are those of the capitalist world system are envisaged, implying a real alternative to capitalism itself that allows for a decrease in the energy intensity of production—and not of this production—the good intentions of economic Malthusianism, based on beliefs more than on science, will remain wishful thinking. As long as the means of technological progress are not found to reduce energy consumption in a more equitable way and to carry out the difficult transition from a waste of fossil energies to a much more balanced management of these energies and of clean renewable resources, while simultaneously building a solidarity, united project of social emancipation of the workers of the North and effective reinforcement of the sovereignty of the peoples of the South, the empty hopes of a fundamentalist and/or a-political ecology will postpone *sine die* the reality of a decrease in greenhouse gas emissions.

Without breaking with this capitalist mode of production and consumption, the arguments will always be deployed, despite nuances and subtleties, within the framework of a representation of a State and economic agents, or citizens, subjected to the forces of globally dominant capital. So, in the absence of substitutes for fossil fuels and of sufficiently dynamic technical progress, the shortage of energy resources, first and foremost oil, is likely to lead the whole system into a "forced degrowth" that would probably not take the path that alterglobalists want to take. And the machinery of capitalism, by depriving the poorest masses of the satisfaction of their most essential needs, in the silence of market price adjustments, would continue to manage their genocide.[27]

9.5 Social, Political, and Democratic Ecology: The Great Challenge of the Left

What we need to build is a world based on the recognition of the non-merchandizable character of nature and all the natural resources of the planet—including agricultural or arable land.[28] The environment is at the heart of the new conquest of modern times launched by neoliberal capitalism, which tends to subjugate all aspects of life. But, as we have said, such "model"—which is anything but a development strategy oriented toward the well-being of the peoples—has dramatically devastating effects, completely unacceptable, on the environmental level, as well as on the social level.[29]

The objective here is not only to achieve a democratic "management" of natural resources, but also and above all to subordinate its definition to a higher vital principle, that of the "right to life," in order to counteract the logic of destruction of the earth. Natural resources must be considered as "public goods of humanity,"[30] for which the decision must not be taken by the market, but by public authorities, themselves democratically placed under the sovereignty of their people. They should not be used beyond their capacity of renewal, but by adjusting them to the needs of each country, and preserving biodiversity and ecosystems. The commodification of life is likely to result in wars for oil, gas, minerals, water, etc.[31] The agribusiness giants privilege cash crops to the detriment of subsistence crops, by imposing techniques that involve both economic dependence and environmental destruction, notably through

[27] Read the words of Nobel Prize in Physics (1979) Abdus Salam on underdevelopment as "silent genocide of the poorest," available at: http://www.unesco.org/courrier/2001_12/fr/droits5.htm.

[28] We refer here to a few recommendations of the Bamako Appeal that some of us launched, within the framework of the World Forum of Alternatives, in January 2006. See: https://mronline.org/2006/01/17/the-bamako-appeal/.

[29] Amin and Herrera (2000).

[30] Herrera (2010), Chapter 4.

[31] Amin and Houtart (2002).

GMOs. Agrofuel production development programs, from African palm to ethanol, risk further aggravating these trends.[32]

In these conditions, a certain number of concrete action proposals deserve to be discussed, well beyond environmentalist circles. Articulated at both the microscopic and macroscopic levels (that is, those of civil societies and States simultaneously), they are part of alternative strategies that seek to strengthen the convergence of popular resistance and promote the emergence of a collective consciousness. Let us mention, among other measures: abolishing the markets of "rights to pollute" and obliging rich countries to reduce their carbon dioxide emissions to allow the poorest countries to develop; fighting against the privatization of water, including in the form of private–public partnerships, and effectively guaranteeing every human being the necessary quantity of water while strictly respecting the renewal of water tables; protecting biological and genetic resources against the "patenting-pillage" practices of transnational firms; making illegal the contracts that impose dependence of farmers on seed producing corporations; establishing an international tribunal in charge of judging the "crimes against the environment" committed by companies and to condemn them to pay damages for their "ecological debts"; contesting the iniquitous rules of the World Trade Organization (WTO) and getting agriculture out of it; creating an international observatory on the environment capable of informing the public and reacting rapidly to the characterized aggressions against the environment, etc. If these themes are presented as being articulated on—and not replacing—those of social transformation, they will win the support of many progressives, at the very heart of the workers' and peasants' forces, who will feel concerned by this fight for protecting environment, which is in fact a struggle for the survival of humanity in the face of destructive capitalism.

And since almost three quarters of the world's population are still peasants, the questions we are dealing with are also closely linked to that of determining a better future for peasant agriculture.[33] This implies seeking conditions that guarantee all peasants in the world the right of access to productive resources, and first of all to land. Its implementation requires adequate reforms of land tenure systems and, where and when necessary,

[32] Houtart (2010).

[33] Herrera and Lau (2015).

deep agrarian reforms.[34] Food sovereignty must be recognized as a fundamental right of States (or regionalization of States), which must be able to determine with sovereignty their internal agricultural policy and their insertion into the world economy.

9.6 Revitalizing Marxism in the Perspective of Modern Socialist Transitions

The urgency is thus to revitalize Marxism by political ecology, so that the Marxists seize the key questions of the environment and the natural resources and place them in the very heart of the rebuilding of their radical social projects, having to exceed the limits and insufficiencies of the really existing socialism of the past.[35] The heterodox thinkers in general certainly can no longer afford to let themselves be divided by useless polemics, renewing now outdated cleavages and reproducing old divisions that are no longer valid. It seems, however, that it is not by advocating "new syntheses" with the economics of neoclassicism and its "reformisms" such as the market for pollution rights—fueling speculation—nor by sinking into a confusion maintained by the authors of dominant ideology, that progressives will succeed in mobilizing the forces of their reconstruction, but, on the contrary, by resisting it and reaffirming their combative radicality and the coherence of alternative projects to capitalism.

To overcome the errors and failures of the past, these alternatives will have to rely on the long history of traditions and experiences of popular resistance, and also take into account the "small steps" indispensable to the most immediate improvement of the daily life of the victims of the capitalist system. For, today more than ever, the question that is posed to us is that of knowing how we will find together the means to continue to hope to determine development strategies for the preservation of the environment and the renewal of energy resources, while at the same time rebuilding authentic and profound social projects. The deep transformation of the current system would be the objective, for a mastery of our collective future and a post-capitalist alternative—whether we want to call it "social" or, better, "socialist."

[34] Amin (2015).

[35] Foster (2000).

Planning this ecological and social transition is imperative. This implies putting under strong political supervision the mechanisms of the capitalist market. Without this, no progress will be possible. The tasks of economic planning are to achieve a stable and sustained development, in a protected environment, but also and above all to meet the basic social needs of the peoples and to promote a satisfactory distribution of income, as well as structural transformations allowing the transition to a more solidary, cohesive society. This requires a coherent strategy to determine the main goals of development and to strictly control their integration into the world economy, but also the means for their implementation, in particular to settle structural problems such as the transformation of the productive base, the improvement of social relations, the impulsion of scientific progress, and the protection of environment. In this respect, modern, democratic, and participative forms of planning would constitute instruments to implement such development strategy, with the associated economic policies to be put into practice, involving processes of forecasting, research of balancing between objectives and resources, optimization programs, etc.[36] Nevertheless, in terms of planning, the mode of functioning of a socialist economy is quite different from that of a capitalist market economy.

As a matter of fact, in a capitalist system, the economic movement is determined by the need to achieve a continuous valorization of capital. When profits decline, the economy is in crisis, and the most affected enterprises are pushed into bankruptcy. Then, capital is destroyed and restructured through concentration and reorganization, thereby creating the conditions for a new cycle of expansion. The starting point of this process is demand. If there is no demand, there is no output growth, nor capital valorization. Thus, the key is that profits have to be realized. Providing resources is achieved by supply and demand through market prices which represent signals of relative scarcity of these resources for producers. This process performs a function of allocating resources, on the basis of the purchasing powers of agents exchanging on markets. Operating mechanisms of competition among producers tend to generate innovation and lower prices. Imbalances that occur during this confrontation of decisions are resolved through crises including destruction of capital, factor under-utilization, or unemployment… The impetus for the

[36] González Gutiérrez (2006).

reproduction of such a system comes from strong material motivations and dynamics is conditioned by a regulatory action designed to smooth cyclical oscillations, to minimize "transaction costs," and to ensure the fulfillment of contracts—for the capitalist division of labor. Here, macroeconomic policy indirectly seeks to influence cycles. The goals aim at preventing recurrent falls in activity level and at controlling inflation. It implies a reactivation of economic growth during recessions through, among other tools, increased budgetary expenditures and/or reduced interest rates to stimulate demand.

In a socialist economy, things are different. The cycle could be driven with respect to a main purpose: that of achieving the best satisfaction of the people's social and environmental needs through political decisions. As the activity risks to be often limited by supply capacities more than by internal demand, generating a surplus in production processes is required to allow an expanded reproduction of resources. But seeking such a surplus is not an absolute imperative in the system, where general criteria, both social and environmental, are considered superior to those of enterprises. By moderating excessive tendencies to profits, the predominance of political priorities is clear both in the decisions of planning management and in the regulation processes, even when significant spaces are reserved to market mechanisms for distributing consumer goods, because of existing subjective factors in the definition of individual needs. Under these conditions, we understand the importance and essence of a social and ecological planning which has to design the economy's development strategy in a sense that oligopolistic private actors ought not to be allowed to impose on the society their exclusive logics of profit, their system of class exploitation and their recurrent crises. If new forms of planning have to mobilize knowledge coming from the maximum number of disciplines, the conceptual, methodological, and theoretical instruments provided by Marxism, especially its class analysis which distinguishes it from other heterodoxies, will be very useful, today, in the current time of the capitalist systemic crisis and of reflections about concrete, difficult and long transition processes toward human societies consistent with equality and solidarity, as well as the respect and protection of nature.

Capitalism is declining, degenerating. It will not find a solution on its own to its systemic crisis, and if it is not collapsing faster, it is because its capitalist State is supporting it at arm's length, as was the case in 2008 when the financial section of the system crumbled, or in the so-called "health crisis" following the COVID-19 pandemic, with the capitalist system surviving on a drip because it is placed under a permanent infusion of public money. Capital under the domination of high finance will never find an internal solution through its logic of profit, not only because its technologies save too much human labor and undermine the creation of value, unproductive labor gains ground on productive labor, or contradictions of capital require State intervention that is increasingly expensive, but also because overaccumulation comes mainly from fictitious capital and high finance locks the whole system into a spiral of military wars and environmental destruction that ends up threatening us all with death.

In conclusion, let us just say that there will be no way out of the environmental problems with procapitalist environmentalists. This is why wanting to embark on a socialist transition is not only a response to a spirit of justice, but also an answer to the call of reason: it is a question of survival for humanity, and for life itself. This is where we are. Socialism is not just a word, but a struggle.[37] It is not an end, but a long and difficult transition process that can take many paths toward the liberation of labor from the domination of capital. It is socialism, a society of solidarity, which walks with history. Capitalism took centuries to emerge through thousands of attempts to extricate itself from feudalism. Socialism, with an infinitely more just, egalitarian and advanced ambition, would not it also be entitled to time to form itself? In this perspective, does not the reference to Marx then appear unavoidable?

Such anti-capitalist alternatives would mean planning to implement a development strategy; strict control of the currency, the banking sector, as well as key strategic sectors, through socialization; collective ownership of natural resources and the urgency of protecting nature; diverse forms of ownership but all oriented toward the socialization of the productive forces; stronger public services as conditions of citizenship; a more rapid increase in labor income and the objective of social justice, as well as the egalitarian perspective; foreign relations based on win–win exchange and peace; and forms of enlarged political democracy, not fictitious as today, but real, deep, participatory, making possible collective strategic choices. Let us delegitimize capitalism, which promises abundance but destroys public services, generalizes scarcity in the midst of a pandemic, sells happiness in advertising but privatizes the commons and only offers the crisis, sacralizes individual freedom but dismantles our rights, which

[37] Herrera (2021).

speaks of democracy but imposes the dictatorship of high finance. We do not manage a dictatorship, we fight it. And the order of financial capital is nothing but a dictatorship. Our duty is to put an end to it.

References

Amin S. (1974), *Accumulation on a World Scale*, New York: Monthly Review Press.

——— (2015), "Theoretical Framework," in Herrera R. and K.-C. Lau (eds.), *The Struggle for Food Sovereignty—Alternative Development and the Renewal of Peasant Societies Today*, London: Pluto Press.

Amin S. and R. Herrera (2000), "Le Sud dans le système mondial en transformation," *Recherches internationales*, n°s 60–61, p. 87–99, Paris.

Amin S. and F. Houtart (2002), *Mondialisation des résistances. L'État des luttes*, CETRI Alternatives Sud - État des résistances dans le Sud, vol. XI, n° 3, Paris: L'Harmattan.

Arrighi G. (1994), *The Long Twentieth Century: Money, Power and the Origins of Our Times*, London: Verso.

Bachram H. (2004), "Climate Fraud and Carbon Colonialism: The New Trade in Greenhouse Gases," *Capitalism Nature Socialism*, vol. 15, n° 4, p. 1–16.

Bergman L. (2005), "CGE Modeling of Environmental Policy and Resource Management," in Mäler K.G. and J. Vincent (eds.), *Handbook of Environmental Economics*, vol. 3, chapter 24, p. 1273–1306, Amsterdam: Elsevier.

Bhagwati J.N. (2004). *In Defense of Globalization*. Oxford University Press.

Brock W. and M.S. Taylor (2005), "Economic Growth and the Environment: A Review of Theory and Empirics," in P. Aghion and S. Durlauf (eds.), *Handbook of Economic Growth*, vol. 1, part B, p. 1749–1821, Amsterdam: Elsevier.

Burniaux J.-M., J.P. Martin, G. Nicoletti and J. Oliveira Martins (1992), "GREEN—A Multi-Sector, Multi-Region Dynamic General Equilibrium Model for Quantifying the Costs of Curbing CO_2 Emissions: A Technical Manual," *Economics Department Working Papers*, n° 116, Organisation for Economic Co-operation and Development, Paris.

Frank A.G. (1979), *Dependent Accumulation and Underdevelopment*, New York: Monthly Review Press.

Foster J.B. (2000), *Marx's Ecology: Materialism and Nature*, New York: Monthly Review Press.

Georgescu-Roegen N. (1971), *The Entropy Law and the Economic Process*, Cambridge (MA): Harvard University Press.

——— (2006), *La Décroissance. Entropie, écologie, économie*, Paris: Éditions Sang de la terre.

González Gutiérrez A. (2006), "La Planification globale de l'économie nationale," *in* R. Herrera (ed.), *Cuba révolutionnaire - Tome 2 : économie et planification*, p. 175–273, Paris: Éditions L'Harmattan.

Herrera R. (2001), "Les Théories du système mondial capitaliste," *in* J. Bidet and E. Kouvélakis, *Dictionnaire Marx contemporain*, p. 201–221, Paris: Presses Universitaires de France.

——— (2008), "Ambiante e crescita: contro l'economia neoclassica e le sue false alternative," *in* L. Vasapollo (ed.), *Capitale, natura e lavoro*, p. 269–282, Milan: Jaca Book.

——— (2010), *Un Autre Capitalisme n'est pas possible*, Paris: Syllepse.

——— (ed.) (2014), La Crise du "Développement", Paris: Éditions L'Harmattan.

——— (ed.) (2021), *Imperialism and Transitions to Socialism*, Bingley (UK): Emerald.

——— (2022), *La Monnaie: du pouvoir de la finance à la souveraineté des peuples*, Geneva: Éditions du Centre Europe - Tiers Monde (CETIM).

Herrera R. and K.-C. Lau (2021), "Agrarian Labor and Peasantry in the Global South," *in* I. Ness and Z. Cope (eds.), *The Palgrave Encyclopedia of Imperialism and Anti-Imperialism*, Chapter 58–1, 12 p., 2nd ed., New York: Palgrave Macmillan and Springer.

Herrera R. and K.-C. Lau (eds.) (2015), *The Struggle for Food Sovereignty—Alternative Development and the Renewal of Peasant Societies Today*, London: Pluto Press.

Houtart F. (2010), *Agrofuels: Big Profits, Ruined Lives and Ecological Destruction*, London: Pluto Press.

Kallis G., C. Kerschner and J. Martinez-Alier (2012), "The Economics of Degrowth," *Ecological Economies*, vol. 841, n° 1, p. 72–180.

Latouche S. (2006), *Le Pari de la décroissance*, Paris: Fayard.

Lomborg B. (ed.) (2001), *The Skeptical Ecologist: Measuring the Real State of the World*, Cambridge (UK): Cambridge University Press.

——— (ed.) (2004), *Global Crises, Global Solutions*, Cambridge MA: Cambridge University Press.

Schelling T.C. (1960), *The Strategy of Conflict*, Cambridge MA: Harvard University Press.

——— (1969), "Models of Segregation," *American Economic Review*, vol. 59, n° 2, p. 488–493.

Shaikh A. (2007), "Globalization and the Myth of Free Trade," *in* A. Shaikh (ed.), *Globalization and the Myths of Free Trade: History, Theory, and Empirical Evidence*, New York: Routledge.

Smith V.L. (2000), *Bargaining and Market Behavior: Essays in Experimental Economics*, New York: Cambridge University Press.

Stokey N. (1991), "The Volume and Composition of Trade Between Rich and Poor Countries," *Review of Economic Studies*, vol. 58, n° 1, p. 63–80.
Tandon Y. (2015), *Trade is War*, New York: OR Books.
Wallerstein I. (2011). *Historical Materialism*. London: Verso.
World Forum of Alternatives (2006), "The Bamako Appeal," January 19, available on: https://mronline.org/2006/01/17/the-bamako-appeal/.
Xepapadeas A. (2005), "Economic Growth and the Environment," *Handbook of Environmental Economics*, vol. 3, p. 1219–1271, Amsterdam: Elsevier.

Appendices: Confronting Mainstream Economists

Appendix A: Jean-Baptiste Say—An Atypical Classic, or a Pre-neoclassical Economist?

This first appendix will offer a critical interpretation, of Marxist inspiration, of the general conception of the economy given by Jean-Baptiste Say. Our intention is not to formulate an analysis of the reading that Karl Marx suggests of the work of J.-B. Say, which he studied in depth, and fought in a tone reserved only for a very limited number of authors.[1] Nevertheless, we will take into account the fact that the contributions of Say were written several decades before those of K. Marx, and in a markedly different historical context. This requires a preliminary reminder, here concise, of some of the strong moments of Say's life likely to shed light on the arguments that we will soon develop.

For, when so many of his contemporaries lost their lives on the European battlefields for the glory of a France that had gone from defensive to conquest, or were languishing in prison for having tried to resist the new authoritarianism which was stifling the ideals of French Revolution, Jean-Baptiste Say, as for him, suffered from other torments. The torments of a privileged, those inflicted on him by the man whose Brumairian coup he

[1] Marx (1974, p. 105), among many other examples. Marx just calls J.-B. Say… shit! But he reads him anyway….

R. Herrera, *Confronting Mainstream Economics for Overcoming Capitalism*, Marx, Engels, and Marxisms,
https://doi.org/10.1007/978-3-031-05851-6

had supported a little earlier. There were certainly these pressures exerted by a Bonaparte still First Consul inviting him (to supper at Malmaison and) to further support his ascent to the top. Then a reissue of the *Traité d'économie politique* (Treatise on Political Economy) delayed by censorship because its author did not agree to add well-chosen and more pleasant passages with regard to the commanding power. Or the exclusion from the Tribunat, where Say had been appointed with some of his *Ideologue* friends like Ginguené (and maintained longer than them after the purge that ousted them in 1802), following his refusal of a generously remunerated offer to occupy the position of Director of Taxes in the department of Allier, France.[2] Or also the forced union of a *Décade philosophique* deemed too restless (and of which Say was the equivalent of editor-in-chief) with the *Mercure de France*...[3]

In brief, not enough to undermine a man of the caliber of J.-B. Say who, without being a hero, knew how to show courage to persist in his liberal principles and oppose Napoleon (whom he called "Buonaparte," as did the reaction), even in the (so short) moments of maximum power of the Emperor. If the reader allows us a daring comparison, it resembles the stubbornness of a F. von Hayek who, in 1947, at the moment when the hegemony of Keynesianism—that of the neoclassical "synthesis"—took hold, created the libertarian Mont Pèlerin Society, before Milton Friedman and George Stigler joined it, while waiting for better days (for them)...

No more, however, than the fractions of the French bourgeoisie who defied Napoleon—starting with the usurers who dragged on releasing the necessary funds for the Russian campaign and brought its launch closer to winter, and therefore to catastrophe—Say did not understand that the Emperor provided this class with the State that it will vitally need to overcome its internal conflicts, affirm its common interest, and thus succeed in dominating the whole of society. And the "penal colony" where he was relegated was not the Fort de Joux, where Toussaint Louverture died, nor the feverish pontoons of Cadiz welcoming the defeated of Baylen, but Auchy-sur-Ternoise, in Pas-de-Calais, where he became an industrial entrepreneur—that is, the "main agent of production" that he admired so much—taking over the management of a cotton mill, in the emblematic

[2] Minart (2003, p. 170).

[3] Benot (2006, p. 234).

sector of capitalism at the time, which obtained its raw material under the conditions that we know and which employed two-thirds of working children in France.[4] His younger brother, Louis, meanwhile—three decades before the abolition of slavery—ran a refinery that imported its sugar from the West Indies. This happened before J.-B. Say's "rehabilitation," under the Restoration. While a Antoine-Augustin Cournot, for example, took almost half a century to be translated into English, and great British classics had to wait to be read in French, Say did not know the least enviable of fates, he whose fame was immediate, in both languages, who made school as far as the United States, and whom his followers raised to the rank of mentor of a French liberalism which was already working to normalize thought in the academy.[5]

Like many others at the time, Jean-Baptiste Say was an enthusiastic disciple of Adam Smith: "I revere him, he is my master, (...) he showed me the right way [and] leaning on his *Wealth of Nations*, which at the same time reveals to us the richness of his genius, I learned to walk alone."[6] Say's own notoriety certainly owes it to his talent as a writer, polemicist journalist and liberal economist at the same time, and to the early success of his Treatise (the first French edition of which dates back to 1803), but also and above all to the resumption by the greatest contemporary classic, David Ricardo, and the innumerable and less prestigious disciples of the latter, such as McCulloch, of what was to come to be called "Say's law" or "law of outlets," as well as to the debates it aroused with opponents of the level of Thomas Malthus and, even more, of Jean C.L.S. de Sismondi.[7]

However, the intrinsic qualities of Say's work, which are real but relatively limited, do not by themselves exhaust the explanation of the surprising longevity of our author's aura. This is also due, in our view, to the fact that by deviating from several of the fundamental contributions of the classics, Jean-Baptiste Say announces, very early on, the rise to power of the analyses of neoclassicism.

This is especially the case with his rejection of the labor value and his conception of a value derived from utility (as with the Abbé de Condillac,

[4] Herrera (2008b).

[5] Blaug (1986).

[6] Say (1848, p. 455).

[7] Guerrero (2011).

one of John Locke's sensualist disciples), which anticipate William S. Jevons and the marginalists, but above all close in the theoretical discussion the ways of passage toward the "secrets" of exploitation (and no longer of abstinence), to return it to subjective judgments. This is also the case of his conception of "capital" as a list of factors serving production stripped of any relationship of domination, or even of his vision of production as an "exchange of productive services," which could be compared to the Walras of the general equilibrium of markets. To this is added an unshakable, and so to speak, communicative faith in the (alleged) virtues of a capitalist system then still in full expansion, which could only seduce, beyond all the disagreements, the theorists of the various classical currents which dominated, as well as the younger generations of neoclassicals which took over.

Let us go further: we will argue here that it is because he is not a classic in the full sense of the term, but rather an atypical economist who does not go beyond the superficial discourse of the apology of the system, because he returns—or regresses, while claiming to be inspired by A. Smith—toward the principles of a priority to be granted to the market and of an exchange value not referring to labor, that J.-B. Say was able to be so useful to neoclassicals forced, after the eruption of Marx, to profoundly revise the analyses of the classics to better preserve the continuity that unites them in their common defense of the capitalist system (Chapter 1).[8]

Say had his role in the *salto mortale* that the economists of neoclassicism carried out above the heads of the "fathers" of classicism, and in the scientific decline and regression that it entailed. And the fact—incredible—that there is no crisis theory at all (or very little) within the current neoclassical mainstream, at the precise moment of the burst of the most serious capitalist crisis since the Great Depression of the 1930s, is only the testimony. As we have seen, for the neoclassicals, in the element of theory, the crisis does not exist.

In this work of rewriting the history of thought and denial of the fact of capitalist crises in which the neoclassicals engaged, the work of J.-B. Say was, for them, in its strengths and discoveries, but also in its inadequacies and ambiguities, extremely precious—much more than that, for example, of the neo-Ricardian McCulloch, about his size, but remained

[8] See: Herrera (2012a). For a position in clear contradiction with our theses, read the studies provided by two of J.-B. Say's specialists: Potier and Tiran (2004).

too faithful to the labor value. The reassuring interpretation that Say gives of the concept of "capital," without historical depth or the slightest social thickness, was therefore not displeasing to them after the trauma of the Marxian "social relationship."

Say defines the capital entering production from the "advances" (a term mobilized differently from the use made of it by the physiocrats who, unlike him, opposed it to the "net product") made for the various categories of producers. According to Say, capital is "the sum of values devoted to making advances to production," which concern factors considered to be all equally useful to production, ranging from material objects to "money."[9] It is associated here with a sense of the "producer"[10] as "one who produces either by his industry, or by his capital, or by his land," that is, a broad acceptance—quite distinct from those stemming from Quesnay's "productive class" or Adam Smith's "productive labor."

And this is a rather vague meaning, because it encompasses both the landowner and the industrial capitalist who, "if they do not produce themselves, (…) contribute to production by means of their instruments." Especially since, for this pre-neoclassical that Say is in our eyes, the "entrepreneur" as "a man not possessing enough capital, or no capital at all,"[11] is not identified with the capitalist; on the contrary—by rediscovering a separation already highlighted by Cantillon, J.-B. Say is once again opposed to the classics, and first of all to Smith. He joins Turgot in reviving the idea of exchange value consisting in comparing commodities with each other, but confusing value and use value, thereby evacuating the centrality of labor revealed by the classics.[12] It is the "sacrifice" of productive services deriving from factors, among which we find labor peacefully associated with capital, which gives utility and creates value. In this scheme, where the harmony of exchange predominates, each factor of production is thus remunerated according to its exact value, or utility, i.e., what its productive service contributes to the creation of wealth.

[9] His *Catéchisme d'économie politique* says, "What is capital? It is a sum of values acquired in advance (…) values [which] can consist of many different objects, as well as a sum of money" (SAY [1839], p. 36).

[10] SAY (1839, Chapter 2, p. 11 et seq).

[11] Ibidem, Chapter 4, p. 19 et seq.

[12] "This quality which makes a thing valuable, it is evident that it is its utility," says SAY (1861).

What supporter of neoclassicism would remain insensitive to the spectacle given by J.-B. Say of this miraculous disappearance of the conflicts of interest between social classes which smoldered under the *Pax Ricardiana*, and on which all his predecessors had insisted? Did not he think that far from the interests of the poor and those of the rich being opposed to each other, they are "strictly the same"? When the Revolution of 1789 and its daughters of 1830, 1848, and 1871, sweeping away the undue privileges of the "*Ancien Régime*" (Old Regime) had also shaken the legitimacy of the "ownership of capital" (the right of which guarantees its owner "disposal at his fantasy to the exclusion of any other person"[13]), which of our neoclassicals would not calm down to the sound of this optimistic unrealism?

We do know, however, that it is thanks to the so-called "law of outlets,"[14] which made him pierce the hearts of many colleagues, that J.-B. Say saw his notoriety rise very largely above that of Sismondi, or that of Stuart Mill, to mention but a few. If "products are exchanged for products"[15]—assuming that we can answer the question of knowing what a worker has to sell, apart from his "labor power," against the purchase of goods of subsistence—if, therefore, all supply is at the same time a demand, then it comes to pass that the accumulation of capital cannot be excessive. And the crises affecting commerce and industry, the existence of which Say obviously does not deny (he witnessed them when his father, Jean-Étienne, went bankrupt during the period of the French Revolution) cannot last long ago.

The origin of the crises is, according to him, to be sought outside an economic sphere which, if the markets are freed from the interference of the State, would be regulated by mechanisms structurally preventing any phenomenon of generalized overproduction. This "outside of the economy" is for him politics—that, in particular, which imposed the continental blockade by the decree of Berlin (in November 1806), i.e.,

[13] SAY (1839, p. 78).

[14] BAUMOL (1999).

[15] See here: SAY (1803), especially Book II (*De la distribution des richesses* [On the distribution of wealth], p. 196 et seq.) and Book III (*De la consommation des richesses* [On the consumption of wealth], p. 274 et seq.).

the prohibition made to the empire and its "allies" of any trade with the British Isles.[16]

Although few people still dare to refer explicitly to this "law of outlets" for more than half a century, we nevertheless measure the late influence of Say by noting that, for those among the economists of neoclassicism who ventured to recognize the fact of the present crisis, the analysis of the latter has almost exclusively been carried out—as with our author—from factors always external to the market and coming to disturb the methods of automatic correction by the price system. This crisis, the very one we are experiencing today, is, however, clearly, in our opinion, and as we have said and repeated in this work, a systemic crisis of overaccumulation of capital, especially in its most abstract forms of "fictitious capital." But in J.-B. Say, whom Marx criticized (and dealt with so harshly,[17] before, and more pertinently than will Keynes), "money" is supposed to be only a "veil"—under which hides the hoarding, but above all the credit system.

And this silence on money still haunts part of the neoclassical mainstream—the theorists of real business cycles are only caricatural examples. More generally, Joan Robinson recalled that orthodox economics justified the hypothesis of full employment by appealing to Say's law—such was the case of Marshall, Pigou, or Aftalion. And she added that, if this view were correct, there could not be the problem of insufficient solvent demand for any production. Until this orthodox axiom was challenged by Keynes' employment theory, it was not criticized by non-Marxist economists. In fact, it provided the test that separated orthodox theorists from "heretics," like Hobson and Gesell in particular.

Marx did not allow himself to be stopped by it. To analyze this problem, he presented a proof where he divided total production into

[16] Central axis of Napoleon's strategy, which motivated the annexation of the Papal States, Holland, and the Hanseatic cities, before constituting one of the reasons for the aggravation of disagreements with Russia and the intervention of the French armies in the Iberian Peninsula, this prohibition responded to the British maritime blockade against the Channel and North Sea coasts. Despite numerous oppositions, including in the circle of French entrepreneurs whom J.-B. Say knew so well, the continental blockade showed its effectiveness by asphyxiating Great Britain—then isolated in Europe—and plunging it repeatedly into crisis (HERRERA [2017b]).

[17] Without explicit reference to the law of the "insipid Say" ("that comic prince of science" whose admirers "celebrated in him, to the sound of a whirlwind, the man who had unearthed this famous treasure of metaphysical equilibrium of purchases and sales"), Marx's criticism of the idea of equilibrium between supply and demand in the markets is without appeal (MARX [1977], p. 121).

two sectors, producer goods and consumer goods. Even a simple reproduction system (where the net investment is zero) is not immune to imbalances. According to J. Robinson, if Marx was the first to confront Say's law, Keynes understood how orthodox theory rests on this law, and even collapses with it.[18]

Oskar Lange and Don Patinkin will come later to ask the supporters of neoclassicism to kindly choose between maintaining Say's law and retaining the quantity theory of money. But, since J.-B. Say, the damage was done, and one always wonders what the analysis of an economic system, capitalist in this case, means without that, *sine qua non*, of the nature and functions of the money...

We thereby also grasp in what way—and this is what interests us here—the general representation of the economy that Say gives is entirely against the idea of a downward trend in the rate of profit in proportion to the accumulation of capital, and therefore against that of the exhaustion of the growth process itself—theses which however are found, more or less implicitly, although on different axiomatic frameworks, in most of the major currents of economic thought, including Keynes.

This is the case, of course, with A. Smith, D. Ricardo, J. Stuart Mill, or an atypical classic like Malthus (atypical, because he was an opponent of Say's law of outlets), but also, later, with a marginalist like W.S. Jevons. Jean-Baptiste Say is not just saying that a lasting crisis of overproduction is impossible. For him, growth would know no limits—especially since he excludes natural resources from the field of economic analysis, because they are generally obtained, he believes, free of charge (Chapter 9).

Besides, it is quite revealing of the dead end in which our discipline is plunged to note the recent flashback of this idea of "perpetual growth" in the long term, through the dissemination of the so-called "new theory of growth," or growth "with endogenous technical progress." As we saw, its canonical formalizations, elaborated by P. Romer and R. Lucas for generic complex models, or S. Rebelo or R. Barro for their simplified versions, fundamentally retain a hypothesis of non-cancelation of the marginal productivity of capital when its stock tends toward an infinitely large value (which corresponds to the relaxation of the third condition of

[18] Robinson (1971, p. 131).

Inada[19]), preventing the extinction of the long-term growth to which the Solowian representation also led.[20]

A majority of these self-sustaining growth models—but not all of them, as we have shown elsewhere[21]—indeed consider, in one way or another, that the elasticity of production to the stock of accumulable factors is at least unitary; which supposes, *in fine*, that the production function is linear in a single input, and therefore characterized simultaneously by the constancy of the returns to scale and that of the marginal return of this same factor. This factor, homogeneous with the output, will be considered to be a "capital" according to a sufficiently loose meaning—just like with Say—to integrate into it almost any factor subject to accumulation on the condition that it is positively linked to the dynamics of productivity: physical capital with externality derived from the investment process, technological knowledge resulting from specific R&D activities, infrastructure expenditure... or "human capital." And we remember that Say included in its "capital" up to scientific knowledge.[22]

In such a scheme, where the driving force of this supposedly unlimited growth is to be sought in the metamorphoses of non-reproducible factors into various accumulable forms of capital, it is therefore understandable now that labor itself could be transformed into "capital"; or, to speak as the neoclassical authors do, into certain "educated" or "skilled" categories of workers—or more precisely what they call "human capital."

However, on closer inspection, what type of "employment contract" corresponds better to this concept than that of slavery, for which the investment represented by the purchase of the slave is, in the most economic sense strict, a fixed capital? With "life annuity," moreover,

19 Inada (1963).

20 For a critical presentation of these models: Herrera (2000b, 2000c), Fine (2000), and Salvadori (2003).

21 We have shown, in writings to which we invite the reader to refer, that endogenous growth is possible, under conditions, in a Solowian framework, thus with a decreasing interest rate, if it takes place asymptotically towards a strictly positive value (Herrera [1998a]). However, these models deserve criticism from Joan Robinson (1971) who recalls that the neoclassicals have fallen back into the habit of identifying the rate of profit with the rate of interest and reaffirmed the doctrine that the rate of return measures marginal productivity of capital, without explaining what that means (p. 72).

22 Say (1861).

because this capital is lost at the death of the slave worker, specifies Jean-Baptiste. A J.-B. Say who was a resolute opponent of slavery…[23]

Appendix B: Walt W. Rostow—An Original Keynesian, from the Non-Communist Manifesto *to the Execution of* Che *Guevara*

It is probable that if W.W. Rostow—the individual who will interest us here—[24] had been born the first of his siblings, he would have been named—as was the case for his older brother – Eugene Victor Debs, in memory of the leader of the great strikes of 1894 in the Pullman factories of Chicago, the founder of the Industrial Workers of the World union and candidate of the Socialist Party of America in the presidential elections of 1904 to 1920. As for him, the youngest of the trio of Rostow brothers won Ralph Waldo Emerson as given names, after the transcendentalist leader who strongly believed in the inherent goodness of human beings, and who was also interested in Buddhism. Nonetheless, it was Walt Whitman (W.W.) which was chosen to name the middle child—and future economist—after the famous Nineteenth-Century libertarian poet, author of *Leaves of Grass* and the hymn to President Abraham Lincoln, *O Captain! My Captain!* The great Walt Whitman, admired by Arthur Rimbaud, Oscar Wilde, and Pablo Neruda, who became the icon of the U.S. left, the one who wrote, in *To the States*: "Obey little, resist much."

The explanation for these eccentric choices lies in the fact that the father of the three Rostow sons, Victor Aaron Rostowsky, was a socialist activist who had fled—long before the Bolshevik revolution—the repression of the Tsarist police of Nikolai II and the anti-Jewish pogroms of his native Ukraine (precisely the town of Orikhiv, in the Zaporijia oblast), to emigrate to the United States. After landing at Ellis Island at the turn of the Twentieth Century, the idealism of this American dreamer was such that he was not afraid, after having crossed out the three most resonant letters of his family name, to give his offspring openly progressive first names. Yet it was diametrically the opposite of his father's socialist ideals that Walt Whitman Rostow decided to position himself. Rarely has Oedipus struck with such rage as in this family.

[23] Herrera (2014b).

[24] See: Herrera (2015a).

Born in 1916 in New York, W.W. Rostow studied economics at Yale University, from which he received his doctorate, and then at Balliol College in Oxford. It was in the 1930s that he "fell in love with Keynesian economics,"[25] of which he taught the basics at Yale and then at Columbia. This is what he says about John Maynard Keynes: "[Keynes] was not a communist. He only tried to produce a policy that would stop unemployment (...) and save capitalism."[26]

At the same time, W.W. Rostow was plotting the ambitious project of settling his account with Karl Marx's conception of history. So he could proudly declare, on the publication of his famous *Non-Communist Manifesto*[27]: "I read Marx [in 1936] and I said to myself that these are big questions and wrong answers. I thought I could do better. I waited twenty-four years and [in 1960] I did it. And it's better!"[28] Actually, it was just mediocre.[29]

Before becoming the intellectual standard-bearer of counter-revolutionary thought, thanks to his *Stages of Economic Growth*, "Walt" had been introduced into the intelligence community, the O.S.S. (Office Strategic Services), created in 1942. It was Richard M. Bissell himself, the future administrator of the Marshall Plan in Germany and head of U.S. intelligence, who was responsible for recruiting him. There, at the Office of Strategic Services, which three years later would become the Central Intelligence Agency, between the generous businessman Paul Mellon (the billionaire banker's "philanthropic" grandson) and the Italian-American mobster, "*capo di tutti capi*," Lucky Luciano, Rostow had the task of designating on beautiful staff maps the targets to be hit by the Allied air force. Unlike other colleagues who did the same job, such as John Kenneth Galbraith and Arthur Meier Schlesinger, the good Walt preferred to decline the offer to participate in the group of experts who were asked in 1946 to evaluate retroactively the real effects of these bombings...

His skills acquired during World War II were not to be lost. But they were soon applied to quite different activities, which had little to do with the operations of destruction of the *Drittes Reich* armies. On the contrary,

[25] Milne (2008, p. 25).

[26] Ibidem, p. 29.

[27] Rostow (1960). A presentation is proposed in: Oman and Wignaraja (1991).

[28] Cited in: Faligot (2013, p. 289).

[29] For a strong criticism: Frank (1970).

the rather large staff led by W.W. Rostow to track down Third World rebels could count on the assistance of some experienced former leaders of the Nazi regime—such as a certain Klaus Altmann, whose real name was Nikolaus Barbie, the former head of Section IV of the German security police in Lyon, France, who was very useful later, in 1967, to "solve the Bolivian problem." We shall soon see how.

For several years, from the "Oversight of United States Covert Operations" to the "Committee 303," W.W. Rostow had the upper hand on the National Security Council. At the height of his art, in January 1966, he was appointed National Security Advisor to President Lyndon Baines Johnson. On the night of January 31 to February 1, the U.S. bombing raids on North Vietnam intensified. Johnson's "Rasputin" was at work.

He declared himself in favor of the war against communism much longer and more inflexibly than others. Through and through, and to the end, in fact. Even when some, including Robert Strange McNamara, wavered, he instead outbid and argued for "intensified counterinsurgency," as the White House put it at the time. Furthermore, remembering President John Fitzgerald Kennedy's speech—which Rostow had written for him in 1961—at the inauguration of the United States Agency for International Development (or U.S.A.I.D.), Walt the "hawk" recommended to President Lyndon B. Johnson the creation and concomitant capitalization of an Asian Development Bank…

As "Bob" McNamara put it: Rostow was "an extraordinarily smart guy and a warm, outgoing guy."[30] Even though "he [was] not critical of the military operations in Vietnam. Because he [was] an optimist by nature, he [was] skeptical of any report that [did] not indicate that [the U.S. armed forces were] making progress."[31] This, of course, did not stop McNamara from going to the Rostows' house to celebrate Thanksgiving. He was not going to miss the turkey cooked by Elspeth ("Popsy" to her friends), Walt's wife, because of some minor disagreements as to the exact number of bombs to drop on the Vietnamese! Furthermore, red!

Let us read W.W. Rostow, on various subjects.

On Vietnam first, of course, in a personal note to Secretary of Defense Robert S. McNamara on November 16, 1964, entitled "Military Dispositions and Political Signals": "Following on our conversation of last night I

[30] Faligot (2013, p. 289).

[31] Idem.

am concerned that too much thought is being given to the actual damage we do in the North [Vietnam], not enough thought to the signal we wish to send. The signal consists of three parts: a) damage to the North is now to be inflicted because they are violating the 1954 and 1962 Accords; b) we are ready and able to go much further than our initial act of damage; c) we are ready and able to meet any level of escalation they might mount in response; if they are so minded. (…) But our force dispositions to accompany an initial retaliatory move against the North should send three further signals lucidly: a. that we are putting in place a capacity subsequently to step up direct and naval pressure on the North (…); b. that we are prepared to face down any form of escalation North Vietnam might mount on the ground; and c. that we are putting forces into place to exact retaliation directly against Communist China, if Peiping [Beijing] should join in an escalatory response from Hanoi. The latter could take the form of increased aircraft on Formosa [Taiwan] plus, perhaps, a carrier force sitting off China as distinguished from the force in the South China Sea. The launching of this track, almost certainly, will require the President to explain to our own people and to the world our intentions and objectives. This will also be perhaps the most persuasive form of communication with Ho and Mao. In addition, I am inclined to think the most direct communication we can mount (perhaps via Vientiane and Warsaw) is desirable, as opposed to the use of cut-outs. They should feel they now confront an LBJ [president Lyndon B. Johnson] who has made up his mind."[32]

He added, to justify an intensification of the bombing against North Vietnam: "Mr. President, you can [perceive] it everywhere. The Hanoi operation, supported by the *Chincoms* [or the *Chicocos* somewhere else], is no longer seen as the wave of opportunity there. American power is beginning to be felt."[33]

Or on Indonesia, in a memo sent to President Lyndon B. Johnson, after the annihilation of the *Partai Komunis Indonesia* (P.K.I.) by the army of the future military dictatorship of Suharto: "Sukarno will be out

[32] Original source: *The Pentagon Papers*, Gravel Edition, Volume 3, pp. 632–633. Personal Note from W.W. Rostow to Robert McNamara on "Military Dispositions and Political Signals," 16 November, 1964. Available on: https://www.mtholyoke.edu/acad/intrel/pentagon3/doc232.htm.

[33] Faligot (2013, p. 497).

of power, probably soon. (…) The Communists will try to pay back the blood debt."[34]

On Ghana, while Rostow was head of the "Committee 303," in a note addressed to the Director of the C.I.A., Admiral W. Francis Raborn, and to Howard T. Bane, in charge of the C.I.A.'s Africa Department, at the time of the coup d'Etat against Kwame Nkrumah carried out by the putschist general Joseph Ankrah—with a copy of this same note to the "head of operations," Desmond Fitzgerald: "No question of blowing up the Chinese. Just overthrow Nkrumah"![35]

On Cuba, of course, because after being consulted by President John F. Kennedy to collaborate on the Bay of Pigs invasion plan, Rostow was to be invited to return to his first love, namely the choice of "targets to bomb," in the manner of today's drone pilots. What he thought: "We must be prepared to respond with overwhelming force."[36]

And finally, on Che, whose tracking in Bolivia he organized—L.B. Johnson having given him *carte blanche* in June 1967 to conduct actions against "Castro subversion," as he saw fit. In close liaison with the C.I.A. and the Pentagon, Rostow's White House team, including William Bowdler, his assistant for Latin American affairs, and the ever-helpful Klaus Barbie, increased the pressure on the guerrilla in October 1967. Our economist (or "economic historian," as he liked to call himself), informed by the head of the C.I.A. station in La Paz, Larry Stenfield, sent the following note to President Johnson, dated May 11, 1967: "[We are getting] the first credible report that 'Che' Guevara is alive and operating in South America. (…) We need more evidence before concluding that Guevara is operational – and not dead, as the intelligence community, with the passage of time, has been more and more inclined to believe."[37]

A little later, on the morning of October 11, 1967, this memo from Walt Whitman Rostow, entitled "Death of 'Che' Guevara," arrived on the

[34] Original source: Memorandum from the President's Special Assistant (Rostow) to President Johnson, § 231, Washington, February 21, 1967. Available on: https://2001-2009.state.gov/r/pa/ho/frus/johnsonlb/xxvi/4435.htm.

[35] Faligot (2013, p. 477).

[36] Ibidem, p. 33.

[37] Original source: National Security Archive, NSC Memorandum, Walt Rostow to President Johnson, May 11, 1967 (declassified November 28, 2013). Available on: https://nsarchive.gwu.edu/document/24583-document-4-nsc-memorandum-walt-rostow-president-johnson-may-11-1967-declassified.

desk of the President of the United States, after Che's hands and head had been cut off and the rest of his body had been buried in a mass grave, along with the bodies of his fallen comrades: "This morning we are about 99% sure that 'Che' Guevara is dead. (…) C.I.A. tells us that the latest information is that Guevara was taken alive. After a short interrogation to establish his identity, General Ovando – chief of the Bolivian Armed Forces – ordered him shoot. (…) The death of Guevara carries these significant implications. It marks the passing of another of the aggressive, romantic revolutionaries like Sukarno, Nkrumah, Ben Bella [error: read Ben Barka, R.H.] and reinforces this trend. In the Latin American context, it will have a strong impact in discouraging would-be guerrillas. It shows the soundness of our 'preventive medicine' assistance to countries facing incipient insurgency – it was the Bolivian 2nd Ranger Battalion, trained by our Green Berets from June- September of this year, that cornered him and got him. We have put these points across to several newsmen."[38]

The next day, October 13, in the afternoon, photos of Che's corpse and his fingerprints reached L.B. Johnson: "Mr. President, this removes any doubt that 'Che' Guevara is dead. Walt Rostow."[39] And on the 14th, just before lunchtime: "The death of 'Che' Guevara (…) represent[s] a serious blow to Castro (…) [because] his leading guerrilla fighter and guerrilla theoretician ha[s] just fallen in Bolivia. We do not know how he will react. Against the possibility that he might try to recoup lost prestige by some dramatic act against United States interests in Latin America – such as bombing of one of our Embassies or kidnapping of diplomatic personnel – we have instructed our missions to be on the alert and take necessary precautions."[40]

As we can see, for the author of the bestselling *The Stages of Economic Growth*, the alternative to war was not necessarily peace. Walt Whitman

[38] Source: NSC Memo, Rostow-LBJ, "Death of 'Che' Guevara," October 11, 1967 (declassified November 28, 2013). Available on: https://nsarchive.gwu.edu/document/24604-document-25-nsc-memo-rostow-lbj-death-che-guevara-october-11-1967-declassified.

[39] Available on: https://www.washingtonpost.com/news/retropolis/wp/2017/10/09/do-not-shoot-the-last-moments-of-communist-revolutionary-che-guevara/.

[40] Original source: Memorandum From the President's Special Assistant (Rostow) to President Johnson, § 173. Available on: https://history.state.gov/historicaldocuments/frus1964-68v31/d173.

Rostow died on February 13, 2003, in Austin, the capital of the State of Texas, where he was also a university professor for a long time, when he was not giving orders to execute Third World revolutionaries.

Appendix C: Robert J. Barro—The Chemically Pure Reactionary Thought

Let us extend our analyses to show how theory and politics hold together, in one of the current thinkers of neoclassicism in macroeconomics: Robert Joseph Barro. Born in 1944 in New York, he is a professor at Harvard University and known worldwide for having revisited in his anti-Keynesian way the "Ricardian equivalence" theorem and contributed to the orthodox theory of growth. Considered one of the most eminent and influential economists of the present day, he is also, among other activities, a columnist for *Business Week* where he regularly gives us real gems.

We could have added in our Chapter 2 that Robert J. Barro proposed a simple (simplistic in fact) formalization of the driving role of public infrastructure expenditure—expressed in flow, not in stock, and assumed to be directly "productive"—[41] very close to an elementary version of endogenous growth of the AK type. His model is consistently cited, far more than the otherwise powerful works of neoclassical predecessors like Kenneth J. Arrow and Mordecai Kurz.[42] It is based on a production function at constant returns to scale with respect to the set of two factors: the private *per capita* capital stock and total public expenditure. This flow of public spending has the effect of increasing returns to scale to make them unitary and of having a positive impact on private productivity.

The State must finance this expenditure through a proportional tax on the product, the rate of which remains constant. This tax rate has a double and contradictory role here: on the one hand, by reducing the incentives (of the single agent) to invest, it negatively influences growth; but, on the other hand, it increases the level of public capital and the productivity of private capital, which has a positive impact on growth. Assessing the net effect involves determining the level of public spending that maximizes the growth of the economy.

[41] Barro (1990).

[42] Arrow and Kurz (1970).

Firms interpret public expenditure as an external production factor. And it is this externality which is at the origin of the suboptimality of the decentralized equilibrium. The competitive equilibrium is thus resolved with the agent taking this expenditure as given, and available at no cost. The solution of the centralized economy is obtained by what R.J. Barro calls a "planner," which takes into account the influence of the private product on the marginal productivity of the capital of all firms of the economy, thanks to a broadening of the tax base and the resulting additional public expenditure.

This leads to a lower competitive equilibrium growth rate than that of the centralized economy. The perpetual nature of growth then comes directly from State action. Any trade-off by the individual between consumption and savings performed in favor of the latter accelerates the accumulation of capital and results in an automatic increase in productive expenditure, which generates an externality disconnecting the decentralized equilibrium from the Paretian optimum.

It is by this very schematic mechanism—since the tax rate used is arbitrarily kept constant—that we must seek the explanation of the non-decrease in marginal returns on capital and ultimately the possibility of obtaining self-sustaining growth. The optimal level of public expenditure is reached when the proportion of resources devoted to it is equal to its relative contribution to production. So one can deduce the optimal size of public spending, as that which maximizes the growth rate in the long period.

Besides, one also understands, and above all, that the question of "optimality," according to the selected criterion, is intrinsically linked to that of the limits of the effectiveness of State intervention. By this, one joins the spirit of the famous "curve" drawn *in abstracto* by Arthur B. Laffer and so dear to the supply-side economists and tax hunters,[43] but still, a "discovery" that Robert J. Barro himself has brought to light, in empirical terms this time, when he studied econometrically the links that may exist between growth and (the idea he has of) "democracy."[44] It is well known that Barro is not close to the U.S. Democratic Party; that he is not a staunch supporter of democracy, either, is perhaps a little less so. Let us read it, in one of his columns: "Throughout this discussion, I

[43] See: Mirrlees (2005).

[44] Barro (1996).

question the romantic focus of U.S. foreign policy on promoting democracy in all times and places. My [econometric] cross-country research has convinced me that the rule of law and property rights are more important than democracy in the promotion of economic growth."[45]

The rest can only be deduced by the force of logic: "Undoubtedly, Chile's outstanding economic performance derived from the free-market reforms instituted by the administration of General Augusto Pinochet from 1973 to 1989. (...) I think that the extent and durability of the leftist animosity toward him reflects the very real economic success; no one has done more than Pinochet and his economic teams to demonstrate the superiority of free-market capitalism over socialism."[46] And R.J. Barro adds that it is fortunate that a Chilean court of justice decided, after the former general returned to Chile, that he could not, due to a bad state of health, be tried for alleged crimes...

How can we forget Gary Becker? The 1992 Nobel Prize winner declared that the willingness of the "Chicago Boys" [University of Chicago economists] to work for General Pinochet was "one of the best things that happened to Chile." As one of their inspirations at the University of Chicago, he said he was "proud of their richly deserved glory."[47]

For fun, here are a host of other quotes from Robert J. Barro. This brilliant mind on the war in the Middle East: "Iraq is almost surely the world's champion for low economic growth (...). [It] was given a well-deserved zero on the Freedom House's index for democracy (...). Another question is which money to install in the new Iraq(s). The U.S. dollar is a reasonable choice, but personally, I prefer the euro. It can be economically justified, since much of Iraq's trade has been with Europe. And the political irony would be too delicious to resist: it would be a proclamation that we Americans are not just evil imperialists."[48] And he added, later: "Amid the continuing violence, people sometimes lose sight of the nobility of the US-led effort to reform Iraq. The success or failure of this mission – not the existence of particular weapons nor the

[45] Barro (2002, p. xix) (introduction).

[46] Ibidem, pp. 105–106 (Chapter 3).

[47] Becker (1997), *Business Week*, June 9.

[48] Barro (2003), *Business Week*, March 31.

deplorable bombings – will greatly influence the prospects for peace and economic development in the Mideast, and elsewhere."[49]

We continue with Latin America, and especially with Argentina, where the economic situation deteriorated sharply in 2001: "My first suggestion would be a full dollarization of the economy, including the use of U.S. dollars as the currency (...), the freeing up of labor markets with a related reduction of the power of labor unions (...), restraint on public expenditures (...)."[50] Or: "[T]he United States is supplying substantial funding for military and other purposes in support of (...) 'Plan Colombia.' (...) Colombia has long stood out in Latin America for its democratic traditions and limited political role of the military. Unfortunately, however, Colombia may now have too much democracy."[51]

Another destination, Asia. R.J. Barro asserts that it was relatively shortly before the publication of his book *Nothing is Sacred!* (in 2002) that the South Korean government allowed the market to determine which companies should survive or not. But he noted that this new attitude of these public authorities was not yet fully anchored in mentalities since in 2001 the government provided assistance to certain sectors in difficulty. He suggested that South Korea abandon its own currency and adopt the U.S. dollar. And the author deplores that his proposal to dollarize South Korea, coupled with his recommendation to buy banks by foreign investors, made him call him a "Yankee imperialist"...[52]

Last stop, in Africa. Regarding the fight against the AIDS epidemic, his position is that the big pharmaceutical companies have given in to pressure to provide drugs against AIDS at a lower cost, but this goodwill stems from the desire of certain governments to seize the assets of pharmaceutical companies. According to him, apart from the opinion that one may have on the morality of the process, it would be a bad idea to want to take away the profitability of the production of drugs, and it would be better for the world, and particularly for Africans, to ensure that innovative companies in this field are well rewarded financially. Furthermore, he thinks that beyond these problems, it is also necessary to be aware of the fact that, insofar as the treatments would prove to be effective, the result

[49] BARRO (2004), *Business Week*, April 5.

[50] BARRO (2002, pp. 52–53) (Chapter 2).

[51] Ibidem, pp. 77–78 (Chapter 2).

[52] Ibidem, pp. 114–115.

would be an increase in the lifespan which, in turn, would have the consequence of favoring a rise in the epidemic. So, as for us, we might wonder if Robert J. Barro considers that there would be too many Africans?[53]

R.J. Barro sometimes remembers being an economist. What does he think of John Maynard Keynes? In fact, he finds it amazing "today" that his first economics classes used Keynes's *General Theory* as a textbook. While this was one of the most influential books of the Twentieth Century, in his view, it is really a "lousy" textbook. Besides, since he thinks he knows that Keynes's analysis is seriously flawed, it is even surprising that he liked this teaching so much. As a student, he appreciated the simple way in which the Keynesian model explained the workings and faults of economics as a whole. What was particularly attractive to Barro were the smart economic policy remedies, such as increased public spending and tax cuts, which Keynes recommended to fight unemployment. And he concludes: too bad he later discovered that the model was theoretically and empirically "flawed"![54]

What about Milton Friedman? At Harvard University, from which Barro graduated in the late 1960s, he writes that Friedman was treated like a right-wing jerk from the Midwest, and that this derision was particularly focused on his conceptions of money, and even the theory of permanent income applied to consumption—Friedman's "scientifically flawless model" where consumer demand depends on expected household income over a long period—does not arouse no interest and little analysis. He adds that Friedman's contributions to public policy, as forcefully expressed in *Capitalism and Freedom*, were dismissed because ignored. And that the unfortunate doctoral students have learned nothing from his "visionary ideas" about training vouchers, low income tax rates, privatized social security, or balanced budgets. Many of the ideas M. Friedman put forward at the time, in the 1950s, have become "mainstream politics," and others still remain "on the agenda." Barro states that one thing is certain: Friedman won the "intellectual battle."[55] And, finally that the economists of his camp, that of neoliberalism, were lucky that Milton

[53] Ibidem, p. 46.

[54] Ibidem, p. xii.

[55] Ibidem, p. 1.

Friedman had a good constitution and enough self-confidence to persevere despite the contempt for so long directed against him by left-wing economists and journalists: "Being right is the best revenge."[56]

What about the libertarian Mont Pèlerin Society? Barro confesses that early in his career, in the 1970s, he was a standard Twentieth Century "liberal," and that his approach to economic problems was mainly to develop "smart" public policies. Later, notably under the influence of his first experience at the University of Chicago between 1972 and 1975, he became more "sensitive" to the effectiveness of private markets and less "enamored" of the curative role of the State. He describes his basic philosophy since that time as being "libertarian" rather than conservative.

He affirms that his views are quite akin to the Nineteenth-Century "liberal" philosophy espoused by Friedman. Barro defends the idea that Milton Friedman, in *Capitalism and Freedom*, proposed various policies consistent with the functioning of free markets, which, according to him, are now receiving the attention they "deserve" in the United States and elsewhere. The list includes freedom of choice in education, low income taxes, monetary stability rules, the privatization of social security, etc.

Barro himself wrote, in *Getting it Right*, that he considers that the government has certain key functions to fulfill, in particular that of defining and protecting property rights. This corresponds to national security and public order, to the establishment and strengthening of a system of laws and contracts. His belief in the applicability of this limited range of public functions is supposed to be consistent with his opinion that most governments have gone way "too far" in their spending, taxes and regulations. And he has found a lot of "interesting things" to study with economic tools, even keeping a fundamentally favorable approach to free markets.[57]

In short, for Robert J. Barro, *nothing is sacred*... except capitalism! No mistake: while he is arguably one of the most creative of neoclassicism today, and certainly one of the most cited in the world in bibliometric rankings, he is also one of the most reactionary. In fact, we could put his thought into one formula: the chemically pure reaction. Just for that, he would obviously also deserve the Sveriges Riksbank Prize in Economic Sciences in Memory of Alfred Nobel!

[56] Ibidem, p. 5.

[57] Idem.

Appendix D: Amartya K. Sen—The Economist of the Poor, or a Guru of the International Institutions?

Amartya Kumar Sen is quite possibly India's best-known economist; and, undoubtedly, one of the extremely rare intellectuals of this country-continent of more than one billion three hundred million inhabitants to have acquired a planetary reputation. This questions us, in passing, on the Western selection criteria of who and what should be globally recognized, or not. On this point, how many people in the discipline could mention a few names of "great economists" from the People's Republic of China, Brazil, South Africa, Russia, or even India, for example? Or even just one with Mexican, Nigerian, Pakistani, or Indonesian nationality? So then are there only "small ones" in these distant lands—but representing, taken together, well over half of the world's population? Or do you have to have a green card (or, failing that, a Schengen area visa) to be able to access the high-level category as well? Let us come instead to our shining Indian…

Amartya K. Sen, therefore, was born in 1933 in Santiniketan, West Bengal, in what was still British India at that time, to a family originally from Dhaka (the capital of Bangladesh today) having emigrated to the Independent Indian Union after the partition of August 1947. He defended his doctoral thesis in economics at the end of the 1950s in the "orthodox" environment of the time—with a high density of neo-Keynesian authors—under the direction of "totally brilliant, but vigorously intolerant" Joan V. Robinson.[58]

New question, always by the way: who could give some names of female "great economists"? Except perhaps the 2009 Nobel Prize winner Elinor A. Ostrom, disciple of Friedrich Hayek and James M. Buchanan, a female theorist of institutions and commons in the framework—more than rightist and radically critical of State intervention—of the Public Choice, and herself besides more a political scientist than an economist, and still relatively unknown.[59] Yet here is (a little more than) another half of humanity…

[58] Cf. A.K. Sen's "Biographical" on the website of *Sveriges Riksbank Prize in Economic Sciences in Memory of Alfred Nobel* (1998): http://www.nobelprize.org/nobel_prizes/economic-sciences/laureates/1998/sen-bio.html.

[59] Ostrom (1990).

Let us come back, this time for good, to the subject. Amartya K. Sen taught economics at various Universities in India, including those in Kolkata and Delhi, then in England, at the London School of Economics (LSE) and at the University of Oxford, before heading the prestigious Trinity College of the University of Cambridge, UK, then taking the direction in early 2004 of the no less famous Harvard University, also in Cambridge, but MA. It was in the latter establishment, as Thomas W. Lamont University Professor, that he completed his career, with colleagues several luminaries of economics such as Eric S. Maskin, Dale W. Jorgenson, and Lawrence H. Summers; or, in business management and strategy, Michael E. Porter.

During this dazzling career, he received numerous honorary awards, including the National Humanities Medal 2011 (in the company of the specialist on Satan, Andrew H. Delbanco, and the anti-Castro historian Teofilo F. Ruiz), but also the highest Indian distinction or Bharat Ratna in 1999 (after Mother Teresa, before cricket star Sachin Tendulkar and the same year as the adulated sitar player Ravi Shankar) as well as, a year earlier, in 1998, the most famous of all the prizes, that of the Bank of Sweden or Nobel Prize in economics. He then became in this discipline the very first winner from a Southern country—and the second black skin laureate, twenty years after the British-Saint Lucian W. Arthur Lewis.

Relatively little mathematized compared to the current standard of the profession, the work of Amartya K. Sen covers a wide range of fields, diversified, ranging from the procedures of social choice (by an attempt to resolve Kenneth J. Arrow's "impossibility theorem") and welfare economics (with an emphasis on individual rights, access to information and, most importantly, political freedom) to theories of human development, by passing through the study of gender inequalities or the institutions of "democracy." His analyses of the causes of famines (notably that of 1943 in Bengal) and the mechanisms of poverty, among others, have been carried around the world.

Essential point: for several decades, the influence of the thought of Amartya K. Sen has been decisive on major international institutions, especially on the United Nations Development Program (UNDP) and, although to a lesser extent, the World Bank. These two organizations both refer to concepts elaborated by A.K. Sen in their respective annual reports, the UNDP *Human Development Reports* and the World Bank's *World Development Reports*. It was he who, along with various collaborators, notably the microeconomist and former Pakistani Finance minister Mahbub-ul-Haq, was behind the development of the "human development index" (HDI) used by the UNDP since the early 1990s.

As an example, and among many other possible illustrations, the World Bank quotes its guru[60] in the 2006 report entitled *Equity and Development*, and this from the very first note of the second introductory page,[61] just before the *Theory of Justice* by John B. Rawls, two publications by Pierre Bourdieu, and an article by Thomas Piketty in the *Quarterly Journal of Economics* (a Harvard University journal of which one of the chief editors was Robert J. Barro, to whom we devoted a few lines in the previous Appendix). Then, Sen is cited again, a little further on, this time between other modest contributors named Plato (in Book V, paragraph 745, of *The Laws*) and Aristotle (in chapter 10 of the *Nicomachean Ethics*)![62]

Note that, in 2008, A.K. Sen accepted a mission of reflection—like so many others—entrusted to him by the President of the French Republic, Nicolas Sarkozy, on the possible modifications to be made to the conceptual, theoretical, and statistical instruments for measuring economic growth. He carried out this in-depth work with another renowned personality, Joseph E. Stiglitz, former chief economist of the World Bank, also winner of the Nobel Prize in economics and also very generally regarded—if not as the "conscience of the profession," at least—as one of the most "critical" of the discipline.

For Amartya K. Sen would be a "critical" economist. He would represent the "economist of the poor," it has been written on the left.[63] It has even been read, in alternative columns: "Strangely enough, he is an economist largely rubbed with orthodoxy who today wears, almost unwillingly, the flag of heterodoxy."[64] It is true that we must recognize that proposing to fit, as he does, in a perspective expressed in terms of "human development," rather than in that of a conception of development which would be reduced to the growth of production or income only—which is the law of the majority among colleagues—may

60 The reference made to A.K. Sen concerns here: Sen (1985).

61 The World Bank (2005, pp. 19 and 233).

62 Ibidem, p. 236.

63 Read: "Amartya Sen, l'économiste des pauvres prix Nobel," *L'Humanité*, October 15, 1998.

64 See: *Alternatives économiques*, November 2005.

in itself appear to be a good thing. Indeed, economists too often lack detailed statistical indicators allowing to assess the real living conditions of populations, starting with families or poorer individuals.

What is generally considered to be the strong originality of the analyzes proposed by Amartya K. Sen is fundamentally due to the formulation of specific economic concepts, such as that of "capability." He also defines the "well-being" of an agent by the quality of his or her existence. This quality is made up of a set of "human functionings" modes, representing more or less complex states and actions: having enough to eat, being in good health, benefiting from an education, but also "to be happy," to remain worthy in his or her own eyes, possibly to participate in the life of the community…

In the vicinity of the austere buildings of the Division of the Humanities at the University of Chicago, where she teaches ethics and law, Professor Martha C. Nussbaum has also gone in search of some unknown specimens of this strange species of "basic functional capabilities with cross-cultural validity." To the short list of the latter, already established by AK Sen, M.C. Nussbaum's explorations, as much inspired by Aristotle as those of the World Bank, have thus made it possible to add a series of discoveries as fundamental as: "to be able to laugh, (…) to be able to cry, (…) to be able to have opportunities for sexual satisfaction"[65]… To understand in what sense this last "capability" is viewed, we would suggest that readers let themselves be carried away by the work full of attractions of the former president of the American Philosophical Association[66]—not without specifying, however, for the attention of wild imaginations who would ignite a little quickly that, in the peaceful spirit of our disciple of the Bengali spiritual master, love, Aristotelian, may also be only platonic.[67] Let us end here.

It remains that the key notion of Sen's argumentation lies in the "capability" to function. Capability corresponds to the different combinations of states and actions of functionings that an agent can achieve. This would be the level of satisfaction of human needs "allowing to behave like a human being." This idea gives an indication of the degree of freedom that this individual has to choose between various possible lifestyles, to

[65] Read: Nussbaum (1990).

[66] From: Nussbaum (2000) to Nussbaum (2009).

[67] Nussbaum (1994).

lead a particular type of personal life. For the author, a number of technical tools, such as "utilization functions" or "conversion functions," for example, are needed to establish a link between freedom of choice and well-being.

The capability analysis, in the case of the study of poverty, focuses on the weakness of the "assets" available to agents (especially "human capital")—which would prevent the poorest among them from leaving their state—as well as on other problems related to the economy (growth) and politics (governance). So, the resumption of this sequence by the UNDP, in its traditional definition of human development, or indirectly, by the World Bank, leads to similar proposals of "sustainable growth" and "good governance."

This is to say the total compatibility between the analytical framework developed by A.K. Sen—in the spirit of which the exit from the state of poverty is done, essentially, by and for an insertion in the markets of a capitalist economy—and the ideological-political line implemented by the major international institutions of the world system. Besides, a careful reading of his writings shows the proximity of his approach to standard microeconomics, that is to say, that of the central current of contemporary neoclassicism, which seeks to account for socio-economic facts based on individual behavior. In reality, and beyond the appearance of conceptual innovations, the theories advanced by Sen, filled with the "obvious injustices" of this world, are a decal of the mainstream economic theory.[68]

However, neoclassicism maintains, as our present work wants to show from cover to cover, dangerous relations with neoliberal economic policies which continue to be imposed today on peoples almost everywhere in the world, against their will and despite the ravages of the crisis. The main strength of Amartya K. Sen is never to have taken a clear position, contenting himself with the role of "expert" of international institutions—including, as has been said, of the World Bank, whose contribution to the improvement of the living conditions of the poorest remains, to say the least, questionable…

If, in his prolific work, the concepts are legion, on the contrary, concrete examples are rare. Commentators have rightly pointed out the

[68] Arrow et al. (2002).

not very operational and ineffective nature of the capability approach.[69] A major difficulty arises from the problems posed by aggregating these capabilities into a composite index—and it should be noted in this regard that in India itself, the usual indicators of international institutions have been radically and appropriately contested.[70] As a consequence, the point is that the various "applications" of this theory, which many of his followers have undertaken, ultimately use the very traditional battery of quantitative indicators for measuring living standards—which can easily do without human functionings and other capabilities...

The non-applicability of A.K. Sen's thought is all the more striking and worrying in that its claimed ethical dimension comes up against insurmountable difficulties, owing to its very methodology. This ethics wants to be pluralist and opposed to the great doctrines in the matter—old (that of utilitarianism, founded on collective happiness or on the satisfaction of desires) or modernized (like natural law and in particular the recent version given by John B. Rawls[71]). In doing so, it no longer succeeds in defining an ultimate criterion which enables it to decide in the presence of incompatible alternatives.

It is hardly surprising here that he attaches little importance to the policies that are put in place to increase the "capability" of the poor. And why not demand, after all, a more extensive redistribution of resources in society, and even social transformations affecting the structures of the economic system? However, if one is unable to arbitrate between several options—all desirable, but not feasible simultaneously, because they involve opposing interests—how then to do *politics*? A.K. Sen's words, so generous and general at the same time, are easily recoverable in these conditions. And they have been taken over.

On closer inspection, Amartya Kumar Sen would not be that "different" than that; and he is ultimately very little "critical." The "other path" he suggests does not really differ from that followed for several decades by the great political leaders of this capitalist world in the "fight against poverty," and whose results are what they are: catastrophic. The "other voice" he makes heard, between Cambridge (UK) and Cambridge

69 See, in particular: SUGDEN (1993) and SRINIVASAN (1994). Also: BÉNICOURT (2004).

70 Consult, among others, the quality publications produced by: ALTERNATIVE SURVEY GROUP (various years), and DELHI SCIENCE FORUM (various years).

71 RAWLS (1971).

(United States), is that of a very talented author, certainly, but in perfect harmony with the dominant ideology of the spirit of the times. The poor do not have much to expect from him.[72]

In brief, A.K. Sen is traditionally presented as proposing "another way" in the struggle against poverty. His analysis concentrates on the paucity of the assets of the poor, preventing them from escaping their poverty by taking an active part in markets. Sen's ideas have influenced considerably the international organizations related to human development. Nevertheless, his reasoning is mainly a perfectly compatible copy of neoclassical theory, including general equilibrium and its methodological individualism. And, in his ethical "pluralist" speeches—which are often very confused—his proposals join those of the good governance crowd at the World Bank and IMF.

Obsessed by the solitary individual and his or her opportunities (and capacities) for choosing, he almost systematically neglects the question of resource distribution between social groups, and above all that of capital ownership inequalities. Just like J. Stiglitz, and so many others, from P. Krugman to Jeffrey Sachs, Sen loses himself in the fiction of the agents' free individual choices. This is closely related to the ideological concept of "democracy" as simply resting on individual choices, concealing the effects of class and/or national domination and the violent relations of forces between exploiters and exploited—that is, the essential contradictions of capitalism since its very origins.

[72] For a selection of readings: Sen (1970, 1973, 1981, 1985, 1987, 1999, and 2002).

Bibliographical References

Abramowitz M. (1956), "Resource and Output Trends in the United States Since 1870," *American Economic Review*, vol. 46, n° 2, p. 5–23.

——— (1986), "Catching Up, Forging Ahead, and Falling Behind," *Journal of Economic History*, vol. 46, n° 2, p. 385–406.

Acemoğlu K.D., S. Johnson and J.A. Robinson (2005), "Institutions as a Fundamental Cause of Long-Run Growth," *in* P. Aghion and S. Durlauf (eds.), *Handbook of Economic Growth*, vol. 1, part A, p. 385–472, Amsterdam: Elsevier.

Adelman I. and S. Robinson (1978), *Income Distribution Policy in Developing Countries: A Case Study of Korea*, A World Bank Research Publication, Oxford: Oxford University Press.

Aghion P.M. and S. Durlauf (eds.) (2005), *Handbook of Economic Growth*, Amsterdam: Elsevier.

Aghion P.M. and P.W. Howitt (1992), "A Model of Growth Through Creative Destruction," *Econometrica*, vol. 60, n° 2, p. 323–351.

——— (1998), *Endogenous Growth Theory*, Cambridge MA: The MIT Press.

——— (2005), "Neoclassical Models of Endogenous Growth," *in* P. Aghion and S. Durlauf (eds.), *Handbook of Economic Growth*, vol. 1, p. 67–110. Amsterdam: Elsevier.

Akerlof G.A. (1976), "The Economics of Caste and of the Rat Race and other Woeful Tales," *Quarterly Journal of Economics*, vol. 90, n° 4, p. 599–617.

——— (1984), *An Economic Theorist's Book of Tale—Essays That Entertain the Consequences of New Assumptions in Economic Theory*, New York: Cambridge University Press.

R. Herrera, *Confronting Mainstream Economics for Overcoming Capitalism*, Marx, Engels, and Marxisms,
https://doi.org/10.1007/978-3-031-05851-6

Alchian A.A. (1977), *Economic Forces at Work*, Minneapolis: Liberty Press.

Alchian A.A. and H. Demsetz (1972), "Production, Information Costs and Economic Costs, and Economic Organization," *American Economic Review*, vol. 62, n° 2, p. 92–101.

Alexander W.R. (1990), "The Impact of Defence Spending on Economic Growth," *Defence Economics*, vol. 2, n° 1, p. 39–55.

Alleg H. (2006), *Retour sur "La Question,"* Brussels: Aden.

Alternative Survey Group (various years), *Alternative Economic Survey*, Liberalisation sans Social Justice, Delhi: Rainbow Publishers.

Althusser L. (1995), *Sur la Reproduction*, Paris: Presses Universitaires de France.

Amin S. (1974), *Accumulation on a World Scale*, New York: Monthly Review Press.

——— (1993), *Itinéraire intellectuel*, Paris: L'Harmattan.

——— (1997), *Critique de l'air du temps*, Paris: L'Harmattan.

——— (2005), *Les luttes paysannes et ouvrières face aux défits du XXIe siècle*, Paris: Les Indes savantes.

——— (2015), "Theoretical Framework," in Herrera R. and K.-C. Lau (eds.), *The Struggle for Food Sovereignty—Alternative Development and the Renewal of Peasant Societies Today*, London: Pluto Press.

Amin S. and R. Herrera (2000), "Le Sud dans le système mondial en transformation," *Recherches internationales*, n°s 60–61, p. 87–99, Paris.

Amin S. and F. Houtart (2002), *Mondialisation des résistances. L'État des luttes*, CETRI Alternatives Sud - État des résistances dans le Sud, vol. XI, n° 3, Paris: L'Harmattan.

Anderton C.H. and J.R. Carter (2007), "A Survey of Peace Economics," *in* K. Hartley and T. Sandler (eds.), *Handbook of Defense Economics*, vol. 2, p. 1211–1258, Amsterdam: Elsevier.

Andréani T. (1999), "Une Explication marxiste. Some Elements of Interpretation of the Crisis of Developed Capitalist Economies," Tony Andréani's personal blog.

Andréani T. and R. Herrera (2015a), "Piketty: Réguler le capitalisme par la fiscalité ?," *La Pensée*, n° 381, p. 105–117, Paris.

——— (2015b), "Which Economic Model for China?," *International Critical Thought—A Journal of the China's Academy of Social Sciences*, p. 105–117, vol. 5, n° 1, p. 111–125, Beijing.

Andréani T., R. Herrera and Z. Long (2021), "Is China Transforming the World?," *Monthly Review*, vol. 73, n° 3, p. 21–30, New York.

Antonakis N. (1999), "Guns vs. Butter: A Multisectoral Approach to Military Expenditure and Growth with Evidence from Greece," *Journal of Conflict Resolution*, vol. 43, n° 4, p. 501–520.

AOKI M. (1986), "Horizontal vs. Vertical Information Structure of the Firm," *American Economic Review*, vol. 76, n° 5, p. 971–983.

ARISTOTLE (1931), *Physique*, Book VI, 239 b, vol. 2, Paris: Les Belles Lettres.

ARRIGHI G. (1994), *The Long Twentieth Century: Money, Power and the Origins of Our Times*, London: Verso.

ARROW K.J. (1962), "The Economic Implications of Learning by Doing," *Review of Economic Studies*, vol. 29, n° 3, p. 155–173.

——— (1972a), "Models of Job Discrimination," *in* A.H. Pascal (ed.), *Racial Discrimination in Economic Life*, p. 83–102, Lexington MA: Lexington Books.

——— (1972b), "Some Mathematical Models of Race in the Labor Market," *in* A.H. Pascal (ed.), *Racial Discrimination in Economic Life*, p. 187–204, Lexington MA.: Lexington Books.

——— (1992), "The Basic Economics of Arms Reduction," *in* W. Isard and C.H. Anderton (eds.), *Economics of Arms Reduction and the Peace Process*, p. 57–67, Amsterdam: North Holland.

ARROW K.J. and G. DEBREU (1954), "Existence of an Equilibrium for a Competitive Economy," *Econometrica*, vol. 22, n° 3, p. 265–290.

ARROW K.J. and M. KURZ (1970), *Public Investment, the Rate of Return, and Optimal Fiscal Policy*, Baltimore: Johns Hopkins Press.

ARROW, K.J. and J.E. LI (1993), "A Note on the Peace Dividend and Reallocation of Knowledge Skills," *in* J. Brauer and M. Chatterji (eds.), *Economic Issues of Disarmament*, p. 26–32, London: Macmillan.

ARROW K.J., A.K. SEN and K. SUZUMURA (2002), *Handbook of Social Choice and Welfare*, 2 volumes, Amsterdam: Elsevier.

ASCHAUER D.A. (1989a), "Public Investment and Productivity Growth in the Group of Seven," *Economic Perspectives*, vol. 13, n° 5, p. 17–25.

——— (1989b), "Is Public Expenditure Productive?," *Journal of Monetary Economics*, vol. 23, n° 1, p. 77–200.

ATHANASSIOU E., C. KOLLIAS and A. ZOGRAFAKIS (2002), "The Effects of Defence Spending Reductions: A CGE Estimation of the Foregone Peace Dividend in the Case of Greece," *Defence and Peace Economics*, vol. 13, n° 2, p. 417–427.

AUMANN R.J.Y. (1996), "A Reply to Binmore," *Games and Economic Behavior*, vol. 17, n° 1, p. 138–146.

AVANT D.D. (2005), *The Market for Force: The Consequences of Privatizing Security*, Cambridge (UK): Cambridge University Press.

AYRES C.E. (1944), *The Theory of Economic Progress*, Chapel Hill: University of North Carolina Press.

AZARIADIS C. and A. DRAZEN (1990), "Threshold Externalities in Economic Development," *Quarterly Journal of Economics*, vol. 105, n° 2, p. 501–526.

BABST D.V. (1964), "Elective Governments: A Force For Peace," *The Wisconsin Sociologist*, vol. 3, n° 1, p. 9–14.

BACHRAM H. (2004), "Climate Fraud and Carbon Colonialism: The New Trade in Greenhouse Gases," *Capitalism Nature Socialism*, vol. 15, n° 4, p. 1–16.

BADIOU A. (1998), *D'un Désastre obscur*, La Tour d'Aigues: Éditions de l'Aube.

BANQUE MONDIALE (1996), "De l'Économie planifiée à l'économie de marché," *Rapport sur le développement dans le monde* de la Banque mondiale, Washington DC: The World Bank.

——— (1997), "L'État dans un monde en mutation," *Rapport sur le développement dans le monde* de la Banque mondiale, Washington DC: The World Bank.

BARNUM H.N. and L. SQUIRE (1979), "An Econometric Application of the Theory of the Farm Household," *Journal of Development Economics*, n° 6, p. 79–102.

BARRÈRE A. (1979), *Déséquilibres économiques et contre-révolution keynésienne*, Paris: Economica.

BARRO R.J. (1974), "Are Government Bonds Net Wealth?," *Journal of Political Economy*, vol. 82, n° 6, p. 1095–1117.

——— (1981), "Output Effects of Government Purchases," *Journal of Political Economy*, vol. 89, n° 6, p. 1086–1121.

——— (1987), *La Macroéconomie*, Paris: Colin.

——— (1990), "Government Spending in a Simple Model of Endogenous Growth," *Journal of Political Economy*, vol. 98, n° 5, p. S103–S125.

——— (1991), "Economic Growth in a Cross Section of Countries," *Quarterly Journal of Economics*, vol. 106, n° 2, p. 407–443.

——— (1996), "Democracy and Growth," *Journal of Economic Growth*, vol. 1, n° 1, p. 1–27.

——— (2002), *Nothing Is Sacred!*, Cambridge (MA): The MIT Press.

——— (2003), "Economic Viewpoint: A Democratic Iraq isn't an Impossible Dream," *Business Week*, March 31.

——— (2004), "Economic Viewpoint: A Step in the Right Direction for Iraq," *Business Week*, April 5.

BARRO R.J. and X. SALA-I-MARTÍN (1992), "Convergence," *Journal of Political Economy*, vol. 100, n° 2, p. 223–251.

——— (1995), *Economic Growth*, New York: McGraw-Hill.

——— (1997), "Technological Diffusion, Convergence, and Growth," *Journal of Economic Growth*, vol. 2, n° 1, p. 1–26.

BASTIAT F. (1864 [1855]), *Harmonies économiques*, *in Œuvres complètes*, Paris: Guillaumin & Cie.

BATCHELOR P., J.P. DUNNE and D.S. SAAL (2000), "Military Spending and Economic Growth in South Africa," *Defence and Peace Economics*, vol. 11, n° 4, p. 553–571.

BAUMOL W. J. (1999), "Retrospectives: Say's Law," *Journal of Economic Perspectives*, vol. 13, n° 1, p. 195–204.

BAUMOL W.J., S. BLACKMAN and E. WOLFF (1989), *Productivity and American Leadership: The Long View*, Cambridge MA: The MIT Press.

BAYOUMI T., D.P. HEWITT and J. SCHIFF (1995), "Economic Consequences of Lower Military Spending," *in* L.R. Klein, F.C. Lo and W.J. McKibbin (eds.), *Arms Reduction*, p. 172–219, Tokyo: United Nations University Press.

BAYOUMI T., D.P. HEWITT and S. SZYMANSKY (1993), "The Impact of Worldwide Military Spending Cuts on Developing Countries," *IMF Working Paper*, p. 93–86, Washington DC: International Monetary Fund.

BECKER G.S. (1964), *Human Capital: A Theoretical and Empirical Analysis, with Special Reference to Education*, New York: Columbia University Press.

——— (1985), "Capital Income Taxation and Perfect Foresight," *Journal of Public Economics*, n° 26, p. 147–167.

——— (1997), "Latin America Owes a Lot to Its 'Chicago Boys,'" *Business Week*, June 9.

BECKER G.S., K.M. MURPHY and R. TAMURA (1990), "Human Capital, Fertility, and Economic Growth," *Journal of Political Economy*, vol. 98, n° 5, part II, p. S12–S37.

BÉNICOURT E. (2004), "Contre Amartya Sen," *L'Économie politique*, n° 23, p. 72–84.

BENOIT E. (1973), *Defense and Economic Growth in Developing Countries*, Lexington Books, Studies in International Development Economics, Cambridge MA: The MIT Press.

BENOIT E. and K.E. BOULDING (1963), *Disarmament and the Economy*, New York: Harper and Row Publishers.

BÉNOT Y. (2006 [1992]), *La Démence coloniale sous Napoléon*, Paris: La Découverte.

BERGMAN L. (2005), "CGE Modeling of Environmental Policy and Resource Management," in Mäler K.G. and J. Vincent (eds.), *Handbook of Environmental Economics*, vol. 3, chapter 24, p. 1273–1306, Amsterdam: Elsevier.

BERNAL M.G. (1996 [1987]), *Black Athena - Les racines afro-asiatiques de la civilisation classique*, Paris: Presses universitaires de France.

BERNANKE B. (2010), "Fiscal Sustainability and Fiscal Rules," *Annual Meeting of the Rhode Island Public Expenditure Council*, Providence, October 4.

BERTRAND É. (2003), "Les 'Théorèmes de Coase:' énoncés et critiques microéconomiques," Ph.D. Dissertation, University of Paris 1 Panthéon-Sorbonne, Paris.

BHADURI A. and D.J. HARRIS (1987), "The Complex Dynamics of the Simple Ricardian System," *Quarterly Journal of Economics*, vol. 102, n° 4, p. 893–901.

Bhagwati J.N. (1982), "Directly Unproductive Profit Seeking Activities," *Journal of Political Economy*, vol. 90, n° 5, p. 988–1002.

——— (2004), *In Defense of Globalization*, New York: Oxford University Press.

Bidet J. (2022), *L'écologie politique du commun du peuple*, Fontainebleau: *Éditions du Croquant*.

Binmore K.G. (2005), *Natural Justice*, New York: Oxford University Press.

Biswas B. and R. Ram (1986), "Military Expenditure and Economic Growth in Less Developed Countries," *Economic Development and Cultural Change*, vol. 34, n° 2, p. 361–372.

Blanchard O.J. (1995), "Comment on 'Establishing Property Rights' by Shleifer," *Proceedings of the World Bank Annual Conference on Development Economics 1994*, p. 118–121, Washington DC: The World Bank.

——— (2008), "Neoclassical Synthesis," *The New Palgrave Dictionary of Economics*, London: Macmillan.

Blanchard O. and S. Fischer (1989), *Lectures on Macroeconomics*, Cambridge MA: MIT Press.

Blaug M. (1986), *La Pensée économique - Origine et développement*, Paris: Economica.

Bloumine I. (1952), "L'économie politique de Keynes," *La Pensée*, n° 42–43, p. 182–186, Paris.

Blum W. (2002), *L'État voyou*, Lyon: Parangon.

Böhm-Bawerk E. (von) (1959 [1890]), *Capital and Interest*, South Holland: Libertarian Press.

Boland L. (1979), "Knowledge and the Role of Institutions in Economic Theory," *Journal of Economic Issues*, vol. 13, n° 4, p. 957–972.

Bukharin N.I. (1972 [1914]), *L'Économie politique du rentier - critique de l'économie marginaliste*, Paris: Études et Documentations Internationales.

Boulding K.E. (1962), *Conflict and Defense*, New York: Harper and Row Publisher.

Bourguignon F., M. Bussolo and L.A. Pereira da Silva (2008), *The Impact of Macroeconomic Policies on Poverty and Income Distribution*, Washington DC: The World Bank.

Bourguignon F., G. Michel and D. Miqueu (1983), "Short-Run Rigidities and Long-Run Adjustments in a Computable General Equilibrium Model of Income Distribution and Development," *Journal of Development Economics*, vol. 13, n° 1, p. 21–43.

Bourguinat H. (1999), *Finance internationale - Après l'euro et les crises*, 4th ed., Paris: Presses Universitaires de France.

Brock W. and M.S. Taylor (2005), "Economic Growth and the Environment: A Review of Theory and Empirics," in P. Aghion and S. Durlauf (eds.), *Handbook of Economic Growth*, vol. 1, part B, p. 1749–1821, Amsterdam: Elsevier.

Broude M., S. Deger and S. Sen (2013), "Defence, Innovation and Development: the Case of Israel," *Journal of Innovation Economics and Management*, n° 2013/2, n° 12, p. 37–57.

Brown M., K. Sato and P. Zarembka (1976), *Essays in Modern Capital Theory*, Amsterdam North Holland.

Buchanan J.M. (1975), *The Limits of Liberty—Between Anarchy and Leviathan*, Chicago: University of Chicago Press.

Buchanan J.M. and R.A. Musgrave (1999), *Public Finance and Public Choice: Two Contrasting Views of the State*, Cambridge MA: The MIT Press.

Buchanan J.M. and G. Tullock (1961), *The Calculus of Consent: Logical Foundations of Constitutional Democracy*, Ann Arbor: The University of Michigan Press.

Burniaux J.-M., J.P. Martin, G. Nicoletti and J. Oliveira Martins (1992), "GREEN—A Multi-Sector, Multi-Region Dynamic General Equilibrium Model for Quantifying the Costs of Curbing CO_2 Emissions: A Technical Manual," *Economics Department Working Papers*, n° 116, Organisation for Economic Co-operation and Development, Paris.

Cambois E., C. Laborde and J.-M. Robine (2008), "La 'double peine' des ouvriers: plus d'années d'incapacité au sein d'une vie plus courte," *Population et Sociétés*, Institut national d'Études démographiques, n° 441, Paris.

Canguilhem G. (1977), *Idéologie et rationalité dans l'histoire des sciences*, Paris: Éditions Vrin.

——— (1996), *Vie et mort de Jean Cavaillès*, Paris: Allia.

Carcanholo R.A. and P. Nakatani (1999), "O Capital especulativo parasitário," *Revista Ensaios*, vol. 20, n° 1, p. 284–304.

Carcanholo R.A. and M. Sabadini (2009), "Capital fictício e lucros fictícios," *Revista da Sociedade Brasileira de Economia Política*, n° 24, p. 66–84.

Casanova A. and R. Herrera (eds.) (2014), *Penser les crises*, Paris: Le Temps des Cerises.

Cass D. (1966), "Optimum Growth in an Aggregative Model of Capital Accumulation: A Turnpike Theorem," *Econometrica*, vol. 34, n° 4, p. 833–850.

Catalinotto J. (2017), *Turn the Guns Around*, New York: World View Forum.

Central Intelligence Agency (various years), *The World Factbook*, Public Affairs, Washington DC.

Chenery H.B. and M. Bruno (1962), "Development Alternatives in an Open Economy: The Case of Israel," *Economic Journal*, vol. 72, n° 285, p. 79–103.

Chenery H.B. and T.N. Srinivasan (eds.) (1988), *Handbooks of Development Economics*, Amsterdam: Elsevier.

Chenery H.B. and A.M. Strout (1966), "Foreign Assistance and Economic Development," *American Economic Review*, vol. 56, n° 4, p. 679–733.

Cheung S.N.-S. (1968), "Private Property Rights and Sharecropping," *Journal of Political Economy*, vol. 76, n° 6, p. 1107–1122.

——— (1969a), *Theory of Share Tenancy*, Chicago: University of Chicago Press.

——— (1969b), "Transaction Costs, Risk Aversion, and the Choice of Contractual Arrangements," *Journal of Law and Economics*, vol. 13, p. 49–70.

Chomsky A.N. (2005), *Les Dessous de la politique de l'Oncle Sam*, Montreal: Écosociété.

Cicchini J. and R. Herrera (2008), "Sociétés militaires privées: la guerre par procuration ? Le cas de la guerre d'Irak," *Recherches internationales*, n° 82, p. 9–26, Paris.

Clark J.M. (1924), "The Socializing of Theoretical Economics," *in* R.G. Tugwell (ed.), *The Trend of Economics*, p. 73–105, New York: Alfred A. Knopf.

——— (1957), *Economic Institutions and Human Welfare*, New York: A.A. Knopf.

Coase R. (1960), "The Problem of Social Cost," *Journal of Law and Economics*, n° 3, p. 1–44, October.

Coase R.H. (1988), *The Firm, the Market and the Law*, Chicago: University of Chicago Press.

——— (1989 [1937]), "La Nature de la firme," *Revue française d'Économie*, vol. 2, n° 1.

Commission Gulbenkian (1996), *Ouvrir les sciences sociales* (Rapport pour la restructuration des sciences sociales), Paris: Descartes & Cie.

Commons J.R. (1931), "Institutional Economics," *American Economic Review*, vol. 21, n° 4, p. 648–657.

Crédit Suisse (2013), *Global Wealth Report 2013*, Research Institute, October, Zurich.

Crespo Cuaresma J. and G. Reitschuler (2003), "A Non-Linear Defence-Growth Nexus? Evidence from US Economy," *Defence and Peace Economics*, vol. 15, n° 1, p. 71–82.

Dahan- Dalmedico A. and J. Peiffer (1986), *Une Histoire des mathématiques*, Paris: Le Seuil.

Dauben J.W. (1979), *Georg Cantor: His Mathematics and Philosophy of the Infinite*, Princeton: Princeton University Press.

De Janvry A., M. Fafchamps and E. Sadoulet (1991), "Peasant Household Behavior with Missing Markets: Some Paradoxes Explained," *Economic Journal*, vol. 101, n° 409, p. 1400–1417.

De Janvry A., E. Sadoulet and E. Thorbecke (1993), "Introduction," *World Development*, vol. 21, n° 4, p. 565–575.

De la Croix D. and P. Michel (2002), *A Theory of Economic Growth—Dynamics and Policy in Overlapping Generations*, Cambridge: Cambridge University Press.

De Long J.B. (1989), "The Protestant Ethic Revisited: A Twentieth Century Look," *Fletcher Forum of World Affairs*, n° 13, p. 229–242.

De Soto H. (1986), *El Otro Sendero*, El Barranco, Lima: Institute for Liberty and Democraty.
Debreu G. (1959), *Theory of Value*, New York: Wiley.
——— (1962), "New Concepts and Techniques for Equilibrium Analysis," *International Economic Review*, vol. 3, n° 2, p. 257–273.
——— (1974), "Excess Demand Functions," *Journal of Mathematical Economics*, vol. 1, n° 1, p. 15–21.
Deger S. (1985), "Human Resources, Government Education Expenditure, and the Military Burden in Less Developed Countries," *Journal of Developing Areas*, vol. 20, n° 1, p. 37–48.
——— (1986a), *Military Expenditure in the Third World Countries: The Economic Effects*, London, Routledge & Kegan Paul.
——— (1986b), "Economic Development and Defense Expenditure," *Economic Development and Cultural Change*, vol. 35, n° 1, p. 180–196.
Deger S. and S. Sen (1995), "Military Security and Developing Countries," *in* K. Hartley and T. Sandler (eds.), *Handbook of Defense Economics*, vol. 1, p. 275–307, Amsterdam: North Holland.
Dejours C. (2010), *Observations cliniques en psychopathologie du travail*, Paris: Presses Universitaires de France.
Delhi Science Forum (various years), *The Indian Economy—An Alternative Survey*, Hyderabad: Prajasakti Book House.
Delong J.B. (1989), "The Protestant Ethic Revisited: A Twentieth Century Look," *Fletcher Forum of World Affairs*, n° 13, p. 229–242.
Denison E.F. (1985), *Trends in American Economic Growth: 1929–1982*, Washington DC: Brookings Institution Press.
Dessus S. and R. Herrera (1999), "Capital public et croissance: une étude en économétrie de panel," *Revue économique*, vol. 50, n° 1, p. 113–126, Paris.
——— (2000), "Public Capital and Growth: A Panel Data Assessment," *Economic Development and Cultural Change*, vol. 48, n° 2, p. 407–418, Chicago.
Devarajan S. and D. Rodrik (1991), "Pro-competitive Effects of Trade Reform: Results from a CGE Model of Cameroon," *European Economic Review*, n° 35, p. 1157–1184.
Diatkine D. (2021), *Adam Smith, the Discovery of Capitalism and of Its Limits*, London: Palgrave Macmillan.
Dierckxsens W. (2000), *The Limits of Capitalism*, London: Zed Books.
Dierckxsens W. and W. Formento (2016), *Geopolítica de la crisis económica mundial - Globalismo vs. Universalismo*, Buenos Aires: Ediciones Fabro.
Diop C.A. (1979), *Nations nègres et culture*, Paris: Présence africaine.
——— (1981), *Civilisation ou barbarie*, Paris: Présence africaine.
Domar E.D. (1946), "Capital Expansion, Rate of Growth, and Employment," *Econometrica*, vol. 14, n° 4, p. 137–147.

——— (1947), *Essays in the Theory of Economic Growth*, New York: Oxford University Press.

Dorigny M. and M.-J. Zins (eds.) (2009), *Les traités négrières coloniales: Histoire d'un crime*, Paris: Cercle d'Art.

Dornbusch R., S. Fischer and P.A. Samuelson (1977), "Comparative Advantage, Trade, and Payments in a Ricardian Model with a Continuum of Goods," *American Economic Review*, vol. 67, n° 5, p. 823–839.

Dupuis M.-C. (1997), *Finance criminelle*, Paris: Presses Universitaires de France.

Easterly W. and R. Levine (1997), "Africa's Growth Tragedy: Policies and Ethnic Divisions," *Quarterly Journal of Economics*, vol. 112, n° 4, p. 1203–1250.

Edgeworth F.Y. (1967 [1881]), *Mathematical Psychics*, New York: Augustus M. Kelley.

Engels F. (1975), *Sur Le Capital de Marx*, Moscow: Éditions du Progrès.

——— (1978), *Anti-Dühring*, Paris: Éditions sociales.

Faligot R. (2013), *Tricontinentale: Quand Che Guevara, Ben Barka, Cabral, Castro et Hô Chi Minh préparaient la révolution mondiale (1964–1968)*, Paris: La Découverte.

Favereau O. (1989), "Marchés internes, marchés externes," *Revue économique*, vol. 40, n° 2, p. 273–328.

Feder G. (1983), "On Exports and Economic Growth," *Journal of Development Economics*, vol. 12, n°s 1–2, p. 59–73.

Fields A. (1981), "The Problem with Neoclassical Institutional Economics: A Critique with Special Reference to the North/Thomas Model of pre-1500 Europe," *Explorations in Economic History*, n° 18, p. 174–198.

Findlay R. and J.D. Wilson (1987), "The Political Economy of the Leviathan," *in* A. Razin and E. Sadka (eds.), *Economic Policy in Theory and Practice*, London: Macmillan.

Fine B. (2000), "Endogenous Growth Theory: A Critical Assessment," *Cambridge Journal of Economics*, vol. 24, n° 1, p. 245–265.

Fogel R.W. (1964), *Without Consent or Contract: The Rise and Fall of American Slavery*, New York: W.W. Norton.

Fogel R.W. and S.L. Engerman (eds.) (1971), *The Reinterpretation of American Economic History*, New York: Harper and Row.

——— (1974a), *Time on the Cross: The Economics of American Negro Slavery*, New York: W.W. Norton and Co.

——— (1974b), *Time on the Cross: Evidence and Methods—A Supplement*, Boston: Little, Brown and Co.

Foster J.B. (2000), *Marx's Ecology: Materialism and Nature*, New York: Monthly Review Press.

FOSTER J.B. and F. MAGDOFF (2009), *The Great Financial Crisis*, New York: Monthly Review Press.

FOSTER J.B. and F. MCCHESNEY (2010), "Listen Keynesians, It's the System! Response to Palley," available on: http://monthlyreview.org/2010/04/01/listen-keynesians-its-thesystem-response-to-palley#.UIWcxm-HWU.

FRANK A.G. (1979), *Dependent Accumulation and Underdevelopment*, New York: Monthly Review Press.

FRIEDMAN D. (1973), *The Machinery of Freedom*, New York: Harper Collophon.

FRIEDMAN M. (1962), *Capitalism and Freedom*, Chicago: The University of Chicago Press.

——— (1976), "The Line We Dare Not Cross," *Encounter*, n° 2, p. 2–14.

——— (1986), *Free to Choose*, London: Penguin Books.

FRYDMAN C. and R.E. SAKS (2008), "Executive Compensation," *National Bureau of Economic Research (NBER) Working Paper*, n° 14145, Cambridge (MA).

FURTADO C. (2003), *Raízes do subdesenvolvimento*, Rio de Janeiro: Civilização Brasileira.

GALVIN H. (2003), "The Impact of Defence Spending on the Economic Growth of Developing Countries: A Cross-Section Study," *Defence and Peace Economics*, vol. 14, n° 1, p. 51–59.

GASTIL R.D. (various years), *Freedom in the World: Political Rights and Civil Liberties*, Westport (CT): Greenwood Press.

GAZIER B. and R. HERRERA (2002), "Escaping from the Crisis: Structural Adjustment and Social Security in the Republic of Korea," *in* K. Marshall and O. Butzbach (eds.), *New Social Policy Agendas for Europe and Asia—Challenges, Experience, and Lessons*, p. 405–417, Washington DC: The World Bank.

GENTILUCCI E. (2010), "La Spesa militare nell'analisi degli economisti contemporanei," Ph.D. Dissertation, Université de Paris 1 and Università di Macerata, Paris and Macerata.

GEORGESCU-ROEGEN N. (1971), *The Entropy Law and the Economic Process*, Cambridge (MA): Harvard University Press.

——— (2006), *La Décroissance. Entropie, écologie, économie*, Paris: Éditions Sang de la terre.

GILLIS M., D.H. PERKINS, M. ROEMER and D.R. SNODGRASS (1990), *Économie du développement*, Brussels: De Boeck.

GOFF B.L. and R.D. TOLLISON (1990), "Is National Defense a Pure Public Good?," *Defense Economics*, vol. 1, n°. 2, p. 141–147.

GOMES H. (eds.) (2015), *Especulação e lucros fictícios: formas parasitárias da acumulação contemporânea*, São Paulo: Outras Expressões.

González Gutiérrez A. (2006), "La Planification globale de l'économie nationale," *in* R. Herrera (ed.), *Cuba révolutionnaire - Tome 2: économie et planification*, p. 175–273, Paris: Éditions L'Harmattan.

Goodwin R.M. (1967), "A Growth Cycle," *in* C.H. Feinstein (ed.), *Socialism, Capitalism and Economic Growth*, p. 54–58, Cambridge: Cambridge University Press.

——— (1983), *Essays in Linear Economic Systems*, London: Macmillan.

Greenspan A. (1996), Speech delivered to the *American Enterprise Institute* in Washington DC, 12 May.

Grossman G. and E. Helpman (1989), "Quality Ladders and Product Cycles," *National Bureau of Economic Research (NBER) Working Paper*, n° 3201, Cambridge (MA).

——— (1991), *Innovation and Growth in the Global Economy*, Cambridge MA: The MIT Press.

Guerrero D. (2011), *Sismondi, precursor de Marx*, Madrid: Maia Ediciones.

Guerrien B. (1989), *La Théorie néo-classique - Bilan et perspectives du modèle d'équilibre général*, Paris: Economica.

——— (1996a), *Dictionnaire d'analyse économique - Microéconomie, macroéconomie, théorie des jeux, etc.*, «Dictionnaires repères», Paris: La Découverte.

——— (1996b), *L'Économie néo-classique*, Paris: La Découverte.

Guillaumont P. (1985), *Économie du développement*, tome 2, Thémis, Paris: Presses Universitaires de France.

Guilluy C. (2014), *La France périphérique - Comment on a sacrifié les classes populaires*, Paris: Éditions Flammarion.

Günlük-Enesen G. (2007), "Accounting for Arms in Input-Output and National Income Accounts," *in* W. Elsner (ed.), *Arms, War and Terrorism in the Global Economy Today*, p. 50–68, Berlin: LIT Verlag.

Haavelmo T.M. (1956), *A Study in the Theory of Economic Evolution*, Amsterdam: North Holland.

Harris R.J. and M.P. Todaro (1970), "Migration, Unemployment and Development: A Two-Sector Analysis," *American Economic Review*, vol. 60, n° 1, p. 126–142.

Harrod R.F. (1939), "An Essay in Dynamic Theory," *Economic Journal*, vol. 49, n° 3, p. 14–33.

——— (1948), *Towards a Dynamic Economics*, London: Macmillan.

——— (1951), *The Life of John Maynard Keynes*, London: Macmillan.

Hartley K. and T. Sandler (eds.) (2007), *Handbook of Defense Economics*, Amsterdam: Elsevier.

Harvey D. (1982), *The Limits to Capital*, London: Basil Blackwell.

——— (2014), *Afterthoughts on Piketty's Capital*, available on: davidharvey.org.

Hayami Y. and V.W. Ruttan (1984), "Toward a Theory of Induced Institutional Innovation," *Journal of Development Studies*, vol. 20, n° 4, p. 203–223.

Hayek F.A. (1953), *Scientisme et sciences sociales: essai sur le mauvais usage de la raison*, Paris: Plon.
——— (1976), *The Constitution of Liberty*, London: Henley-Routledge & Kegan Paul.
——— (1981), *Droit, législation, liberté*, Paris: Presses universitaires de France.
Helliwell J.F. (1994), "Empirical Linkages Between Democracy *and Economic* Growth," *British Journal of Political Science*, n° 24, p. 225–248.
Helliwell J.F., P.R. Layard and J.D. Sachs (2013), *World Happiness Report 2013*, New York: Sustainable Development Solutions Network.
Herrera R. (1994), *Statistics on Military Expenditure in Developing Countries: Concepts, Methodological Problems, and Sources*, Paris: OECD Development Centre.
——— (1996), "Institutions et croissance: une étude appliquée aux pays en développement," *mimeo*, Paris: OECD Development Centre.
——— (1997), "Productivités et externalités des dépenses publiques: une étude économétrique sur séries temporelles," *Économie & Prévision*, vol. 5, n° 131, p. 145–153, Paris.
——— (1998a), "Dépenses publiques d'éducation et capital humain dans un modèle convexe de croissance endogène," *Revue économique*, vol. 49, n° 3, p. 831–844, Paris.
——— (1998b), "Dépenses militaires: quels effets sur les finances publiques et la croissance économique?," *Revue d'économie politique*, vol. 108, n° 4, p. 503–530, Paris.
——— (2000a), "Critique de l'économie 'apolitique'," *L'Homme et la Société*, n° 135, p. 87–104, Paris.
——— (2000b), "Éléments pour une critique de la 'nouvelle théorie' néoclassique de la croissance," *Cahier de la Maison des Sciences économiques de l'Université de Paris 1*, n° 75, Paris.
——— (2000c), "Por uma crítica da nova teoria neoclássica do crescimento," *Revista da Sociedade Brasileira de Economia Política*, n° 7, p. 55–73, Rio de Janeiro.
——— (2000d), "Le Rôle des dépenses militaires dans les pays en développement: une analyse critique théorique et empirique," *Mondes en développement*, n° 112, p. 39–58, Brussels.
——— (2001a), "Y a-t-il une pensée unique en économie politique?," *La Pensée*, n° 325, p. 99–111, Paris.
——— (2001b), "Les Théories du système mondial capitaliste," *in* J. Bidet and E. Kouvélakis, *Dictionnaire Marx contemporain*, p. 201–221, Paris: Presses Universitaires de France.
——— (2001c), "Brève introduction à la Théorie de l'État chez Marx et Engels," *Cahier de la Maison des Sciences économiques de l'Université de Paris 1*, n° 1, Paris, available on: https://vimeo.com/144550507.

——— (ed.) (2001d), *L'Empire en guerre - Le Monde après le 11 septembre*, Paris and Brussels: Le Temps des Cerises and EPO.

——— (2003a), "L'État contre le service public?," *Actuel Marx*, n° 34, p. 147–160, Paris.

——— (2003b), "Why Israel Should Vote to Lift the Embargo of the United States Against Cuba?," *Haaretz*, (in English and Hebrew), heshvan 7, 5764, vol. 85, n° 25662, Tel Aviv.

——— (ed.) (2003c), *Cuba révolutionnaire: Histoire et culture*, Tome 1, Paris: Éditions L'Harmattan.

——— (2004a), "Un Renouveau de l'économie du développement?," *Recherches internationales* (Paris), n° 72, p. 51–68, Paris.

——— (2004b), "Good Governance against Good Government?," Joint Written Statement of the Centre Europe Tiers-Monde and the American Association of Jurists for the Human Rights Commission of the United Nations, 60th Session, Point 17, E/CN.4/2004/NGO/124, July, Geneva.

——— (2004c), "IMF: A Bad Governance Model?," *Third World Economics*, n° 324, p. 15–21, Penang.

——— (2004d), "On the Free Trade Area of the Americas (FTAA)," Joint Written Statement of the Centre Europe Tiers-Monde and the American Association of Jurists for the Human Rights Commission of the United Nations, Geneva.

——— (2004e), "Cuba: Why Lift the Embargo?," *Monthly Review*, vol. 55, n° 8, p. 49–54, New York.

——— (2005), "When the Names of the Emperors were Morgan and Rockefeller," *International Journal of Political Economy*, vol. 34, n° 4, p. 25–49, New York.

——— (2006a), "The Hidden Face of Endogenous Growth Theory," *Review of Radical Political Economics*, vol. 38, n° 2, p. 243–257, New York.

——— (2006b), "The 'New' Development Economics: A Neoliberal *Con*?," *Monthly Review*, vol. 58, n° 1, p. 38–50, New York.

——— (2006c), "Objectifs du Millénaire pour le Développement: lutte contre la pauvreté ou guerre contre les pauvres ?," *Alternatives Sud*, vol. 13, n° 1, p. 185–199, Louvain-la-Neuve.

——— (ed.) (2006d), *Cuba révolutionnaire: Économie et planification*, Tome 2, Paris: Éditions L'Harmattan.

——— (2007), "War and Crisis," *Political Affairs*, vol. 86, n° 4, p. 34–38, New York.

——— (2008a), "Ambiante e crescita: contro l'economia neoclassica e le sue false alternative," *in* L. Vasapollo (ed.), *Capitale, natura e lavoro*, p. 269–282, Milan: Jaca Book.

——— (2008b), "Les Enfants travailleurs au cœur du capitalisme," *La Pensée*, n° 354, p. 31–45, Paris.

——— (2010a), *Dépenses publiques et croissance économique - Pour sortir de la science(-fiction) néoclassique*, Paris: L'Harmattan.
——— (2010b), *Un Autre Capitalisme n'est pas possible*, Paris: Syllepse.
——— (2010c), *Estado y crecimiento*, Madrid: Maia Ediciones.
——— (2010d), *Les Avancées révolutionnaires en Amérique latine - Des transitions socialistes au XXIe siècle?*, Lyon: Parangon.
——— (2011a), "A Critique of Mainstream Growth Theory," *Research in Political Economy*, vol. 27, n° 1, p. 3–64, London and New York.
——— (2011b), "Tendances de l'économie étasunienne sous la mandature de Barack H. Obama," *Recherches internationales*, n° 91, p. 151–169, Paris.
——— (2012a), "Neoclassical Economic Fiction and Neoliberal Political Reality," *International Critical Thought—A Review of the Chinese Academy of Social Sciences*, vol. 3, n° 1, p. 98–107, London: Routledge.
——— (2012b), *Gastos públicos y crecimiento económico*, Caracas: Banco Central de Venezuela.
——— (2012c), "Reflections on the Current Crisis and Its Effects," *Economic and Political Weekly*, vol. XLVII, n° 23, p. 62–71, Mumbai.
——— (2013a), "La Domination de la haute finance états-unienne: origines, mécanismes, alternatives," *Marché & Organisations*, n° 19, p. 127–146, Paris.
——— (2013b), "Defense and the Economy," *Journal of Innovation Economics and Management*, n° 2013/2, p. 3–11, Brussels.
——— (2013c), "Between Crisis and Wars—Where Is the United States Heading?," *Journal of Innovation Economics and Management*, n° 2013/2, p. 151–174, Brussels.
——— (2013d), "Crise et guerre sont-elles liées?," *Innovations - Cahiers d'Économie et de Management de l'Innovation*, vol. 2013/3, n° 42, p. 175–194, Brussels.
——— (2013e), "On the Lifting of the Embargo Against Cuba," Joint Written Statement of the Centre Europe Tiers-Monde, the International Association of Democratic Lawyers and the American Association of Jurists for the Human Rights Council of the United Nations, Geneva.
——— (2014a), "A Marxist Interpretation of the Crisis," *World Review of Political Economy*, vol. 5, n° 2, p. 128–148, Shanghai.
——— (2014b), "Notes sur Jean-Baptiste Say: Conception de l'économie en général et position face à l'esclavage en particulier," *Innovations - Revue d'économie et de management de l'innovation*, vol. 3, n° 45, p. 135–157, Brussels.
——— (ed.) (2014c), *La Crise du "Développement"*, Paris: Éditions L'Harmattan.
——— (2015a), *La Maladie dégénérative de l'économie: le "néoclassicisme"*, Paris: Éditions Delga.

——— (2015b), "Defense and Security (Economics of)," *International Encyclopedia of Social and Behavioral Sciences*, 2nd ed., Amsterdam and London: Elsevier.

——— (2017a), "La Colombie telle que l'a vécue Marulanda," *in* R. Herrera, *Figures révolutionnaires de l'Amérique latine*, p. 65–72, Paris: Éditions Delga.

——— (2017b), "Le Temps et l'espace de Bolívar - Les Bouleversements européens et leurs effets en Amérique hispanique entre 1795 et 1815," *in* R. Herrera, *Figures révolutionnaires de l'Amérique latine*, p. 7–50, Paris: Éditions Delga.

——— (2018), "La colonisation vue par Marx et Engels: évolutions (et limites) d'une réflexion commune," *in Le Colonialisme - Textes de Marx et Engels*, p. 3–73, Paris: Éditions Critiques.

——— (2019), "Pushback on Human Rights in France: The Republic on the Move, in Reverse Gear," *Social Justice—A Journal of Crime, Conflict & World Order*, digital version, San Francisco.

——— (2020), *En Lutte! Les résistances populaires en France de 1981 à nos jours*, Paris: Éditions Critiques.

——— (2021a), "Guerre(s) et crise(s) globales: sur leurs relations systémiques," *Marchés & Organisations*, vol. 2021/2, n° 41, p. 139–155, Paris.

——— (2021b), "De los ciclos de no-especialización a la era del azúcar: Elementos de historia de Cuba en un largo período (1492–1958)," *International Journal of Cuban Studies*, vol. 12, n° 2, p. 182–212, London.

——— (ed.) (2021c), *Imperialism and Transitions to Socialism*, Bingley (UK): Emerald.

——— (2022a), *La Monnaie: du pouvoir de la finance à la souveraineté des peuples*, Geneva: Éditions du Centre Europe - Tiers Monde (CETIM).

——— (2022b), "Les Métamorphoses de la pensée de Marx sur la colonisation," *Revue de Philosophie économique*, Paris, to be published.

Herrera R. and J. Cicchini (2013), "Notes sur les bases et les effectifs militaires étasuniens à l'étranger," *Innovations - Revue d'économie et de management de l'innovation*, vol. 3, n° 42, p. 147–173.

Herrera R., W. Dierckxsens and P. Nakatani (2014), *Beyond the Systemic Crisis and Capital-led Chaos—Theoretical and Applied Studies*, Brussels and Berlin: P.I.E. Peter Lang.

Herrera R. and E. Gentilucci (2013), "Military Spending, Technical Progress, and Economic Growth," *Journal of Innovation Economics and Management*, n° 2013/2, n° 12, p. 13–35, Brussels.

Herrera R. and K.-C. Lau (eds.) (2015), *The Struggle for Food Sovereignty—Alternative Development and the Renewal of Peasant Societies Today*, London: Pluto Press.

——— (2021), "Agrarian Labor and Peasantry in the Global South," *in* I. Ness and Z. Cope (eds.), *The Palgrave Encyclopedia of Imperialism and Anti-Imperialism*, Chapter 58–1, 12 p., 2nd ed., New York: Palgrave Macmillan and Springer.

Herrera R. and Z. Long (2017), "Las Leyes del Capital en el Siglo XXI de Piketty en China," *Economía y Desarrollo*, año XLVIII, vol. 158, n° 2, p. 6–21, Havana.

——— (2018), "The Enigma of China's Economic Growth," *Monthly Review*, vol. 70, n° 7, p. 52–62, New York.

——— (2019), *La Chine est-elle capitaliste?*, Paris: Éditions Critiques.

——— (2021), *Dynamique de l'économie chinoise: croissance, cycles et crises de 1949 à nos jours*, Paris: Éditions Critiques.

Herrera R., Z. Long, Z. Feng and B. Li (2021), "¿El que pierde gana? La guerra comercial sino-estadunidense en perspectiva," *El Trimester Económico*, vol. LXXXVIII, n° 4, n° 352, p. 1073–1097, Mexico.

Herrera R. and P. Nakatani (2008), "La Crise financière: racines, raisons, perspectives," *La Pensée*, n° 353, p. 109–113, Paris.

——— (2010), "Keynes (et Marx), la monnaie et la crise," *La Pensée*, n° 364, p. 57–68, Paris.

Herrera R. and P. Tetoe (2011), "Le Capital étranger dans le secteur des mines en Papouasie Nouvelle-Guinée," *Économies et Sociétés*, série F, tome XLV, n° 2, p. 321–336, Paris.

——— (2012), "Le Paradoxe *Papua Niugini*: archaïsme de la propriété de la terre, modernité des résistances paysannes?," *Revue française de Socio-économie*, n° 9, 2012/1, p. 133–152, Paris.

——— (2015), "The *Papua Niugini* Paradox," *in* R. Herrera and K.-C. Lau (eds.) *The Struggle for Food Sovereignty—Alternative Development and the Renewal of Peasant Societies Today*, p. 119–135, London: Pluto Press.

Hicks J.R. (1937), "Mr. Keynes and the Classics: A Suggested Interpretation," *Econometrica*, vol. 5, n° 2, p. 147–159.

——— (1969), *A Theory of Economic History*, Oxford: Oxford University Press.

——— (1974), *The Crisis in Keynesian Economics*, New York: Basic Books.

Hicks J.R. and S. Hollander (1977), "Mr. Ricardo and the Moderns," *Quarterly Journal of Economics*, vol. 91, n° 3, p. 351–369.

Hirschman A.O. (1958), *The Strategy of Economic Development*, New Haven: Yale University Press.

——— (1986), *Vers une Économie politique élargie*, Paris: Éditions de Minuit.

Horny G. (2012), *La Bourse pour les nuls*, 2nd ed., Paris: Éditions First-Gründ.

Houtart F. (2010), *Agrofuels: Big Profits, Ruined Lives and Ecological Destruction*, London: Pluto Press.

Inada K. (1963), "On a Two-Sector Model of Economic Growth," *Review of Economic Studies*, vol. 30, n° 2, p. 119–127.

INTERNATIONAL INSTITUTE FOR STRATEGIC STUDIES (various years), *Strategic Survey*, I.I.S.S., London.

INTERNATIONAL MONETARY FUND (various years), *Government Finance Statistics Yearbook*, IMF. Statistics Department, Washington DC.

——— (2003), *Good Governance: The IMF Role*, Washington DC: IMF.

INTRILIGATOR M.D. (1990), "On the Nature and Scope of Defence Economics," *Defence and Peace Economics*, vol. 1, n° 1, p. 3–11.

ISARD W. (1988), *Arms Races, Arms Control and Conflict Analysis*, New York: Cambridge University Press.

JEVONS W.S. (1957 [1871]), *The Theory of Political Economy*, New York: Kelley and Millman.

JOHNSON C. (2010), *Dismantling the Empire—America's Last Best Hope*, New York: Metropolitan Books Henry Holt and Co.

JOHNSON D.G. (1950), "Resource Allocation Under Share Contracts," *Journal of Political Economy*, vol. 58, n° 1, p. 111–123.

KALDOR N. (1956), "Alternative Theories of Distribution," *Review of Economic Studies*, vol. 23, n° 2, p. 83–100.

——— (1957), "A Model of Economic Growth," *The Economic Journal*, vol. 67, n° 268, p. 591–624.

——— (1961), "Capital Accumulation and Economic Growth," *in* F.A. Lutz and D.C. Hague (eds.), *The Theory of Capital*, p. 177–222, New York: St.Martin Press.

——— (1982), *The Scourge of Monetarism*, New York: Oxford University Press.

KALECKI M. (1986), *Selected Essays on Economic Planning*, Cambridge (UK): The University Press.

——— (1993). *Introduction to the Theory of Growth in a Socialist Economy* (1963). *in* J. Osiatyński and B. Jung (eds.), *Collected Works of Michal Kalecki*, vol. IV, New York: Oxford University Press.

KALLIS G., C. KERSCHNER and J. MARTINEZ-ALIER (2012), "The Economics of Degrowth," *Ecological Economies*, vol. 841, n° 1, p. 72–180.

KEEFER P. and S. KNACK (1995), "Institutions and Economic Performance: Cross-Country Tests Using Alternative Institutional Measures," *Economics & Politics*, vol. 7, n° 3, p. 207–227.

KENNEDY P. (1987), *The Rise and Fall of Great Powers: Economic Change and Military Conflict from 1500 to 2000*, New York: Random House.

KENNEDY S.W. (2008 [1955]), *Introduction à l'Amérique raciste*, Paris: L'Aube.

KEYNES J.M. (1920), *The Economic Consequences of the Peace*, London: Macmillan.

——— (1926), *Laissez-faire and Communism*, New York: New Republic Inc.

——— (1930), *Treatise on Money*, 2 volumes, London: Macmillan.

——— (1933), *Essais de persuasion*, Paris: Gallimard.

——— (1936), *The General Theory of Employment, Interest and* Money, Cambridge (UK): Macmillan Cambridge University Press (for Royal Economic Society).

——— (1951), *Essays in Bibliography* (first edition in 1933), Rupert Hart-Davis, Londres.

——— (1971 [1920]), *A Tract on Monetary Reform*, The Collected Writings of J.M. Keynes, vol. IV, London: Macmillan.

——— (1987), *The Collected Writings of John Maynard Keynes*, London: Cambridge University Press, Macmillan.

KICILLOF A. (2007), *Fundamentos de la Teoria General: las consecuencias teoricas de Lord Keynes*, Buenos Aires: Eudeba.

KIRMAN A.P. (1989), "The Intrinsic Limits of Modern Economic Theory: The Emperor Has No Clothes," *The Economic Journal*, vol. 99, n° 395, p. 126–139 (Supplement Conference Papers).

——— (1992), "Whom or What Does the Representative Individual Represent?," *Journal of Economic Perspectives*, vol. 6, n° 2, p. 117–126.

KLAMER A. (1988), "Conversations with Economists: New Classical Economists and their Opponents Speak Out on the Current Controversy in Macroeconomics," *Rowman & Littlefield Publishers*, New Jersey: Totowa.

KLEIN T. (2004), "Military Expenditure and Economic Growth: Peru, 1970–1996," *Defence and Peace Economics*, vol. 15, n° 3, p. 275–288.

KNACK S. (1996), "Institutions and the Convergence Hypothesis: The Cross-national Evidence," *Public Choice*, n° 87, p. 207–228.

KNIGHT M., N. LOAYZA and D. VILLANUEVA (1995), "The Peace Dividend: Military Spending Cuts and Economic Growth," *IMF Working Paper*, n° 53, IMF Middle Eastern Department, International Monetary Fund, Washington DC.

KOJM C. (2012), *Global Trends 2030: Alternative Worlds*, Washington DC: National Intelligence Council.

KOOPMANS T. (ed.) (1965), *The Econometric Approach to Development Planning*, Amsterdam: North Holland.

KREGEL J. (2010), "Minsky Moments and Minsky's Proposals for Regulation of an Unstable Financial System," Draft of Opening Remarks for the 19th Annual H.P. Minsky Conference, available on: http://www.levyinstitute.org/pubs/conf_april10/19th_Minsky_Kregel_drt.pdf.

KRUEGER A.O. (1974), "The Political Economy of the *Rent-Seeking* Society," *American Economic Review*, vol. 64, n° 3, p. 291–303.

——— (1990), "Government Failures in Development," *National Bureau of Economic Research (NBER) Working Paper*, n° 3340, Cambridge (MA).

——— (1993), *Political Economy of Policy Reform in Developing Countries*, Cambridge MA: MIT Press.

Krueger A.O. *et al.* (1981), *Trade and Employment in Developing Countries*, National Bureau of Economic Research, London: The University of Chicago Press.

Krugman P.R. (1989), *Rethinking International Trade*, Cambridge (MA): The MIT Press.

——— (1990), "Increasing Returns and Economic Geography," *National Bureau of Economics Research Working Papers*, n° 3275, Cambridge MA.

——— (1993a), "Economic Geography: on the Number and Location of Cities," *European Economic Review*, vol. 37, n°s 2–3, p. 293–298.

——— (1993b), "The Fall and Rise of Development Economics," available on: http://www.wws.princeton.edu/pkrugman/dishpan.html.

——— (1995), *Development, Geography, and Economic Theory*, Cambridge (MA): The MIT Press.

——— (2009), *The Return of Depression Economics and the Crisis of 2008*, New York: W.W. Norton & Co.

Krugman P.R. and M. Obstfeld (2003), *Économie internationale*, Brussels: De Boeck.

Kuhn T.S. (1996), *The Structure of Scientific Revolutions*, 3rd ed., Chicago: University of Chicago Press.

Kuznets S.S. (1955), "Economic Growth and Income Inequality," *American Economic Review*, vol. 45, n° 1, p. 1–28.

——— (1966), *Modern Economic Growth: Rate, Structure, and Spread*, New Haven: Yale University Press.

——— (1971), *Economic Growth of Nations: Total Output and Production Structure*, Cambridge (MA): Harvard University Press.

Kydland F.E. and E.C. Prescott (1977), "Rules Rather than Discretion: The Inconsistency of Optimal Plans," *Journal of Political Economy*, vol. 85, n° 3, p. 473–492.

——— (1982), "Time to Build and Aggregate Fluctuations," *Econometrica*, vol. 50, n° 6, p. 1345–1370.

Laffont J.-J. (1982), *Cours d'analyse microéconomique - Tome 1: Fondements de l'économie publique*, Paris: Economica.

Laffont J.-J. and M.S. Matoussi (1995), "Moral Hazard, Financial Constraints and Sharecropping in El Oulja," *Review of Economic Studies*, vol. 62, n° 3, p. 381–399.

Landau D. (1983), "Government Expenditure and Economic Growth: A Cross-Country Study," *Southern Economic Journal*, vol. 49, n° 3, p. 783–792.

——— (1986), "Government Expenditure and Economic Growth in Less Developed Countries: An Empirical Study for 1960–1980," *Economic Development and Cultural Change*, vol. 35, n° 1, p. 35–75.

——— (1993), "The Economic Impact of Military Expenditure Best," *World Bank Policy Research Working Paper*, n° 1138, Washington DC: The World Bank.

LANGE O.R. (1967), *Essays on Economic Planning*, London: Asia Publishing House.

LATOUCHE S. (2006), *Le Pari de la décroissance*, Paris: Fayard.

LAVOIE M. (1985), "La Théorie générale et l'inflation de sous-emploi," *in* F. Poulon (ed.), *Les Écrits de Keynes*, p. 131–152, Paris: Dunod.

LENIN V.I. (1965 [1920]), *Collected Works*, 4th ed., vol. 31, Moscow: Progress Publishers.

——— (1969 [1916]), *L'Impérialisme, stade suprême du capitalisme*, Moscow: Éditions du Progrès.

——— (1970 [1916]), *Œuvres - tome 39: Cahiers de l'impérialisme*, Paris and Moscow: Éditions sociales and Éditions du Progrès.

LEONTIEF W.W. (1941), *The Structure of the American Economy: 1919–1929*, Cambridge (MA): Harvard University Press.

LEONTIEF W.W. and F. DUCHIN (1983), *Military Spending—Facts and Figures, Worldwide Implications and Future Outlook*, New York: Oxford University Press.

LEONTIEF W.W. and M. HOFFENBERG (1961), "The Economic Effects of Disarmament," *Scientific American*, vol. 204, n° 4, p. 47–55.

LEONTIEF W.W., A. MORGAN, K. POLENSKE, D. SIMPSON and E. TURNER (1965), "The Economic Impact (Industrial and Regional) of an Arms Cut," *Review of Economics and Statistics*, vol. 47, n° 3, p. 217–241.

LEONTIEF W.W. and P.A. PETRI (1971), *Impact of Disarmament on Strategic Raw Materials Demand*, United Nations Department of Political and Security Council Affairs, New York: United Nations.

LEVINE R. (2005), "Finance and Growth: Theory and Evidence," *in* P. Aghion and S. Durlauf (eds.), *Handbook of Economic Growth*, vol. 1, p. 865–934. Amsterdam: Elsevier.

LÉVI-STRAUSS C. (1962), *La Pensée sauvage*, Paris: Plon.

LEWIS W.A. (1955), *Theory of Economic Growth*, London: Harper & Row.

LIN J.Y. and J.B. NUGENT (1995), "Institutions and Economic Development," *in* J. Behrman and T.N. Srinivasan (eds.), *Handbook of Development Economics*, vol. III, Chapter 38, p. 2302–2369, Amsterdam: Elsevier.

LIPSET S.M. (1959), "Some Social Requisites of Democracy: Economic Development and Political Legitimacy," *American Political Science Review*, vol. 53, n° 1, p. 69–105.

LOMBORG B. (ed.) (2001), *The Skeptical Ecologist: Measuring the Real State of the World*, Cambridge (UK): Cambridge University Press.

——— (ed.) (2004), *Global Crises, Global Solutions*, Cambridge MA: Cambridge University Press.

LONG J.B. and C.I. PLOSSER (1983), "Real Business Cycles," *Journal of Political Economy*, vol. 91, n° 1, p. 39–69.

LONG Z., Z. FENG, B. LI and R. HERRERA (2020), "U.S.-China Trade War: Has the Real 'Thief' Finally Been Unmasked?," *Monthly Review*, vol. 72, n° 5, p. 32–43, New York.

LONG Z. and R. HERRERA (2018), "The Laws of Capital in the Twenty-First Century in China. Piketty in Beijing," *China Economic Review*, online on March 11, Columbus (OH).

——— (2021), "'21世纪资本论'在中国:皮凯蒂的资本定律在中国成立吗?," *政治经济学报* (*zhèngzhì jīngjì xuébào, Tsinghua University Review of Political Economics*), vol. 21, n° 4, p. 94–116, Beijing.

——— (2022), *Dynamics of China's Economy: Growth, Cycles and Crises from 1949 to the Present Day*, Amsterdam and Chicago: Brill and Haymarket, to be published.

LUCAS R.E. (1981), *Studies in Business Cycle Theory*, Cambridge MA: The MIT Press.

——— (1988), "On the Mechanisms of Economic Growth," *Journal of Monetary Economics*, vol. 22, n° 1, p. 3–42.

MACEDO E SILVA A.C. (2008), "Do Treatise à General Theory: o extravio dos 'detalhes monetários'," *in* J. Sicsú and C. Vidotto (eds.), *Economia do desenvolvimento: Teoria e políticas keynesianas*, p. 241–265, Rio de Janeiro: Elsevier.

MAHALANOBIS P.C. (1953), "Some Observations on the Process of Growth of National Income," *Sankhya—The Indian Journal of Statistics*, vol. 12, n° 4, p. 307–312.

——— (1955), "The Approach of Operational Research to Planning in India," *Sankhya—The Indian Journal of Statistics*, vol. 16, n°s 1–2, p. 3–130.

MAHIEU F.R. (1989), "Transferts et communauté africaine," *Stateco*, n°s 58–59, p. 107–136.

MALINVAUD E. (1993), "Regard d'un ancien sur les nouvelles théories de la croissance," *Revue d'économie politique*, vol. 44, n° 2, p. 171–188.

——— (1994), "Éducation et développement économique," *Économie et Prévision*, n° 116, p. 1–15.

——— (1996), "Pourquoi les économistes ne font pas de découvertes," *Revue d'économie politique*, vol. 106, n° 6, p. 929–942.

MALTHUS T.R. (1986 [1798]), *An Essay on the Principle of Population*, London: Pickering.

MAMPAEY L. (2010), *Finance, technologie et production d'armements aux États-Unis: une lecture institutionnaliste*, Saarbrücken: Éditions universitaires européenne.

MANDEL E. (1985), *La Crise*, Paris: Flammarion.

Mantel R.R. (1974), "On the Characterization of Aggregate Excess Demand," *Journal of Economic Theory*, vol. 7, n° 3, p. 348–353.
Mao Z. (1968), *Écrits militaires de Mao Tsé-Toung*, Beijing: Éditions en langues étrangères.
Marini R.M. (1969), *Subdesarrollo y revolución*, México: Siglo XXI.
Marques R.M. and P. Nakatani (2009), *O que é capital fictício e sua crise*, São Paulo: Ed. Brasiliense.
Marshall A. (1920 [1890]), *Principles of Economics*, 8th ed., London: Macmillan.
Marx K. (1964), *Das Kapital - Kritik der politischen Ökonomie*, *Buch* III: *Der Gesamtprozeß der kapitalistischen Produktion* (*Band* 25), Institut für Marxismus-Leninismus, Berlin: Dietz Verlag.
——— (1972 [1859]), *Contribution à la critique de l'économie politique*, Paris: Éditions sociales.
——— (1974), *Théories sur la plus-value*, vol. 1, Paris: Éditions sociales.
——— (1978), *Le Capital - Critique de l'économie politique*, Paris: Éditions sociales.
——— (1980), *Manuscrits de 1857–1858*, Paris: Éditions sociales.
——— (1984 [1850]), *Les Luttes de classes en France 1848–1850*, Paris: Messidor - Éditions sociales.
Marx K. and F. Engels (1965 [1848]), *Le Manifeste du Parti communiste*, *in* Économie I, La Pléiade, Paris: Gallimard.
——— (1968 [1846]), *L'Idéologie allemande*, Paris: Éditions sociales.
——— (1973), *Werke*, Band 17, 5th ed., Berlin (GDR): Dietz Verlag.
Massé P. (1965), *Le Plan ou l'anti-hasard*, Collection Idées, Paris: Gallimard.
Matoussi M.S. and J.B. Nugent (1989), "The Switch to Sharecropping in Medjez-el-Bab," *in* M. Nabli and J.B. Nugent (eds.), *The New Institutional Economics and Development*, p. 140–157, Amsterdam: North Holland.
Matthews R.C.O. (1986), "The Economics of Institutions and the Sources of Growth," *The Economic Journal*, vol. 96, n° 384, p. 903–918.
Mattick P. (1972), *Marx et Keynes: les limites de l'économie mixte*, Paris: Gallimard.
McKinnon R. (1964), "Foreign Exchange Constraints in Economic Development and Efficient Aid Allocation," *Economic Journal*, vol. 74, n° 293, p. 388–409.
McNamara R.S. (1995), *In Retrospect: The Tragedy and Lessons of Vietnam* (with B. Van De *Mark*), New York: Times Books.
Ménard C. (1990), *L'Économie des organisations*, collection «Repères», n° 86, Paris: La Découverte.
Menger C. (1950 [1871]), *Principles of Economics*, Glencoe: Free Press.
——— (1996 [1833]), *Investigations into the Method of the Social Sciences*, Grove City: Libertarian Press.

MILL J.S. (1865 [1848]), *Principles of Political Economy with Some of Their Applications to Social Philosophy*, London: Longmans.

MILNE D. (2008), *America's Rasputin: Walt Rostow and the Vietnam War*, New York: Hill and Wang.

MINART G. (2003), *Les Opposants à Napoléon: 1800–1815 - L'élimination des royalistes et des républicains*, Toulouse: Éditions Privat.

MINSKY H. (2008), *Stabilizing an Unstable Economy*, New York: MacGraw Hill.

MIRRLEES J.A. (2005), "The Theory of Optimal Taxation," *in* K.J. Arrow and M.D. Intriligator (eds.), *Handbook of Mathematical Economics*, vol. 3, p. 1197–1249, Amsterdam: Elsevier.

MISHKIN F.S. (2010), *Monnaie, banque et marchés financiers*, Chapter 27, 9th ed., Paris: Pearson Education.

MITCHELL W.C. (1913), *Business Cycles*, Berkeley: University of California Press.

MONTCHESTIEN A. (de) (1889 [1615]), *Traicté de l'œconomie politique*, Paris: E. Plon, Nourrit et Cie.

MORIN F. (2006), *Le Nouveau Mur de l'argent - Essai sur la finance globalisée*, Paris: Le Seuil.

MURPHY K.M., A. SHLEIFER and R.W. VISHNY (1989), "Industrialization and the Big Push," *Journal of Political Economy*, vol. 106, n° 2, p. 503–530.

MYRDAL G. (1968), *Asian Drama: An Inquiry into the Poverty of Nations*, New York: Twentieth Century Fund.

NABLI M.K. and J.B. NUGENT (eds.) (1989), *The New Institutional Economics and Development*, Amsterdam: North Holland.

NAKATANI, P. et R. CARCANHOLO (2001), "Capital especulativo parasitário versus capital financier," *Problemas del Desarrollo*, vol. 32, n° 124, p. 9–31.

NAKATANI P. and H. GOMES (2010), «Dinheiro: natureza e funções», *mimeo*, Vitoria: Federal University of Espirito Santo.

NAKATANI P. and R. HERRERA (2007), "What Rich Countries Owe Poor Ones," *Monthly Review*, vol. 59, n° 2, p. 31–36, New York.

——— (2009), "Critique des politiques anticrise orthodoxes," *La Pensée*, n° 360, p. 31–42, Paris.

——— (2013), "Keynes et la crise: hier et aujourd'hui," *Actuel Marx*, n° 53, p. 153–168, Paris.

NAKATANI, P. and R.M. MARQUES (2020), *O Capitalismo em crise*, São Paulo: Expressão Popular.

NAOUSSI C.F. and F. TRIPIER (2012), "La Modélisation en équilibre général dynamique et stochastique des cycles économiques en Afrique sub-saharienne," *Revue d'économie politique*, n° 5, p. 657–683.

NASH J. (1950), "Equilibrium Points in N-Person Games," *Proceedings of the National Academy of Sciences*, vol. 36, n° 1, p. 48–49.

——— (1951), "Non-Cooperative Games," *Annals of Mathematics*, vol. 54, n° 2, p. 286–295.

Nicolas J. (2002), *La Rébellion française - Mouvements populaires et conscience sociale: 1661–1789*, Paris: Le Seuil.

Nietzsche F.W. (1899), *Humain, trop humain*, Paris: Mercure de France.

Niskanen W.A. (1971), *Bureaucracy and Representative Government*, Chicago: Aldine.

——— (1975), "Bureaucrats and Politicians," *Journal of Law and Economics*, vol. 18, n° 3, p. 617–643.

North D.C. (1979), "A Framework for Analyzing the State in Economic History," *Explorations in Economic History*, vol. 16, n° 3, p. 249–259.

——— (1981), *Structure and Change in Economic History*, New York: W.W. Norton.

——— (1984), "Government and the Cost of Exchange in History," *Journal of Economic History*, vol. XLIV, n° 2, p. 255–264.

——— (1987), "Institutions, Transaction Cost and Economic Growth," *Economic Inquiry*, vol. 25, n° 3, p. 419–428.

——— (1990a), *Institutions, Institutional Change and Economic Performance*, Political Economy of Institutions and Decisions, Cambridge (UK): Cambridge University Press.

——— (1990b), "Institutions and a Transaction-Cost Theory *of* Exchange," *in* J.E. Alt and K.A. Shepsle (eds.), *Perspectives on Positive Political Economy*, Cambridge: Cambridge University Press.

——— (1991), "Institutions," *Journal of Economic Perspectives*, vol. 5, n° 1, p. 97–112.

North D.C. and R.P. Thomas (1970), "An Economic Theory of the Growth in the Western World," *Economic History Review*, vol. 23, n° 1, p. 1–17.

——— (1973), *The Rise of the Western World—A New Economic History*, Cambridge: Cambridge University Press.

Nussbaum M.C. (1990), "Aristotelian Social Democracy," *in* R.B. Douglass, G.M. Mara and H.S. Richardson (eds.), *Liberalism and the Good*, London: Routledge.

——— (1994), "Platonic Love and Colorado Law," *Virginia Law Review*, vol. 80, n° 7, p. 1515–1651.

——— (2000), *Sex and Social Justice*, Oxford and New York: Oxford University Press.

——— (2009), *The Therapy of Desire*, Woodstock Princeton NJ: Princeton University Press.

Observatoire des inégalités (2011), "Les inégalités d'espérance de vie dans le monde," April, available on: http://www.inegalites.fr/.

Observatoire international de la Crise (2019), *Le Capitalisme face à son déclin*, Paris: Éditions Critiques.

Olson M. (1996), "Distinguished Lecture on Economics in Government—Big Bills Left on the Sidewalk: Why Some Nations Are Rich, and the Other Poor," *Journal of Economic Perspectives*, vol. 10, n° 2, p. 3–24.

Oman C.P. and G. Wignaraja (1991), *Postwar Evolution of Development Thinking*, Paris: OECD Development Centre.

Ortiz I. and M. Cummings (2011), *Global Inequality: Beyond the Bottom Billion*, Social and Economic Policy Working Paper, April, New York: UNICEF.

Ostrom E. (1990), *Governing the Commons—The Evolution of Institutions for Collective Action*, Cambridge (UK): Cambridge University Press.

Oxfam (2014), "Working for the Few: Political Capture and Economic Inequality," *Briefing Paper*, n° 178, January, Oxford.

——— (2022), *Inequality Kills: The Unparalleled Action Needed to Combat Unprecedented Inequality in the Wake of COVID-19*, available on: https://www.oxfam.org/en/research/inequality-kills.

Pagano M. (1993), "Financial Markets and Growth: An Overview," *European Economic Review*, vol. 37, n°s 2–3, p. 613–622.

Palley T. (2010), "The Limits of Minsky's Financial Instability Hypothesis as an Explanation of the Crisis," available on: http://monthlyreview.org/2010/04/01/thelimits-of-minskys-financial-instability-hypothesis-as-an-explanation-ofthecrisis#.UIWZv2–_HWU.

Papadimitriou D.B. and L.R. Wray (2008), "Minsky's Stabilizing an Unstable Economy: Two Decades Later," in H. Minsky (ed.), *Stabilizing an Unstable Economy*, p. xxv et s., New York: MacGraw Hill.

Pareto V. (1964 [1897]), *Cours d'Economie politique*, Paris: Droz.

Pasinetti L.L. (1960), "A Mathematical Formulation of the Ricardian System," *Review of Economic Studies*, vol. 27, n° 2, p. 78–98.

Petty W. (1690), *Political Arithmetick* (1690), available on: https://la.utexas.edu/users/hcleaver/368/368PettyPolArithtableedit.pdf.

Piketty T. (1995), "On the Long-Run Evolution of Inheritance: France 1820–2050," *Quarterly Journal of Economics*, vol. CXXVI, n° 3, p. 1071–1131.

——— (2003), "Income Inequality in France, 1901–1998," *Journal of Political Economy*, vol. 111, n° 5, p. 1004–1042.

——— (2013), *Le Capital au XXᵉ siècle*, Paris: Éditions du Seuil.

Piketty T., Y. Li and G. Zucman (2017), "Capital Accumulation, Private Property and Rising Inequality in China, 1978–2015," *National Bureau of Economic Research (NBER) Working Paper*, n° 23368, Cambridge (MA).

Piketty T. and N. Qian (2011), "Income Inequality and Progressive Income Taxation in China and India, 1986–2015," *in* A.B. Atkinson and T. Piketty (eds.), *Top Incomes: A Global Perspective*, p. 40–75, New York: Oxford University Press.

Piketty T. and E. Saez (2003), "Income Inequality in the United States, 1913–1998," *Quarterly Journal of Economics*, vol. 118, n° 1, p. 1–39.

Piketty T. and G. Zucman (2014), "Capital Is Back: Wealth-Income Ratios in Rich Countries 1700–2010," *Quarterly Journal of Economics*, vol. 129, n° 3, p. 1255–1310.

Piqueras A. (2017), "El Capital ficticio especulativo-parasitario se pone al mando del capitalismo," *Áreas - Revista Internacional de Ciencias Sociales*, n° 36, p. 11–23.

Potier J.-P. and A. Tiran (eds.) (2004), *Jean-Baptiste Say: nouveaux regards sur son œuvre*, Paris: Economica.

Poulon F. (2000), *La Pensée économique de Keynes*, Paris: Dunod.

Prebisch R. (1973), *Problemas teóricos y prácticos del crecimiento económico*, New York: Naciones Unidas, Comisión Económica para América Latina.

Preiswerk R. and D. Perrot (1975), *Ethnocentrisme et histoire - L'Afrique, l'Amérique indienne et l'Asie dans les manuels occidentaux*, Paris: Éditions Anthropos.

Pritchett L. (1999), *Where Has All the Education Gone?*, Washington DC: The World Bank.

Ram R. (1985), "Exports and Economic Growth: Some Additional Evidence," *Economic Development and Cultural Change*, vol. 33, n° 1, p. 415–425.

Ramonet I. (1995), "La Pensée unique," *Le Monde diplomatique*, January.

Rawls J.B. (1971), *A Theory of Justice*, Cambridge MA: Harvard University Press.

Rebelo S. (1990), "Long Run Policy Analysis and Long Run Growth," *National Bureau of Economic Research*, *Working Paper*, n° 3325, Cambridge MA.

Ricardo D. (1951 [1817]), *On the Principles of Political Economy and Taxation*, Cambridge (UK): Cambridge University Press.

Richter J. (2003), *Building on Quicksand: The Global Compact, Democratic Governance and Nestlé*, Geneva: Éditions CETIM / IBFAN-GIFA / Déclaration de Berne.

Robinson J.V. (1938), "The Classification of Inventions," *Review of Economic Studies*, vol. 5, n° 2, p. 139–142.

——— (1953), "The Production Function and the Theory of Capital," *Review of Economic Studies*, vol. 21, n° 55, p. 81–106.

——— (1964), *Theory of Economic Growth*, London: Macmillan.

——— (1971), *Essai sur l'économie de Marx*, Paris: Dunod.

——— (1972), *Hérésies économiques*, Paris: Calmann-Lévy.

Rodrik D. and M. Rosenzweig (2010), *Handbooks of Development Economics*, Amsterdam: Elsevier - North Holland.

Romer P.M. (1983), *Dynamic Competitive Equilibria with Externalities, Increasing Returns and Unbounded Growth*, Ph.D. Dissertation, University of Chicago.

——— (1986), "Increasing Returns and Long-Run Growth," *Journal of Political Economy*, vol. 94, n° 5, p. 1002–1037.

——— (1990a), "Endogenous Technological Change," *Journal of Political Economy*, vol. 98, S71–S10277.

——— (1990b), "Growth Based on Increasing Returns Due to Specialisation," *American Economic Review*, vol. 77, n° 2, p. 56–62.

Rosenstein-Rodan P.N. (1943), "Industrialization of Eastern and South Eastern Europe," *Economic Journal*, vol. 53, n° 210, p. 202–211.

Rostow W.W. (1960), *The Stages of Economic Growth: A Non-Communist Manifesto*, Cambridge: Cambridge University Press.

Rothbard M. (1973), *For a New Liberty*, New York: Macmillan.

Rubel M. (1997), *Guerre et paix nucléaires*, Paris: Paris Méditerranée.

Rutherford M. (1989), "What Is Wrong with the New Institutional Economics (and What Is Still Wrong with the Old)?," *Review of Political Economy*, vol. 1, n° 3, p. 299–318.

Sachs J. (2005), *The End of Poverty*, London: Penguin Press.

Saez E. (2013), "Striking It Richer: The Evolution of Top Incomes in the United States," Department of Economics, University of California, Berkeley, available on: http://elsa.berkeley.edu/~saez/saez-UStopincomes-2012.

Said E.W. (2000), *Culture et impérialisme*, Paris: Fayard and Le Monde diplomatique.

Sala-i-Martín X. (1990), "Lectures Notes on Economic Growth," *National Bureau of Economic Research, Working Papers*, n°s 3563 & 3564, Cambridge MA.

Salvadori N. (ed.) (2003), *Old and New Growth Theories: An Assessment*, London: Edward Elgar Publishing.

Samuelson P.A. (1978), "The Canonical Classical Model of Political Economy," *Journal of Economic Literature*, vol. 16, n° 2, p. 1415–1434.

——— (1983 [1947]), *Foundations of Economic Analysis*, Cambridge MA: Harvard Economic Studies.

Say J.-B. (1803), *Traité d'économie politique*, 1st ed., Paris: Imprimerie de Chapelet.

——— (1839), *Catéchisme d'économie politique*, Brussels: Société belge de Librairie.

——— (1848), *De l'Angleterre et des Anglais*, in *Œuvres diverses*, Paris: Guillaumin.

——— (1852), *Cours complet d'économie politique pratique*, Paris: Guillaumin.

——— (1996), *Cours d'économie politique et autres essais*, Paris: Flammarion.

SCHELLING T.C. (1960), *The Strategy of Conflict*, Cambridge MA: Harvard University Press.
——— (1969), "Models of Segregation," *American Economic Review*, vol. 59, n° 2, p. 488–493.
SCHNEIDER H. and M.H. LIBERCIER (1995), *Mettre en œuvre le développement participatif*, Centre de Développement de l'OCDE, Séminaires du Centre de Développement, Paris.
SCHULTZ T.P. and J. STRAUSS (2008), *Handbooks of Development Economics*, Amsterdam: Elsevier - North Holland.
SCHULTZ T.W. (1968), "Institutions and the Rising Economic Value of Man," *American Journal of Agricultural Economics*, vol. 50, n° 5, p. 1113–1122.
SCHUMACHER G. (2006), *A Bloody Business: America's War Zone Contractors and the Occupation of Iraq*, London: Zenith Press.
SCHUMPETER J.A. (1951), *Ten Great Economists*, London: George Allen & Unwin Ldt.
SCHWARZ G. (1992), "Democracy and Market-Oriented Reform: A Love-Hate Relationship?," *Economic Education Bulletin*, vol. 32, n° 5, p. 13–128.
SCULLY G.W. (2002), "Economic Freedom, Government Policy and the Trade-Off Between Equity and Economic Growth," *Public Choice*, vol. 113, n°s 1–2, p. 77–96.
SCULLY G.W. and D.J. SLOTTJE (1991), "Ranking Economic Liberty Across Countries," *Public Choice*, vol. 69, n° 2, p. 121–152.
SEN A.K. (1970), *Collective Choice and Social Welfare*, San Francisco CA: Holden-Day.
——— (1973), *On Economic Inequality*, New York: Norton.
——— (1981), *Poverty and Famines: An Essay on Entitlements and Deprivation*, Oxford: Clarendon Press.
——— (1985), *Commodities and Capabilities*, Amsterdam: North Holland.
——— (1987), *On Ethics and Economics*, Oxford: Basil Blackwell.
——— (1992), "Wars and Famines: On Divisions and Incentives," *in* W. Isard and C.H. Anderton (eds.), *Economics of Arms Reduction and Peace Process*, p. 219–234, Amsterdam: North Holland.
——— (1999), *Reason Before Identity*, Oxford: Oxford University Press.
——— (2002), *Rationality and Freedom*, Harvard: Belknap Press.
SHAIKH A. (2007), "Globalization and the Myth of Free Trade," *in* A. Shaikh (ed.), *Globalization and the Myths of Free Trade: History, Theory, and Empirical Evidence*, New York: Routledge.
SHIEH J.-Y., C.-C. LAI and W.-Y. CHANG (2002), "The Impact of Military Burden on Long-Run Growth and Welfare," *Journal of Development Economics*, vol. 68, n° 2, p. 443–454.

Shleifer A. (1995), "Establishing Property Rights," *Proceedings of the World Bank Annual Conference on Development Economics 1994*, p. 93–107, Washington DC: The World Bank.

Singh I.J., L.Squire et J. Strauss (dir.) (1986), *Agricultural Household Models: Extension, Application and Policy*, Baltimore: Johns Hopkins University Press.

Sismondi J.-C. L. (1971 [1815]), *Nouveaux Principes d'économie politique*, Paris: Calmann-Lévy.

Smith A. (1937 [1776]), *An Inquiry into the Nature and Causes of the Wealth of Nations*, New York: Random House.

Smith R. (1977), "Military Expenditure and Capitalism," *Cambridge Journal of Economics*, vol. 1, n° 1, p. 61–76.

——— (1980), "Military Expenditure and Investment in OECD Countries: 1954–1973," *Journal of Comparative Economics*, vol. 4, n° 1, p. 19–32.

Smith V.L. (2000), *Bargaining and Market Behavior: Essays in Experimental Economics*, New York: Cambridge University Press.

Snowdon B. and H.R. Vane (2005), *Modern Macroeconomics: Its Origin, Development, and Current State*, Cheltenham (UK) and Northampton (MA): Edward Elgar.

Soboul A. (2014), "Du Féodalisme au capitalisme: la Révolution française et la problématique des voies de passage," *in* A. Casanova et R. Herrera (eds.), *Penser les crises*, p. 34–58, Paris: Le Temps des Cerises.

Solow R.M. (1956), "A Contribution to the Theory of Economic Growth," *Quarterly Journal of Economics*, vol. 70, n° 1, p. 65–94.

——— (1983), "Discussion," *World Development*, vol. 11, p. 892.

——— (1988), "Growth Theory and After," *American Economic Review*, vol. 78, n° 3, p. 307–317.

——— (2000), *Growth Theory: An Exposition*, Oxford: Oxford University Press.

Sonnenschein H. (1972), "Market Excess Demand Functions," *Econometrica*, vol. 40, n° 3, p. 549–563.

——— (1973), "Do Walras' Identity and Continuity Characterize the Class of Excess Demand Functions?," *Journal of Economic Theory*, vol. 6, n° 4, p. 345–354.

Soros G. (1998), *La Crise du capitalisme mondial*, Paris: Plon.

Squire L. and H.B. Van der Tak (1975), *Economic Analvsis of Projects*, Baltimore and London: Johns Hopkins University Press (for The World Bank).

Srinivasan T.N. (1994), "Human Development: A New Paradigm or Reinvention of the Wheel?," *American Economic Review*, vol. 84, n° 2, p. 238–243.

Stigler G.J. (1971), "The Theory of Economic Regulation," *Bell Journal of Economics*, vol. 2, n° 1, p. 3–21.

——— (2003), *Memoirs of an Unregulated Economist*, Chicago: University of Chicago Press.

STIGLITZ J.E. (1974), "Incentives and Risk Sharing in Sharecropping," *Review of Economic Studies*, vol. 41, n° 2, p. 219–256.

——— (1988), *Economics of the Public Sector*, New York: W.W. Norton & Co.

——— (1995), "Economic Organization, Information, and Development," *in* H. Chenery and T.N. Srinivasan (eds.), *Handbook of Development Economics*, vol. I, Chapter 5, p. 94–160, Amsterdam: Elsevier.

——— (2001), "Information and the Change in the Paradigm in Economics," *Prize Lecture at Columbia Business School*, Columbia University, December 8.

——— (2003), *Quand le Capitalisme perd la tête*, Paris: Le Livre de poche.

STIGLITZ J.E. and L. BILMES (2008), *The Three Trillion Dollar War*, New York: W.W. Norton & Co.

STOCKHOLM INTERNATIONAL PEACE RESEARCH INSTITUTE (various years), *SIPRI Yearbook*, Oxford: Oxford University Press.

STOKEY N. (1991), "The Volume and Composition of Trade Between Rich and Poor Countries," *Review of Economic Studies*, vol. 58, n° 1, p. 63–80.

STRAUSS L. (1989), *La Persécution et l'art d'écrire*, Paris: Agora.

SUGDEN R. (1993), "Welfare, Resources and Capabilities: A Review of Inequality Re-examined by Amartya Sen," *Journal of Economic Literature*, vol. XXXVI, p. 1947–1962.

SUMMERS L.H. (1986), "Some Skeptical Observations on Real Business Cycle Theory," *Quarterly Review*, Federal Reserve Bank of Minneapolis, vol. 10, n° 4, p. 23–27.

SZMRECZANYI T. (ed.) (1978), *John Maynard Keynes*, São Paulo: Ática.

TANDON Y. (2015), *Trade Is War*, New York: OR Books.

TANZI V. (1985), "Fiscal Management and External Debt Problems," *in* H. Mehran (ed.), *External Debt Management*, p. 65–67, Washington DC: International Monetary Fund.

TINBERGEN J. (1990), "Conventional and New Thinking in Defence Economics," *Defence and Peace Economics*, vol. 1, n° 2, p. 121–128.

TIROLE J. (1988), *The Theory of Industrial Organization*, Cambridge MA: The MIT Press.

TOBIN J. (1955), "A Dynamic Aggregative Model," *Journal of Political Economy*, vol. 63, n° 2, p. 103–115.

TODARO M.P. (1982), *Economics for a Developing World*, Essex: Longman.

TOSEL A. (1992), "L'Impensable du libéralisme," *in* J. Bidet and G. Labica (eds.), *Libéralisme et État de droit*, Paris: Méridiens Klincksieck.

TRAN D.L. (2021), "Imperialism and Transition to Socialism in Vietnam," *in* R. Herrera (ed.), *Imperialism and Transitions to Socialism*, p. 141–156, Bingley (UK): Emerald.

TULLOCK G. (1967), "The Welfare Costs of Tariffs, Monopolies and Theft," *Western Economic Journal*, n° 5, p. 224–232.

——— (1993), *Rent Seeking*, Brookfield: Edward Elgar.

Turgot A.R.J. (1788 [1766]), *Réflections sur la formation et la distribution des richesses*, In.12, R 24520, Bibliothèque nationale de France, Paris.

Turner A. (2004), "Estimated U.K. Employment Dependent of Ministry of Defence Expenditure and Defence Exports," *Defence and Peace Economics*, vol. 15, n° 4, p. 331–342.

UNICEF (2001), *A Decade of Transition*, Regional Monitoring Report (MONEE), n° 8, Florence.

United Nations (1991), *The U.N. Disarmament Yearbook*, Department of Disarmament Affairs, vol. 15, New York.

United Nations Development Programme (1992), *Human Development Report*, Paris: Economica.

United Nations Institute for Disarmament Research (1992), *Aspects économiques du désarmement: le désarmement en tant qu'investissement*, UNIDIR, A/47/346, August, Geneva.

U.S. Department of Defense (various years), *Active Duty Military Personnel Strengths by Regional*, Area and by Country (309A), Washington DC.

U.S. Arms Control and Disarmament Agency (various years), *World Military Expenditures and Arms Transfers*, U.S.A.C.D.A., Library of Congress, Washington DC.

Uzawa H. (1965), "Optimal Technique Change in an Aggregative Model of Economic Growth," *International Economic Review*, vol. 6, n° 1, p. 18–31.

Varian H.R. (1984), *Microeconomic Analysis*, 2nd ed., New York and London: W.W. Norton & Co.

Veblen T.B. (1899a), "Preconceptions of Economic Science (I)," *Quarterly Journal of Economics*, vol. 13, p. 121–150, January.

——— (1899b), "Preconceptions of Economic Science (II)," *Quarterly Journal of Economics*, vol. 13, p. 396–426, July.

——— (1900), "Preconceptions of Economic Science (III)," *Quarterly Journal of Economics*, vol. 14, p. 240–269, February.

Vergara F. (2002), *Les Fondements philosophiques du libéralisme*, Paris: La Découverte and Syros.

Vilar P. (1974), *Or et monnaie dans l'histoire*, Paris: Éditions Flammarion.

Vitali S., J.B. Glattfelder and S. Battiston (2009), *The Network of Global Corporate Control*, Zurick: ETH.

Von Mises L. (1938), *Le Socialisme - Étude économique et sociologique*, Paris: Éditions M.-Th. Génin - Librairie de Médicis.

Wallerstein I. (1997), *Impenser la science sociale*, Paris: Presses universitaires de France.

——— (2011), *Historical Materialism*, London: Verso.

Walras L. (1988 [1874–1877]), *Éléments d'économie politique pure ou théorie de la richesse sociale, in Œuvres économiques complètes*, tome 8, Paris: Economica.

——— (2009), *Œuvres économiques complètes*, Paris: Economica.

WARD M.D., M. COCHRAN, D.R. DAVIS, M. PENUBARTI and S. RAJMAIRA (1991), "Military Spending in India: Country Survey," *Defence and Peace Economics*, n° 3, p. 41–64.

WELLISZ S. and R. FINDLAY (1986), "Central Planning and the Second Economy in Soviet-Type Systems," *Economic Journal*, vol. 96, n° 383, p. 646–658.

WILKINSON R. and K. PICKET (2013), *Pourquoi l'égalité est meilleure pour tous*, Paris: Éditions Les Petits Matins.

WILLIAMSON O.E. (1975), *Markets and Hierarchies: Analysis and Antitrust Implications*, London and New York: Free Press - Macmillan.

——— (1985), *The Economic Institutions of Capitalism: Firms, Markets, Relational Contracting*, New York: Free Press.

——— (1995), "The Institutions and Governance of Economic Development and Reform," *Proceedings of the World Bank Annual Conference on Development Economics 1994*, p. 171–205, Washington DC.

WORLD BANK (THE) (1994), *Governance: The World Bank's Experience*, Washington DC: The World Bank.

——— (2005), *World Development Report 2006: Equity and Development*, Washington DC: The World Bank and Oxford University Press.

——— (2013), *World Development Report*, The World Bank: Washington DC.

——— (2014), "Gross National Income per capita Atlas Method and PPP," *World Development Indicators Database 2012*, April, The World Bank: Washington DC.

WORLD F*orum of* ALTERNATIVES (2006), "The Bamako Appeal," January 19, available on: https://mronline.org/2006/01/17/the-bamako-appeal/.

XEPAPADEAS A. (2005), "Economic Growth and the Environment," *Handbook of Environmental Economics*, vol. 3, p. 1219–1271, Amsterdam: Elsevier.

YILDIRIM J., S. SEZGINE and N. OCAL (2005), "Military Expenditure and Economic Growth in Middle Eastern Countries," *Defence and Peace Economics*, vol. 16, n° 4, p. 283–295.

ZAREMBKA P. (1975), "Capital Heterogeneity, Aggregation, and the Two-Sector Model," *Quarterly Journal of Economics*, vol. 89, n° 1, p. 103–114.

ZIEGLER J. (2005), *L'Empire de la honte*, Paris: Fayard.

ZINN H. (1980), *A People's History of the United States*, New York: Harper & Row / HarperCollins.

Author Index

R. Herrera, *Confronting Mainstream Economics for Overcoming Capitalism*, Marx, Engels, and Marxisms,
https://doi.org/10.1007/978-3-031-05851-6

Subject Index

R. Herrera, *Confronting Mainstream Economics for Overcoming Capitalism*, Marx, Engels, and Marxisms,
https://doi.org/10.1007/978-3-031-05851-6

N

O

P

R

FSC
www.fsc.org
MIX
Papier | Fördert
gute Waldnutzung
FSC® C083411

Kolibri 360 GmbH
Ferdinand-Jühlke-Straße 7
99095 Erfurt, Deutschland
produktsicherheit@kolibri360.de